# AL-GHAZĀLĪ'S
# *Moderation in Belief*

# Al-Ghazālī's *Moderation in Belief*

AL-IQTIṢĀD FĪ AL-IʿTIQĀD

Translated, with an Interpretive Essay and Notes by

Aladdin M. Yaqub

THE UNIVERSITY OF CHICAGO PRESS
CHICAGO AND LONDON

The University of Chicago Press, Chicago 60637
The University of Chicago Press, Ltd., London

Published 2013
Paperback edition 2017

Printed in the United States of America

23 22 21 20 19 18 17 2 3 4 5 6

ISBN-13: 978-0-226-06087-3 (cloth)
ISBN-13: 978-0-226-52647-8 (paper)
ISBN-13: 978-0-226-06090-3 (e-book)
DOI: https://doi.org/10.7208/chicago/9780226060903.001.0001

Library of Congress Cataloging-in-Publication Data

Ghazali, 1058–1111.
[Iqtisad fi al-i'tiqad. English]
Al-Ghazali's Moderation in belief: al-Iqtisad fi al-i'tiqad / translated, with an interpretive essay and notes by Aladdin M. Yaqub.
pages. cm.
Includes bibliographical references and index.
ISBN 978-0-226-06087-3 (cloth : alk. paper)—ISBN 978-0-226-06090-3 (e-book) 1. Ghazzali, 1050–1111. Iqtisad fi al-i'tiqad. 2. Islam—Doctrines—Early works to 1800. I. Yaqub, Aladdin Mahmud. II. Title.
BP166.G513 2013
297.2—dc23
2013005909

⊗ This paper meets the requirements of ANSI/NISO Z39.48-1992 (Permanence of Paper).

*To Connie,*
*who kept a candle burning*
*during the darkest time of my life*

# Contents

## SECOND TREATISE



## THIRD TREATISE

# Note on the Translation

This is the first complete English translation of *al-Iqtiṣād fī al-Iʿtiqād* (*Moderation in Belief*). To the best of my knowledge, there are only three partial English translations of this work. The first appears in a 1968 M.A. thesis by Abdu-r-Rahman Abu Zayd at McGill University. It covers only the Second Treatise of the *Iqtiṣād*. It was published as a book in 1970 by Sh. Muhammad Ashraf of Lahore under the title *Al-Ghazālī on Divine Predicates and Other Properties*, and was republished in 1994 under the same title by Kitab Bhavan of New Delhi. The second is Michael E. Marmura's translation of the first chapter of the Second Treatise—the chapter on the divine attribute of power. It was published with an interpretive introduction in *Arabic Sciences and Philosophy* (vol. 4, 1994, pp. 279–315) under the title "Ghazālī's Chapter on Divine Power in the *Iqtiṣād*." The third is a translation of the four introductions and the First Treatise of the *Iqtiṣād* and is found in a 2005 Ph.D. dissertation by Dennis Morgan Davis, Jr., at the University of Utah, titled "Al-Ghazālī on Divine Essence."

There are two critical editions of the *Iqtiṣād*: Çubukçu and Atay's (Ankara: Nur Matbaasi, 1962) and al-Sharafāwī's (Jeddah: Dār al-Minhāj, 2008). There are also several noncritical editions, the oldest of which was published in Cairo in 1891 by Maktabat Muṣṭafā al-Bābī al-Ḥalabī and reprinted most recently in 1966. I refer to these editions as the Ankara, Jeddah, and Cairo editions, respectively. My translation is based on the two critical editions. Where the two critical editions offer different readings, both are indicated in the notes. When the reading in the Cairo edition is adopted, the alternative readings found in the Ankara and Jeddah editions are provided in a note. Although I examined almost all the noncritical editions available, I elected to consult only the edition published by Maktabat Muṣṭafā al-Bābī al-Ḥalabī because it is the oldest and the one most widely used in seminaries.

I make some uncommon choices in translating certain Arabic terms. I defend and explain most of my choices in notes. Most notable are the following. I depart from the usual practice of always, in all contexts, translating *ʿaraḍ* as 'accident'. It is recognized that philosophers and theologians use the term in two primary senses. The first is contrasted with *dhāt* (essence), or more commonly with *dhātī* (essential), and it refers to a quality of a thing whose presence or absence does not change the identity of the thing. The second is contrasted with *jawhar* (substance) and it refers to that which does not subsist (or exist) in itself but in a subject. I translate *'araḍ* in the first sense as 'accident' (and the adjective *'araḍī* as 'accidental'), in the second sense as 'mode'.

The distinction between these two senses of *'araḍ* is frequently noted. Al-Ghazālī says in *Mi'yār al-'Ilm* that the quiddity of an object does not subsist in any of its *a'rāḍ* (plural of *'araḍ*), such as heat and cold, which are unlike the form of liquidity in water whose removal would change the water into something else, such as vapor: the presence or absence of heat and cold does not change the quiddity of water (p. 293). So it is clear that this sense of *a'rāḍ* corresponds to what philosophers call *accidental qualities*, which are to be contrasted with *essential qualities* (*dhātī*). Al-Ghazālī then says that the form of liquidity in water would be described by theologians as *'araḍ*, since they mean by *'araḍ* that which subsists in a receptacle, while *jawhar* refers to that which does not subsist in a receptacle (p. 294). This sense corresponds to what modern philosophers call *mode*. For instance, Spinoza in *The Ethics* defines 'substance' as "that which is in itself, and is conceived through itself," and 'mode' as "the modification of substance, or that which exists in, and is conceived through, something other than itself" (p. 45); Descartes in *Principles of Philosophy* says, "We employ the term *mode* when we are thinking of a substance as being affected or modified" (Cottingham et al., vol. i, p. 211); and Locke writes in *An Essay Concerning Human Understanding*, "*Modes* I call such complex *ideas*, which however compounded contain not in them the supposition of subsisting in themselves but are considered as dependences on, or affections of substances" (p. 165).

Ibn Sīnā (Avicenna) also makes this distinction clear. He writes in *al-Najāt* that every universal is either *dhātī* or *'araḍī*. As for *dhātī*, it is that which constitutes the quiddity of a thing (vol. i, p. 12). By contrast, the *'araḍī* is "everything that is not designated as *dhātī*." He adds that it is possible "to err and assume that this is the *'araḍ* that is contrasted with *jawhar* . . . which is not so" (vol. i, p. 14). Later in the book he defines *jawhar* as "any essence that is not in a subject" and *'araḍ* as "any essence whose subsistence is in a subject" (vol. ii, p. 49). It is clear that the former *'araḍ* corresponds to *accident* and the latter *'araḍ* corresponds to *mode*.

Linguistic sources also mark this distinction. For example, *al-Munjid fī al-Lugha* (p. 497, s.v. *al-'araḍ*), Muṣṭafā et al., *al-Mu'jam al-Wasīṭ* (p. 594, s.v. *al-'araḍ* and *al-'araḍī*), and al-Jurr, *Lārūs*: *al-Mu'jam al-'Arabī al-Ḥadīth* (p. 824, s.v. *al-'araḍ*) all distinguish between two senses of *'araḍ*: that which has no permanence or is not part of a thing's essence, and that which subsists in something other than itself or subsists in a *jawhar* but is not a *jawhar* itself. It is unfortunate that even when an author explicitly recognizes the distinction between these two senses, he might still treat *'araḍ* in all cases as 'accident'. For example, Ṣalībā in *al-Mu'jam al-Falsafī* states that all the various meanings of *'araḍ* may be reduced to two primary meanings: (1) "*'araḍ* is opposite to essence, and it is that which does not enter into the presence of a thing's quiddity or essence; for example, sitting and standing with respect to man do not enter into the presence of his quiddity"; and (2) "*'araḍ* is opposite to substance, for substance is that which subsists in itself and requires nothing other than itself for its subsistence, while *'araḍ* is that which requires something other than itself for its subsistence; body therefore is substance, which subsists in itself, but color is *'araḍ* since it could not subsist in anything other than a body" (p. 69, s.v. *'araḍ*; for consistency, I inverted the order of the two meanings). In spite of this clarity, Ṣalībā gives only one translation of *'araḍ*: 'accident'. I believe that the evidence leaves no doubt that *'araḍ* in the first sense, which is contrasted with *dhāt*, should be translated 'accident'; and that *'araḍ* in the second sense, which is contrasted with *jawhar*, should be translated 'mode'.

I translate *ḥādith* as 'occurrent'. Translators do not agree on a single English term for this word. They variously use such expressions as 'temporally originated thing', 'temporal thing', 'transient thing', and 'thing produced in time'. 'Occurrent' has the advantage of being concise and to the point. It designates something that occurs at a particular time or place—a meaning that is almost identical with the meaning of the Arabic term. Also, like its Arabic counterpart, 'occurrent' may be used as both a noun and an adjective. One may say "Soul and body are two occurrents" (*al-nafs wa-l-jasad ḥādithān*), and also "God created the occurrent power" (*Allāh khalaq al-qudra al-ḥāditha*).

Translators have invented the odd-sounding 'pre-eternal' and 'post-eternal' to capture the sense of being without a beginning and without an end, respectively. Following a suggestion by my colleague Roslyn Weiss, I prefer to translate *qadīm* in this sense as 'anteriorly eternal' and *bāqī* as 'posteriorly eternal', and the noun forms *qidam* and *azal* as 'anterior eternity' and *baqā'* and *abad* as 'posterior eternity'. *Qadīm* literally means old or ancient, but in theological and philosophical contexts it means either eternal or not having a beginning. *Bāqī* literally means remaining or persisting in existence, but, again, in theological and philosophical contexts it means not having an end. Unless these terms are used to indicate eternity on specifically one end or the other I use simply 'eternal' (or 'eternity').

Arabic makes extensive use of "exclusive negation," which is marked by the expression *lā . . . illā* ('not . . . except' or 'not . . . unless'). The most famous use of exclusive negation is in the Islamic declaration of faith (*shahāda*): *there is no deity except God* (*lā ilāh illā Allāh*). Al-Ghazālī is no exception, employing this construction frequently in the *Iqtiṣād*. Translating exclusive negations literally tends to produce tedious and cumbersome expressions. I translate this construction literally wherever the resulting English expression sounds natural, but sometimes I translate it as an "exclusive affirmation." Thus, for instance, rather than translating *al-ʿālam lā yakūn qadīman illā idhā kān ṣādiran ʿan al-awwal ḍarūratan* as 'The world cannot be eternal unless it proceeds from the First by necessity', I might translate it as 'The world can be eternal only if it proceeds from the First by necessity'.

Every translator faces the difficult choice between faithfulness and readability. Faithfulness pulls the translator towards a more literal translation and readability towards a more liberal translation. I sought to be as literal as possible without sacrificing readability. To help achieve this balance I relied partly on brackets and notes. However, brackets and notes about matters of translation can be impeding, so I tried to minimize their number as much as possible. I employed the following convention: if the alteration to the text is clearly implied by the context, I did not enclose the alteration in brackets, and if it is not clearly implied by the context, I either enclosed the alteration in brackets or gave a literal translation in the notes. For example, if al-Ghazālī uses a pronoun to refer to an opponent, say, a philosopher, I might replace that pronoun with the expression 'the philosopher' without indicating this addition by using brackets.

I supplement al-Ghazālī's discussion with extensive notes that demanded as much time and effort as the translation itself. Since my goal is to make al-Ghazālī's arguments and doctrines accessible to the modern reader, I sometimes provide elaborations of his arguments and sometimes offer actual reconstructions. I also try to explain every difficult or opaque passage, and supply the intellectual and historical backgrounds of some of his discussions. These notes are best viewed as my interpretation of al-Ghazālī's arguments and doctrines. In addition to the running commentary in the notes, I appended to this translation a substantive Interpretive Essay, in which I attempt to summarize and reconstruct the argument of the *Iqtiṣād*, explaining its central facets and describing its main contours. Unlike the notes, which mostly deal with the details of al-Ghazālī's analyses, the Interpretive Essay deals with the big picture: the implications of these analyses and the relations between their elements. I believe that it is best if the Interpretive Essay is read after reading the whole translation; a reader may elect, however, to read it before reading the translation, or to read each of its four sections before reading the corresponding treatise.

In the end, I hope to have done justice to al-Ghazālī's book and to have provided a valuable service to my readers.

# Acknowledgments

The work on this book consumed the better part of four years. In the spring semester of 2008, in preparation for undertaking this translation, I led the philosophy faculty seminar at Lehigh University in a careful study of al-Ghazālī's *Tahāfut al-Falāsifa*, since one cannot understand fully the *Iqtiṣād* without coming to terms with the *Tahāfut*. I benefited greatly from the discussion, comments, and critiques of my colleagues. For the fall semester of 2008 Lehigh University granted me an academic leave that was invaluable in enabling me to complete a large portion of the translation and commentary. The National Endowment for the Humanities awarded me a stipend for the summer of 2009 to continue the work on this translation. I thank both institutions for their financial support.

I am deeply indebted to my colleague Professor Roslyn Weiss, who generously read a draft of the whole book, reviewing certain passages more than once, and offered numerous linguistic and philosophical corrections and suggestions. This work was much improved as a result of her efforts. Furthermore, Professor Weiss contributed generously to my acquisition of many of the Arabic sources that I consulted during my translation of and commentary on the *Iqtiṣād*, all of which are listed in the bibliography whether I cite them explicitly in the book or not. I am also grateful to the two anonymous colleagues who advised the University of Chicago Press regarding the publication of this book. Alongside their kind praise of the translation, they offered valuable critical remarks and constructive suggestions, in response to which I made changes in and additions to the manuscript that enhanced the quality of the book. Professor Yasir Ibrahim's knowledge of the Near East collection of Princeton University Library was invaluable for identifying the *ḥadīth*s mentioned in this book; I am very grateful for his help. Ranah Yaqub proofread a large portion of the manuscript before I submitted it to the University of Chicago Press; I thank her for her diligent work. Thanks are also due to John Tryneski, executive editor at the University of Chicago Press, for his belief in the value of and support for this project. I am thankful as well to Michael Koplow for his meticulous copyediting of the manuscript of this book. Finally,

I am most grateful to my wife, Connie, who endured my endless requests for her judgment on matters of linguistic usage, and who was immensely supportive during the time it took to complete this project. Needless to say, all errors and shortcomings that might remain in this work are exclusively mine.

# Translator's Introduction

## I

Abū Ḥāmid Muḥammad al-Ghazālī (AH 450/1058 CE–AH 505/1111 CE) is without doubt one of the most important thinkers in the Islamic intellectual tradition. Indeed, in the judgment of many Muslim and Western scholars, no other thinker is quite his equal. R. J. McCarthy (1980, pp. 12–13) compiled a short list of adulatory references to al-Ghazālī, containing such remarks as: "if there had been a prophet after Muḥammad, it would have been al-Ghazālī"; "the greatest, certainly the most sympathetic figure in the history of Islam"; "the greatest Muslim after Muḥammad"; "the pivot of existence and the common pool of refreshing waters for all"; "without doubt the most remarkable figure in all Islam"; and "this man, if ever any have deserved the name, was truly a 'divine.'" And McCarthy's list is just a small sample of the encomia lavished upon al-Ghazālī by classical and contemporary scholars. His admirers also bestowed upon him many honorary titles, such as *ḥujjat al-Islām* ("the argument of Islam"), *zayn al-dīn* ("the beauty of religion"), *barakat al-inām* ("a blessing for mankind"), and *jāmiʿ al-ʿulūm* ("the gatherer of the sciences").

These remarks and honorifics might strike us as hyperbolic, but those who study al-Ghazālī's history, influence, and works appreciate their accuracy. His vast knowledge, his command of logical reasoning and argumentation, and the clarity and thoroughness of his expositions all indicate exceptional intellectual power. His work also exhibits remarkable originality. Several of al-Ghazālī's important books, such as *Iḥyāʾ ʿUlūm al-Dīn* (*The Revival of the Religious Sciences*) and *Tahāfut al-Falāsifa* (*The Incoherence of the Philosophers*), are products of an unquestionably fiercely independent and original mind.[1] Yet in spite of this independence and originality,

1. By saying that these books are original, I do not mean to deny that they are influenced by other works. *Tahāfut al-Falāsifa* contains expositions of philosophers' views and arguments and al-Ghazālī's refutations of them. Some of al-Ghazālī's polemics are influenced by arguments and positions advocated by other theological schools. *Iḥyāʾ ʿUlūm al-Dīn* is significantly influenced by other Sufi books, especially Abū Ṭālib al-Makkī's *Qūt al-Qulūb* (*The Sustenance of the Hearts*), a book that al-Ghazālī in his *al-Munqidh min al-Ḍalāl* (*The Deliverer from Error*) says he has read (p. 131).

al-Ghazālī never shed the deep influence of his education under Imam al-Juwaynī. To the end of his life he remained Shāfiʿite in jurisprudence (*fiqh*) and Ashʿarite in theology (*kalām*).

*Al-Iqtiṣād fī al-Iʿtiqād* (*Moderation in Belief*), which is al-Ghazālī's most profound work of philosophical theology, is a strikingly original defense of his theological commitment to Ashʿarism. Although all the central doctrines in the *Iqtiṣād*, except for the one concerning the anthropomorphic descriptions of God in the Qurʾān and the Ḥadīth,[2] are standard Ashʿarite views, many of the arguments and intermediary conclusions found in the book are al-Ghazālī's own. Al-Ghazālī describes the *Iqtiṣād* in *Kitāb al-Arbaʿīn fī Uṣūl al-Dīn* (*The Book of Forty Principles of Religion*) as follows:

> It is a stand-alone book, and contains the core of the science of the theologians. It is more elaborate in its investigations, however, and closer to reaching the entrance to knowledge than are the formal discussions one encounters in the books of theologians. (p. 16)

In the third century AH (the ninth century CE) Muʿtazilism attained the status of official state theology. As a result, Muʿtazilites incurred the enmity of many distinguished scholars of theology and jurisprudence. By the fifth century AH (the eleventh century CE), Ashʿarism, founded by Abū al-Ḥasan ʿAlī al-Ashʿarī (AH 260/873 CE–AH 324/935 CE) as a reaction against Muʿtazilite theology, was becoming the dominant Sunni theology. The powerful vizier Niẓām al-Mulk (AH 408/1017 CE–AH 485/1092 CE), who was appointed by the Seljuk sultans, subscribed to the Shāfiʿī school of jurisprudence and to the Ashʿarī school of theology. He was widely considered the principal defender of Sunni Islam against the propaganda and activism of various Shīʿa groups, such as the Fāṭimid caliphs of Egypt and the Ismāʿīlī militants. To oppose the rising Shīʿa influence in the Muslim world,

2. A *ḥadīth* is a saying or a description of a practice attributed to the Prophet Muḥammad. The Ḥadīth is the corpus consisting of the sayings and the descriptions of the practices attributed to the Prophet Muḥammad. In other words, Ḥadīth is considered to embody the Sunna, which is the collective tradition of the Prophet Muḥammad. The term 'Hadith' has been part of the English vocabulary since the eighteenth century. As for the token term *ḥadīth*, it has not yet, to the best of my knowledge, entered the "official" English vocabulary. However, an increasing number of translators and writers are using the Arabic term *ḥadīth* instead of the English expression 'a saying (or, a tradition) of the Prophet Muḥammad', or more cautiously, the expression 'a saying (or, a tradition) attributed to the Prophet Muḥammad'. The concept is sufficiently complex to warrant its own term. By using the Arabic term, one hopes that the word 'hadith' would one day enter into the English vocabulary as 'Hadith' has. It should be noted, however, that some scholars are already using the term 'Hadith' to refer to the corpus of *ḥadīth*s as well as to a single *ḥadīth* or a collection of *ḥadīth*s.

Niẓām al-Mulk established several schools of higher education that focused on teaching Shāfiʿite jurisprudence and Ashʿarite theology. He appointed as professors in these schools some of the most distinguished scholars of the time, such as al-Juwaynī at the Niẓāmiyya School of Nishapur and al-Ghazālī at the Niẓāmiyya School of Baghdad. These efforts, together with the great influence of al-Ghazālī's book *al-Iqtiṣād fī al-Iʿtiqād*, were largely responsible for the establishment of Ashʿarism in the second half of the sixth century AH (the twelfth century CE) as the orthodox Sunni theology—a status it has maintained until the present day.

## II

There is near universal agreement among al-Ghazālī's biographers concerning certain aspects of his life and career, but concerning others there are contradictory accounts. Al-Ghazālī's own autobiographical account, found in *al-Munqidh min al-Ḍalāl* (*The Deliverer from Error*),[3] appears to be a faithful record of the main events of his life and their chronology.[4] The account that follows relies on al-Ghazālī's autobiography, filling in gaps where necessary and where there is good evidence to support the reconstruction.

Muḥammad al-Ghazālī was born in Tus, which is part of the Persian province of Khorasan, in AH 450/1058 CE. His father was an impoverished, illiterate man, who shortly before his death entrusted a Sufi friend to educate his sons Muḥammad and Aḥmad. After the father's death, the friend did what he was asked until he exhausted the little money the boys inherited from their father. He then advised them to attend a madrasa that provides financial and other support for its students. Around AH 465/1072 CE, Muḥammad and Aḥmad went to such a madrasa in Tus. There al-Ghazālī studied Islamic law with Aḥmad al-Rādhkānī. He went next to Jurjan to study with Abū al-Qāsim al-Ismāʿīlī,[5] and remained there until about AH 470/1077 CE, when he returned to Tus and stayed for three years studying and memorizing what he learned in Jurjan. Around AH 473/1080 CE, he went to the prestigious Niẓāmiyya School of Nishapur. He was then about twenty-two years old. At the Niẓāmiyya, he studied under Imam al-Ḥaramayn Abū al-Maʿālī ʿAbd al-Malik al-Juwaynī (AH 419/1028 CE–AH 478/1085 CE), who was then the principal scholar of the Shāfiʿī school of jurisprudence and of the Ashʿarī school of theology. Al-Ghazālī never

3. The book is famously known in the English-speaking world as *Deliverance from Error*.

4. ʿAbd al-Karīm al-ʿUthmān's *Sirat al-Ghazālī wa-Aqwāl al-Mutaqaddimīn fīh* is a compilation of the classical Arabic biographies of al-Ghazālī.

5. In some biographies, he is called Abū Naṣr al-Ismāʿīlī.

explicitly admits or denies the great influence al-Juwaynī had on him. But it is remarkable that throughout the whole of his intellectual and moral development, including his adoption of the teachings and practices of the Sufis, al-Ghazālī never abandons his zeal for Ashʿarism or his allegiance to the Shāfiʿī school of jurisprudence. His legal convictions did not interfere with his respect for and openness to the other orthodox schools of jurisprudence, such as the Ḥanafī and Mālikī schools, but his theological convictions prompted him to impute heresy or even infidelity to all the other theological and philosophical schools, with the exception of the equally orthodox theological school of al-Māturīdī.

After the death of Imam al-Juwaynī in AH 478/1085 CE, al-Ghazālī went to the court-camp of the vizier Niẓām al-Mulk, which was a center for scholars who discussed and debated a wide variety of issues and problems in theology and law. Al-Ghazālī remained there for six years. In AH 484/1091 CE, Niẓām al-Mulk appointed him professor of jurisprudence and theology at the Niẓāmiyya School of Baghdad, then the most prestigious madrasa in the eastern part of the Muslim world. Thus at the age of thirty-three, al-Ghazālī found himself occupying a post of great stature, which was the envy of many scholars at the time.

Al-Ghazālī tells us in *al-Munqidh min al-Ḍalāl* that early in his life he rejected conformism (*taqlīd*), and strove to acquire "certain knowledge, in which what is sought is fully disclosed, so that no doubt would linger, no error or mistaken appearance could be associated with it, and the mind could not allow for any of these things; the safety from making a mistake should accompany the certainty [of the belief], such that if its falsity is argued for by, say, transforming a rock into gold or a rod into a serpent, no doubt or denial would be engendered" (p. 82). It is likely that at some time between al-Ghazālī's decision to devote himself to the pursuit of certain knowledge and his departure for Baghdad, he experienced an intellectual crisis—a severe bout of skepticism that lasted for two months. Al-Ghazālī says that he could not find solace in conformist belief since "a necessary condition for a conformist is that he not know that he is a conformist; for if he were to know, the glass of his conformism would be cracked; and such a crack could not be mended, nor could it be fixed by self-deception and telling tales" (pp. 89–90). He therefore decided to seek certain knowledge either through the senses or through pure reason. Unfortunately, he had doubts concerning both. On the one hand, he could not trust the evidence of the senses, for even sight, which is the most powerful sense, tends to deceive us by giving us images of perceptibles that do not agree with their reality. On the other hand, if the evidence of the senses is found wanting when examined by pure reason, what guarantee is there that a faculty higher than reason, one that we do not possess, would not impugn the evidence of pure reason? These skeptical thoughts left him intellectually paralyzed. He could not employ arguments to dispel these doubts, for any argument would necessarily invoke reason, yet reason itself is now seen to require justification. Al-Ghazālī says that this skeptical period ended when God illuminated his heart with the light of knowledge, which restored to him his trust in reason. The necessary truths of reason returned to their secure status as certain knowledge.

After his recovery from this "illness," he decided to study the four groups of seekers: the theologians, the Esotericists,[6] the philosophers, and the Sufis. He thought that surely one of these groups would have attained the truth, and that if none had, there would then be little hope for his discovering it. According to the narrative in al-Ghazālī's *Munqidh*, he investigated theology first, then philosophy, then the teachings of the Esotericists, and finally the teachings of the Sufis, before deciding to follow the Sufi path to knowledge (*maʿrifa*). There is no doubt that al-Ghazālī studied theology while he was a student at the Niẓāmiyya School of Nishapur. It is also likely that his serious study of philosophy came later, after his arrival in Baghdad. What seems unlikely is that his investigation of the Esotericists post-dated his study of philosophy, particularly since it was before he went to Baghdad that he spent six years at the court-camp of Niẓām al-Mulk, who was occupied with maintaining the hegemony of the Seljuk sultans and with defending Sunni Islam against the rising influence of the Esotericists. It is virtually inconceivable that al-Ghazālī could have been part of Niẓām al-Mulk's intellectual circle without being aware of the teachings of the Esotericists.

We might reasonably vindicate al-Ghazālī's seemingly inaccurate chronology by viewing it as a record not of the sequence in which he encountered certain views but of the order in which he composed his books. According to the most authoritative chronicle of al-Ghazālī's works,[7] he wrote the following ten books, in the given order, during his time in Baghdad: (1) *Ghāyat al-Ghawr fī Masāʾil al-Dawr* (*The Outcome of a Thorough In-*

6. The term 'Esotericists' (*al-Bāṭiniyya*) is used to refer to several Shīʿa sects. The most notable of these sects is a group of militant Shīʿa also called *al-Ismāʿīliyya*. They are called "Esotericists" (as well as "Instructionists") because they claim that they follow the *instructions* of infallible hidden imams, who understand the *esoteric* interpretations of all Qurʾānic verses.

7. I take ʿAbd al-Raḥmān Badawī's *Muʾallafāt al-Ghazālī* to be the most authoritative of the chronicles because it is one of the latest and most complete. Badawī had the benefit of studying many other chronicles before he compiled his own; he also makes extensive use of al-Ghazālī's internal cross-references and of chronicles of some of al-Ghazālī's works found in the historical sources. The most recent chronicle of al-Ghazālī's works is George F. Hourani's "A Revised Chronology of Ghazālī's Writings" (1984).

*vestigation into the Problems of Reiteration*),[8] (2) *Maqāṣid al-Falāsifa* (*The Aims of the Philosophers*), (3) *Tahāfut al-Falāsifa* (*The Incoherence of the Philosophers*), (4) *Miʿyār al-ʿIlm* (*The Standard for Knowledge*),[9] (5) *Miḥak al-Naẓar* (*The Touchstone of Theorization*), (6) *Mīzān al-ʿAmal* (*The Balance of Practice*), (7) *Kitāb al-Mustaẓhirī fī al-Radd ʿalā al-Bāṭiniyya* (*The Mustaẓhirī Book for Refuting the Esotericists*),[10] (8) *Kitāb Ḥujjat al-Ḥaqq* (*The Book of the Argument for the Truth*), (9) *Qawāṣim al-Bāṭiniyya* (*The Breaking Points of the Esotericists*), and (10) *al-Iqtiṣād fī al-Iʿtiqād* (*Moderation in Belief*). The first book deals with a specific issue of Islamic law. The second book is a summary of Ibn Sīnā's philosophy, the third book consists of a systematic refutation of Ibn Sīnā's and al-Fārābī's philosophies, the fourth and fifth books are summaries of Ibn Sīnā's logic, and the tenth is a book of philosophical theology, which is the last of his philosophical books of this period and the last book he wrote in Baghdad. The seventh, eighth, and ninth books are all meant as refutations of the teachings of the Esotericists. The sixth book is a book of applied ethics, in which al-Ghazālī shows early signs of his inclination towards Sufism. Since al-Ghazālī wrote his philosophical books before he wrote his refutations of the Esotericists, his careful study of the philosophers indeed preceded his careful study of the Esotericists—even though he surely became acquainted with Esotericist teachings earlier. According to almost all those who chronicle al-Ghazālī's works, his philosophical writings were completed during his stay at the Niẓāmiyya School of Baghdad. And so, if, as al-Ghazālī himself says in the *Munqidh*, he spent two years studying the books of the philosophers, it would appear that al-Ghazālī studied philosophy during the first half of his stay in Baghdad, and wrote his philosophical works during the second half of this period.[11]

8. The problem of reiteration is a legal issue in Islamic law. It concerns the validity of a divorce when a man says to his wife, "If I divorce you three times, you will be divorced," but then says only once, "You are divorced." In al-Ghazālī's day, this was a hotly debated matter among Shāfiʿite scholars. Al-Ghazālī provides in this work a thorough investigation and elaboration of the relevant factors, concluding that in this case the divorce is not valid. Much later in life he returned to this issue and reversed his initial fatwa, declaring that a reiterated divorce was valid.

9. There are cross-references between the *Tahāfut* and the *Miʿyār*. According to Badawī, however, the references to the *Miʿyār* are found in only some of the copies of the former work—suggesting that al-Ghazālī added this cross-reference later, that is, after composing the latter work.

10. The book was written at the request of the ʿAbbāsid caliph al-Mustaẓhir bi-Allāh to counter the propaganda of the Ismāʿīlites.

11. Most of al-Ghazālī's early biographers state that al-Ghazālī studied philosophy and Sufism during his years at the Niẓāmiyya School of Nishapur. All of this is consistent with al-Ghazālī's chronology of his studies in the *Munqidh*, so long as he is understood to be chroni-

In the month of Rajab (the seventh month of the Hijrī calendar) of AH 488/1095 CE, al-Ghazālī experienced a severe spiritual crisis. He lost the ability to talk, became melancholy, and no longer had an appetite for food. This crisis lasted about six months. Al-Ghazālī interpreted this experience and his recovery from it as a clear sign from God to give up his academic post, to leave Baghdad, and to follow the path of the Sufis. Al-Ghazālī made arrangements for his family; and at the end of AH 488/1095 CE, under the pretense of traveling to perform the pilgrimage, he left Baghdad and traveled to Damascus. He stayed there for about two years, living the Sufi life of seclusion and worship. He then traveled to Jerusalem and secluded himself daily in the Dome of the Rock. There he wrote *al-Risāla al-Qudsiyya* (*The Jerusalem Epistle*),[12] which is the first *complete* work he wrote after the *Iqtiṣād* and provides a summary of it. Later he included this book in his magnum opus *Iḥyā' 'Ulūm al-Dīn* as part of *Kitāb Qawā'id al-'Aqā'id* (*The Book of the Foundations of Belief*).[13] From Jerusalem he went to Hebron to visit the Mosque of the prophet Abraham. After staying there for a short time he headed to Mecca and Medina to perform the pilgrimage.

Al-Ghazālī tells us in the *Munqidh* that after he performed the pilgrimage, the needs of his family and children made it necessary for him to return home to Tus. There is, however, strong evidence suggesting that he first went to Baghdad for a short time, during which he taught his book the *Iḥyā'*. Since his family was in Baghdad at the time, it was reasonable for him to go first to Baghdad and from there to take his family with him to Tus. He most likely returned to Baghdad in AH 490/1096 CE. From Baghdad he went to Tus and remained there for about ten years. He says in the *Munqidh* that despite the demands placed on his time by family responsibilities, he managed to find opportunities for seclusion. In AH 499/1106 CE, the vizier Fakhr al-Mulk, who was the son of Niẓām al-Mulk, came to Tus and pressured al-Ghazālī to return to teaching in the Niẓāmiyya School of Nishapur. Al-Ghazālī complied. It is unknown how long al-Ghazālī stayed in Nishapur. We know that Fakhr al-Mulk was assassinated in AH 500/1106 CE

---

cling his careful and thorough studies of the various disciplines. Khalidi (2005, pp. xxv–xxvi) and others suggest that al-Ghazālī could not have immersed himself in all these areas of study, taught about three hundred students (as he tells us in the *Munqidh*), and written several books during four years only. I am not persuaded. Al-Ghazālī was a prodigious writer and reader. The fact that he wrote more than one hundred works, some of which are multivolume, in his relatively short life is a testimony to his extraordinary ability to accomplish much in little time. We may note that he did not start from scratch: he had studied Arabic, law, theology, philosophy, and Sufism before taking up his many ventures in Baghdad.

12. The work is so named because it was written in Jerusalem (*al-Quds*).

13. It is very likely that al-Ghazālī began writing the *Iḥyā'* during his stay in Damascus and that he completed it sometime after he wrote *al-Risāla al-Qudsiyya*.

by an Ismāʿīlī militant (Niẓām al-Mulk was also assassinated by an Ismāʿīlī militant). Perhaps al-Ghazālī returned to Tus shortly after the death of Fakhr al-Mulk. At any rate, al-Ghazālī spent the last years of his life in Tus. He established near his home a madrasa and a Sufi center for worship and seclusion. Al-Ghazālī devoted the remaining years of his life to the study of Ḥadīth, prompted perhaps by the criticism some scholars leveled against *Iḥyāʾ ʿUlūm al-Dīn*, challenging his inclusion in it of many *ḥadīth*s of questionable authenticity. Al-Ghazālī's untimely death at the age of fifty-three came on Monday, AH 14 Jumādā al-Thānī 505/18 December 1111 CE.

Al-Ghazālī left behind an extensive body of work. Badawī (1977) lists 72 works that were definitely written by al-Ghazālī, of which 48 are extant, 23 works that might have been written by him, and 32 works that have been attributed to him and that were most likely not written by him. Ṣalībā and ʿAyyād (in al-Ghazālī, *al-Munqidh*, 1956) list 228 works by al-Ghazālī, of which 57 are extant. Hence a conservative estimate would easily place al-Ghazālī's intellectual output at over a hundred volumes. These books cover a wide range of fields: jurisprudence, theology, logic, philosophy, Sufism, education, politics, and ethics. Many of these books contain commentaries on Qurʾānic verses and *ḥadīth*s, as well as explanations and interpretations of Islamic practices and invocations.

The only religious science on which al-Ghazālī did not compose a work is Ḥadīth. It was reported that he said that his expertise in Ḥadīth was limited. This is surprising, given the large number of *ḥadīth*s included in his works. It is thus almost certain that al-Ghazālī was referring to his lack of formal training in Ḥadīth. It is a common complaint that *Iḥyāʾ ʿUlūm al-Dīn* is filled with *ḥadīth*s of questionable authenticity. The charge, however, is overstated. Several early scholars, such as al-Ḥāfiẓ al-ʿIrāqī and Murtaḍā al-Zabīdī, carried out the difficult task of identifying the *ḥadīth*s mentioned in the *Iḥyāʾ*, and according to them most of these *ḥadīth*s are either authentic (*ṣaḥīḥ*) or acceptable (*ḥasan*). At any rate, the charge was made during the life of al-Ghazālī, and it is evident that it troubled him greatly. As was mentioned previously, al-Ghazālī devoted the last years of his life to the study of Ḥadīth, and it was said that he memorized a substantial portion of al-Bukhāri's *Ṣaḥīḥ*, which is a large collection of authentic *ḥadīth*s.

## III

The *Iqtiṣād* consists of two prefaces, four introductions, and four treatises (*aqṭāb*). The first preface is partly an invocation, enumerating the good qualities of *ahl al-sunna* (orthodox Sunnis), and partly a religious justification for writing a book on the foundations of belief. Al-Ghazālī addresses himself to one who seeks the true doctrines and their proofs regarding matters of belief. He says that *ahl al-sunna* aim at moderation in belief (hence the title of the book), which lies between two extremes: excess and deficiency in relying on reason. Some groups were deficient in the sense that they neglected reason and relied on a literal interpretation of revelation; and others were excessive in the sense that they ignored revelation and relied solely on reason. He says that reason is like sight and revelation like sunlight; one needs both in order to see clearly.

It is important to keep in mind that the intended audience of the book consists of nonspecialists in theology "who [long] to know the foundations of the beliefs of *ahl al-sunna* and who [aspire] to establish them by conclusive proofs." This is no ordinary audience. It contains neither specialists nor average believers who conform to orthodox doctrines without asking for conclusive proofs. The intended reader of this book seems to be an intelligent person who is no longer satisfied with the comfort of conformism (*taqlīd*), but is also not well-versed in the theological debates; rather he is troubled with many questions about God, His attributes, acts, and prophecy, and he longs to learn the true doctrines about these matters based on conclusive proofs. To a considerable degree, this imagined reader guides the writing of the book. Al-Ghazālī eschews the use of technical logical and theological terms, and tries to explain all specialized notions as he introduces them. He also repeats himself frequently. Moreover, he supplies the background needed to understand the various theological schools and debates. But he is not entirely consistent. Many parts of the *Iqtiṣād* are dense and presuppose specialized theological and philosophical knowledge, making the *Iqtiṣād* a very difficult work—indeed, by far al-Ghazālī's most difficult work on philosophical theology. Nevertheless, there are parts of the *Iqtiṣād* that are clearly aimed at a general reader who seeks to know the "true" doctrines on the basis of conclusive proofs.

The second preface is a brief analytical table of contents, including a definition of the science of theology (*kalām*). The first three introductions discuss, in order, the importance, danger, and legal status of the science of theology. The First Introduction explains why the science of theology is important. Theology consists in a rational investigation into whether what we are told by the prophets is true or not: do we, as the prophets say, actually have a God who can send messengers, assign duties and rights, punish and reward? And if we do, what are His attributes, acts, and relationship to us and our world? The aims of the science of theology is to answer these questions and related ones. Of course, not everyone is troubled by these questions, and not everyone who is troubled by these questions is best served by the methods of the science of theology. Al-Ghazālī explains in the Second Introduction that, although this science is important for certain people, it is not important in general; and most people should be shielded from its questions, arguments, and debates. He divides people into four groups: (1) those who have intuitive belief and are not troubled by any of these questions; (2) those who follow error obstinately and rigidly and for whom no rational discourse is fruitful; (3) those whose sincere belief has been clouded with some questions and doubts; and (4) those who follow error but are discontent with their belief and are skeptical about the doctrines they are taught. Al-Ghazālī recommends a limited amount of theology only for members of the third and fourth groups. The questions and arguments of theology are dangerous for the first group and useless for the second. The doubts of members of the third group must be examined carefully and dispelled with the least amount of argumentation and analysis. If a doubt can be erased by citing a Qurʾānic verse or a *ḥadīth*, then one should not administer any more complex remedy by invoking theological answers and arguments. Only when more benign methods fail in dispelling the doubt and the person is sufficiently intelligent to comprehend theological analysis and reasoning should one rely on the methods and the resources of theology. As for the last group, al-Ghazālī thinks that one is justified in invoking the resources of theology to bring these people into the ranks of the believers; but even here he cautions that one should invoke the fewest theological resources adequate for the task and he should act with mercy and gentleness.

The Third Introduction is a discussion of the legal status of the science of theology. Al-Ghazālī decrees that theology is a collective, and not an individual, obligation—that is, an obligation upon the Muslim community as whole, and not upon every individual Muslim. The Second Introduction makes it clear that the majority of people are harmed by being exposed to the questions and arguments of theology; hence it cannot be an individual obligation. But it is important for every Muslim community to have a specialist in theology for three reasons: (1) to restore faith to those whose minds become disturbed with certain doubts; (2) to bring those nonbelievers who are intelligent and can only be moved by demonstrative proofs into Islam; and (3) to counter the propaganda of heretics and expose the weakness and ugliness of their doctrines. Al-Ghazālī is quick to say, however, that if a community lacks a jurist and a theologian, and there is someone who can master only one of these arts, he should study jurisprudence (*fiqh*) and not theology; for only the few who are troubled by doubts need theology, while everyone needs the decrees of jurisprudence.

The Fourth Introduction is a short logical treatise. In it al-Ghazālī discusses the methods of proof that he employs in the book. He enumerates three methods of demonstrative proof. Since these are three valid forms of inference, any conclusion inferred via these rules from true premises must also be true. It is natural to ask here how the truth of the premises is ascertained. Al-Ghazālī lists six "apprehensions" through which the truth of a premise may be established. It could be (1) based on sense perception (*al-ḥiss*), (2) based on pure reason (*al-ʿaql al-maḥḍ*), (3) based on widely transmitted reports (*al-mutawātirāt*), (4) validly inferred from other premises, which are themselves established by either sense perception, pure reason, or widely transmitted reports, (5) conveyed in a revelation, or (6) presupposed as something the disputant already accepts. Al-Ghazālī explains that each one of these apprehensions has its utility and limitation. For instance, someone who is not part of a community in which certain reports are widely transmitted cannot be expected to accept premises based on such reports, and someone who does not believe in revelation will not be moved by a premise derived from a revelation.

The First Treatise is on the existence, essence, and nature of God. It consists of ten propositions and their proofs. Collectively these proofs are meant to establish the existence of a transcendent, eternal, uncaused cause of the world, who is one and seeable. The Second Treatise is devoted to the seven divine attributes: power, knowledge, will, life, hearing, sight, and speech. In the first section of the treatise, each attribute is established, and its characteristics and some of their implications are discussed. In the second section, some general characteristics of the seven attributes are discussed, such as their eternity and their being additional to the divine essence. The Third Treatise concerns the acts of God and His relation to the creation. In it, al-Ghazālī states and defends seven propositions. At the outset of the treatise, al-Ghazālī introduces an ethical theory that is a form of ethical egoism. This ethical theory, together with the seven propositions, gives an account of absolute divine freedom that is not subject to any constraint other than the constraint of logical possibility. The Fourth Treatise discusses prophecy in general and the prophecy of the Prophet Muḥammad in particular; matters of the hereafter, such as the torment of the grave and resurrection; the imamate and its requirements; and the canon according to which a sect might be charged with infidelity. Certain aspects of these treatises are discussed with some elaboration in the Interpretive Essay, which is appended to the translation.

# [Religious Preface]

*In the Name of God, the Compassionate, the Merciful*

Praise be to God, who selected among the best of His servants the league of the followers of the truth, the followers of the Sunna;[1] and distinguished them from all the other sects with merits through His benevolence and grace; and bestowed upon them light through His guidance, which uncovered for them the truths of the religion; and made their tongues articulate His arguments, with which He quelled the errors of the atheists; and cleared their souls from the insinuations of the devils; and purified their consciences from the incitements of the deviants; and filled their hearts with the light of certitude, through which they understood the secrets of what He sent down through the tongue of His Prophet and chosen one, Muḥammad (may God bless him and grant him peace), the master of the messengers. So they came to know the way of integrating the requirements

1. 'Sunna' has been part of the English vocabulary since the eighteenth century. It designates the body of traditions attributed to the Prophet Muḥammad. I translate *ahl al-sunna* literally as the followers of the Sunna. It might be objected that this translation is biased since the Shīʿa consider themselves also followers of the Sunna; it is only that these groups have different interpretations of the Sunna as well as different traditions attributed to the Prophet. *Ahl al-sunna*, it might be said, really refers to the adherents of Sunni orthodoxy, and thus it should be translated as such. All of this is true, but still my translation is defensible. A translation ideally should capture the intent of the author—his meaning, even if this meaning conflicts with historical or ideological facts. When al-Ghazālī, and other defenders of Sunni orthodoxy, use *ahl al-sunna*, they mean by it the followers of the prophetic tradition, that is, the followers of the Sunna. Since this is a translation of a text written by al-Ghazālī and not a commentary on it, I find it inescapable to adhere to the meanings of the terms as he understood them. He definitely would not think of *ahl al-sunna* as merely a group adhering to orthodoxy, but rather, true followers of the prophetic tradition. The term 'orthodoxy' itself, of course, could connote a system of religious belief that is widely held as right or as the norm. Thus being an adherent of Sunni orthodoxy could simply mean an adherent of the Sunni tradition that is widely held as the right tradition, which is not far from al-Ghazālī's intended meaning. However, I still would argue that 'orthodoxy' could carry with it a connotation of convention, which al-Ghazālī would reject. For him what is conventional or accepted at certain time may not be consistent with the Sunna, and hence it should not be part of the belief or practice of *ahl al-sunna*.

of the law[2] and the demands of reason, and ascertained that there is no conflict between the transmitted revelation[3] and the intellectual truth. They knew that the Ḥashawites,[4] who thought it necessary to adhere rigidly to conformism[5] and to follow literalism, put forward what can only be based on feeble intellects and dim visions, and that the philosophers and the extremists among the Muʿtazilites,[6] who relied excessively on the dictates of

2. In the original it is *sharāʾiʿ* (laws), which is the plural of *sharīʿa* (law). *Sharīʿa* is usually translated as religious (or Islamic or divine) law. Since during the time of al-Ghazālī Islamic law was the law of the land, I use 'law' without a modifier.

3. I translated *sharʿ* as revelation. *Sharʿ*, unlike *sharīʿa*, could mean in certain contexts divine revelation or, in general, divine teaching. The contrast here between what is transmitted and what is intellectualized strongly suggests that the intended meaning of *sharʿ* is divine revelation, whether this revelation is contained in the Qurʾān or the Ḥadīth (that is, the corpus of the sayings and the descriptions of the practices attributed to the Prophet Muḥammad). I believe that al-Ghazālī almost always uses *sharʿ* in the *Iqtiṣād* to mean divine revelation. Hence I will translate it almost uniformly as 'revelation'. In certain contexts, however, I find it more appropriate to translate *sharʿ* as 'law' or 'divine teaching'.

4. The Ḥashawiyya was an Islamic theological school. The Ḥashawites were extreme literalists in their interpretation of the Qurʾān. Thus they attributed corporeal characteristics to God based on literal reading of the anthropomorphic Qurʾānic verses and *ḥadīth*s (i.e., sayings attributed to the Prophet Muḥammad), such as the verse: *It is God who created the heavens and the earth and all between them in six days, then He seated Himself on the throne . . .* (32:4). Some of the Ḥashawites went so far as to assert the possibility of physical contact between humans and God. They also believed that the written script of the Qurʾān and the sounds made when it is recited are eternal. (See al-Shahrastānī, *al-Milal wa-l-Niḥal*, vol. 1, pp. 120–122.)

5. The Arabic word that I translate as 'conformism' is *taqlīd*. A conformist is *muqallid*, which literally means imitator. (Hence *taqlīd* literally means imitation.) *Muqallid* is a technical term of Islamic law. It refers to a follower of a *madhhab* (i.e., a school of Islamic law) who has no specialized legal knowledge but merely adheres to the decrees of a jurist or a group of jurists of that *madhhab*. Hence it is said that he "imitates" that specific jurist or jurists. In general, a *muqallid* is someone who adheres to a tradition without rational scrutiny, and *taqlīd* is such an adherence.

6. The Muʿtazila was one of the oldest and largest schools of Islamic theology. It comprised many subschools (al-Baghdādī lists twenty-two of them), but they were united in their belief in absolute divine justice and divine unity. Divine justice, for the Muʿtazilites, implies that all the acts of God are good, that God fulfills all His obligations, that humans have free will and the power to produce their actions according to their free will, and hence they are responsible for their good deeds and for their evil deeds, and that God's promise to reward His obedient servants and His threat to punish His disobedient servants were true and just consequences. One of the earliest manifestations of the Muʿtazilites' commitment to divine justice was their doctrine of the "intermediary position" (*al-manzila bayn al-manzilatayn*; literally, a position between the two positions). They held that a Muslim who committed a major sin (*kabīra*) and died without atoning for his sin was neither a believer (*muʾmin*) nor an infidel (*kāfir*), but rather he was a grave sinner (*fāsiq*), which is an intermediary position between that of a believer and that of an infidel. They argued that it was unjust to place a grave sinner among the believers because faith (*īmān*) was achieved through acquiring the characteristics of goodness, yet a grave sinner lacked a significant part

the intellect, so as to collide against the absolutes of the revelation, put forward what can only be based on malefic consciences. The former were inclined towards deficiency and the latter towards excess; and both were far from judiciousness and caution. The definitive obligation in [investigating] the foundations of belief is to maintain moderation and steadiness on the straight path, for either extreme in pursuing the matter is reprehensible.

How could right guidance be attained by one who is content with conforming to a tradition and a testimony and rejects the methods of investigation and theorization? Does he not know that there is no basis for the divine teaching other than the statements of the master of mankind,[7] and that his truthfulness in what he relates is established by a demonstration of the intellect? And how could one be guided to what is right if he confines himself to pure reason and does not illuminate his eyesight with the light of the revelation? I wish I knew how one could take refuge in the intellect when he is afflicted with dyslogia[8] and anguish. Does he not know that the intellect's steps do not reach far and its scope is narrow and limited?

Far from it! He who is not able to bring together the distinctive aspects of reason and revelation would fail decidedly and categorically and would

---

of these characteristics; and it was equally unjust to place him among the infidels because he professed the articles of faith and possessed many of the characteristics of goodness; so he must be placed in an intermediary position. However, they also argued that since in the hereafter there are only two groups, those who deserve paradise and those who deserve hell, and since only the believers deserve paradise, a grave sinner will be condemned to hell for eternity but his punishment will be less than that of an infidel. Divine unity means, for the Muʿtazilites, that God is one in all respects. They denied that God had eternal attributes that were additional to His essence, because they saw in this multiplicity and composition in God that were contrary to His absolute unity (the Islamic philosophers maintained a similar doctrine about the divine attributes). They believed that the Qurʾān was created and not eternally coexisting with and subsisting in God's essence. The Muʿtazilites gave metaphorical readings of many of the divine attributes and of all the anthropomorphic descriptions of God found in the tradition. For example, they interpreted the verse cited in note 4 above about God's sitting on the throne as a metaphor for God's assuming authority over the heavens and the earth. In general, the Muʿtazilites were rationalists, in the sense that they believed that following reason was adequate for discovering all the fundamental truths of religion. (See al-Shahrastānī, *al-Milal wa-l-Niḥal*, vol. I, pp. 56–96; al-Baghdādī, *al-Farq bayn al-Firaq*, pp. 81–138; Badawī, *Madhāhib al-Islāmiyyīn*, pp. 37–484; Amīn, *Ḍuḥā al-Islām*, vol. III, pp. 21–150, and *Ẓuhr al-Islām*, vol. IV, pp. 17–56.)

7. The expression 'the master of mankind' refers to the Prophet Muḥammad.

8. 'Dyslogia' is the translation of *ʿiyy*, which means the temporary (or permanent) loss of the ability to express thoughts in spoken language. As mentioned in the Translator's Introduction, the *Iqtiṣād* was most likely written in, or shortly before AH 488/1095 CE, and al-Ghazālī suffered his major spiritual crisis in 1095. Part of that crisis was the loss of his ability to speak. I do not think that one should infer that there is a connection between al-Ghazālī's mentioning of *ʿiyy* and his own predicament, since it is very likely that al-Ghazālī was not in a position to write a major work immediately after his "illness."

be entangled in the webs of errors.[9] The example of the intellect is that of eyesight that is free from diseases and ailments, and the example of the Qur'ān is that of the sun, whose light radiates throughout. It is more appropriate for the seeker of right guidance who dispenses with one of them for the sake of the other to be among the dim-witted. For the one who forsakes the intellect, relying only on the light of the Qur'ān, is like the one who dwells in the sunlight with his eyelids shut, so that there is no difference between him and the blind. Reason together with revelation is light upon light. He who tries to observe one of them specifically with his blind eye is hanging from an illusory rope.

It will become clear to you, O you who long to know the foundations of the beliefs of the followers of the Sunna and who aspire to establish them by conclusive proofs, that no sect other than this one succeeded in integrating the revelation and theoretical verification.[10] So be grateful to God (Exalted is He) for your following in their footsteps, your enrolling in their order, your entering into their multitude, and your mixing with their group, so that you may be resurrected on the Day of Resurrection with their company.

We ask God (Exalted is He) to clear our hearts from the murkiness of error, to fill them with the light of truth, to mute our tongues from uttering what is false, and to make them articulate what is true and wise. He is Most Generous, whose grace is bountiful, and whose mercy is most wide.

9. The Arabic idiom is *ta'aththar bi-adhyāl al-ḍalālāt* (literally, "would trip on the coattails of errors").

10. The Arabic term is *taḥqīq*, which could mean, in philosophical contexts, verification, establishment by means of proof or evidence, examination, or investigation. Since al-Ghazālī mentioned earlier the reader's aspiration to establish these beliefs (*taḥqīqahā*), 'theoretical verification' seems to be an appropriate translation.

# [Preface]

*Chapter*

Let us begin our discussion by stating the title of the book, and describe its division into introductions, parts, and chapters. As for the title of the book, it is *Moderation in Belief*. As for its organization, it consists of four introductions, serving as prologues and forwards, and four treatises, serving as aims and objectives.

*The First Introduction*: on showing that this science[1] is one of the important matters for the religion.

*The Second Introduction*: on showing that it is not important for all Muslims but for a specific group of them.

*The Third Introduction*: on showing that it is one of the collective, and not of the individual, obligations.[2]

*The Fourth Introduction*: on explaining the methods of proof that I employ in this book.

As for the intended treatises, there are four. Most of them are concerned with theoretical reflection on God (Exalted is He). For if we reflect on the world, we do not reflect on it insofar as it is world, body, heaven, and earth, but insofar as it is the work of God. And if we reflect on the Prophet, we do not reflect on him insofar as he is a man, honorable, knowledgeable, and righteous, but insofar as he is the Messenger of God. And if we reflect on

1. *The science* of which al-Ghazālī speaks throughout this book is the science of *kalām*, which is theology. Sometimes, it is referred to as 'scholastic theology' and, though rarely, as 'philosophical theology'. 'Scholastic theology' is a reasonable translation since some jurists discussed theological issues although they were not considered practitioners of *kalām*. On the other hand, *kalām* is more generic than the phrase 'philosophical theology' suggests. I prefer to translate it as simply 'theology'. (A theologian is a *mutakallim* and theologians are *mutakallimūn* or *mutakallimīn*.)

2. According to Islamic law, an individual obligation (*farḍ 'ayn*) is a religious obligation incumbent upon every individual Muslim who meets certain conditions. For example, fasting during Ramaḍān is such an obligation. A collective obligation (*farḍ kifāya*), on the other hand, is an obligation that devolves upon the Muslim community as a whole, and not upon every member of the community who meets certain conditions. For instance, the funeral prayer is a collective obligation: if some members of the Muslim community perform the prayer, then the community as a whole has met its obligation, even if most members of the community might have not participated in the prayer.

his sayings, we do not reflect on them insofar as they are sayings, addresses, and explanations, but insofar as they are information from God conveyed by him. Thus there is no reflection but on God, and there is nothing sought but God. All parts of this science are confined to theoretical reflection on the essence of God, on the attributes of God, on the acts of God, and on the Messenger of God and what he related in the way of informing about God. They are, therefore, four treatises.

*The First Treatise*: theoretical reflection on the essence of God (Exalted is He). We show in it that He exists, that He is eternal anteriorly, that He is eternal posteriorly, that He is not a substance,[3] not a body, not a mode,[4] not bounded by a limit, not specified by a direction, that He can be seen[5] as well as known, and that He is one. These are, then, ten propositions that we establish in this treatise, God willing.

*The Second Treatise*: on the attributes of God (Exalted is He). We show in it that He is living, knower, powerful, willer, hearer, seer, sayer, and that He is endowed with life, knowledge, power, will, hearing, sight, and speech. We state the characteristics of these attributes and their necessary consequences,[6] and which characteristics are shared among them and in which characteristics they differ, and that these attributes are additional to the essence, eternal, and subsisting in the essence, and that it is not possible that any of the attributes is an occurrent.[7]

*The Third Treatise*: on the acts of God (Exalted is He). In it there are

3. By 'substance' (*jawhar*) al-Ghazālī means here *extended substance*. Like most theologians and philosophers, al-Ghazālī would be willing to describe God as non-extended substance, if 'substance' simply refers to that which subsists in itself and not in a subject.

4. 'Mode' is my translation of *'araḍ* when it is contrasted with substance (*jawhar*), that is, when it is used to mean that which does not subsist in itself but subsists in a subject. See Note on the Translation for further discussion of this choice.

5. The traditional doctrine is that God will be seen by His righteous servants in the hereafter. This doctrine is based on literal interpretations of certain Qur'ānic verses and sayings of the Prophet Muḥammad. The following Qur'ānic verse is an example of these statements: *Faces, on that day, will be radiant, looking towards their Lord* (75:22–23).

6. 'Their necessary consequences' can be understood as referring to the divine attributes or to their characteristics. The Arabic original, *wa-nadhkur aḥkām hādhih al-ṣifāt wa-lawāzimahā/lawāzimihā*, contains the same ambiguity as the English: if it is *lawāzimahā* (their necessary consequences), then it refers to *aḥkām* (characteristics); and if it is *lawāzimihā*, then it refers to *al-ṣifāt* (the attributes). As it is standard in most Arabic texts, the short vowels are not written. Except for the Jeddah edition, all the editions in my possession do not distinguish between *lawāzimahā* and *lawāzimihā*. The Jeddah edition selects *lawāzimahā* (and hence makes 'their necessary consequences' refer to the characteristics). I have no knowledge whether this choice is based on a manuscript or is due to the editor. It should also be noted that both *aḥkām* and *ṣifāt* are feminine.

7. 'Occurrent' is my translation of *ḥādith*. See Note on the Translation for further discussion of this choice.

seven propositions. They are: it is not incumbent upon God to assign obligations, nor to create, nor to reward for fulfilling the obligations, nor to care for the well-being of His servants, nor is it impossible for Him to assign obligations that exceeds the ability [of the one obligated], nor is it incumbent upon Him to punish for committing sins, nor is it impossible for Him to send prophets. Rather, all of these are contingent.[8] At the outset of this treatise, there is an explanation of the meanings of 'obligatory', 'good', and 'bad'.

*The Fourth Treatise*: on the messengers of God and what was related by His Messenger (may God bless him and grant him peace) regarding the resurrection and congregation, paradise and hellfire, intercession, the torment of the grave, the balance, and the path. In it there are four chapters. The First Chapter: on establishing the prophethood of Muḥammad (may God bless him and grant him peace). The Second Chapter: on what is related by him regarding the affairs of the hereafter. The Third Chapter: on the imamate and its requirements. The Fourth Chapter: on explaining the canon for imputing infidelity to heretical sects.

# First Introduction

*On showing that to wade into this science is important for the religion*

Know that devoting efforts to what is insignificant and wasting time on what is superfluous is the height of misguidedness and the extreme of loss, whether that to which the efforts are devoted is a science or an activity. We take refuge in God from [the pursuit of] useless science.

The most important of affairs for all mankind is the attainment of eternal happiness and the avoidance of everlasting misery. Prophets came who told mankind that God (Exalted is He) has rights and is owed duties by His servants in their activities, utterances, and beliefs, and that he whose tongue does not speak truly, whose heart does not embrace the truth, and whose limbs are not adorned with justice[9] is destined to hellfire and to utter ruin. They did not confine themselves to merely relating news but they attested to their own truthfulness by performing strange things and

8. 'Are contingent' is my translation of the verb *yajūz*. Its noun and adjective are *jā'iz*, which means permissible, possible, or contingent. By saying that God's acts are contingent, al-Ghazālī means that God can do them, if He wills, or can refrain from doing them, if He wills. (See First Treatise, note 4, for further elaboration.)

9. The reading in the Cairo edition is *bi-l-ʿadl* (with justice); in the Jeddah and Ankara editions it is *bi-l-ʿamal* (with work).

wondrous acts that transcended the habitual course of things[10] and were beyond[11] the abilities of human beings. So for one who has seen them or has heard about them through widely transmitted reports,[12] the possibility of their truthfulness would readily be impressed on his mind; indeed, their truthfulness would be most probable for him as soon as he hears about them—even before he examines carefully the distinction between miracles and merely wondrous crafts.

This intuitive probability or necessary possibility removes equanimity from the heart and fills it with foreboding and fear. It moves [a person] to investigate and to contemplate. It robs him of calmness and contentment. It warns him against the consequences of indulgence and negligence. It impresses upon him that death is surely coming, that what is after death is hidden from the eyes of mankind, and that what the prophets related is not beyond the realm of possibility.

Thus it is judicious to abandon any procrastination in discovering the truth of this matter. The prophets—given the wondrous acts they performed and the possibility of their truthfulness even before investigating to verify their claims—are no less [to be heeded] than someone who tells us, after we exited our home and place of residence, that a lion has entered the house, and so we should take precautions and protect ourselves from it. By merely hearing this, and realizing that what we were told is within the realms of possibility and probability, we do not venture to enter the house, but we go to extremes in being cautious. Death is decidedly *the* home and *the* residence; how then could it be that being cautious with respect to what comes after it is not important?

Therefore the most important matter is to investigate the prophet's testimony, which the mind determined by initial opinion and first reflection to be possible. Is it, upon verification, impossible in itself or is it undoubtedly true? Among his statements is: "You have a Lord who obliged you with

10. Al-Ghazālī uses *ʿādāt*, which literally means habits. He avoids describing miracles as transcending natural causation because, as an Ashʿarite, he believes in occasionalism, which is the doctrine that all occurrents, including all effects and all acts of living beings, are directly caused by God, and that "natural causes" are not really true causes but simply "occasions" for God to bring about the expected effects. Hence what appears to be an event e1 causing an event e2 is merely the habitual conjunction of e1 and e2 due to the *direct* action of God. Al-Ghazālī discusses this doctrine in the Second Treatise.

11. *Khārija ʿan* (outside of) is the reading in the Jeddah edition. It is *baʿīda ʿan* (far from) in the Ankara edition.

12. In the original it is *al-akhbār al-mutawātira*. *Akhbār* here is news, reports, or testimonies, and *mutawātira* means a statement that is transmitted and related through many different sources, so that it is extremely unlikely that it is the product of liars. Different translators use different translations for this term. I have seen it translated as 'recurrent testimony', 'corroborated testimony', and 'recurrently corroborated testimony'. See Fourth Introduction, note 47, for further elaboration.

respect to rights, and He will punish you for ignoring them and will reward you for fulfilling them, and He has sent me as a messenger to you to explain this to you." It is incumbent upon us, without a doubt, to know whether we indeed have a Lord. And if we do, is it possible that He is a sayer in order to command and forbid, assign obligations, and send messengers? And if He is a sayer, is He powerful so as to punish and reward if we obey or disobey Him? And if He is powerful, is this specific person truthful in saying "I am the messenger to you"? If this becomes clear for us, then it is definitely incumbent upon us, if we are rational, to be cautious, look out for ourselves, and devalue this perishing worldly life in relation to the everlasting hereafter. For the prudent is the one who prepares for his hereafter and is not deluded by his worldly life.

The objective of this science is to erect a demonstration for the existence of the Lord (Exalted is He), His attributes, and His acts, and for the truthfulness of the messengers, as we specified in the table of contents.[13] All of this is important and is indispensable for an intelligent person.

If you say, "I do not deny this incitation in my soul to seek, but I do not know whether it is a product of my disposition and nature, a dictate of the intellect, or a religious obligation, for people have different opinions regarding the sources of obligation," then you will indeed know this at the end of the book, when we deal with the sources of obligation. To deal with it now is impertinence. The only appropriate course of action, after the occurrence of the incitation, is to rise and seek deliverance. Analogous to someone who is occupied with the source of the incitation is a man who is bitten by a snake or a scorpion that will bite again, and the man is able to escape but stands still in order to ascertain whether the snake came from the right side or from the left side. This is the behavior of the dim-witted and the ignorant. We take refuge in God from busying ourselves with what is impertinent and neglecting what is important and fundamental.

# Second Introduction

*On showing that to wade into this science, although it is important, is unimportant for some people but what is important for them is to avoid it*

Know that the proofs we erect in this science are analogous to the remedies used to treat the ailments of the heart. The physician who prescribes them, if he is not skilled and does not have acumen and sound judgment, may cause more damage by his remedies than he effects cures. So let him who

13. The "table of contents" refers to the Preface.

comprehends the content of this book and benefits from these sciences know that people are of four classes.

*The first class* is a group of people who have faith in God, believe His Messenger, believe and embrace the truth, and occupy themselves with either worship or trades. They ought to be left as they are without disturbing their beliefs by encouraging them to study this science. For the man with the revelation (may God bless him) did not ask the Arabs, when he preached to them, for more than their conviction; and he did not differentiate between its being due to faith and conventional adherence or to the certitude of a demonstration. This is necessarily known from his common practice of approving of the faith of the Bedouin Arabs, who were quick to believe him based not on any investigation or demonstration but merely on indications and conjectures that entered their hearts and led them to submit to the truth and follow their conviction. They are true believers. Their beliefs should not be disturbed. For if these demonstrations are mentioned to them, together with the problems that surround them and their solutions, it cannot be guaranteed that one of these problems would not persist in their minds and control them, or that it would be erased from their minds by what might be presented in the way of a solution. It is for this reason that it was not reported that the companions of the Prophet engaged in this art in terms of investigation, study, or composition; but their occupation was only with worship, inviting others to worship,[14] and prompting people to seek the right paths and what benefits them in their affairs, activities, and livelihoods.

*The second class* is a group of people who stray from believing the truth, such as the infidels and the heretics. The whip and the sword are the only useful means for dealing with those of them who are harsh and coarse, weak-minded, rigid in following a tradition, and raised on falsehood from infancy to maturity.[15] The majority of the infidels converted to Islam in the shadows of the swords; for God does by means of the sword and spear what he does not do by means of demonstration. This is why if you survey the historical narratives, you will not encounter a battle between the Muslims and the infidels that did not result in a group of the followers of error being inclined towards submission,[16] and you will not encounter a session of

14. Literally, and the invitation to it (*wa-l-daʿwa ilayhā*).

15. Al-Ghazālī's readers are sometimes struck by his oscillation between harsh intolerance and compassionate tolerance. Both extremes are evident in this introduction. It is wroth noting that this harsh judgment is not in agreement with many Islamic texts, such as the Qurʾānic verse: *Let there be no compulsion in religion; the right way stands out clearly from error . . .* (2:256).

16. That is, submission to Islam.

debate and argument that did not result in more insistence and obstinacy.[17] Do not think that what we just mentioned belittles the status of the intellect and its demonstrations; but the light of the intellect is a grace with which God distinguishes the few among his devout servants. What is for the most part characteristic of mankind is inadequacy and ignorance. Because of their inadequacy, they do not apprehend the demonstrations of the intellect, just as bats' eyes do not perceive the sunlight.[18] They are harmed by the sciences the way the floral breeze harms the dung beetle. Al-Shāfiʿī (may God have mercy upon him) said about such people:

He who gives the ignorant knowledge squanders it
And he who withholds it from those who deserve it acts unjustly.

*The third class* is a group of people who believe the truth by conforming to tradition and convention, but are distinguished by being endowed with intelligence and perspicacity. They become aware by themselves of difficulties that make them doubt their beliefs and shake their contentment, or they hear a skeptical opinion and it persists in their hearts. They must be treated gently by restoring their contentment and dispelling their doubts by whatever speech they find convincing and agreeable, even by merely making their doubts improbable and repugnant, or reciting a Qur'ānic verse, or relating a *ḥadīth*, or conveying the statements of someone who is well known to them in terms of virtue. If the doubt [of one of them] is dispelled with just this, then he should not be presented with the proofs that are delivered in the course of argumentation; for this might open the door for other difficulties for him. However, if he is intelligent and perspicacious, so that he can be convinced only by a discussion that follows the course of[19] theoretical verification, then it is permissible to present him with the actual proof; but that should be based on the extent of the need and be specific to the exact difficulty.

*The fourth class* is a group of the followers of error, in whom the signs of intelligence and perspicacity are detected, and who are expected to accept the truth, because their beliefs are infected with doubt and their hearts, by nature and disposition, are receptive to skepticism. They must be dealt with gently in attracting them to the truth and in guiding them to the right belief. It should not be through heated debate and zealotry;

17. The debate and argument are understood to be between Muslims and infidels.

18. The simile in the original is more vivid, because the Arabic sentence uses one verb *yudrik* (or, *tudrik*) for both 'apprehend' and 'perceive'.

19. The reading in the Cairo edition is *yasīr ʿalā* (in this context, it follows the course of). In the Jeddah and Ankara editions, it is *yaṣir ʿalā* (in this context, it turns into, or it results in).

for this strengthens the motivations for going astray and excites the causes for extremism and obstinacy. Most of the ignorant beliefs took root in the minds of the common people because of the zealotry of some imprudent followers of the truth. They presented their true doctrines in a challenging and arrogant manner, and they looked upon the weak among their opponents with disdain and disparagement. Thus there rose inside them the causes for obstinacy and contrariness; false beliefs were firmly established in their souls, and it became difficult for the gentle scholars to erase them despite the beliefs' apparent corruption.[20] The zealotry of some people reached such an extreme, that they believed that the letters they uttered for the first time, after not having spoken them throughout their lives, were eternal.[21] Were it not for the devil taking over, fostering obstinacy and the zealousness of whims, such a belief would have had no place in the mind of a madman, let alone in the mind of a sane man.

Heated debate and obstinacy are pure disease for which there is no remedy. So let one who is devout exert effort to stay clear from it, abandon malevolence and spite, look upon all mankind[22] with a merciful eye, rely on kindness and gentleness in guiding those who go astray among this nation, and be wary of harassment, which awakens the cause for going astray.[23] And let him be assured that whoever excites the cause for persistence in a heresy by being obstinate and zealous aids in the persistence in the heresy and will be held accountable for this aid on the Day of Judgment.

# Third Introduction

*On showing that the occupation with this science is a collective obligation*

Know that [the occupation with] penetrating the depths of this science and mastering its breadth is not an individual but a collective obligation.[24] As

20. It should be clear from the context that the obstinate contrarian people, to whose souls false beliefs are affixed, are the common people who were treated with disdain and disparagement by the imprudent zealous followers of the truth. Al-Ghazālī uses the third-person plural pronouns to refer to both groups of people without specifying to which group he is referring.

21. Al-Ghazālī is referring to minor groups, such as the Ḥashawiyya (see Religious Preface, note 4), who maintained that the letters of the physical script of the Qur'ān and the sounds made when it is recited were not occurrents but eternal.

22. Alternatively, God's creation (*khalq Allāh*).

23. The Jeddah and Ankara editions add *min al-ḍāl* (for the one who goes astray). The sentence is stated in the Cairo edition without this addition.

24. See Preface, note 2, for an explanation of the difference between individual and collective obligation.

for its not being an individual obligation, the demonstration of this should be clear to you from the Second Introduction,[25] since there it is shown that what is obligatory for all mankind is only resolute conviction and purifying the heart from skepticism and doubt about faith. However, the dispelling of doubt becomes an individual obligation for the one who is overcome with doubt.

You might say: "Why is it a collective obligation, when you have stated that most classes of people are harmed by it and do not benefit from it?" Know then, as previously stated, that the dispelling of doubts about the fundamentals of beliefs is obligatory, and that to be overcome with doubt is not impossible, even though it occurs only to the few. Furthermore, using demonstrations to invite to the truth the one who is insistent on falsehood and who is likely, due to his intelligence, to comprehend the demonstrations is important for the religion. Furthermore, it is not improbable that a heretic may rebel and undertake seducing the people who follow the truth by introducing a dubious doctrine. So there must be someone who strives against his dubious doctrine by exposing it and counters his seduction by uncovering its ugliness; and this is possible only through this science. There is no city that is immune from such events. Hence, it is obligatory that in every country and every region there be a defender of the truth,[26] who is occupied with this science, strives against the propaganda of the heretics, redirects those who stray from the truth, and purifies the hearts of the followers of the Sunna from the ills of the dubious doctrine. If a country lacks such a person, the whole population of the country would be at fault, exactly as if it lacks a physician or a jurist.

So it is; if one perceives in himself an aptitude for learning jurisprudence or theology, and the region lacks specialists in them,[27] and he does not have sufficient time for mastering both of them, and he requests a decree specifying the one in which he should be occupied, then we would oblige him to be occupied with jurisprudence. For the need for it is more common

25. It is possible to construe al-Ghazālī's argument in the Second Introduction as a demonstration (*burhān*). It may be reconstructed as follows.
(1) If $x$ is an individual obligation and $p$ is a person who is able to perform $x$, then $x$ is obligatory for $p$.
(2) If $x$ is obligatory for $p$, then $p$ cannot be harmed by $x$.
(3) Many people who are able to study the science of theology will be harmed by their studying theology.
(4) From 2 and 3 it follows that the study of theology is not obligatory for many people who are able to study theology.
(5) Therefore, from 1 and 4, the study of theology is not an individual obligation.

26. The Arabic phrase is *qā'im bi-l-ḥaq* (literally, someone who is in charge of the truth).

27. The Arabic phrase is *al-qā'im bi-himā* (literally, the one who is in charge of them).

and its applications are more numerous. No one can dispense, in his nights and days, with the aid of jurisprudence. On the other hand, the occurrence of doubts that present a need for the science of theology is rare in relation to jurisprudence. Similarly if a city lacks a physician and a jurist, studying jurisprudence would be more important; because the need for it is shared by the nobility and the populace; as for medicine, the healthy do not need it and the sick are fewer in number in relation to them. Moreover, the one who is sick cannot dispense with jurisprudence as he cannot dispense with medicine, and his need for medicine is for this fleeting life and for jurisprudence is for his everlasting life—and what a difference there is between these two lives. If you compare the fruit of medicine to the fruit of jurisprudence, you would know that the difference between the bearers of the fruit is the same as the difference between the fruit.[28]

What proves for you that jurisprudence is the most important science is the engagement of the companions of the Prophet in researching it in their consultations and negotiations. Do not be misled by the exaggeration of those who glorify the practice of theology by claiming that it is the principle and jurisprudence is a branch of it. It is a true statement but it is useless in this context. The principle is right belief and resolute conviction, and these are attainable through conformity. The need for demonstration and for the subtleties of argumentation is rare. The physician, too, may equivocate by saying, "Your existence is first, then your beneficence;[29] and the existence of your body is conditional on my art and your life is dependent on me; hence life and health are first, then comes occupation with religion." The distortion behind these statements is apparent, and we have cautioned against it.

# Fourth Introduction

*On explaining the methods of proof that we employ in this book*

Know that the methods of proof ramify. We mentioned some of them in the book *The Touchstone of Theorization*[30] and discussed them with elaboration in the book *The Standard for Knowledge*.[31] In this book, however, we stay

28. Literally, if you relate the fruit of medicine to the fruit of jurisprudence, you would know that what is between the fruit-bearers is what is between the fruits.

29. The clause 'Your existence is first, then your beneficence' is in the Ankara edition. It is dropped from the Jeddah edition.

30. *Miḥak al-Naẓar*.

31. *Mi'yār al-'Ilm*.

away from dead-end paths and obscure trails, aiming at clarity, inclining towards brevity, and avoiding long-windedness. We confine ourselves to three methods.

*The first method*: *al-sabr wa-l-taqsīm*.[32] This one is restricting the matter to two cases; we then refute one of them; from this the affirmation of the second necessarily follows.[33] For example, we may say, "The world is either occurrent or anteriorly eternal, and it is impossible that it is anteriorly eternal; thus it necessarily follows from these that it must be occurrent." This necessary consequence is what we seek. It is an intended cognition, which we gain from two other cognitions. One of them is our statement that the world is either anteriorly eternal or occurrent. To affirm this disjunction is a cognition. The second is our statement that it is impossible for it to be anteriorly eternal. This is another cognition. The third is what necessarily follows from them; it is what is sought—namely, that the world is occurrent. Every cognition that is sought can only be gained from two cognitions, which are principles—not any two principles; rather, a relation should obtain between them according to a specific manner and a specific condition. If this relation obtains according to its condition, a third cognition is gained, which is what is sought. We may call this third cognition "a claim" if we have an opponent; we may call it "what is sought" if we do not have an opponent, because it is what the theorist seeks; and we may call it "a yield"[34] or "a branch" in relation to the two principles, because it is what is gained from them. So long as our opponent grants the two principles, it is inevitable that he necessarily grant the branch that is gained from them, and thus the truth of the claim.[35]

32. The literal translation of *al-sabr wa-l-taqsīm* is 'principle and division'. This is a technical term used by jurists and theologians to refer to a type of syllogism that logicians and philosophers call *al-qiyās al-sharṭī al-munfaṣil* (literally, disjunctive conditional syllogism). The example al-Ghazālī gives in what follows is a standard disjunctive syllogism: (i) P or Q, (ii) not-P, (iii) therefore Q. But in the books of Islamic logic, such as al-Ghazālī's *Miʿyār al-ʿIlm* (pp. 130–131), this syllogism is in fact better described as an *exclusive* disjunctive syllogism, whose disjunctive premise, 'Either P or Q', is true if and only if either P or Q is true, but not both. (*Inclusive* truth conditions allow for both P and Q to be true). If we read the disjunctive premise exclusively, four inferences are licensed by this syllogism.

| Either P or Q | Either P or Q | Either P or Q | Either P or Q |
|---|---|---|---|
| not-P | not-Q | P | Q |
| Therefore, Q | Therefore, P | Therefore, not-Q | Therefore, not-P |

33. *Yalzam* (it necessarily follows) is the reading in the Cairo edition. The reading in the Jeddah and Ankara editions is *naʿlam* (we know).

34. Literally, benefit or gain (*istifāda*).

35. 'Cognition' is my translation of *ʿilm*, which in this context means roughly an item or a piece of knowledge. It is worth noting that al-Ghazālī eschews the use of standard logical

*The second method.* This one is arranging two principles in a different manner, such as our statements: "Whatever is not devoid of occurrents is itself an occurrent" (this is a principle); and "The world is not devoid of occurrents" (this is another principle). The truth of our claim that the world is an occurrent necessarily follows from them, and this is what is sought. So consider: is it imaginable that our opponent would grant the two principles and then deny the truth of the claim? You know conclusively that this is impossible.

*The third method.* This one is that we do not directly establish our claim, but we claim that our opponent's position is impossible by showing that since it leads to an absurdity, it is inevitably absurd.[36] An example of this is our saying: "If our opponent's claim that the revolutions of the celestial sphere are infinite is true, then the truth of the statement that the infinite has been concluded and completed necessarily follows; it is known that this necessary consequence is absurd; hence it necessarily follows[37] that what leads to it, namely the doctrine of our opponent, is surely absurd."[38] So here are two principles. One of them is our statement that if the revolutions

---

terminology in this introduction. For example, he does not use the familiar terms *muqaddima* (premise) and *natīja* (conclusion). We encounter, instead, *aṣl* (principle), *istifāda* (benefit or gain), *'ilm* (cognition), *da'wā* (claim), and other nonstandard terminology. It seems, therefore, that al-Ghazālī in this work is addressing himself to readers who lack prior knowledge of logic or philosophy.

36. The third method is the first part of the inference rule reductio ad absurdum. The first part asserts that if P leads to absurdity, then conclude not-P. The second part asserts that if not-P leads to absurdity, then conclude P. It is well known that both parts must be included and supplemented with other standard rules to account for classical logic. Intuitionistic logic accepts the first part but rejects the second. There are strong reasons to believe that al-Ghazālī also accepts the law of excluded middle, which asserts that 'P or not-P' is always true. We know from the first method that al-Ghazālī accepts the inference rule disjunctive syllogism. The first part of reductio ad absurdum, together with the law of excluded middle and disjunctive syllogism, entails the second part of reductio ad absurdum. Here is a short demonstration.

1. Suppose that not-P leads to absurdity.
2. By the first part of reductio ad absurdum: not-not-P.
3. By the law of excluded middle: P or not-P.
4. From 2 and 3, and by disjunctive syllogism: P.

37. *Yalzam* (it necessarily follows) is the reading in the Jeddah edition; in the Ankara edition it is *yu'lam* (it is known).

38. Al-Ghazālī will invoke the same line of argumentation later in the book. It is clear that al-Ghazālī believes that the concept of actual infinity is incoherent. He argues for this conclusion in many places, most notably in this book and in *Tahāfut al-Falāsifa*. The problem he sees here that is implied by the concept of actual infinity is the *completion* of actually infinitely many terms. His point is that the concept of the actual infinite implies both (1) that it has no end and (2) that an infinity of terms has been completed. He sees these propositions as inconsistent with each other, because he takes (1) to imply that no infinite sequence has been completed.

of the celestial sphere are infinite, then the infinite has been concluded. The judgment that the concluding of the infinite is a necessary consequence of denying the finitude of the revolutions of the celestial sphere is knowledge that we claim to have and that we assert. It is imaginable, however, that our opponent would affirm his claim and deny our statement by saying: "I do not concede that this is a necessary consequence."[39] The second is our statement that this necessary consequence is absurd. This, too, is a principle for which it is imaginable that there would be a denial, as he might say: "I concede the first principle but I do not concede the second one, which asserts the impossibility of concluding the infinite." But if he were to affirm the two principles, it would be a necessary requirement to affirm the third cognition, which necessarily follows from them; this would be the acknowledgment of the impossibility of his doctrine insofar as it leads to this absurdity.[40]

These are three clear methods of proof; to deny that through them knowledge is obtained is unimaginable. The knowledge that is obtained and sought is what is proved, and the conjoining of the two principles that necessarily imply this knowledge is the evidence. To know the manner in which what is sought necessarily follows from the conjoining of the two principles is to know the manner in which the evidence provides proof. Theoretical reflection is the reflection that consists in your bringing the two

39. What the opponent is made to say, however, does not express the thought fully. The missing portion is implicit. The first principle is that the completion of the infinite is a consequence of the *claim* that the number of the revolutions of the celestial sphere is infinite. This is the opponent's claim and the part he would affirm. He would deny the second part—namely, that his claim leads to the "absurd" consequence that the infinite is completed.

40. Al-Ghazālī sets up the reductio ad absurdum argument against the opponent as a standard modus tollens argument. As is well known, every reductio ad absurdum argument can be transformed into a modus tollens argument. A reductio ad absurdum argument has the following general form.

Suppose P and infer Q from P.
Q is absurd.

---

Therefore, not-P
The argument can be given a modus tollens form.
If P, then Q (first principle)
not-Q (second principle)

---

Therefore, not-P
The modus tollens form of the actual argument that al-Ghazālī considers is this.
First principle: If the revolutions of the celestial sphere are infinite, then the infinite has been concluded.
Second principle: The concluding of the infinite is impossible (or absurd).

---

Conclusion: The claim that the revolutions of the celestial sphere are infinite is impossible (or absurd).

principles to mind and your seeking an awareness of the manner in which the third cognition necessarily follows from the two cognitions that are the two principles. Therefore, two tasks are required of you in order to attain the cognition that is sought. One of them is to bring the two principles to mind—this is called "reflection." The other is to look for an awareness of the manner in which what is sought necessarily follows from the conjoining of the two principles—this is called "seeking."

For this reason the one who restricts his attention to the first task, when aiming for a definition of theoretical reflection, would say that it is reflection. And the one who restricts his attention to the second task, when defining theoretical reflection, would say that it is the seeking of either knowledge or the most likely opinion. And the one who pays attention to both matters would say that it is the reflection through which the one who reflects seeks knowledge or the most likely opinion.

This is how you ought to understand evidence, what is proved, the manner of proof, and the nature of theoretical reflection. Set aside the elaborations and the reiterating of statements, with which many sheets of paper are inked, and which do not satisfy the fervor of a seeker and do not quench the desire of a thirsty one. No one appreciates the value of these brief statements but he who has abandoned his quest in disappointment after having read many treatises. That you now, in searching for the correct definition, consult what has been said about the definition of theoretical reflection shows that you did not gain any benefit from this discussion and did not return from it with any result. Thus if you learn that there are only three cognitions—two cognitions that are two principles arranged in a specific manner and a third cognition that necessarily follows from them—and that what is required of you is only two tasks, one of them, to bring the first two cognitions to mind, and the second, to be aware of the manner in which the third cognition necessarily follows from them, then you have a choice after that of using the term 'theoretical reflection' to denote either the reflection through which you bring the two cognitions to mind, or the anticipation that is the seeking of an awareness of the manner in which the third cognition necessarily follows, or the two matters jointly. For the expressions are open to all and there should be no quarrel over terminology.

You might say: "My purpose is to learn the terminology of the theologians; what do they denote by 'theoretical reflection'?" Then know that if you were to hear one person define theoretical reflection as reflection, another as seeking, and another as the reflection through which one seeks, you would not doubt that their terminology is used in three different ways. What is surprising is the one who is not aware of this. He supposes that the statements regarding the definition of theoretical reflection are a disputed matter; he presents evidence for the correctness of one of the definitions; and he does not know that the meaning understood from these definitions is not disputed and that it is senseless to have disagreement over terminology. If you look closely and are guided to the right path, you will surely know that most mistakes arise from the error of seeking meanings from terms, when it is incumbent upon one, first, to determine the meanings and, second, to look into the terms, and to know that they are terms that do not change the intelligibles. But he who is denied success travels backward and abandons verification.

You might say: "I do not doubt that the truth of the claim necessarily follows from the two principles, if my opponent affirms them in this way; but what makes it incumbent upon the opponent to affirm them? And where do the principles that must be conceded come from?"[41] Then know that these have many ways of being apprehended, but we will labor to restrict what we use in this book to no more than six apprehensions.

*The first*: the sensibles. I mean that which can be apprehended by external or internal perception.[42] An example of this is our statements: "Every occurrent has a cause; there are occurrents in the world; hence they must have a cause." Thus our statement that there are occurrents in the world is a principle that our opponent must affirm, since he apprehends by external perception the occurrence of individual animals, plants, clouds, and rain, and, among the modes, sounds and colors. If he imagines that they are transferable, then the transfer is an occurrent.[43] We claim that there is an occurrent, and we do not specify whether that occurrent is a substance, mode, transfer, or something else. Similarly, he knows by internal perception the occurrence of pains, joys, and sorrows in his heart and body. Hence, he cannot deny it.[44]

*The second*: the pure intelligibles. If we say that the world is either occurrent or anteriorly eternal, and there is no option beyond these two options, this is something that it is incumbent upon every rational person to admit. An example of this is that we say: "Whatever does not precede an occurrent is an occurrent; the world does not precede the occurrents;[45] therefore, it is an occurrent." One of the two principles is our statement that whatever

41. The Arabic reads *al-uṣūl al-musallama al-wājibat al-taslīm*, which literally means "the accepted principles whose acceptance is necessary."

42. Literally, seeing (*mushāhada*).

43. Al-Ghazālī is addressing here the possible objection that these modes are never originated but are rather transferred from one substance to another.

44. The opponent cannot deny the principle that there are occurrents in the world.

45. *Ḥawādith* (occurrents) is the reading in the Cairo edition. The reading in the Jeddah and Ankara editions is *ḥādith* (occurrent).

does not precede an occurrent is an occurrent. Our opponent must affirm it, because that which does not precede an occurrent either is concurrent with it or exists after it, and no third option is possible. If he were to claim that there is a third option, he would be denying what is self-evident to the intellect. And if he were to deny that what is concurrent with an occurrent or exists after it is an occurrent,[46] he would also be denying what is self-evident.

*The third*: widely transmitted reports.[47] An example is that we say: "Muḥammad (may God bless him and grant him peace) is truthful, because whoever performs a miracle is truthful, and he performed a miracle, therefore he is truthful." If it is said, "I do not concede that he performed a miracle"; then we say, "He brought forth the Qur'ān, and the Qur'ān is a miracle, hence he brought forth a miracle." If our opponent[48] accepts, either on his own or because of a proof, one of the two principles, namely, that the Qur'ān is a miracle, and wants to deny the second principle, which is that Muḥammad brought forth the Qur'ān, and says "I do not concede that the Qur'ān is brought forth by Muḥammad," then this is a denial that is not possible for him.[49] For widely transmitted reports produced this knowledge for us, as they produced our knowledge of Muḥammad's existence, of his

46. Following the Jeddah edition, I read *fahū ḥādith* (it is an occurrent) instead of *fahū ghayr ḥādith* (it is *not* an occurrent), which is the reading in the Ankara edition. It is clear that the negation in the Ankara edition conflicts with the verb *ankar* (deny).

47. The Arabic word is *mutawātir*. I discussed my translation of *mutawātira*, which is the feminine form of *mutawātir*, in the First Introduction, note 12. Here is some further elaboration. The word *mutawātir* implies the existence of multiple sources and unbroken testimonial chains. In the science of Ḥadīth, which is the discipline that studies the sayings and the practices of the Prophet Muḥammad, *mutawātir* describes a statement or a description of a practice that is attributed to the Prophet by several sources and that has reached us via unbroken testimonial chains. It is assumed to be virtually impossible that all those witnesses propagated a lie. In Islamic law, the evidentiary status of the *mutawātir* Ḥadīth is similar to that of the Qur'ān. Al-Ghazālī does not use *mutawātir* here in this strict technical sense. Instead he is referring to reports, commonly communicated in the community, that have been transmitted via many testimonial chains that go back to the original events or sources. For example, you know that Mecca exists. But how do you know that it does without your having been there? Perhaps you heard of its existence from many people who heard it from others who heard the same from others who visited Mecca. This is an example of the kind of information that al-Ghazālī here calls *mutawātir*. Of course, his usage covers *mutawātir* Ḥadīth as well.

48. 'Opponent' (*al-khaṣm*) is in the Cairo edition. It is left out in the Jeddah and Ankara editions.

49. The notion of possibility at work here is epistemic. It cannot be logical, metaphysical, or physical, since in these senses the opponent can deny whatever he pleases. From an epistemic point of view, however, given what he knows, he *cannot* deny that Muḥammad brought forth the Qur'ān. Al-Ghazālī argues that since the opponent is a member of the community, part of his knowledge is the acquaintance with such widely transmitted reports

claim to prophethood, of the existence of Mecca, and of the existence of Jesus, Moses, and the rest of the prophets (may God bless them all).

*The fourth*: this is for a principle to be established by another inference[50] that is founded—on one or many levels—on either sensibles, intelligibles, or widely transmitted reports; for something that is a branch of two principles can be made a principle in another inference.[51] An example is that after we conclude our proof for the occurrence of the world, we may make the occurrence of the world a principle in a syllogism. For instance, we may say: "Every occurrent has a cause; the world is an occurrent; therefore it has a cause." They cannot deny that the world is an occurrent after we have established it by a proof.

*The fifth*: revealed truths.[52] An example is that we claim that sins are in accordance with God's will, and we say: "Everything that exists is in accordance with God's will; sins exist; therefore they are in accordance with God's will." As for our statement that they exist: their existence is known through the senses; and that they are sins is known on the basis of the revelation. As for our statement that everything that exists is in accordance with God's will: if our opponent would deny this, he would be prevented by the revelation, so long as he affirms the revelation or it was established for him by a proof. For we establish this principle by the consensus of the community regarding the truthfulness of the one who says: "Whatever God willed was and whatever He did not was not." Thus the revealed truth prevents the denial.

*The sixth*: this is for the principle to be taken from the opponent's beliefs

---

as that Muḥammad brought forth the Qur'ān. Since such reports are a source of knowledge, the opponent must know that Muḥammad brought forth the Qur'ān.

50. The Arabic term *qiyās* can mean syllogism, inference, or analogy. Translators of Arabic medieval texts usually use 'syllogism'. Contemporary Arabic logic texts, however, use *qiyās* to mean inference. (In books of Islamic jurisprudence *qiyās* is usually translated as 'legal analogy'.) I use either 'syllogism' or 'inference', depending on the context. Since the current context speaks of multiple levels on which a proposition may be proved, *qiyās* is best understood here as inference.

51. A branch of two principles is one of their consequences. In logical terms, the sentence says that a conclusion inferred from two premises may be used as a premise in another inference.

52. The Arabic term is *samʿiyyāt*. It is a technical term used in the study of Islamic beliefs (*al-ʿaqāʾid*). The feminine plural noun *samʿiyyāt* almost never appears in any other context. (A contemporary phrase is *ʿilm al-samʿiyyāt*, which refers to the science of acoustics or the science of phonics.) It is safe to assume that al-Ghazālī intends to use the term in its technical sense to denote the information that is based solely on revelation, such as descriptions of paradise and hell. The translation 'revealed truths' captures this technical sense. The example al-Ghazālī discusses in the passage supports this understanding of *samʿiyyāt*. (See al-Jurr, *Lārūs*: *al-Muʿjam al-ʿArabī al-Ḥadīth*, p. 676, s.v. *samʿiyyāt*; and Muṣṭafā et al., *al-Muʿjam al-Wasīṭ*, p. 450, s.v. *samʿiyyāt*.)

or concessions. Even though we may have no proof for it, and it is not a sensible or an intelligible, we could still benefit from invoking it as a principle in our syllogism. Our opponent is prevented from denying it, because a denial would be destructive to his position.[53] The examples of this are numerous, so there is no need to specify any one of them.

You might say: "Is there a difference among these apprehensions in their usefulness for theoretical inferences?" Then know that they differ in how widespread their usefulness is. The intellectual and perceptual apprehensions are common to all mankind except those who have no intellect or no sense. The principle that is known through a sense that one lacks has no value for him, such as a principle that is known through the sense of sight when it is presented to a congenitally blind person; if the congenitally blind person is the theorist, then he could not invoke it as a principle. The same applies to what is based on hearing as pertains to a deaf person.

As for the widely transmitted reports, they are useful but only to someone to whom they were transmitted. If someone were to arrive to us now from a faraway place, having never heard the call to Islam, and we wanted to show him, based on widely transmitted reports, that Muḥammad (may God bless him and grant him peace) challenged people with the Qur'ān,[54] then he would not be able to see it unless we allowed him time, so that the reports could be transmitted to him. Something might be widely reported within one group of people but not within another. The position of Abū Ḥanīfa (may God be pleased with him) regarding killing a Muslim [who murders] a non-Muslim residing in a Muslim country[55] is widely reported among his peers of jurists but not among the common people who are conformists.[56] Many schools of Islamic law have positions on isolated issues that are not widely reported among most jurists.

53. 'Because the denial is destructive to his position' (*li'ann al-inkār hādim li-madhhabih*) is the reading in the Jeddah edition. The reading in the Ankara edition is 'which is destructive to his position (*al-hādim li-madhhabih*).

54. According to Islamic tradition, the Prophet Muḥammad challenged people to produce a chapter (*sūra*) that is similar to the chapters of the Qur'ān in form and content. The challenge is reported in several Qur'ānic verses, such as the following: *And if you are in doubt as to what we have revealed to Our servant, then produce a sūra like it, and call your helpers apart from God, if you are truthful* (2:23).

55. A non-Muslim who resides in an Islamic land is denoted in Arabic by a single word—namely, *dhimmī*.

56. The Jeddah edition follows a correction made in one of the manuscripts in reporting Abū Ḥanīfa as the holder of this position instead of al-Shāfi'ī, who is mentioned in all the other editions and manuscripts. The Jeddah edition is correct. Al-Shāfi'ī holds precisely the opposite position. Abū Ḥanīfa's position is that if a Muslim murders a *dhimmī* (i.e., a non-Muslim who lives in a Muslim country), the family of the victim has the same rights as Muslims: they can choose to pardon the killer and be paid "blood money," or they can choose

As for a principle that is obtained from another inference, it only benefits the one who accepts that inference. As for the presuppositions of a doctrine, they do not benefit the theorist, but they benefit the one who is challenging[57] the one who believes that doctrine. As for the revealed truths, they benefit only the one who affirms the revelation.[58]

These are, then, the apprehensions for having knowledge of the principles—apprehensions, which, through their arrangement and structure, yield knowledge of unknown matters that are sought.

Now that we have concluded the introductions, we will be occupied with the treatises, which are the aims of this book.

---

to have him killed. Al-Shāfiʿī's position is that a Muslim should not be killed as a retribution for murdering a *dhimmī*. It is not clear what the source of the confusion is. Al-Ghazālī was a celebrated professor of Islamic jurisprudence and a prominent Shāfiʿite jurist. It is unthinkable that he was unacquainted with al-Shāfiʿī's position.

57. I followed the Cairo edition in reading *munāẓir* (debater or disputant) instead of *nāẓir* (theorist), which is the reading in the Jeddah and Ankara editions.

58. Alternatively, the one for whom the revelation has been established (*man thabat al-samʿ ʿindah*).

# FIRST TREATISE

∵

## *Theoretical Reflection on the Essence of God (Exalted is He)*

IT CONSISTS OF TEN PROPOSITIONS.

# First Proposition

*The existence of God (Exalted and Sanctified is He)*

Its proof is that we say: "The occurrence of every occurrent has a cause; the world is an occurrent; it necessarily follows that it has a cause." We mean by 'the world' all existents other than God (Exalted is He). And we mean by 'all existents other than God' all the bodies and their modes. The explanation of all of this in details is that we do not doubt the principle of existence. Furthermore, we know that every existent is either extended or non-extended, and that every extended thing, if there is no combination in it, is called "a single substance," and if it comprises something other than itself, is called "a body," and that the existence of a non-extended thing either requires a body in which it subsists, and hence we call it "a mode," or it does not, and this is God (Glorious and Exalted is He).

As for the existence of bodies and their modes, this is known by observation. No attention should be paid to the one who disputes the existence of modes, even if he quibbles loudly and beseeches you to offer a proof for it. For if his commotion, disputation, beseeching, and shouting did not exist, then how could they be engaged through responding and listening to him? If they do exist, then they are inevitably other than the disputant's body, since his body existed earlier when the disputation did not exist.[1] Thus you know that body and mode are apprehended by observation.

Regarding an existent that is neither a body, nor an extended substance, nor a mode, it cannot be apprehended by perception. We claim that it exists and that the world exists by virtue of it and its power. This can be ap-

1. This style of argument is common to many arguments against skeptical hypotheses. Its strategy is to show that the skeptical hypothesis is self-defeating. Perhaps the simplest of those arguments is the one that attempts to refute the hypothesis that knowledge is impossible. The argument runs as follows: it is either possible or not possible to know that knowledge is impossible; if it is not possible, then there is no position to be concerned with; but if it is possible, then knowledge is possible after all, and hence the skeptical hypothesis is false. Al-Ghazālī's argument follows the same general strategy. Assume there is a person who disputes that modes exist. Either his disputing is real or not. If it is not real, then there is no dispute to address. If it is real, then it is clearly not identical with the disputant's body, since his body existed even without his disputing; hence his disputing must be a mode. Therefore, modes exist.

prehended by a proof, not by perception. The proof is what we stated.[2] Let us return to its verification.

We have included in it two principles. Our opponent might deny them. We say to him: "Which principle do you dispute?" He might say: "I dispute your statement that every occurrent has a cause; how did you know this?" We say: "This principle must be affirmed; for it is a priori and necessary according to reason." The one who is not moved by it is, perhaps, not moved because it is unclear to him what we intend by the term 'occurrent' and the term 'cause'. If he understood them, his mind would necessarily believe that every occurrent has a cause. For we mean by 'occurrent' that which was nonexistent and then became existent. Thus we say: "Was its existence before it existed impossible or contingent?"[3] It is false that it was impossible, since what is impossible can never exist. If it was contingent, then we

2. Al-Ghazālī is referring to the original argument presented at the beginning of the First Proposition—namely, that every occurrent has a cause; the world is an occurrent; therefore the world has a cause.

3. 'Contingent' is my translation here of *mumkin*. The word *mumkin* has two usages in the Islamic philosophical and theological literature. The first indicates that which is the opposite of impossible, that is, that whose existence is not impossible. The second indicates that whose existence and nonexistence are not impossible. The second usage is the more common and the one that Ibn Sīnā describes in *al-Najāt* (vol. I, pp. 27–30, and vol. II, p. 77) as the usage of the select (*al-khāṣṣa*), while he describes the first usage as that of the populace (*al-ʿāmma*). In *al-Ishārāt wa-l-Tanbīhāt* (pp. 90–91) he calls the first usage 'the general *mumkin*' and the second 'the special *mumkin*'. Al-Ghazālī in *Miʿyār al-ʿIlm* (pp. 325–330) lists several meanings of *mumkin*, the first of which is that whose existence is not impossible (this is our first usage) and the second of which is that whose existence and nonexistence are not necessary, or, equivalently, whose existence and nonexistence are not impossible (this is our second usage). Al-Ghazālī and Ibn Sīnā say that the first sense includes the necessary, and the second sense excludes the necessary. They also say that *mumkin* in the second sense forms one of three categories: that whose existence is impossible (which is the *mumtaniʿ*), that whose existence is necessary (which is the *wājib*), and that whose existence and nonexistence are not necessary (which is the *mumkin*). It is typical (though by no means universal) to translate *mumkin* as 'possible' whether it is used in the first or second sense. However, given the way modalities are defined in the logical literature, 'possible' is the correct translation of *mumkin* when it is used in the first sense, and 'contingent' is the correct translation when it is used in the second sense. The notions of necessity, impossibility, and contingency are mutually exclusive and collectively exhaustive. We can say that an object is necessary when the supposition of its nonexistence is contradictory; an object is impossible when the supposition of its existence is contradictory; and an object is contingent when the suppositions of its existence and of its nonexistence are both not contradictory. We may define a possible object as an object the supposition of whose nonexistence is not contradictory. Nevertheless, even well-known authorities use 'possible' to translate *mumkin* when it is used in the second sense. For instance, Jamīl Ṣalībā in his *al-Muʿjam al-Falsafī* (vol. II, pp. 424–426) lists 'possible' as the *only* translation of *mumkin*, and he defines it as that for which existence and nonexistence are on a par (*yatasāwā fīh al-wujūd wa-l-ʿadam*) and contrasts it with *mumtaniʿ* and *wājib* (this, in fact, is *mumkin* in the sense of contingent); he later says,

mean by 'contingent' only that which is possible[4] to exist and is possible not to exist. However, it was not a necessary[5] existent, because its existence is not necessitated by its essence; for if its existence were necessitated by its essence, it would be necessary, not contingent. In fact, its existence was deprived of that which would give it preponderance over nonexistence—preponderance, which would change nonexistence into existence. If its nonexistence continues, then that is because there is nothing that gives preponderance to existence over nonexistence; for so long as there is nothing that gives this preponderance, existence does not come about.[6] We do not intend by 'a cause' anything other than the giver of preponderance.

In summation, for a nonexistent whose nonexistence continues, its nonexistence would not change into existence unless something comes along that gives preponderance to the side of existence over the continuation of nonexistence. If the meanings of these terms are fixed in the mind, the intellect would have to accept this principle.[7] This is the validation of this principle—a validation that is established by explaining the terms 'occurrent' and 'cause', not by erecting a proof for it.[8]

---

however, that whatever is free from contradictions is *mumkin* in the absolute or logical sense (this is *mumkin* in the sense of possible).

4. 'Is possible' is my translation of the verb *yajūz*; its noun is *jā'iz*, which means permissible, possible, or contingent. *Jā'iz* is sometimes used synonymously with *mumkin* (see the preceding note). Ṣalībā in *al-Mu'jam al-Falsafī* (vol. 1, pp. 385–386) mentions several meanings for *jā'iz*. One meaning is that which is conceptually not impossible (hence, it is conceptually *possible*) and a second meaning is that for which existence and nonexistence are conceivable (hence, it is conceptually *contingent*). However, Ṣalībā lists 'contingent' as the only translation of *jā'iz*. As in the case of *mumkin*, 'possible' is the correct translation of *jā'iz* when it is used in the first sense but 'contingent' is the correct translation when it is used in the second sense.

5. 'Necessary' (*wājib*) is in the Jeddah edition. The Ankara edition leaves it out.

6. The Cairo edition has *lā yūjad al-wujūd* (existence does not come about), and the Ankara and Jeddah editions have *lā yūjad* ([the occurrent] does not exist).

7. The expression 'this principle' refers to the premise that states that every occurrent has a cause.

8. The expression 'not by erecting a proof for it' (*lā iqāmat dalīl 'alayh*) is the choice of the Ankara and Jeddah editions. The Cairo edition has 'as a proof for it' (*li-iqāmat dalīl 'alayh*). I adopted the first reading. It seems to me that al-Ghazālī is correct in saying that he need not give a proof showing that every occurrent has a cause, because this premise (principle) is an a priori one, and hence its truth follows immediately from the meaning of the terms involved. It is clear that al-Ghazālī does not distinguish, as Kant does, between analytic and a priori propositions. Kant defines a priori propositions as those that are known independent of experience (such as the propositions of mathematics) and a posteriori (or empirical) propositions as those that are known through experience (such as existential propositions about the objects of our experience). In addition, an analytic proposition is one whose predicate is contained in the concept of its subject (such as the proposition 'All bodies are extended') and a synthetic proposition is one whose predicate is not contained

It might be said: "How do you refute the one who disputes the second principle, which is your statement that the world is an occurrent?" We say that this principle is not a priori, but we establish it by a proof containing two other principles. We say: "If we say that the world is an occurrent, then we now intend by 'the world' only bodies and substances."[9] So we say: "No body is devoid of occurrents; whatever is not devoid of occurrents is an occurrent; it necessarily follows that every body is an occurrent."[10] About which of these two principles is there a dispute?

It might be said: "Why did you say that every body and extended sub-

---

in the concept of its subject (such as the proposition 'All bodies are heavy'). Kant famously asserts that there are synthetic a priori propositions. On Kant's view, almost all the propositions of mathematics and metaphysics are synthetic a priori. An example that is of particular interest to us here is the metaphysical proposition 'Everything that happens has a cause'. This is just another version of al-Ghazālī's first premise 'Every occurrent has a cause'. Kant says that the proposition is a priori because it cannot be known through experience, since its universality extends beyond the scope of all experiences and it makes an assertion about a necessary connection—namely, causation—which cannot be learned through experience. According to Kant, the proposition is not analytic, however, because the concept of cause is not included in the concept of that which happens. Hence the proposition is said to be synthetic a priori. Notice that this is contrary to al-Ghazālī's position. Al-Ghazālī argues that the proposition is a priori (*awwalī*) and necessary (*ḍarūrī*) precisely because its truth is established without recourse to experience but merely by understanding the concepts involved—namely, occurrent and cause—and seeing that the concept of the predicate (has a cause) is contained in the concept of the subject (occurrent). For to be an occurrent simply means to be existent after having been nonexistent, but the concept of becoming existent after having been nonexistent contains the concept of a giver of preponderance, which is the very meaning of a cause. This is why al-Ghazālī says that he did not erect a proof for it. (See Kant, *Critique of Pure Reason*, Introduction , A1–A13, and Introduction <B>, B1–B24.)

9. In this book al-Ghazālī almost always uses 'substance' (*jawhar*) to mean extended substance (*jawhar mutaḥayyiz*). When he uses 'substance' to include non-extended substance, he usually makes his usage explicit.

10. There are two ways in which this argument establishes that the world is an occurrent. The first is to say that since the world contains bodies and since bodies are not devoid of occurrents, the world is not devoid of occurrents; but whatever is not devoid of occurrents is itself an occurrent, therefore the world is an occurrent. The second way is to modify the conclusion of the argument such that it asserts that every body *and* extended substance is an occurrent; given that the world is the collection of all bodies and extended substances, it follows that the world is an occurrent. To reach the modified conclusion, the first premise must be changed to state that every body *and* extended substance is not devoid of occurrents. It is clear from the following paragraph that al-Ghazālī has this modified version of the premise in mind. It is worth noting that there is a standard objection to the latter inference. If the world consists of infinitely many objects, then even if one understands by 'occurrent' that which has a beginning, and by 'world' the collection of all bodies and extended substances, and even if one accepts, too, that all bodies and extended substances are occurrents, it would not follow that the world itself had a beginning. For if the world consists of infinitely many objects, then it is possible that there is no point in time after which all those objects origi-

stance is not devoid of occurrents?" We say: "Because it is not devoid of motion or rest, and they are occurrents." If it is said, "You have claimed that they exist and, moreover, that they occur; we concede neither their existence nor their occurrence,"[11] then we say, "This question was answered with much elaboration in the books of theology, and it does not even deserve this elaboration; for it is never posed by a reasonable person." No rational person would ever doubt that modes, such as aches, sicknesses, hunger, thirst, and other states truly exist in himself or that they actually occur. Similarly, if he observes the bodies of the world, he would not doubt the alteration of their states and that these alterations are occurrents. If an opponent disputes this, then it is senseless to engage his position; and if it is supposed that an opponent accepts what we have said, then it is an absurd supposition, assuming that the opponent is rational.[12]

Indeed, the opponents with respect to the occurrence of the world are the philosophers. They affirm that the bodies of the world are divided into the heavens, which move constantly, and the units of whose movements are occurrents but are perpetual and sequential, following each other eternally both anteriorly and posteriorly,[13] and into the four elements,[14] which are contained in the sublunar world.[15] They affirm, too, that these elements share matter, which is the bearer of their forms and accidents, and that

---

nated. Al-Ghazālī, however, does not believe that actual infinities exist and he asserts, as we will see later, that the existents are finite.

11. Note that al-Ghazālī distinguishes occurrence from mere existence. To occur is to exist after having been nonexistent. Thus the assumption that rest and motion exist does not necessarily imply that they occur, but, of course, to assume that they occur is to assume that they exist (or at least, that they have existed at some time).

12. The two opponents deny the premise stated at the beginning of the paragraph—namely, that every body and extended substance is not devoid of occurrents. The first opponent is a "disputing opponent" (*khaṣm muʿānid*) because he also disputes the import of the observation that the states of bodies change and that these changes are occurrents. Al-Ghazālī thinks that this position denies the obvious and is unworthy of consideration. The second opponent is a "believing opponent" (*khaṣm muʿtaqid*) because he accepts the truth of the observation that bodies undergo change and that changes are occurrents. Al-Ghazālī thinks that this position is inconsistent, for the truth of the observation, which the "believing opponent" accepts, implies the truth of the original premise, which this opponent rejects.

13. 'Eternally anteriorly' is a translation of *azalan*, that is, eternally without a beginning; and 'eternally posteriorly' is a translation of *abadan*, that is, eternally without an end.

14. These are the familiar four elements of the ancient Greeks: earth, water, air, and fire.

15. The expression 'the sublunar world' is part of the medieval Islamic philosophers' idiom. It is borrowed from the ancient philosophers, and it refers to the terrestrial world. The term is embedded in the philosophers' descriptions of their various emanation (*fayḍ*) schemes. (For an account of these emanation schemes see Deborah L. Black, "al-Fārābī," and Charles Genequand, "Metaphysics," both in *History of Islamic Philosophy*, edited by Seyyed Hossein Nasr and Oliver Leman, pp. 187–189 and pp. 787–796, respectively.)

this matter is eternal though the forms and accidents are occurrents and alternate in it eternally both anteriorly and posteriorly.[16] For water is transformed by heat into air, and air is transformed by heat into fire, and so the rest of the elements. They mix in various ways, which are occurrents, thereby producing minerals, plants, and animals. The elements never cease from acquiring these occurrent forms, and the heavens never cease from exhibiting these occurrent movements. What the philosophers dispute is our statement that whatever is not devoid of occurrents is an occurrent.

Therefore there is no point in elaborating on this principle.[17] However, in order to supply an outline, we say that a substance is necessarily not devoid of motion and rest, which are occurrents. As for motion, its occurrence is perceptible. If a stationary substance, such as the earth, is considered, then positing a motion for it is not impossible; in fact, its possibility is known necessarily. If this possible motion takes place, it would be an occurrent and it would annihilate rest. Hence, the rest that is prior to this motion would also be an occurrent, since what is eternal anteriorly does not cease to exist, as we will state when giving a proof for the posterior eternity of God (Exalted is He).[18]

If we want to give a proof for the existence of motion as additional to the body, we say: "If we state that this substance is moving, we affirm the existence of something other than the substance." The proof of this is that if we say that this substance is not moving, our statement would be true, assuming that the substance is still, in a state of rest. If the concept of motion is precisely that of substance, then to deny it would be to deny the substance

16. In the preceding sentence, I translated *aʿrāḍ* as 'accidents' instead of 'modes', since the contrast is not with substances but with forms, and forms are standardly understood as the essences of things. I said in the Note on the Translation that when *ʿaraḍ* (singular of *aʿrāḍ*) is contrasted with *jawhar* (substance), its most likely meaning is mode; and when it is contrasted with *dhāt* (essence), its most likely meaning is accident.

17. The principle here remains the premise that every body and extended substance is not devoid of occurrents.

18. The point here is that if the stationary substance had been in a state of rest since eternity, it would *have to* continue to be in this state forever, and motion could not be a possible state for it. Al-Ghazālī needs this point in order to establish that the earth's state of rest is occurrent (i.e., that it had a beginning in time). He reasons as follows: if a stationary substance, such as the earth, had been in a state of rest since eternity, then it would necessarily stay at rest forever, and motion would never be a possible state for it; but it is necessarily known that motion is a possible state for the earth; therefore the earth could not be in a state of rest since eternity; and since the earth could not be in a state of rest since eternity, its state of rest is occurrent. It is true that al-Ghazālī had said that what is anteriorly eternal is posteriorly eternal, but that alone does not tell us whether the posterior eternity is a matter of fact or of necessity, yet the argument depends on its being a matter of necessity. Al-Ghazālī will therefore argue, in the Third Proposition of the First Treatise, that what is anteriorly eternal *cannot* cease to exist.

itself. A similar proof applies regarding the affirmation of the existence of rest and its denial. In sum, contriving a proof for the obvious adds obscurity to it and does not enhance its clarity.

It might be said: "How do you know that motion is an occurrent? It might have been latent and only subsequently emerged." We say that if we were occupied in this book with curiosities that lie beyond our purpose, we would have independently refuted the affirmation of latency and emergence for modes. However, we do not occupy ourselves with that which does not undermine our purpose. Rather we say that a substance is not devoid of the latency or the emergence of motion in it, and both are occurrents.[19] It is established, therefore, that it is not devoid of occurrents.

It might be said: "Motion could have transferred to it from another place; how do you know the falsity of affirming that modes transfer?" We say that weak proofs have been given to refute this, and we will not lengthen the book by rehearsing and rebuffing them. The correct approach to showing its falsity is to explain that deeming such a transfer possible is not allowed by an intellect unless it lacks an understanding of the true nature of mode and the true nature of transfer; and the one who understands the true nature of mode ascertains the impossibility of its transfer.

The explanation of this matter is that transfer is a notion borrowed from the transfer of a substance from one region to another.[20] The notion of mode's transfer arises in the mind when it understands substance, region, and the substance's attachment to a region as additional to the essence of the substance. Subsequently the mind knows that a mode must have a locus just as a substance must have a region. Hence it imagines that relating a mode to a locus is similar to relating a substance to a region. This leads "the estimation"[21] to posit the possibility of the transfer of a mode just as there

19. Emergence is clearly an occurrent, since to emerge is to come into existence after having been latent. That latency is an occurrent is shown on the basis of the argument discussed in note 18 above. If $x$ is latent for anterior eternity, then it would not be possible for $x$ to emerge later. So if it is ever possible for $x$ to emerge at any point, it could not be latent for anterior eternity, that is, its latency must be an occurrent.

20. Al-Ghazālī uses the word *maḥall*, which means place or locus , in association with the transfer of a mode (*'araḍ*), and the word *ḥayyiz*, which means bounded area or region, in association with the transfer of a substance (*jawhar*). By 'region' he actually means spatial region but by 'locus' he means that in which the mode subsists. So it is a receptacle for or a holder of the mode. This is typically a body or an extended substance.

21. "The estimation" (*al-wahm*) or the estimative faculty (*al-quwwa al-wahmiyya*) is, according to Ibn Sīnā, one of the five internal senses. It is above imagination and below recollection. A representation in the imagination is never divorced from matter (what is represented in the imagination is always represented as existing in a material object), but "the estimation" applies a value judgment to the representation, such as "good," "bad," "frightening," and "pleasant." These evaluations are not among the sensibles, and hence the

is a transfer of a substance. If this analogy were correct, the mode's attachment to a locus would be something additional to the essence of the mode and the locus, just as the substance's attachment to a region is something additional to the essences of the substance and the region.[22] As a result, a mode would subsist in a mode, and the subsistence of the mode in a mode would require that yet another attachment be additional to the subsistent and to that in which the subsistent subsists.[23] Thus the process would lead to a regress such that there could not be one mode without there being an infinity of modes.[24]

Let us search for the reason behind the differentiation between the attachment of a mode to a locus and the attachment of a substance to a re-

---

estimative faculty deals with concepts (*ma'ānī*) that need not (but might) be instantiated by sensibles. (See Ibn Sīnā, *al-Najāt*, vol. II, pp. 8–10.) When this technical sense is intended by the noun 'estimation' and the verb 'estimate', I will enclose these two words in double quotation marks ("scare quotes").

22. The ambiguity in the English sentences reflects an ambiguity in the Arabic original. The sentence 'the mode's attachment to a locus would be something *additional to the essence of the mode and the locus*' (*zā'idan 'alā dhāt al-'araḍ wa-l-maḥall*) could be understood to mean that the attachment is additional to the mode's essence and to the locus's essence or that the attachment is additional to the mode's essence and to the locus. The same applies to the sentence concerning the substance's attachment to a region being *additional to the essence of the substance and the region* (*zā'idan 'alā dhāt al-jawhar wa-l-ḥayyiz*).

23. I decided to use the archaic 'subsistent' instead of 'that which subsists', because the clause would read 'that in which that which subsists subsists', which is quite cumbersome.

24. The infinite-regress argument requires some clarification. First, suppose that if the attachment of a mode $x$ to a locus is additional to the essence of $x$, then $x$ must subsist in another mode $y$. This supposition gives us infinite regress; for there would be an attachment of $y$ to a locus, and this attachment would be additional to the essence of $y$. Hence, by the supposition, $y$ subsists in a third mode $z$. Medieval philosophers and theologians did not permit cyclic chains; thus we cannot have $x$ subsists in $y$, $y$ subsists in $z$, and $z$ subsists in $x$. So this regress would have to continue ad infinitum, which is also rejected by the medieval philosophers and theologians. One, of course, might reject the original supposition and assume that if the attachment of a mode $x$ to a locus is additional to the essence of $x$, then $x$ must subsist in a substance, not in another mode. This assumption implies that $x$'s subsistence in the substance is additional to $x$'s essence, since the "locus" is the receptacle of the mode—i.e., the locus here is the substance—and the attachment relation (of a mode to a locus) is here just the subsistence relation (of a mode in a substance). But this is absurd; for part of the essence of any mode is its subsistence in a substance. Thus it cannot be the case that $x$'s subsistence in the substance is both *additional to* $x$'s essence and *part of* $x$'s essence. It follows from these two cases that if the attachment of a mode to a locus is additional to the mode's essence, then the mode can neither subsist in another mode nor can it subsist in a substance. But the consequent is absurd: a mode by definition must subsist in something. We conclude, therefore, that the attachment of a mode to a locus (i.e., receptacle) is not additional to its essence but part of its essence. Hence to transfer a mode from one locus to another is to change the essence of the mode, which implies that *the original* mode was not really transferred after all. Al-Ghazālī's goal of this argument is to deny that transfer is possible for modes.

gion, inasmuch as one of the two attachments is additional to the essence of that which has the attachment, but the other attachment is not. This would make clear the mistake of the estimative faculty in positing the transfer.[25] The secret to it is that although a locus is required for a mode just as a region is required for a substance, there is a difference between the two requirements. For a requirement might be essential to an object or it might be inessential to an object.[26] I mean by 'essential' that whose annulment necessarily annuls the object: if it is annulled in reality, the object would cease to exist; and if it is annulled in the intellect, the knowledge of the object would cease to exist in the intellect.

A region is not essential to substance. For we know a body and substance first, and only afterwards do we theorize about the region: is it an invariant or an "estimated" matter?[27] We arrive at a verification of [the answer to this question] through a proof, but we apprehend a body through sensation and observation without proof.[28] Thus the region occupied by Zayd's body is not essential to Zayd; for the loss or alteration of that region does not necessitate the annulment of Zayd's body. This is not so with, for example, Zayd's height, since it is a mode of Zayd, which we do not conceive in itself apart from Zayd. Indeed, we conceive Zayd as being tall. Zayd's height

25. Literally, the mistake in "estimating" the transfer. It is clear that 'the transfer' here refers to the transfer of a mode from one locus to another.

26. Al-Ghazālī's distinction between *required* (*lāzim*) and *essential* (*dhātī*) will be made clear as the argument unfolds. Having extension, that is, occupying space, is essential to extended substance: there can be no extended substance without extension. But occupying *a specific region* of space, though required, is not essential. It is required in the sense that an extended substance must occupy a specific region of space. It is not essential, however, because a substance might be *transferred* from one specific region to another while remaining the same substance, that is, its essence persists. As al-Ghazālī will argue below, *specific loci* (receptacles) are both required for and essential to mode: unlike a substance, if a mode is *transferred* from one specific locus to another, its essence is annihilated, and hence it ceases to exist.

27. An *estimated matter* here is a matter that is produced by the estimative faculty. The question may be explained, on the basis of the rest of the passage, as follows: is the presence of a particular region an invariant aspect of a body (or a substance) or is it only posited by the estimative faculty as belonging to the concept of a body (or a substance)?

28. The proof here is an intellectual proof and not a perceptual one. Al-Ghazālī's point seems to be this: whereas a body is apprehended by perception, only an intellectual proof can determine whether the presence of a specific region is an invariant part of this apprehension (*idrāk*) or not; hence the particular region that a body occupies cannot be part of the essence of the body. If this is a correct understanding of al-Ghazālī's point, then he must think that if an aspect is essential to an object, then an apprehension of the object carries with it an apprehension of the essentiality of that aspect. In order for this claim to be plausible, 'an apprehension of *x*' must be taken to mean something like "a conceptual awareness of the nature of *x*." Thus one might *see* a person without *apprehending* him. To apprehend a person one must be conceptually aware that what one is seeing is a *person*, that is, a rational animal.

is known as a consequence of Zayd's existence. The annulment of Zayd's height necessarily follows from supposing the nonexistence of Zayd; for Zayd's height does not subsist in reality or in the intellect apart from Zayd. Its attachment to Zayd is essential to it, that is, it is part of its essence, not something[29] additional to it; so it is specific to it. If this specificity is annulled, then the essence of Zayd's height is annulled. Transfer annuls specificity; thus its transfer would annul its essence.[30] For its being specific to Zayd is not additional to its essence—I mean the essence of the mode.[31] This is contrary to the way in which a substance is attached to a region: here the attachment is additional to its essence. Annulling the attachment by transfer would in no way annul the essence of the substance.

The discussion is based on this: transfer annuls attachment to a locus. If the attachment to a locus is additional to the essence of a thing, the essence is not annulled by [the annulment of the attachment to the locus], but if it is not additional, then the essence is annulled by the attachment's annulment. This has become clear. The conclusion of the theoretical reflection is that the attachment of a mode to a locus is not additional to the mode's essence, while the attachment of a substance to a region is.[32] And that is because of what we mentioned, namely, that a substance is conceived through itself and a region is conceived through itself,[33] but a substance is not conceived through its region. As for a mode, it is conceived through a substance, and not through itself. The essence of a mode is its being attached to a specific substance, and it has no essence other than this. If its separation from that specific substance is posited, then the annihilation of its essence is posited.

We have discussed the example of height to make our purpose understood. Even though height is not a mode—but it is the accumulation of

29. The Arabic word is *ma'nā*, which literally means "meaning." The Islamic medieval philosophers and theologians make wide use of it. It could be employed to mean "meaning," "concept," "notion", or even "thing" and "existent." Thus, depending on the context, I might translate it as 'meaning', 'concept', 'notion', or 'thing'.

30. Literally, thus its essence is annulled.

31. The sentence 'I mean the essence of the mode' is a translation of the reading in the Jeddah edition. The translation of the reading in the Ankara edition is 'I mean what is annulled; and the discussion returns to the essence of the mode'.

32. The meaning is that the attachment of a substance to a region is additional to the substance's essence.

33. In the original it is 'in it' (*bih*). The pronoun 'it' could be understood as referring to substance. Thus the meaning would be that a region is conceived through a substance. This implies that a space that is empty of any substance is inconceivable. This is not an absurd position; some philosophers hold that space is conceivable only through the spatial relations that obtain between objects. However, the editor of the Jeddah edition reports that a marginal note in the oldest manuscript asserts that 'it' here refers to the region itself. My translation is based on that interpretation.

bodies in one direction—it brings our purpose close enough to the understanding. Once it is understood, we can transfer the explanation to the case of modes.

This exploration and investigation, although inconsonant with brevity, was needed because what has been said about this issue is neither convincing nor satisfying. Thus we have concluded the establishment of one of the two principles, which is that the world is not devoid of occurrents; for it is not devoid of motion and rest, and they are occurrents that do not transfer. Our elaboration is not in response to a "believing opponent,"[34] nor to the philosophers who all agree that the bodies of the world are not devoid of occurrents but deny the occurrence of the world.

It might be said: "The second principle remains, namely, your statement that whatever is not devoid of occurrents is an occurrent; what is its proof?" We say: "It is because if the world were anteriorly eternal yet not devoid of occurrents, then there would be occurrents that have no beginning, from which it would necessarily follow that the revolutions of the celestial spheres are infinite in number; and that is absurd, because it leads to absurdity, and what leads to absurdity is absurd."[35]

We show that three absurdities necessarily follow from it. First, if this were the case, then what is infinite would have passed, would have been followed by void, and would have concluded. There is no difference between saying that it has passed, that it has concluded, and that it has ended. Hence it would be necessary to say that the infinite has ended. The notion that the infinite ends or that it concludes and passes is a glaring absurdity.[36]

Second, if the revolutions of the celestial spheres are infinite, then their number is either even, odd, neither even nor odd, or both even and odd. These four[37] cases are impossible, so what leads to them is impossible as well. It is impossible that a number is neither even nor odd, or is both even

34. As explained in note 12 above, a "believing opponent" is someone who rejects the premise that every body or extended substance is not devoid of occurrents yet accepts the truth of the observation that bodies undergo change and that the changes are occurrents. Al-Ghazālī previously said that such a position is absurd, because the truth of the observation (which the "believing opponent" accepts) entails the truth of the premise (which the "believing opponent" rejects).

35. The statement that is absurd (because it leads to absurdity) is the conclusion that the revolutions of the celestial spheres are infinite. In the next passage al-Ghazālī discusses three absurdities that follow from this statement.

36. As mentioned in note 38 of the Fourth Introduction, al-Ghazālī is troubled by the notion of actual infinity. He raises objections to this notion in other places, most notably, in *Tahāfut al-Falāsifa*. The objection of this paragraph is already discussed in that note. To summarize, al-Ghazālī sees the notion of actual infinity as implying two "contradictory" propositions: (1) an infinity of terms has been completed and (2) the progression of terms has no end.

37. The Jeddah edition has 'four', the Ankara edition 'three'.

and odd. For an even number is that which can be divided into two equal parts, such as ten, and an odd number is that which cannot be divided into two equal parts, such as seven. Every number that is composed of units either can be divided into two equal parts or cannot.[38] But to be described as capable and incapable of such division or as lacking both is impossible. It is false that it is even. For an even number is not odd because it is short of one; hence if one is added to it, it becomes odd; but how can the infinite be short of one? It is impossible that it is odd. For an odd number becomes even by adding one; hence it is odd because it is short of one; but how can the infinite be short of one?

Third, it necessarily follows from it[39] that there are two numbers, each of which is infinite, yet one is smaller than the other. It is impossible for an infinite to be smaller than an infinite, since a smaller number is that which is short of something: if [the missing something] is added to it, it becomes equal. Yet how can the infinite be short of something? The manifestation of this is that Saturn, according to them,[40] revolves once every thirty years and the sun revolves once every year. Thus the number of Saturn's revolutions is equal to one third of one tenth of the sun's revolutions. For the sun revolves thirty times in thirty years and Saturn revolves once; and one to thirty is one third of one tenth. Furthermore, the revolutions of Saturn are infinite, and they are fewer than the revolutions of the sun, since it is necessarily known that one third of one tenth of a magnitude is smaller than the magnitude. The moon revolves twelve times in a year. Thus the number of the revolutions of the sun is equal to one half of one sixth of the revolutions of the moon. Although every one of these numbers is infinite, nevertheless some of them are smaller than others. This is clearly impossible.[41]

38. The original literally says that every number that is composed of units either divides into two equal parts or into two unequal parts. Yet every number greater than two, whether odd or even, divides into two unequal parts (for instance, six divides into four and two). It may therefore be assumed that what al-Ghazālī intends is that some numbers can be divided *only* into two unequal parts; in other words, they cannot be divided into two equal parts.

39. The pronoun 'it' refers to the assertion that the revolutions of the celestial spheres are infinite.

40. Al-Ghazālī is arguing against the philosophers, who say that the world is anteriorly eternal. Hence 'them' refers to the philosophers.

41. Here is a contemporary mathematical response to the second and third objections: these and similar objections are standard difficulties encountered when *finite* concepts are mistakenly applied to the infinite. For instance, even, odd, prime, and composite are all finite notions that are not applicable to infinite numbers. The same applies to relative magnitudes. In the case of finite magnitudes, the part is always smaller than the whole, but not so in the case of actual infinities. For example, the set of even numbers, {0, 2, 4, 6, . . .}, is a proper subset of the set of natural numbers, {0, 1, 2, 3, 4, . . .}, but they have demonstratively the same magnitude: the mapping "$n \to 2n$" is a one-to-one correspondence between the two sets, which demonstrates that the two sets have the same number of members. It is

It might be said: "According to you, the objects of God's power are infinite, and so are the objects of His knowledge; yet there are more objects of His knowledge than there are objects of His power, since the essence of the Eternal and His attributes are known to Him and so is the Existent whose existence is persistent, and none of these is an object of power."[42] We say: "If we state that the objects of His power are infinite, we do not intend by it what we intend by our saying that the objects of His knowledge are infinite." In fact, we intend by it that God (Exalted is He) has an attribute represented as power through which the origination of things can be produced, and this capacity to produce never ceases.[43] Our statement that this capacity to produce never ceases does not imply the positing of actual objects, let alone describing them as finite or infinite. This mistake occurs for someone who looks at the meanings of expressions and sees the symmetry between the expressions 'objects of knowledge' and 'objects of power' with regard to their linguistic declension, and hence he thinks that what is intended by them is the same.[44] Far from it! There is no relation between them at all.

Moreover, our statement that the objects of knowledge are infinite is based on a secret that is contrary to what immediately comes to mind. For what immediately comes to mind is the positing of actual objects that are called "objects of knowledge" and are infinite; yet this is absurd. Indeed,

---

interesting to note that al-Ghazālī is aware of this response. He considers it and dismisses it in *Tahāfut al-Falāsifa*. In the First Discussion of the *Tahāfut*, which contains his polemics against the philosophers' doctrine of the anterior eternity of the world, he offers the second and third objections we find here. After describing the even-odd objection, he considers a possible rebuttal to his objection: "What is described as even or odd is the finite, and the infinite is not [so described]", but he rejects it: "A number that is composed of units and has a sixth and a tenth, as previously mentioned, and that cannot then be described as even or odd is known not to exist by necessity without [need for] theoretical reflection." (See al-Ghazālī, *Tahāfut al-Falāsifa*, pp. 99–100.)

42. The counterargument here is that al-Ghazālī is equally committed to the existence of actual infinities and to their relative magnitudes. He must be committed to the claim that the things that God can do and the things that He knows are actually infinite. Furthermore, the objects of His knowledge (i.e., what is known to Him) are more than the objects of His power (i.e., what is within the reach of His power); for he knows His essence, attributes, and eternal existence, and none of these is something He can create. Hence, al-Ghazālī is committed not only to the existence of two actual infinities but to one's being greater than the other. As we will see below, al-Ghazālī will argue that there is confusion here: saying that the objects of God's power are infinite does not imply that there is an infinity of actually existing objects that are the objects of His power.

43. My translation of the 'which' clause is liberal. Here is a very literal translation: through which the origination is made available, and this "making available" never becomes nonexistent.

44. The Arabic terms are *maqdūrāt* (objects of power) and *ma'lūmāt* (objects of knowledge). They share form, gender, number, and declension.

the actual objects are the existents, which are finite. However, the explanation of this matter requires much elaboration. The difficulty has been resolved by uncovering what is meant by denying the finiteness of the objects of power. Hence there is no need to address the second case, namely, the objects of knowledge, in order to discredit the inference.[45]

The correctness of this principle has been demonstrated using the third method of proof discussed in the Fourth Introduction of the book.[46] At

45. The inference here is the inference of the opponent's counterargument presented at the outset of the previous paragraph (see also note 42 above). The counterargument is aimed at showing that al-Ghazālī is committed to the existence of two actual infinities (the objects of divine power and the objects of divine knowledge), one of which is greater than the other. Al-Ghazālī says that by explaining the true meaning of the statement "The objects of God's power are infinite," we show that the inference of the opponent's counterargument is not necessary (i.e., invalid). He does not discuss the meaning of the statement "The objects of God's knowledge are infinite"; he maintains that explaining the meaning of the first statement should be adequate for invalidating the inference. His point is that just as we were able to show that there is a way of understanding the statement "The objects of God's power are infinite" that does not commit us to the existence of infinitely many objects, there is also a way of understanding the corresponding statement regarding God's knowledge that does not imply the existence of infinitely many objects. Thus neither statement justifies the opponent's claim that an actual infinity exists.

46. The principle that has been demonstrated is the premise that whatever is not devoid of occurrents is itself an occurrent, and the method of the demonstration is that of reductio ad absurdum. Al-Ghazālī first argues that if this premise were false, that is, if there are anteriorly eternal things that are not devoid of occurrents, then the world, which is not devoid of occurrents, could be anteriorly eternal; but if the world could be anteriorly eternal and is not devoid of occurrents, then there could exist actual infinities. He then argues that the existence of actual infinities is absurd, because it leads to three absurdities. Hence, by reductio ad absurdum, the original (reductio) assumption, which asserts that there are anteriorly eternal things that are not devoid of occurrents, is false. This establishes the truth of the premise that whatever is not devoid of occurrents is itself an occurrent. There are two points that require some elaboration. First, the claim that the world, which is not devoid of occurrents, could be anteriorly eternal does not necessarily follow from the reductio assumption that there are anteriorly eternal things that are not devoid of occurrents; for the world might not be such a thing. Al-Ghazālī applies the reductio assumption to the case of the world, because the world is the opponents' (here, the philosophers') primary example of an anteriorly eternal thing that is not devoid of occurrents, and because the main goal of al-Ghazālī's argument is to establish the occurrence of the world. In other words, al-Ghazālī and the philosophers accept the following conditional as true: if there are anteriorly eternal things that are not devoid of occurrents, then the world is such a thing. Al-Ghazālī's argument is supposed to show that the consequent of this conditional leads to absurdity. Second, even if the world is anteriorly eternal and not devoid of occurrents, it seems possible that the number of these occurrents need not be infinite. One might argue that the world contains finitely many occurrents but it has been in existence since eternity. In this case, since these occurrents are finite, there would have been a point in time at which occurrents first began to occur, and prior to which no occurrent ever occurred. This entails that the world was at an immutable state of rest for eternity, and at some point change began to occur. This conclusion, however, contradicts a central principle that al-Ghazālī presupposes, namely, that

this stage you know the existence of the Maker, since it is established by the syllogism that we mentioned, which is our statements: "The world is an occurrent; every occurrent has a cause; hence the world has a cause." This proposition has been established by this method. However, only the existence of the cause is now known to us. Whether it is eternal or occurrent and its attributes are not yet known to us. So let us be occupied with these matters.[47]

# Second Proposition

*[God is eternal anteriorly]*

We claim that the cause we have established for the existence of the world is eternal anteriorly. For if it were occurrent, it would require another cause, and so would this other cause; and either there would be an infinite regress, which is impossible, or the regress would necessarily arrive at something anteriorly eternal, at which it would terminate. This anteriorly eternal thing is what we seek and call "the Maker of the world." It is inescapable to acknowledge necessarily His existence. We do not mean by our saying that He is eternal anteriorly anything other than that His existence is not preceded by nonexistence. The term 'eternal anteriorly' implies only the affirmation of an existent and the denial of a preceding nonexistence. Do not think that being eternal anteriorly is something additional to the essence of the anteriorly eternal. Otherwise you will be required to say that this thing is itself anteriorly eternal and that its anterior eternity is additional to it; and this would regress ad infinitum.

# Third Proposition

*[God is eternal posteriorly]*

We claim that the Maker of the world, in addition to His being an existent who has never failed to exist, is eternal posteriorly, and will never cease to

---

whatever is eternal anteriorly cannot cease to exist. Hence, if the world were at an immutable state of rest for eternity, then it would remain at this state forever. Al-Ghazālī will argue for this principle later in this treatise. Again, it is important to keep in mind that al-Ghazālī here is arguing against the Islamic philosophers who affirm the anterior eternity of the world and the existence of infinitely many revolutions of heavenly bodies.

47. The Jeddah edition adds: "God is the one who grants success and guides."

exist, since it is impossible for an existent whose anterior eternity is established to cease to exist. We say this because if the anteriorly eternal were to cease to exist, its cessation would require a cause; for its cessation is incidental,[48] since its existence persisted from eternity;[49] and we have already mentioned that every incidental thing must have a cause insofar as it is incidental, not insofar as it is existent.[50] As the change from nonexistence to existence requires something that gives preponderance to existence over nonexistence, so the change from existence to nonexistence requires something that gives preponderance to nonexistence over existence.[51]

The giver of preponderance is either an agent who annuls existence through power, a contrary [of that whose existence is annulled], or the termination of one of the conditions for existence. It is impossible to assign [the annulment of existence] to power. Existence is an actual thing, which might be produced by power; thus the powerful agent who produces it does do something. Nonexistence is not a thing; hence it is impossible for it to be an actual act produced by power. We ask: "Does the author of nonexistence do something?" To answer "Yes" would be absurd, since annulment is not a thing. Even though a Muʿtazilite might say that a nonexistent

48. The Arabic word is *ṭāriʾ*, which literally means "foreign to the object." In Islamic philosophy *ṭāriʾ* is a technical term that refers to that which is extrinsic or incidental to a thing, and not part of the thing's nature or definition. Al-Ghazālī's point here is that for a thing that is anteriorly eternal nonexistence is foreign to its nature. Hence if nonexistence were to happen to something that is anteriorly eternal, it would require a cause. This is a general rule: when something that happens is foreign to a thing's nature, it will not happen without a cause, since it will not happen as a result of the thing's nature.

49. I think that al-Ghazālī's reason for saying that the cessation of the anteriorly eternal (if it were ever possible) would have to be incidental to it is that it is inconceivable that the cessation of the anteriorly eternal might be produced by something intrinsic to it. For, whatever this intrinsic condition might be, how could it have remained "dormant" from eternity and then suddenly become active? Yet anything that is intrinsic to the anteriorly eternal and thus part of its nature would have to have been present from eternity.

50. Al-Ghazālī did not previously mention that whatever is incidental (*ṭāriʾ*) to an object must have a cause—at least, not in these exact words. What he did say is that all occurrents must have causes, and it is not hard to see why all incidental things must have causes. Since incidental things are foreign to an object's nature, they could not exist simply by virtue of that nature and therefore must have a cause.

51. According to al-Ghazālī, as we will see, the termination of nonexistence and the termination of existence are not symmetrical: something that is nonexistent from eternity might be brought into existence (such as the world), but something that is anteriorly eternal cannot cease to exist. This lack of symmetry is due to the fact that existence, insofar as it is an "actual thing," can be created, but nonexistence, insofar as it is not an "actual thing," cannot be directly created. For al-Ghazālī, the existence of an occurrent can be terminated by removing one of its necessary conditions for existence or by introducing into it a contrary, which would make its continued existence logically impossible. Al-Ghazālī will argue below that none of these things is possible for what is anteriorly eternal.

is a thing and an essence, still that essence is not an effect of power. It is unimaginable that even he would say that an act, produced by power, authored that essence,[52] since it is anteriorly eternal.[53] His act,[54] in fact, would be to annul the existence of an essence;[55] but the annulment of the existence of an essence is not a thing. Therefore, he does not do anything. And if our statement that he does not do anything is true, then our statement that he did not invoke power at all is also true. Hence, he remained as he was and did not do anything.[56]

It is false to say that the anteriorly eternal is annihilated by its contrary; because the existence of the contrary, if it is assumed to be occurrent, would be annulled by its being contrary to the anteriorly eternal. This would be

52. The Arabic expression can be read in two ways: (1) *fa'ala tilk al-dhāt*, which means "authored that essence," and (2) *fi'lu tilk al-dhāt*, which might mean "the act of that essence." The Jeddah edition is the only one that attempts to resolve this issue. It chooses the second reading, but I adopted the first. The second reading yields the following translation: 'It is unimaginable that even he would say that the act produced by the power is the act of that essence.' It is most odd, however, to claim that an act that is produced by power and that creates nonexistence is the act of the essence of a nonexistent. Even a Mu'tazilite is unlikely to claim that an act produced by power is the work of a nonexistent.

53. It is likely that what al-Ghazālī means here is that the existence of each occurrent is preceded by anteriorly eternal nonexistence. Until an occurrent comes into existence, its prior nonexistence stretches back to eternity.

54. 'His' refers to the agent who authored the nonexistence.

55. The essence now spoken of is not the essence of a nonexistent as per the Mu'tazilite view but is, once again, that of an existent. Al-Ghazālī's point is that the act of an agent in annulling the existence of an existent is not an act at all, so that the annulment of existence is not an exercise of power. If annulling an existent is not doing anything at all and is not an exercise of power, then annulling an anteriorly eternal existent cannot be accomplished by an act that is the exercise of power.

56. Arguments in this style are common in medieval Islamic philosophy and theology. Al-Ghazālī considers critically several of them in *Tahāfut al-Falāsifa*. One is the philosophers' argument that the substances of the world are posteriorly eternal. The argument runs as follows. If God were to cause the substances of the world to cease to exist, then He would have to perform an act that is the creation of nonexistence. But nonexistence is not *a thing*, and every act must have a thing as its object. But if God did not perform an act by annihilating the substances, then He did nothing and so did not, after all, annihilate substances. It is interesting to note that al-Ghazālī suggests in the *Tahāfut* that God's perfection implies that He is able to originate existence if He wills, and to annihilate existence if He wills, and that when He annihilates existence, His act is indeed the annihilation of existence. One possible way to explain what appears to be contradictory positions in the *Tahāfut* and the *Iqtiṣād* is to note that al-Ghazālī's task in the *Tahāfut* is largely destructive—rather than state what he actually believes, he presents counterexamples to show that the philosophers' arguments are invalid—but in the *Iqtiṣād* his task is constructive: he affirms doctrines and presents proofs for them. Whether this explanation is successful may be debated. (See al-Ghazālī, *Tahāfut al-Falāsifa*, pp. 128–133; al-Ghazālī ends the section with "And God knows best," which is not a typical practice for him.)

more proper than the termination of the existence of the anteriorly eternal by virtue of its contrary. Moreover, it is impossible that the anteriorly eternal had an anteriorly eternal contrary that coexisted with it since eternity yet did not annihilate it earlier but rather annihilated it now.

It is false to say that the anteriorly eternal is annihilated due to the annulment of a condition for its existence. For if the condition is occurrent, it is impossible for the existence of the anteriorly eternal to be conditional upon an occurrent; and if it is anteriorly eternal, then the argument for the impossibility of the annulment of the condition is similar to the argument for the impossibility of the annulment of what is conditional upon it. Hence its annulment is unimaginable.[57]

It might be said: "Through what are substances and modes annihilated according to you?" We say: "Regarding modes, they are annihilated through themselves." We mean by 'through themselves' that their essences cannot be imagined to persist. The doctrine may be explained by considering the case of motion. The states that follow each other through continuous periods of time are described as movements only because they alternate by continuously originating anew and continuously ceasing to exist. Indeed, if these states are supposed to remain unchanging, they would be states of rest, not motion. The essence of motion is inconceivable without also conceiving nonexistence to follow existence. This can be understood regarding motion even without a demonstration. As for colors and the rest of the modes, their annihilation is understood according to what we have said—namely, that if they were to persist, it would be impossible for their annihilation to be produced through power or through a contrary, as discussed in the case of the anteriorly eternal.[58]

57. The argument is a standard infinite-regress argument. If the anteriorly eternal were to be annihilated through the annulment of a condition necessary for its existence, the condition would have to be either occurrent or anteriorly eternal (these alternatives are mutually exclusive and collectively exhaustive). It cannot be occurrent, for then the anteriorly eternal would exist before its necessary condition did. The only other possibility is that the annulled condition is itself anteriorly eternal. But if this condition is anteriorly eternal and annulled, we again have to ask how something anteriorly eternal might be annulled. Once we eliminate the possibilities that it might be annulled by an act of powerful agent or by the presence of a contrary, the only remaining option is that it is annulled by the annulment of a condition necessary for its existence. Again, we would say that the condition would have to be either occurrent or anteriorly eternal, and the process would continue without end. The only way the regress would end is if the condition were occurrent. But an occurrent, as al-Ghazālī has already demonstrated, cannot be a necessary condition for what is anteriorly eternal.

58. This is an interesting doctrine. It is not totally foreign to Western philosophy. The doctrine asserts that modes do not persist; instead there is a new mode (presumably, of the same type) at every moment of time. Al-Ghazālī explains that if a mode were to persist even for a short period of time, its annihilation would be impossible thorough an act of power or

Such annihilation is impossible regarding God (Exalted is He). We have shown first His anterior eternity and then the continuation of His existence through posterior eternity. His annihilation following His existence is not a reality that is necessitated by His existence, unlike motion, where its annihilation following its existence is a reality that is necessitated by its existence.

Regarding the substances, their annihilation is brought about by creating neither motion nor rest in them, so the condition for their existence is annulled. Their persistence would then be inconceivable.[59]

# Fourth Proposition

*[God is not an extended substance]*

We claim that the Maker of the world is not an extended substance. For His anterior eternity is established; and if He were extended, He would not be devoid of motion and rest within His region; and whatever is not devoid of occurrents is an occurrent, as previously stated.

It might be said: "In what way do you object to the one who calls God substance and does not believe Him to be extended?"

We say:

Reason, for us, does not require the prevention of using terms in any way. This usage may be prevented due either to linguistic or to legal considerations. As for linguistic considerations: if one claims that it is consistent with linguistic practice, then the matter must be examined. If the one who describes God with this term[60] claims that it is a true name of Him, that is, that those who established the language assigned this term to Him, then he

---

through the presence of a contrary, by an argument similar to the one given in the case of the anteriorly eternal. Hence, the only way that a mode is annihilated is by the removal of a condition necessary for its existence, and this removal takes place by the simple passing of the moment (i.e., a temporal *atom*) at which the mode exists. Part of the essence of a mode is to exist, as we were told previously, in a specific receptacle (locus) and, as we are told now, at a specific moment. In other words, the essence of a mode entails an existence *here and now*; if one of these conditions should be changed, the mode is replaced by a new mode. As an occasionalist (see First Introduction, note 10), al-Ghazālī holds that God is constantly creating the modes to give them the *appearance* of continuity.

59. The doctrines concerning both the annihilation of modes through themselves and the annihilation of substances by creating neither motion nor rest in them are standard Ashʿarite doctrines. (See, e.g., al-Ghazālī, *Tahāfut al-Falāsifa*, p. 130.)

60. I followed the Jeddah edition in reading *wāṣifuh bih* (the one who describes Him with it) instead of *wāḍiʿuh lah* (its user), which is the reading in the Ankara edition.

has lied about linguistic practice. On the other hand, if he claims that it is a metaphor based on the meaning that it shares with the term from which the metaphor is borrowed, then if it is suitable as a metaphor, no objection is raised against him from a linguistic viewpoint. But if it is not suitable, he would be told that he erred linguistically. The extent of the error should be as great as the extent of the remoteness of the metaphor [from the original term]. Investigating this matter is not appropriate for intellectual research.[61]

As for legal considerations and whether this usage is permissible or forbidden: it is a legal examination, which must be conducted by jurists, since there is no difference between examining the permissibility of using terms without intending erroneous meanings and between examining the permissibility of acts. There are two opinions here. One of them is to say that no name may be used to refer to God (Exalted is He) without permission, and no permission is reported for this usage; hence it is forbidden. The other is to say that it is not forbidden without prohibition, and no prohibition is reported against this; hence it must be examined. If it implies an erroneous notion,[62] then it must be guarded against, because implying an erroneous notion with respect to the attributes of God (Exalted is He) is forbidden. If it does not imply an erroneous notion, it may not be deemed forbidden. Both sides are probable. Furthermore, implication varies across languages and habits of linguistic usage. The use of a term might imply something for certain people and might not imply the same thing for other people.

# Fifth Proposition

*[God is not a body]*

We claim that the Maker of the world is not a body, since every body is composed of two extended substances.[63] Thus if it is impossible for Him to

61. By 'intellectual research' al-Ghazālī intends theoretical investigation—theological, logical, or philosophical. The matter of whether the term 'substance' may be applied to God is to be decided by a semantical or literary investigation. It is clear that al-Ghazālī does not consider linguistics and literary analysis theoretical disciplines.

62. The Arabic expression is *yūhim khaṭa'an*, which may be translated loosely as "leading the imagination into error."

63. Perhaps, al-Ghazālī is not using the number two restrictively here. Perhaps, he means that a body is divisible into *at least* two extended substances. It is clear from this treatise that al-Ghazālī is using 'substance' to mean matter occupying a region of space. In this sense a *solid* body is composed of at least two extended substances. A footnote in the Jeddah edition indicates that one of the manuscripts has 'and the least of bodies is composed of two sub-

be a substance, it is impossible for Him to be a body. We do not mean by 'body' other than this. If one calls Him body and does not intend this meaning, he might run into a difficulty with respect to the language or the law, but not with respect to reason; for reason does not decree about the use of terms and the concatenation of letters and sounds, which are conventions. Moreover, if God were a body, He would have a measure of a specific magnitude, and it would be possible for Him to be smaller or larger than this magnitude. Neither possibility would be more likely than the other without a specifier and a determinant, as stated previously.[64] Hence there would be a need for a specifier to act on Him and determine for Him a specific magnitude; thus He would be made, not maker, and created, not creator.

# Sixth Proposition

*[God is not a mode]*

We claim that the Maker of the world is not a mode; for we mean by 'mode' that whose existence requires an entity in which it subsists, and that entity is either a body or a substance. Insofar as the body is necessarily an occurrent, what resides in it must be an occurrent as well, since it is shown that modes do not transfer. We have proved that the Maker of the world is eternal. Hence He cannot be a mode.

If a mode is understood to be an attribute of a thing without this thing being extended, then we do not deny its existence; for in this way we understand the attributes of God (Exalted is He). So it is; the debate is centered on how to use the names 'maker' and 'agent'.[65] Using them to name the essence, of which the attributes are predicated, is more proper than using them to name the attributes. If we say that "the maker" is not an attri-

---

stances' instead of 'every body is composed of two extended substances'. This lends support to our interpretation here.

64. 'Determinant' here is the translation of *murajjiḥ*, which I have translated elsewhere as "giver of preponderance." Thus the sentence implies that what is needed in order to specify a certain magnitude is something that gives preponderance to one possibility over another. Al-Ghazālī had spoken earlier of the need for there to be givers of preponderance to determine various possibilities; hence his expression 'as stated previously'.

65. 'Agent' is the unfortunate translation of *fāʿil*. It is a common translation but by no means universal. *Fāʿil* is a doer of an action, its author, and its enactor. However, none of these words, either, captures the meaning correctly. A case might be made, and al-Ghazālī makes it in *Tahāfut al-Falāsifa*, that *fāʿil* requires agency, which requires will and intention. It is this sense that justifies translating *fāʿil* into 'agent'. It should be noted, however, that linguistically a *fāʿil* is the subject of a verb phrase.

bute, we mean by this that the activity of making is related to the essence, in which the attributes subsist, and not to the attributes. Similarly, if we say that "the carpenter" is neither a mode nor an attribute, we mean by this that the trade of carpentry is not related to the attributes but to the essence, which must be described by a set of attributes in order to be "a maker." The same analysis applies to "the Maker of the world." If by calling a thing "a mode" the opponent intends something other than what resides in a body and other than an attribute, which subsists in an essence, then it is for language or the law, but not for reason, to prevent his usage.

# Seventh Proposition

*[God is not located in a direction]*

We claim that God is not located in any specific one of the six directions. He who understands the meaning of the expression 'direction' and the meaning of the expression 'belonging to'[66] decidedly understands that it is impossible for directions to apply to anything other than a substance or a mode.[67] [The notion of] region is intelligible: it is what belongs to a substance. But it becomes a direction once it is related to something else—namely, an extended thing. There are six directions: above, below, front, back, right, and left. Thus the meaning of a thing's being above us is that it is in a region that is next to the side of the head, and the meaning of its being below us is that it is in a region that is next to the side of the foot, and similarly with respect to the rest of the directions. Hence saying that a thing is in a certain direction is saying that it is in a region in conjunction with a relation.

Our statement that a thing occupies a region can be understood in two ways. One of them is that the region belongs to the thing, so that it prevents its likes from existing where it is, and that is substance. The other is that the thing resides in the substance; hence it may be said that it is located in a direction but only in a way that follows from that of the substance. A mode's being located in a direction is not the same thing as a substance's being located in a direction. A direction belongs primarily to a substance and only

66. I translated *ikhtiṣāṣ* as 'belonging to'. The translation serves its purpose when we are talking about regions of space as belonging to substances; because the sense here is that the substance occupies the region, that is, it prevents other substances from existing in that region. Al-Ghazālī derives the *ikhtiṣāṣ* of a direction from the *ikhtiṣāṣ* of a region. For him, we have a region that belongs to a substance, and that region is related to a certain object (such as a head), and because of that relation the region acquires direction.

67. We should note again that almost always in this book al-Ghazālī uses 'substance' to mean extended substance and 'mode' to mean a mode of an extended substance.

derivatively to a mode. So these are two intelligible senses of a direction's belonging to a thing.

If our opponent intends either one of these meanings, then whatever proves the falsehood of God's being a substance or a mode also proves the falsehood of His being located in a direction. If he intends something other than these, then it is not comprehensible. It is for language or the law, and not for reason, to deal with the usage of this term, which is then detached from a comprehended meaning.

Our opponent might say: "I intend by 'He is located in a direction' a meaning other than these; so why do you deny it?"

I say:

As for your expression, I, in fact, deny it insofar as it implies its apparent sense, which is understood to apply to substance and mode, and is a lie about God (Exalted is He). As for what you intend by this expression, that I do not deny; for how can I deny that which I do not understand? You might intend by it His knowledge and His power. I do not deny that God is located in a direction in the sense that He is a knower and powerful. If you were to open this door, which is to intend by an expression a meaning different from what is commonly assigned to it and what it generally indicates in communication, then there would be no end to what you may intend. I would not deny you this unless you specify what you intend in such a way that I would understand by it something that implies occurrence; for whatever implies occurrence is impossible with respect to the essence of God.

Another proof against positing a direction for God is that this would make Him subject to possibility, and thus in need of a determinant to specify for Him one specific possibility. This is impossible in two ways. One of them is that the direction that is specific to Him is not specific to Him by virtue of His essence, since all the directions are equal in their relation to that which is capable of receiving a direction. Hence His being specified with certain directions is not a necessity of His essence, but a possibility; thus it needs a determinant to specify it. This specification of a possibility is a notion that is additional to His essence. It is impossible for anything that is subject to possibility to be eternal. The eternal, indeed, is that whose existence is necessary in all respects.

If it is said that the direction "above" is specific to God because it is the most sublime of all the directions, then we say that, in fact, the direction "above" became this direction due to His creation of the world in the region in which He created it. Originally, before the creation of the world, there was no "above" or "below," since these directions are derived from the head and the foot, and there was as yet no animal so that one could call the region next to its head "above" and the one opposite to it "below."

The second way is that if God were located in a direction, He would be located alongside the body of the world. And whatever is located alongside something is either smaller than it, larger than it, or equal to it. All of that requires determining a magnitude, and since it is possible for the intellect to entertain that this magnitude might be smaller or larger than what it is, it would need a determinant and a specifier. It might be said that if being specified with a direction requires determining a magnitude, then a mode would have a magnitude. We say, however, that a mode is not located in a direction on its own but by residing in a substance. Hence, similarly, its magnitude is derived; for we know that ten similar[68] modes can exist only in ten substances, and it is unimaginable that they exist in twenty substances. Hence assigning the magnitude of ten to the modes is necessarily derived from the magnitude of the substances, just as a mode's being located in a direction is derived.

It might be said: "If the direction 'above' is not specific to God, then why, according to natural inclination and divine teaching, are the faces directed and the hands raised towards the heavens when supplicating? And why did the Prophet (may God bless him and grant him peace) ask the slave girl whom he intended to free and wanted to confirm her belief where God is, and why, when she pointed to the heavens, did he say that she is a believer?"[69]

The answer to the first question is that this is analogous to one's saying: "If God is not in the Kaʿba, which is His house,[70] then why do we make pilgrimage to it and visit it, and why do we direct our faces towards it during prayer? And if God is not in the earth, then why do we humble ourselves by placing our faces on the earth during prostration?" But this is madness. Rather, it should be said that the purpose of the revelation for people's worship through the act of facing the Kaʿba during the prayers is to fix one direction; for this is without a doubt more conducive to feeling devotion and to the heedfulness of the heart than constantly changing direction. Furthermore, since every direction is equally suitable to be the direction of the prayer, God has specified one site to be distinguished with veneration and glorification, and He has honored it by relating it to Himself. By conferring such honor He attracted the hearts to it, so that He may reward

68. *Mutamāthila* (similar) is in the Jeddah edition. It is omitted in the Ankara edition.

69. Reported by Abū Dawūd, *Sunan*, XVI.19, no. 3284; Aḥmad ibn Ḥanbal, *Musnad*, II.291, no. 7888; Bayhaqī, *al-Sunan al-Kubrā*: VII.15266; Malik, *Muwaṭṭa'*, XXV.6, no. 1464; Muslim, *Ṣaḥīḥ*, V.7, no. 537; and Nasā'ī, *Sunan*, XIII.20, no. 1218.

70. The Kaʿba is the holiest shrine in Islam and is located in Mecca. As is common in the monotheistic traditions, every place of worship, including a mosque, is referred to as the house of God.

people for directing themselves towards it. Just as the Kaʿba is the kiblah[71] for the prayers, the heavens are the kiblah for the supplication. The one who is worshiped through the prayers and asked through the supplication is too exalted to reside in the Kaʿba or the heavens.

Moreover, there is a subtle secret in turning towards the heavens during supplication—a secret, the likes of which can be known only by the few. It is that the salvation of a servant of God and his success in the hereafter are reached by humbling himself to God and believing in glorifying his Lord. Humbleness and glorification are acts of the heart and their instrument is the intellect. The external organs may be employed to purify and chasten the heart; for the heart is so created that it may be influenced by the diligence of the external organs in performing their acts. Conversely, the external organs are so created that they may be influenced by what the hearts believe. Since the purpose is for the servant of God to humble himself in his mind and heart by realizing his true value, so he may know the abjectness of his status in existence when compared to the loftiness of God (Exalted is He) and His highness,[72] and since among the greatest indications of his abjectness, which makes it incumbent upon him to be humble, is that he was created from dust, he was commanded to place his face, which is the noblest of all organs, on the dust, which is the lowliest of all things, so that his heart may truly feel humility through the act of his forehead touching the ground. Thus the body is humbled in its matter, person, and form in a manner suitable for it, which is to embrace the lowly, abject dust. The mind is humbled before its Lord in a manner suitable for it, which is to realize its lowliness, the lowness of its rank, and the abjectness of its status, when it is reminded of that from which man is created.[73]

Similarly, glorifying God (Exalted is He) is a task for the heart, in which lies its salvation. The external organs must also participate in this task to the extent that these organs can be made to contribute. The heart glorifies by asserting the greatness of God's rank through knowledge and belief, and the organs glorify by turning towards the direction of the heavens,[74] which is the highest of all directions and, according to what is believed,

71. 'Kiblah' is the English equivalent of the Arabic *qiblah*, which is the direction Muslims face during prayers. It is now the direction of the Kaʿba.

72. The sentence is a translation of the reading in the Ankara edition. The Jeddah edition has a different reading, which may be translated as 'so he may know through the abjectness of his status in existence the loftiness of God (Exalted is He) and His highness'.

73. Al-Ghazālī indicates at the beginning of this paragraph that he will offer an explanation for the practice of turning towards the heavens during supplication. Yet the explanation he offers concerns placing the forehead on the earth during prostration, which is part of the ritual of the Muslim's prayer. He will offer the promised explanation in what follows.

74. The Arabic is *jihat al-ʿuluww* (literally, the direction of "height").

the noblest of them. The highest form of glorifying God that an organ can perform involves being oriented in the right direction. In fact, it is a common understanding in communication that a man may assert the loftiness of the rank of another and the greatness of his authority by stating that his status belongs to the seventh heaven. He is indicating the greatness of the person's status by using the metaphor of a high place. He might even point to the heavens with his head in order to glorify the status of whomever he wants to glorify, indicating that his status belongs to the heavens, that is, it is high—the heavens here represent that which is high.

Thus observe how the revelation treats with care the hearts and organs of mankind in driving them to glorify God (Exalted is He), and how ignorant is the one whose perception is dim, who is aware only of the surface acts of the external organs and bodies. He is heedless of the secrets of the hearts in their glorifying God without the need to specify any direction. He thinks that the truth of the matter lies in that to which the external organs point. And he does not know that the primary seat for glorification is the heart,[75] that it glorifies by believing in the loftiness of His rank, and not of His place, and that the external organs are, in this task, servants and followers, serving the heart by participating in the glorification to the extent that is possible for them; and what is possible for the external organs is only their pointing in certain directions.

That is the secret behind the act of turning the faces towards the heavens when the glorification of God is intended. Another meaning is added to this when one is supplicating. It is that supplication in essence is a request for one of God's blessings, and the treasures of God's blessings are the heavens, and the keepers of God's provisions are the angels, whose abode is the kingdom of the heavens and who are trusted with the sustenance of the creation. God (Exalted is He) says: *And in heaven is your sustenance and that which you are promised.*[76] It is a natural disposition to direct one's face towards the coffers that contain the sought-after provision. Those who seek provisions from kings, once they are told that the provisions are being distributed at

75. This is the translation of the reading in the Jeddah edition. The translation of the reading in the Ankara edition is: 'And he does not know that the glorification that is most suited for the heart is the glorification of God'.

76. The Arabic word is *samā'*, which denotes the skies, the heavens, and the occult heaven. It is interesting that al-Ghazālī's interpretation of the Qur'ānic reference to heaven in this regard is the heavens of this world. Most commentators think that the heaven mentioned in the Qur'ānic verse above (60:22) refers to both the skies and the occult heaven. The wind, clouds, sun, and revolutions of the Earth, etc., are responsible for the rain, seasons, and growth—all matters of sustenance. However, the promises made to mankind regarding paradise, hellfire, and similar matters belong to the occult heaven.

the gates of the coffers,[77] turn their faces and hearts in the direction of the coffers, although they do not believe that the king is in the coffers. That is what motivates religious scholars to direct their faces towards the heavens by natural inclination and according to the revelation. As for the populace, they might believe that the one they worship is in the heavens, and this would be one of their reasons for pointing towards the heavens. May the Lord of lords be greatly exalted above what the misguided believe.

As for the Prophet's decree that the slave girl is a believer when she pointed to the heavens, the matter may be explained similarly. For it is apparent that the only way the mute can indicate the loftiness of a rank is by pointing to the direction of the heavens. As it was narrated, she was mute and was thought to have been a worshiper of idols and to have believed that her god was in the temple of idols. Hence when she was asked about her belief, she informed, by pointing to the heavens, that the one she worshiped was not in the temple of idols as the idolaters believed.[78]

It might be said: "Denying direction leads to absurdity, for it posits an existent that is not located in any of the six directions; such an existent would be neither inside nor outside the world, neither contiguous to nor disconnected from the world; and that is impossible."

77. In the Ankara edition it is *al-khizāna* (the coffers), in the Jeddah edition *al-malik* (the king).

78. In denying that God is in the heavens, where by 'the heavens' is understood 'the skies', and in attributing metaphorical interpretations to the slave girl's pointing to the heavens and to the faithful's directing their faces and raising their hands towards the heavens when supplicating, al-Ghazālī is transcending the influence of al-Ash'arī, the founder of the Ash'ariyya school of Islamic theology, to which al-Gazālī subscribes. (See Second Treatise, note 34, for a brief description of this school.) Al-Ash'arī takes literally the Islamic texts and rituals that appear to suggest that God is above in (or above) the heavens. For example, al-Ash'arī writes:

> God (Great and Glorious is He) is seated on His throne. . . . The Pharaoh accused the prophet of God, Moses, of lying when Moses said that God (Great and Glorious is He) is above the heavens. . . . Above the heavens is the throne. . . . [God] is seated on the throne, which is above the heavens; everything that is high is a heaven and the throne is the highest heaven. . . . We see the Muslims all raise their hands towards the heavens when they supplicate. This is because God (Great and Glorious is He) is on the throne, which is above the heavens. If God were not on the throne, they would not raise their hands towards the throne. . . . The Prophet asked [the slave girl], "Where is God?" She said that He is in the heavens. He asked, "Who am I?" She said that he is the Messenger of God. The Prophet said: "Free her, for she is a believer." This [*ḥadīth*] proves that God (Great and Glorious is He) is on His throne above the heavens. (al-Ash'arī, *al-Ibāna 'an Uṣūl al-Diyāna*, pp. 46–50)

The interpretations that al-Ghazālī advances in these passages are closer to the ones typically put forward by the Mu'tazilites and the Islamic philosophers.

We say:

It is conceded that it is impossible for an existent that is receptive of contiguity[79] to be neither contiguous nor disconnected, and that it is impossible for an existent that is receptive of direction not to be located in any of the six directions. However, it is not impossible for an existent that is not receptive of contiguity or directionality not to be a subject to either one of the two contraries.[80]

This objection is similar to one's stating that it is impossible to have an existent that is neither impotent nor powerful, that is neither knowledgeable nor ignorant, for a thing must be subject to one of two contraries. It is said to him: "If a thing is receptive of the contraries, it is impossible for it to be independent of both of them; but if it is not receptive of them, it is not impossible for it to be independent of both of them." An inanimate object, for instance, is not receptive of either one,[81] because it lacks their condition—namely, being alive—thus its independence of them is not impossible. Similarly, if a thing lacks the condition for contiguity and direction—namely, being extended or subsisting in an extended thing—then it is not impossible for it to be independent of all these contraries.

The object of the theoretical reflection, therefore, is whether it is impossible or not for an existent neither to be extended nor to reside in an extended thing, and hence lack the condition for contiguity and direction. If our opponent claims that it is impossible for such a thing to exist, then we prove its existence by stating that every extended thing is an occurrent and every occurrent requires an agent that is not an occurrent; the establishment of an existent that is not extended necessarily follows from these two premises. Regarding these two principles, we have already established them; as for the claim that follows from them, it cannot be denied while affirming the two principles.

If our opponent says, "Such an existent that your proof aims to establish is not comprehensible," then we say to him, "What do you mean by saying that it is not comprehensible?" If you mean by it that it cannot be visualized, imagined, or envisaged,[82] then what you say is true. For nothing is

79. The expression *yaqbal al-ittiṣāl* (is receptive of contiguity) is the reading in the Ankara edition. The Jeddah edition adds *bijiha* (in a direction); hence the expression becomes 'is receptive of contiguity in a direction'.

80. 'The two contraries' refers to each of the pairs of opposites alluded to above—namely, inside/outside, contiguous/disconnected, above/below, front/back, and right/left.

81. The relevant pairs of contraries, which do not apply to an inanimate object, are impotence and power, and knowledge and ignorance.

82. I translated *dākhil fī al-wahm* as 'envisaged'. It is possible that al-Ghazālī is using *wahm* here in its technical sense; thus the expression could mean "subject to (or, apprehended by) the estimative faculty." The rest of the passage, however, makes this usage quite unlikely.

envisaged, imagined, or visualized except a body that has color and size. Visualization cannot form an image of that which has no color or size. Visualization has an affinity to what can be seen; it can envisage a thing only in accordance with the way it sees, and it cannot envisage what does not accord with it.

If our opponent means that it is not intelligible, that is, that it is not known through a proof of the intellect, then this is absurd, since we have already presented a proof for its existence. The only meaning to its being intelligible is that the intellect is required to submit to believing in it due to a proof that cannot be revoked. And that has been established.

If our opponent says that whatever cannot be imagined by visualization has no existence, let us judge, then, that visualization has no existence in itself, for visualization itself is not subject to visualization. Vision is not subject to visualization, neither are knowledge and power, nor sound and smell.[83] If one were to envisage the essence of sound, he would fashion a color and size for it and imagine it like that. The same applies to all the states of the soul, such as embarrassment, fear, love, anger, joy, sadness, and vanity. He who necessarily apprehends these states in his soul and forces his imagination to examine the essences of these states finds that it fails to achieve this end and, instead, posits errors. In spite of this, our opponent denies the existence of that which he cannot imagine. This is, then, the right approach to explaining this issue.

We have exceeded the limits of brevity. However, I find concise beliefs are given by this science much elaboration regarding what is obvious, and are approached with many digressions that are beside what is important, together with inadequate exploration of difficult problems. Thus I decided that it was more important and proper to provide an elaborate discussion of what is obscure rather than of what is clear.

## Eighth Proposition

*[No anthropomorphic description is true of God]*

We claim that God is too exalted to be described as being settled on the throne.[84] Whatever is established and settled on a body must have magnitude, for it is either smaller than, larger than, or equal to it,[85] and all of that requires magnitude. Moreover, if it is possible for the body of the throne to

83. The Ankara edition adds 'nor motion'.
84. As indicated earlier, this is different from al-Ashʿarī's position. (See note 78 above.)
85. The pronoun 'it' refers to the body.

be contiguous to God at one side, it would be possible for it to be contiguous to Him at all sides; hence He would be surrounded by it. Our opponent surely does not believe that, but it necessarily follows from his position. In general, nothing settles on a body except a body and nothing resides in a body except a mode. It has been shown that the Exalted is neither a body nor a mode. This proposition is not discussed independently for the sake of giving a demonstration of it.

It might be said: "So what is the meaning of the Exalted's statement: *The Compassionate seated Himself on the throne*,[86] and what is the meaning of the Prophet's statement: 'God descends every night to the nearest heaven'?"[87] We say: "The discussion about the surface meanings regarding this category [of statements] is very elaborate.[88] We describe, however, a methodology for dealing with these two surface meanings, which is a guide for dealing with the rest of them."

We say that with respect to this matter people form two groups: populace and scholars. What we see suitable for the populace is that they should not be engaged with these interpretations. Rather whatever necessitates anthropomorphism or indicates occurrence with respect to God should be removed from their beliefs. It should be made firm for them that God is an existent such that: *There is nothing like Him and He is the Hearer and Seer.*[89] If they ask about the meanings of these verses,[90] they should be rebuked and told: "This is not your pursuit, so stay clear of it; for every science has its men." The answer to be given is the answer given by one of the earlier scholars.[91] When asked about God's sitting on the throne, he said: "The sitting is known, its modality is unknown, to ask about it is a heresy, and to believe in it is a duty." This is because the minds of the populace are inadequate to receive the intelligibles, and their knowledge of the language is not broad enough to understand the Arabs' expansive use of metaphors.

As for the scholars, what is suitable for them is to comprehend and understand this matter.[92] I do not say that this is an individual obligation; for it

86. Qur'ān, 20:5

87. Reported by Abū Dawūd, *Sunan*, II.311, no. 1315; Aḥmad ibn Ḥanbal, *Musnad*, II.504, no. 10523; Bukhārī, *Ṣaḥīḥ*, XIX.14, no. 1145; LXXX.14, no. 6321; and Muslim, *Ṣaḥīḥ*, VI.24, no. 758.

88. 'This category of statements' here refers to the category of anthropomorphic Qur'ānic verses and *ḥadīth*s.

89. Qur'ān, 42:11.

90. The expression 'these verses' refers to the anthropomorphic Qur'ānic verses.

91. The earlier scholar is most likely Mālik ibn Anas, the founder of the Mālikī school of Islamic jurisprudence.

92. The matter under consideration is how to interpret the anthropomorphic Qur'ānic verses and *ḥadīth*s in a way that does not attribute anthropomorphic qualities to God.

is not reported that this is obligatory. What is obligatory is the exaltation of God above any attribution to Him of a likeness to something else. As for the meanings of the Qur'ānic verses, the law does not obligate every individual scholar to understand all of them.

We reject, however, the statement of the one who says that these are among the obscure verses, such as the letters that open some of the Qur'ānic chapters.[93] For the letters that open these chapters are not employed as part of an earlier convention of the Arabs for conveying certain meanings. If one utters letters or words that are not part of a convention, his meaning is necessarily unknown unless he defines what he means. If he states his definition, these letters become like a language invented by him. As for the Prophet's saying "God (Exalted is He) descends to the nearest heaven," it is a comprehensible expression that is asserted in order to convey something. It is known that its literal or metaphorical meaning may readily be understood. How can it, then, be said that it is obscure? Indeed, the ignorant envisages an erroneous meaning of it, while the scholar comprehends the right meaning.

This is similar to the Exalted's statement: *And He is with you wherever you may be.*[94] The ignorant envisages an association that is contrary to His being on the throne, and the scholar understands that He is with everyone by complete awareness and knowledge.

This is also similar to the Prophet's saying: "The heart of the believer is between two fingers of the Compassionate."[95] The ignorant envisages two organs that are composed of flesh, bones, and nerves, include fingertips and fingernails, and are attached to the palm. For the scholar, it indicates a metaphorical meaning rather than a literal one. It signifies what the finger is for. It is as if He called His power "a finger" because the function of the finger—and its spirit and nature—is the ability to turn things as it pleases. Similarly, the association in the Exalted's statement, *And He is with you wherever you may be*, conveys the purpose of the association—namely,

93. Many Qur'ānic chapters begin with groups of letters. For instance, the second chapter, *al-Baqara* (the Cow), begins with *alaf lām mīm* ('a', 'l', 'm'). These verses are considered obscure or ambiguous (*mutashābiha*). Some scholars said that a *mutashābiha* verse is one that allows for multiple interpretations (in this sense, it should be translated as 'ambiguous'). It is clear that this is not al-Ghazālī's definition. For him, a *mutashābiha* verse is one whose meaning cannot be discerned (in this sense, the correct translation is 'obscure'). If that is what a *mutashābiha* verse is, then Muslims are required to avoid seeking an interpretation of it.

94. Qur'ān, 57:4.

95. Reported by Aḥmad ibn Ḥanbal, *Musnad*, II.173, no. 6607; Ibn Māja, *Sunan*, INTRODUCTION.13, no. 199; Muslim, *Ṣaḥīḥ*, XLVI.3, no. 2645; and Tirmidhī, *al-Jāmiʿ al-Ṣaḥīḥ*, XXXIII.7, no. 2141.

to have knowledge and awareness. It is a common practice of the Arabs to express the effect by mentioning the cause, and hence to borrow the cause as a metaphor for the effect.

A similar case is the Exalted's statement in the holy *ḥadīth*: "If one comes closer to Me by a hand's span, I come closer to him by an arm's length; and if one comes to Me walking, I come to him trotting."[96] 'Trotting', for the ignorant, indicates the transposing of the feet and the quickness of the pace and 'coming' indicates the closeness in terms of distance. For the rational, 'coming' indicates the meaning conveyed by having close proximity between people, which is a closeness of bounty and blessing. Its meaning is: "My mercy and blessing are flowing towards My servants more bountifully than their obedience towards Me."

This is analogous to what the Exalted says as reported in the tradition: "The longing of the righteous to meet Me is great, and My longing to meet them is even greater."[97] God is exalted above what is understood from the literal sense of 'longing'; for it is a kind of pain and a need for relief, which are in fact a form of deficiency. Longing, however, is a cause for accepting the one who is longed for, receiving him with enthusiasm, and showering him with favors. Hence 'longing' is used to express its effect. Similarly, 'anger' and 'pleasure' are used to express the will to reward and punish, which are the fruits of anger and pleasure and their usual effects.

When the Prophet says "The black stone is God's right hand on His earth,"[98] the ignorant thinks that what is intended is the right hand, which is opposite to the left hand, and which is an organ composed of flesh, blood, and bones, and divided into five fingers. If he invokes his discernment, he would know that if God is on the throne, then His right hand cannot be in the Kaʿba, let alone a black stone. With a little discernment, he would realize that the black stone is borrowed as a metaphor for the holding of a hand; for he is commanded to hold the stone and kiss it, exactly as he is commanded by kings to kiss their right hands. The expression is borrowed metaphorically for this purpose. The one who has intellectual wholeness and linguistic discernment is not overwhelmed by these matters. Rather, he understands their meanings by relying on his intuition.

96. Reported by Bukhārī, *Ṣaḥīḥ*, XCVII.15 no. 7405; Ibn Māja, *Sunan*, XXXIII.58, no. 3822; Muslim, *Ṣaḥīḥ*, XLVIII.1, no. 2675; and Tirmidhī, *al-Jāmiʿ al-Ṣaḥīḥ*, XLIX.132, no. 3603.

97. Reported by Daylamī, *al-Firdaws bi-Maʾthūr al-Khiṭāb*: V.8067.

98. Reported by al-Khaṭīb al-Baghdādī, *Tārikh Baghdād*: VII.3324; al-Muttaqī al-Hindī, *Kanz al-ʿUmmāl*, XII.34744; and Ṭabarānī, *al-Mauʿjam al-Awsaṭ*: I.563.

The black stone is a stone located in the Kaʿba. It is part of the Islamic pilgrimage (*ḥajj*) rituals that the pilgrim holds and kisses the black stone. However, given the great number of pilgrims every year, almost no pilgrims are able to fulfill this ritual.

Let us return to the meaning of 'sitting' and 'descending'. As for sitting, it unquestionably involves the throne's having a relation to God. It is not possible for the throne to have a relation to Him unless it is something known, or willed, or is an object of God's power, or is a locus such as the locus of a mode, or is a place such as where a body resides. Some of these relations are conceptually impossible and some are linguistically unsuitable for metaphorical analogy. If there is among these relations a relation—even if it is the only one—that reason does not deem impossible and with which linguistic usage does not conflict, then let it be known that this is the intended one.

Regarding its being a place or a locus, which is what it would be for a substance and mode, its expression is suitable linguistically but reason deems it impossible, as was previously shown. As for its being something known or willed, reason does not deem it impossible but its expression is unsuitable linguistically. Regarding its being within God's power, under the control of this power,[99] and subject to it, while it is the greatest of all created things and is suitable for possession—for it brings praise and notice when compared to what is less than it in greatness—this is what reason does not deem impossible and its expression is suitable linguistically. Hence it is most proper that this is definitely what is intended.

Regarding the linguistic suitability for its expression, it should be obvious to whoever has expertise with the Arabic tongue. Those who fail to understand such matters are obtruders into the Arabic language, who examine it from afar, and who are concerned with it as much as the Arabs are concerned with the Turkish tongue, for they have learned nothing but its fundamentals. It is considered eloquent in Arabic to say that the prince "sits over" his kingdom. To this end the poet says:

Bishr has sat over Iraq
Without using a sword or spilling blood.[100]

It is for this reason, some of the earlier scholars said that we should understand from God's statement: *The Compassionate seated Himself on the throne,*[101] what we understand from His statement: *He then directed Himself to the heaven when it was smoke.*[102]

99. Literally, placed in the fist of power.

100. Al-Sharafāwī, the editor of the Jeddah edition, states that the poet is either Buʿayth or Akhṭal.

101. Qur'ān, 20:5.

102. Qur'ān, 41:11. The point of the Arabic sentence is totally lost in the translation. Both verses share a key word *istawā* accompanied by a different preposition in each verse. The

As for the saying of the Prophet (may God bless him and grant him peace), "God descends to the nearest heaven," it can be interpreted in two ways. One of them is to relate the descent to God metaphorically, when in reality it is related to an angel. This is similar to God's statement: *And ask the village,*[103] when the ones who are asked are in reality the inhabitants of the village. This, too, is part of linguistic practice. I mean relating the states of what is dependent to that on which it depends. Thus it is said that the king arrived at the gates of the city, though what is intended is his army. The informer about the arrival of the king at the gates of the city might be asked: "Will you go to visit him?" He might say: "No, because on his way he digressed to go to the hunt, and he has not arrived yet." It is incorrect to say to him: "Why did you say that he has arrived and now say that he has not arrived yet?" Thus what is understood by the arrival of the king is the arrival of the army. This is evident and obvious.

The second is that the expression 'descent' may be used to indicate gentleness and humbleness with respect to mankind, just as 'ascent' is used to indicate pride. It may be said, "So-and-so raised his head to the firmament," that is, he became proud. It may also be said, "He rose to the highest of the highs," that is, he became great. If one's status is elevated, it may be said that his status is in the seventh heaven. Conversely, if his rank is debased, it may be said that he has fallen to the lowest of the lows. If he became humble and gentle, it may be said that he came down to earth and descended to the lowest steps. If this is understood, and it becomes known that 'descent' may be used to describe descending in place, descending in rank by leaving it or falling from it, and descending in rank through gentleness and the abandonment of the acts that are commensurate with the elevation of rank and perfect independence, then these three meanings, which the expression 'descent' may assume alternately, should be examined to see which one reason permits.

With respect to descent as locomotion, reason has deemed it impossible, as was previously shown. For this is possible only for an extended object. As for the falling in rank, this is impossible, since the Exalted is eternal in His attributes and sublimity and it is impossible for Him to lose His grandeur. Regarding descending in the sense of being gentle and merciful

---

first verse reads: *The Compassionate "istawā on" the throne. Istawā on* (*'alā*) means "to settle on," "to be seated on," or "to be established on." The second verse is: *He then "istawā to" the heaven when it was smoke. Istawā to* (*ilā*) means "to direct oneself to" or "to rise to." Thus the claim made by the earlier scholars is substantive. They propose to understand *istawā* in the same metaphorical manner in both verses in spite of the different prepositions.

103. Qur'ān, 12:82.

and abandoning any act that is commensurate with being independent of and indifferent to others, this is possible, and hence this sense is identified and 'descent' must be understood according to it.

It was relayed that when the Exalted's statement: *The Exalter of ranks, the Possessor of the throne*,[104] was revealed, the Prophet's companions were overcome with a feeling of great veneration, so that they felt discouraged from being comfortable in asking God and supplicating to Him given His great sublimity. So they were told that God (Exalted is He), in spite of the greatness of His sublimity and the loftiness of His status, is gentle and merciful with His servants and answers them if they supplicate to him, even though He has no need for them.

It is as if[105] answering a supplication is a descent when considered in relation to what is required by His sublimity—namely, independence of and indifference to others. Thus it was described as 'descent' in order to encourage the hearts of the servants of God to supplicate with ease, indeed [to encourage them] to bow and prostrate themselves. For he who feels, within his capacity, the signs of God's sublimity sees his bowing and prostrating as insignificant.[106]

The devotion of all the servants of God in relation to God's sublimity is less significant than a servant's moving his finger for the purpose of gaining favor with one of the world's kings. If he should think that devotion glorifies a king, he would deserve rebuke. In fact, it is customary for kings to deter their ignoble subjects from serving them, prostrating themselves before them, and kissing their doorsteps, because they consider them too base to serve them and because they are too proud to employ anyone other than princes and nobility, as is the habit of some of the caliphs.

If it were not for descending from the requirements of sublimity through gentleness, mercy, and the answering of supplications, such a sublimity would have required the minds to be too stunned to have a thought, the tongues to be too muted to utter a word, and the limbs to be too numbed to make a move. Hence he who comprehends this sublimity and this gentleness clearly and decidedly understands that the expression of descent is

104. Qur'ān, 40:15.

105. The reading in the Jeddah edition is *ka'anna* (as if); in the Ankara edition, it is *kāna* (it was). According to the latter, the sentence asserts that God's answering a supplication is a descent. This is an unlikely assertion.

106. *Istab'ada* (found it difficult, found it insignificant, felt discouraged, or deemed it improbable) is the reading in the Jeddah edition. The reading in the Ankara edition is *istaḥaqqa* (deserved, or was deserving of).

commensurate with sublimity, and the term is used properly,[107] but not according to what the ignorant understands.

It might be said: "Why is the nearest heaven specified?" We say: "It represents the last level, after which there is no level." This is similar to saying that he fell down to Earth and he rose up to Pleiades, as it is supposed that Pleiades are the highest of the stars and Earth is the lowest of places.

It might be said: "Why are the nights specified, so that he said: 'He descends every night'?" We say: "The states of seclusion are more proper for supplications to be answered, and nighttime is suitable for that; for it is when people settle down, the hearts are cleared from remembering people, and remembrance is devoted to God (Exalted is He)." For this kind of supplication there is hope of being answered, but not for the kind produced by heedless hearts busied with all sorts of tasks.[108]

107. The term is 'descent'.

108. Al-Ghazālī describes two attitudes towards the anthropomorphic verses and *ḥadīth*s: one that is suitable for the populace and one for the scholars. He first says that the populace should not busy themselves with interpreting these texts but rather should be told that God is too exalted to have likeness to any aspect of His creation. But he then cites the Muslim scholar who famously said regarding God's sitting on the throne that it is obligatory to believe in it without attempting to describe it and that it is heretical to ask anything about it. Al-Ghazālī also tells us that what is appropriate for the scholars is to try to understand the true meaning of these texts. The position he advances is that of *ta'wīl*, which is to interpret these texts metaphorically. While the details of his interpretations differ from those put forward by the Mu'tazilites, the approach is the same. Regarding these texts, Islamic scholars are divided into three groups: those who interpret them literally and attribute to God anthropomorphic qualities, those who interpret them literally yet affirm that God is unlike any aspect of His creation, and those who interpret them metaphorically. The second position is the one embodied in the scholar's famous words cited by al-Ghazālī and endorsed by many scholars, most notably Ibn Ḥanbal, al-Ash'arī, and Ibn Taymiyya. These scholars accept the literal meaning of these texts but they say that the *modality* is unknown (*bilā kayf*). Al-Ash'arī, for instance, writes:

> The statement we affirm and the religion we believe is to hold fast to the Book of our Lord (Great and Glorious is He), to the Sunna of our Prophet (peace be upon him), and to what is reported from his companions, their followers, and the principal scholars of Ḥadīth . . . , and to what is affirmed by Abū 'Abd Allāh Aḥmad ibn Ḥanbal. . . .
>
> The sum of our position is that we believe in God, His angels, His books, His messengers, what they delivered, and what the principal scholars reported from the Messenger of God, and that we reject none of this . . . , and that God is seated on his throne . . . , and that He has a face . . . , and that He has two hands without [specifying their] modality . . . , and that He has two eyes without [specifying their] modality. . . .
>
> God (Great and Glorious is He) indeed spoke to the Arabs in their language according to what is understood in their speech and dialogue. It is not permissible in the speech of those who are eloquent to say "I performed this with my hand" where

# Ninth Proposition

*[God is seeable]*

We claim, contrary to the Muʿtazilites, that God (Glorious and Exalted is He) is seeable. We mention this issue in the treatise dedicated to theoretical reflection on God's essence for two reasons. One of them is that denying seeing is considered among the necessary consequences of denying direction.[109] Thus we want to show how to combine the denial of direction and the affirmation of seeing. The second is that, for us, the Exalted is seeable due to His existence and the existence of His essence. That He is seeable is due only to His essence, and not due to an act or an attribute of His. Indeed, every existent that is an essence must be seeable as it must be knowable. I do not mean that it must be knowable and seeable in actuality but in potentiality, that is, with respect to its essence it is capable of being seen, and there is nothing in its essence that prevents this or makes it impossible. If the existence of seeing is prevented, then this is because of a matter that is extraneous to the existent's essence. This is similar to your saying that the water in the river is thirst-quenching and the wine in the cask is intoxicating. They are not so, because they intoxicate and quench the thirst only when they are drunk. The meaning is that their essences are capable [of having those qualities].

If you understand what is intended by ['God's being seeable'], then you need to reflect theoretically on two aspects. One of them is its rational *possibility* and the second is its *reality*, which can be known only through a revelation. And if the revelation proves the reality of something, it inevitably proves that it is possible. However, we prove its possibility by two effective rational approaches.

---

what is meant is "with my grace." (Al-Ashʿarī, *al-Ibāna ʿan Uṣūl al-Diyāna*, pp. 14–16 and pp. 51–52)

Since al-Gazālī thinks this position is appropriate not for scholars but for the populace, it is clear that he does not follow al-Ashʿarī's standard doctrine in interpreting the anthropomorphic verses and *ḥadīth*s.

109. That is, the denial that God is seeable is thought to follow necessarily from the denial that God is located in a direction; or, as al-Ghazālī will state below, it is thought that affirming that God is seeable entails that God is located in a direction. If this were correct, then al-Ghazālī would be committed to denying that God is seeable, since he denies that God is located in a direction (see the Seventh Proposition). Al-Ghazālī will argue below, however, that this entailment is invalid, that is, God is seeable even though He is not located in a direction.

## [FIRST ASPECT: FIRST RATIONAL APPROACH]

The first is that we say that the Creator is an existent and an essence, who has constancy and true nature; but He is different from the rest of the existents by the impossibility of His being an occurrent, of having a quality that indicates occurrence, or of having an attribute that contradicts the divine attributes, such as knowledge, power, and so forth. Whatever is true of an existent is true of Him unless it indicates occurrence or contradicts one of His attributes.

The proof of this is that knowledge attaches to Him.[110] Since being knowable does not lead to any change in His essence, to anything contradicting His attributes, or to anything indicating occurrence, He is considered on a par with the bodies and modes with respect to the possibility of knowledge's attaching to His essence and attributes. Seeing is a form of knowledge, whose attachment to what is seen does not necessitate a change in an attribute and does not indicate occurrence. Hence it must be affirmed that every existent is seeable.

It might be said:

His being seen necessitates His being located in a direction. And His being located in a direction necessitates His being a mode or a substance; and this is impossible. The syllogism is this: if He is seen, then He is in the same direction as the seer; this necessary consequence is impossible; thus what leads to His being seen is impossible.[111]

We say that one of the two principles of this syllogism, which is that the necessary consequence is impossible, is conceded to you; but the first principle, which is the claim that this necessarily follows from affirming the seeing, is invalid.

Hence we say: "Why do you say that if He is seen, then he is in the direction of the seer? Did you know this by necessity or through theoretical re-

110. Al-Ghazālī uses the language of "attachment" to indicate that the thing is an object of the designated attribute. Thus to say that knowledge attaches to God's essence is to say that His essence is an object of knowledge, that is, His essence is known (or, at least, knowable); and to say that power does *not* attach to God's essence is to say that His essence is *not* an object of power, that is, no power can create the essence of God.

111. Since the necessary consequence ('He is in the same direction as the seer') is impossible, the premise ('He is seen') must be impossible as well. Instead of concluding that His being seen is impossible, however, al-Ghazālī states that what *leads* to His being seen is impossible. It is true, of course, that if there is a proposition that entails the premise, then the proposition is impossible too. Yet it is not clear what proposition al-Ghazālī has in mind as leading to the premise. Perhaps, he is referring to the orthodox doctrine that the righteous will see God in the hereafter, or simply to the claim that someone sees Him.

flection?" It cannot be claimed that it is known by necessity. As for theoretical reflection, it must be shown.[112] Their main point is that they have never seen anything that is not located in a direction specifically related to the seer. To this, it may be said that what has not been seen cannot be judged to be impossible. If this were permissible,[113] it would be permissible for the one who believes in the corporeity of God[114] to say that God (Exalted is He) is a body, because He is an agent, and we have never seen an agent who is not a body. Or he might say that if He is an agent and an existent, then He is either inside or outside the world, is either contiguous to or disconnected from the world, and cannot be devoid of all six directions; for we have not known an existent that is not so. Thus there is no difference between you and those people.

In summation, this position is based on the judgment that things can be known only in accordance with what is already observed and known. This is similar to one who knows body but denies mode, and says: "If a mode were to exist, it would occupy a region and prevent other things from existing where it is, exactly like a body." This position leads to[115] the impossibility for existents to differ in particular facts if they share general characteristics. This is arbitrary and has no basis.

Furthermore, in spite of their objections, they are aware that God (Exalted is He) sees Himself and sees the world, and He is not located in a direction related to Himself or to the world. If this is possible, then that conception is invalid.[116] This is what most of the Muʿtazilites admit,[117] and no one who admits that can evade this conclusion.

Those of them who deny this[118] cannot deny that a man may see himself in a mirror. It is clear that he is not in front of himself. If they claim that he does not see himself but an image that resembles his form and is imprinted in the mirror as an engraving is imprinted on a wall, then it would be said that this claim is clearly impossible. For if one moves away by two ells from

112. The pronoun 'it' refers to the claim that God's being in the same direction as the seer follows from that it is possible to see Him.

113. That is, if it were permissible to judge that which has never been seen as impossible.

114. 'The one who believes in the corporeity of God' is the translation of a single Arabic word, *mujassimī* (or *mujassim*).

115. Reading *yansha' min hādhā* (it results from this), which is the reading in the Ankara edition, instead of *mansha' hādhā* (the source of this), which is the reading in the Jeddah edition.

116. The conception referred to in this sentence is the belief that being seen entails being located in a direction that is related to the seer.

117. Most of the Muʿtazilites believe that God, indeed, sees Himself and the world. Some affirm the former and deny the latter and some deny both of them. However, all the Muʿtazilites believe that God is not located in a direction.

118. The demonstrative 'this' refers to the position that God sees Himself and the world.

a mirror attached to a wall, he sees his image two ells away from the body of the mirror; and if he moves away by three ells, so does the image. How is it possible for that which is two ells away from a mirror to be imprinted in the mirror when the thickness of the mirror might be no more than the thickness of a barley spike? It is impossible that the image is in something behind the mirror, for there is nothing behind the mirror except a wall, air, or another person, each of which is hidden from him and is something he does not see. The same applies to what is to the right of the mirror and to the left of it, to what is above it and below it, and to what is in each of its six directions. He sees an image that is two ells away from the mirror. So let this image be sought in the sides of the mirror. Where this image is found, that is where the thing seen is. This seen image does not exist in the bodies around the mirror except in the body of the seer. Therefore *he* is necessarily what is seen, since his being in front of himself or his image being in any direction has been disproved.[119] This necessary implication should not be belittled, for the Muʿtazilites cannot evade it.

We know by necessity that if a man has never seen himself and does not know of mirrors, and he is told that he can see himself in a mirror, he would deem it impossible. He would say: "It is inescapable that either I see myself and I am in the mirror, which is impossible, or I see a likeness of my form in the body of the mirror or in a body behind the mirror, which is also impossible; for the mirror itself has a form and the bodies near it have forms, and two forms cannot combine in one body. It is impossible for the forms of man, iron, and wall to exist in one body.[120] On the other hand, it is impossible that I see myself where I am, for I am not opposite to myself. How can then I see myself, when there must be an opposition between the seer and what is seen?"

This division into cases is correct according to the Muʿtazilite. But it is known that it is false. Its falsity, according to us, is due to his saying: "I am not opposite to myself, so I do not see myself." Otherwise, the remaining cases are correct. This clearly shows the narrow-mindedness of those opponents in their refusal to believe that which is not familiar to them and that with which their senses are not acquainted.

119. Literally, being in front or in a direction has been disapproved (*baṭalat al-muqābala wa-l-jiha*).

120. The point here is this. If the image in the mirror (or in a body behind the mirror) is a likeness of my form, I can say that my form is in the mirror (or in that body). (Al-Ghazālī does not exactly say this but it seems to be part of the argument). If my form is in the mirror, then there are two forms combined in the mirror: the form of the mirror itself and my form. But multiple forms cannot combine in one object. Therefore my image is not in the mirror (or in a body behind the mirror). Needless to say, this argument is problematic.

## [FIRST ASPECT: SECOND RATIONAL APPROACH]

The second rational approach is based on *considerable illumination*.[121] It is that we say: "Our opponent denies the seeing because he does not understand what we intend by 'seeing', does not comprehend its correct meaning, and thinks that we intend by it a state equivalent to the state attained by a seer when he looks at bodies and colors." Far from it. We, in fact, admit that such a state is impossible with respect to God (Exalted is He). We must comprehend the meaning of this term as used in the manner that is agreed upon, clarify it, and exclude from it what is impossible with respect to God. If there remains an aspect of its meaning that is not impossible with respect to God and can be described as "true seeing," then we affirm it regarding God and judge that He is indeed seeable. On the other hand, if it is not possible to apply the term 'seeable' to Him except figuratively, then we apply the term to Him with the permission of the revelation, but we understand its meaning according to the dictates of reason.

In sum, 'seeing' implies a meaning that involves a locus, which is the eye, and an object, which is color, size, body, and the rest of the visible things. So let us reflect theoretically on its true meaning, locus, and object, and ponder which one of these three is the basis for using the term.

We say:

Regarding locus, it is not the basis for the correctness of this usage. For if the state that we attain through the eye by virtue of what is seen should be attained, for instance, through the heart or the forehead,[122] then we would say that we have seen the thing and perceived it, and our statement would be true. The eye is a locus and a tool, which is not sought specifically but as that in which this state resides. Wherever the state resides, the true nature of seeing is fulfilled and the use of the term is correct. We may say that we have known with our hearts or our brains if we apprehend a thing with our hearts or brains; and similarly if we have seen a thing with our hearts, foreheads, or eyes.

As for the object of seeing, it is not specifically the basis for using the term and for fulfilling the true nature of seeing. For if seeing is "seeing" because it attaches to the color black, then what attaches to the color white is not seeing. If it is "seeing" because it attaches to color, then what attaches to motion is not seeing. If it is "seeing" because it attaches to a mode, then

121. 'Considerable illumination' refers to the experience of sight when compared to mental visualization, and not to the approach itself.

122. *Jabha* (forehead or front) is the reading in the Jeddah edition. The reading in the Ankara edition is *jiha* (direction).

what attaches to a body is not seeing. This shows that the specific qualities of the object of seeing are not the basis for the existence of the true nature of seeing and for the use of the term. Rather, the basis for its being an attribute that attaches to something is that it has an existent object, whatever the existent or essence might be. Therefore the basis for the use of the term is the third aspect—namely, the true meaning of seeing without considering its locus or object.

So let us search for its true nature: what is it? Seeing's true nature is nothing but a type of apprehension that is a perfection and an increased illumination in relation to the imagination. We see a friend, for instance, then we close our eyes. The image of the friend becomes present in our brain by way of visualization and imagination. If we open our eyes, we would perceive a difference. This difference is not due to our having perceived another image that is different from the visualized image. Rather, the seen image corresponds to the visualized image without a difference. The only difference between them is that the second state is like a perfection and an illumination of the state of visualization. An image of the friend occurs in us, when we open our eyes, that is clearer, fuller, and more perfect than the image formed by visualization.[123] Therefore visualization is a type of apprehension of a certain degree. Beyond it there is another degree, which is more complete in clarity and illumination—indeed, it is like a perfection of it. This perfection, in relation to visualization, is called "seeing" and "vision."

Similarly, there are things that we know but cannot visualize. These are God's essence and His attributes and all things that have no forms, that is, no color or size, such as power, knowledge, love, vision, and imagination. For these are matters that we know but cannot visualize. Knowledge about these matters is a type of apprehension. Let us reflect whether reason deems it impossible that there should be greater perfection of this apprehension, such that this greater perfection is related to this apprehension[124] the way seeing relates to visualization. If this is possible, then this illumination and perfection, in relation to knowledge, would be called "seeing," just as in relation to visualization we call [the greater illumination and perfection] "seeing."

It is known that positing such a perfection in clarity and illumination is not impossible regarding the known existents that cannot be visualized, such as knowledge, power, God's essence, His attributes, and so forth. In fact, we almost apprehend that our nature by necessity seeks more clar-

123. The clause 'than the image formed by visualization' is in the Cairo edition. It is omitted in the Ankara and Jeddah editions.

124. Literally, its relation to it (*nisbatah ilayh*).

ity in comprehending God's essence, His attributes, and the essences of all these known things.

We say that this is not impossible; there is nothing that renders it impossible. Indeed, the intellect proves[125] that it is possible and, furthermore, that our nature seeks it. However, this perfection in illumination is not available in this world, where, because the soul is occupied with the body and its turbid qualities, this perfection is veiled from it. Just as it is not unexpected that the eyelid, a cover, or a blackness in the eye might be a cause, according to the habitual course of things,[126] that prevents seeing what has been visualized, it is not unexpected that the turbidity of the soul and the accumulation of the veils of worldly occupations might be, according to the habitual course of things, an obstacle to seeing what is known.

Hence when what is in the graves is scattered out, what is in the breasts is disclosed,[127] and hearts are sanctified with immaculate drink and purified by all forms of purification and cleansing, nothing, because of this, prevents them from being occupied[128] with attaining more perfection and clarity in their comprehension of God's essence or of the rest of the knowables. The superiority of the degree of this comprehension over familiar knowledge is similar to the superiority of the degree of seeing over visualization. Thus it would be expressed as meeting God (Exalted is He), having a vision of Him, seeing Him, perceiving Him, or whatever expression you wish; for there need be no quarrel over expressions once the meaning is made clear.

If this is possible, then if this state is created in the eye, the use of the term 'seeing' would be more proper according to linguistic practice. Its creation in the eye is not impossible; similarly its creation in the heart is not impossible. If it is understood what the people who follow the truth intend by the use of 'seeing', it would be known that reason does not deem it impossible—on the contrary, it deems it necessary—and that the revelation has affirmed it. There remains no room for disputation other than being obstinate, quarrelling over how to use the expression 'seeing', or falling

125. Reading *yadullu ʿalā* (proves that) instead of *dalīlun ʿalā* (a proof for), which is the reading in the original.

126. The reader might have observed that al-Ghazālī is always careful to avoid the language of causation and that he consistently refers to causal relations as what is habitual or the habitual course of things. This is in accordance with his occasionalism, which he expounds in the Second Treatise, when he discusses the Ashʿarite doctrine of acquisition (*kasb*).

127. These clauses are borrowed from the following Qurʾānic verses: *Does he not know that when what is in the graves is scattered out, and what is in the breasts is disclosed, that their Lord is fully acquainted with them on that day*? (100:9–11).

128. The pronoun 'them' refers to the sanctified hearts. *Tashtaghil* (they are occupied) is in the Cairo edition. In the Ankara edition, it is *yashtaghil* (he, or it, is occupied). The Jeddah edition has *yastaʿid* (he, or it, is prepared).

short of comprehending the subtle meanings we discussed. Let us limit our summary to this.

### [SECOND ASPECT: THE EVIDENCE OF THE REVELATION]

The second aspect is the reality of seeing God according to the revelation. The revelation indicates that this will take place. Its sources are considerable. Because they are so considerable, it is feasible to claim that there was a consensus of the early Muslims in their supplication to God (Glorified is He), requesting the pleasure of looking at His noble face. We certainly know from their beliefs that they were expecting this and that they understood that it was permissible to expect it and request it from God (Exalted is He), on the basis of evidence concerning the affairs of God's Messenger (may God bless him and grant him peace) and many of his explicit sayings, which cannot be recounted here. The consensus indicates that the sources are beyond enumeration.

One of its strongest proofs is the statement of Moses (peace be upon him): *Show me [Yourself] that I may look upon You.*[129] It is impossible that this[130] would be hidden from one of God's prophets, whose status was so elevated that God spoke directly to him, and that he would fail to know about the attributes of God's essence what the Muʿtazilites came to know. This is necessarily known to be false. Our opponents regard one's being ignorant of the impossibility of seeing God as grounds for declaring one an infidel or one who has gone astray. For this ignorance is ignorance of an attribute of God's essence, since, for them, seeing God is an impossibility that is due to His essence and to His not being located in a direction. Yet, how is it possible that Moses (peace be upon him) did not know that God was not located in a direction, or that he knew that God was not located in a direction but did not know that seeing what has no direction is impossible?

I wish I knew what our opponent believes and supposes about Moses' confusion. Does he suppose that Moses believes God to be a body that is located in a direction and has color? Accusing the prophets of this is a manifest infidelity, because it is imputing infidelity to the prophets (peace be upon them). For the one who says that God (Glorified is He) is a body is on a par with the one who worships idols and the sun. Or does he say that Moses knows that it is impossible for God to be located in a direction but does not know that whatever has no direction cannot be seen? This

129. Qur'ān, 7:143.

130. The demonstrative 'this' refers to the impossibility of seeing God.

would be to accuse the prophet (peace be upon him) of ignorance. For our opponent thinks this is an obvious truth and not a theoretical one.[131] So now, my heedful reader,[132] you have a choice between being inclined to attribute ignorance to a prophet and being inclined to attribute ignorance to a Muʿtazilite. Thus choose what is more appropriate for you, and peace be upon you.

It might be said: "If this is evidence for you, then it is evidence against you that Moses asked to see God in this worldly life, that God says: *You will not see Me,*[133] and that God says: *No vision can perceive Him.*"[134]

We say:

Regarding his asking to see God in this worldly life, it shows his lack of knowledge of when what is possible in itself may be actualized. All the prophets (peace be upon them) have no knowledge of the occult except what they are taught, which is little. How frequent it is that a prophet may pray for the dispelling of a trouble and the removal of a calamity and hope that his prayer will be answered at a certain time, when it is already established in God's knowledge that this is not when the prayer will be answered. Our response is of the same sort as this.[135]

As for the Exalted's statement: *You will not see Me,* it is a denial of a solicitation, in which Moses made an immediate request. Had he said "Show me [Yourself] so that I may look upon You in the hereafter," and God said *You will not see Me,* then this would be a proof for negating the seeing of God, but only with respect to Moses specifically and not in general. And hence it would not be a proof of its impossibility. So how can it be [considered a proof against seeing God], when it is a response to a request to have something now?

Regarding the Exalted's statement: *No vision will perceive Him,* this might mean that sight cannot encompass Him and embrace Him from His sides as sight encompasses bodies, and that is true. Or it might mean perception in general,[136] and what is intended by it is perception in this worldly life, and

131. The Muʿtazilites believe that it is obvious that the nature of seeing requires what is seen to be located in space and bounded by limits, both of which are obviously contrary to God's essence. Hence, for them, it is a manifest truth that God cannot be seen. However, many Muʿtazilites interpret Moses' request of God to show him Himself as an indication of doubt, that is, of his not having been certain about every aspect of God's nature, so that God had to make it clear to him that He cannot be seen.

132. Literally, O heedful.

133. Qurʾān, 7:143.

134. Qurʾān, 6:103.

135. Literally, this is of the same sort as that.

136. Literally, or it could be general.

that is true as well, and it is what He intended by His saying: *You will not see Me*, that is, in this worldly life.

Let us confine our discussion of the issue of seeing God to this extent. The fair reader should examine how the different sects are divided and grouped into those whose belief is excessive and those whose belief is deficient.

The Ḥashawites could not comprehend an existent that is not located in a direction.[137] Thus they affirm a direction for God, which makes it necessary for them to attribute to God corporeity, magnitude, and qualities that are particular to occurrents. The Muʿtazilites, on the other hand, deny that God has direction, and could not affirm the seeing of God without direction. So they contradict definite assertions of the revelation. They think that in affirming the seeing of God they also affirm direction for Him. These people have gone too far in their exaltation of God, trying to avoid anthropomorphism; they end up being excessive. The Ḥashawites affirm direction for God, trying to avoid nullifying His attributes;[138] they end up anthropomorphizing.

God (Exalted is He) guided the followers of the Sunna to stand up for the truth. They became aware of the straight path, they knew that direction must be denied because it is an outcome and a completion of having a body, and that seeing God is established because it is an analogue of knowledge and is related to it, and is a perfection of it.[139] Hence the rejection of corporeity necessitates a rejection of direction, which is one of its necessary consequences. The affirmation of knowledge necessitates the affirmation of seeing God,[140] which is one of its analogues and perfections and shares with it a characteristic. This characteristic is that seeing does not entail a change in the essence of what is seen, but is attached to it as it is, just as the case of knowledge. It is not veiled from a rational man that this is moderation in belief.

137. See Religious Preface, note 4, for a brief description of the beliefs of this theological school.

138. Literally, being cautious of nullification.

139. Al-Ghazālī literally says: "and that the seeing is established because it is an analogue of knowledge and. . . ." However, the meaning must be "and that the *possibility* of seeing God is established because seeing God is an analogue of knowledge and. . . ." According to al-Ghazālī, God's being seeable is a consequence of His essence, because if He can be known, then He can be seen. It does not follow, however, that people *will see* God. The seeing of God is not a consequence of His essence.

140. The knowledge here is the human knowledge of God's essence and His attributes—not divine knowledge—since there is no higher degree of apprehension than God's knowledge. In a sense, then, one can claim that all of God's knowledge, insofar as it is perfect, is a form of seeing.

# Tenth Proposition

*[God is one]*

We claim that God (Exalted is He) is one. His being one is based on affirming the existence of His essence and denying the existence of other such essences.[141] Since [the matter of God's oneness] is not a theoretical reflection on an attribute that is additional to His essence, this issue should be discussed in this treatise.[142]

We say that 'being one' might be used to indicate that the thing is indivisible, that is, it has no quantity, part,[143] or magnitude. The Creator (Exalted is He) is one in the sense[144] that a quantity, which brings divisibility, is negated of Him. He is indivisible, for divisibility applies to that which has quantity. To divide a thing is to act on its quantity through separation and diminution. If a thing has no quantity, its division is inconceivable.

'Being one' might also be used to indicate that the thing has no analogue of its kind, as we say that the sun is one. The Creator (Exalted is He) is also one in this sense. There is no counterpart to Him.

As for His having no alternate, this is obvious. By 'alternate' is understood that which alternates with the thing in one locus, and never combines with it. Whatever has no locus has no alternate. The Creator has no locus; hence He has no alternate.

Regarding our saying that there is no counterpart to Him, we mean by it that He, and no other, is the creator of everything other than Himself. The proof for this claim is that if a partner for Him were posited, it would be either similar to Him in all respects, higher than Him in rank, or lower than Him in rank. Since each of these is impossible, what leads to them is also impossible.

The reason for the impossibility of its being similar to Him in all respects is that every two things must be different. If there were no difference at all,

141. Literally, denying the existence of other than Himself.

142. What al-Ghazālī means is that the reason the issue of the divine unity should be discussed in this treatise is that this treatise is concerned with theoretical reflection on the essence of God, and the oneness of God pertains to his essence. God's oneness is not an attribute, such as knowledge or will, that is additional to His essence.

143. The reading in the Cairo edition is *juz'* (part) and in the Jeddah and Ankara editions is *ḥadd* (in this context, limit or boundary).

144. In the Ankara edition the expression *annah lā kammiyya lah* (that it has no quantity) is inserted here. It is omitted in the Jeddah edition.

duality would be inconceivable.[145] For we do not conceive of two blacks except in two loci, or in one locus but at two times, so that one of them would be separate, dissimilar, and different from the other either in locus or in time. Two things might differ in their definitions and true natures, just as motion and color differ, since they are two things even if they coexist in one locus at the same time. For one of them is different from the other in its true nature. If two things are equal in their true nature and definition, such as black, the difference between them would be either in locus or in time. To posit two similar blacks in the same substance and in one state is impossible, for duality could not then be apprehended. If it were permissible to say that they are two things without there being any difference between them,[146] then it would be permissible to point to a man and say that he is two men, or even ten, but that they are identical and parallel in qualities, place, all accidents, and all necessary conditions without any distinction. This is necessarily impossible. Thus if there were a counterpart to God (Exalted is He) that was identical to Him in its true nature and attributes, its existence would be impossible. For it could not be distinguished from Him by place, since there is no place, nor in time, since there is no time, because they would both be eternal; therefore there would be no differentiation. If every difference is removed, multiplicity is necessarily removed, and hence unity is necessitated.

It is also impossible to say that it differs from Him by being superior to Him, because the one who is superior is the god. The god is the most sublime and supreme of all existents. The posited other is deficient; hence not the god. We reject a multiplicity of gods. The god is the one who is described in superlative terms: He is the most supreme and most sublime of all existents.

On the other hand, if it were inferior to Him, that, too, would be impossible, because it would then be deficient. We designate by 'god' the most sublime of all existents. The most sublime, then, must be one, and that is the god. It is inconceivable that there are two who are equal in all qualities of majesty, for differentiation would be removed, and there could be no multiplicity,[147] as mentioned previously.

It might be said:

What objection do you have against the one who does not dispute with you concerning the existence of what is designated by the name 'god' inasmuch as the god is identified with the most sublime of all existents, but

145. That is, indiscernibles are identical. In Western philosophy this is referred to as "Leibniz's law."

146. Literally, without variation (*bilā mughāyara*).

147. Literally, and multiplicity would be annulled.

he says: "The world as a whole is not the creation of one creator; rather it is the creation of two creators; for instance, one of them is the creator of the heavens and the other is the creator of the earth, or one of them is the creator of inanimate objects and the other is the creator of animals and plants"? What is impossible about this? If there is no proof for the impossibility of this, of what use is your statement that none of those can be called by the name 'god'? Such a speaker designates by 'god' a creator. He might even say that one of them is the creator of good and the other is the creator of evil, or that one of them is the creator of substances and the other is the creator of modes. So there must be a proof for the impossibility of this.

We say:

The impossibility of this is proved by showing that, according to this questioner, the distribution of the created things among the creators is inescapably one of two kinds. Either it requires dividing bodies and modes together, so that one of them creates some of the bodies and modes, but not others, or it is said that all the bodies are created by one and all the modes by the other.

It is false to claim that some of the bodies, such as the heavens but not the earth, are created by one. We would ask whether the creator of the heavens is capable of creating the earth or not. If he is capable, just as the other is,[148] then neither one can be differentiated from the other in terms of power. And so, neither one can be differentiated by what is within his power. The object of power would be within the domain of both creators, so that attributing it to one of them would be no more fitting than attributing it to the other. The impossibility here arises from what we already mentioned with respect to positing a multiplicity of similar things without there being a difference between them—which is impossible. On the other hand, if he is not capable, this, too, would be impossible, because the substances are similar, and their forms of being, which are their occupying specific regions, are also similar. The one who has power over one thing would, if his power is eternal, have power over things that are like it, so that his power can attach to both things. Since the power of each one of them attaches to a number of bodies and substances, why should it be restricted to one object? If this eternal power, unlike any occurrent power, has more than one object, then it is no more fitting for some things rather than others to be objects of this power.[149] It becomes necessary, therefore, to deny that

148. The reading in the Jeddah edition is *ka-qudratih* (similar to his power) and in the Ankara edition is *bi-qudratih* (through his power).

149. This is a liberal translation. The original literally says: "If it, unlike an occurrent power, has more than one object, then some numbers are not more proper than others."

there is a limit to what is within his power; all substances whose existence is possible are within his power.

The second case is to say that one of them is capable of creating substances[150] and the other modes; so they are different; for having power over one kind of things does not entail having power over the other kind. This is impossible, because mode cannot dispense with substance and substance cannot dispense with mode. Thus the act of each one of them would be dependent on the other. If the creator of modes wants to create a mode, how would he create it? The creator of substances might not cooperate with him by creating a substance when he wants to create a mode. Hence he would remain impotent and confounded, and the impotent cannot be powerful. Similarly for the creator of substances: the creator of modes might be at variance with him, so that he would not be able to create substances. This leads to "co-obstruction."[151]

It might be said: "Whenever one of them wants to create a substance, the other cooperates with him by creating a mode, and conversely." We say: "Is this cooperation necessary, such that the intellect cannot conceive of its absence, or not?" If you claim that it is necessary, your claim is arbitrary; moreover, it nullifies power. For it is as if the creation of substance by one of them would make it incumbent upon the other to create a mode, and conversely. Hence, he would have no power to abstain. Under this condition, power cannot be established.

In summation, if it were possible to abstain from cooperation, then the act of creation might not be carried out, and the meaning of power would be nullified. If cooperation is necessary, then the one who has to cooperate would be compelled to act and would have no power.[152]

If it is said that one of them is the creator of evil and the other is the creator of benevolence, then we say: "This is madness, for evil is not evil due

150. Literally, has power over the substances.

151. This is a literal translation of the Arabic word *tamānuʿ* ("co-obstruction," "co-inhibition," or "co-prevention"). The meaning of the sentence is that this leads each creator to obstruct (or prevent, or inhibit) the act of the other.

152. The claim would have been stronger had al-Ghazālī said that the one who must cooperate would have no *free will* instead of no power. However, as it will become clear from the chapter on power of the Second Treatise, al-Ghazālī understands by the expression '*x* is an object of *A*'s power' or '*A*'s power is attached to *x*' that *x* is under *A*'s control. Given this understanding, the claim that an act of a person is the object of two powers—God's power and the person's power—will pose a difficulty for al-Ghazālī when he affirms the Ashʿarite doctrine of acquisition, which asserts that although a person's voluntary act is created directly by God, it is simultaneously an object of the person's power, which is also created by God, and of God's power. Al-Ghazālī will try to make sense of saying that a person's act is an object of his power, even though his power did not and could not produce the act.

to its essence, rather in essence it is equivalent to benevolence and similar to it." To have power over something is to have power over things that are like it. The burning by fire of the body of a Muslim is evil, but the burning of the body of an infidel is benevolent and is a repelling of evil. The burning of the same person, if he utters the declaration of Islam,[153] would transform into an evil act. The one who is able to burn the flesh of a person when he abstains from uttering the declaration of faith is inevitably able to burn him when he utters it, since his utterance is a vanishing sound, which does not alter the essence of flesh, the essence of fire, or the essence of burning, and does not transform one genus [into another]. Thus all kinds of burning are equivalent. Power, therefore, must attach to all of them. This necessitates either "co-obstruction" or "crowding."[154]

In general, however that matter is supposed to be, disarray and corruption result from it. This is what God (Exalted is He) intends by His saying: *Had there been deities apart from God, both [the heaven and the earth] would have been corrupted.*[155] Nothing can be added to the explanation of the Qur'ān.

Let us conclude this treatise with the Tenth Proposition. All that remains that is relevant to this topic is to show that it is impossible for God to be a receptacle of occurrents. We will visit this issue during our discussion of divine attributes, when we respond to those who say that knowledge, will, and other attributes are occurrents.

153. The declaration of Islam, or of faith (*al-shahāda*), is the following statement: "I bear witness that there is no deity but God, and I bear witness that Muḥammad is the Messenger of God."

154. This is an extremely condensed sentence. As explained in note 151, 'co-obstruction' is the literal translation of *tamānu'*. The word 'crowding' is the literal translation of *tazāḥum*. Here is an unpacking of the sentence: 'This necessitates the existence of either a multiplicity of creators who obstruct the acts of each other or a multiplicity of creators who are identical to each other.' In the original, the sentence is a conjunction, 'co-obstruction *and* crowding', but the meaning clearly calls for a disjunctive form, '*either* co-obstruction *or* crowding', which is my reading.

155. Qur'ān, 21:22.

# SECOND TREATISE

∵

## *On the Divine Attributes*

IT INCLUDES SEVEN PROPOSITIONS.[1]

We claim that God is knower, powerful, living, willer, hearer, seer, and sayer. These are seven attributes.[2] A consideration of them branches into theoretical reflections on two matters. One of them concerns what is specific to each attribute. The second concerns what is common to all the attributes. Let us begin with the first part, in which we establish the principal attributes and explain their specific characteristics.

1. The discussion of each attribute begins with a proposition—seven propositions for seven attributes.

2. This is a central Ashʿarite doctrine—namely, that there are only seven principal attributes and that all other attributes, such as being a sustainer, steadfast, and sanctified, are derived from the principal ones. Al-Ghazālī will address the "secondary attributes" near the end of this treatise.

# [FIRST PART]

# First Attribute: Power

We claim that the Originator of the world is powerful, since the world is a product[3] that is well-designed, well-ordered, exquisite, and well-composed, and contains all kinds of wonders and marvels; and this is a demonstration of power. To present a syllogism, we say: "Every well-designed product is produced by a powerful agent; the world is a well-designed[4] product; therefore it is produced by a powerful agent." Which of the two principles would one dispute?

It might be said: "Why do you say that the world is a well-designed product?" We reply that we signify by its being well-designed its excellent organization, excellent composition, and exactness. He who examines his organs—the external and internal—would become aware of wonders of exquisiteness, which would take very long to enumerate. The knowledge of this principle, then, is attained through sensation and observation. Thus this principle cannot be denied.

It might be said: "How do you know the other principle, which is that the agent who produces a well-designed, well-ordered product is powerful?"[5] We reply that this is apprehended by a necessity of reason. The intellect believes its truth without a proof. No rational person can deny it. In spite of this, we present a proof for it in order to eliminate any trace of denial and obstinacy.

We say that we mean by God's being powerful that the act that proceeds from Him must proceed from Him either through His essence or through something additional to His essence. It is false to say that it proceeds from Him through His essence, since if it did, it would be eternal, coexisting with

3. The Arabic word is *fiʿl*, which literally means "act"; it is something that an agent (*fāʿil*) performs. However, it sounds odd in English to speak of a well-designed act. *Fiʿl* could mean "work" as well, and it is natural to speak of a well-designed work. The difficulty is that translating *fiʿl* as 'work' fails to give the implication that the world, since it is a *fiʿl*, must be produced by an agent. 'Product', on the other hand, is a possible translation of *fiʿl* and it carries with it the implication that there must be an agent who made the product.

4. The Ankara addition adds 'and well-ordered'.

5. Al-Ghazālī paraphrases here the first premise. He originally said that every well-designed product is produced by a powerful agent. The two statements are equivalent because the word *fiʿl* (which I translated here as 'product') implies that there is an agent who produced this *fiʿl*.

the essence. This shows that it proceeds from Him through something additional to His essence. We call the attribute that is additional to His essence through which He becomes prepared [to perform] the existing act "power."[6] For 'power', according to linguistic usage, designates an attribute through which the agent becomes prepared for the act and the act comes to fruition. This description is indicated by the exclusive disjunction we mentioned.[7] We do not mean by power anything but this attribute, and we have established its existence. If it is said, "One thing that counts against you with respect to power is that it is eternal yet the act[8] is not eternal," then we say that the answer to this will be discussed when the characteristics of will[9] are considered. Now that we have established [the existence of the divine attribute of] power, let us discuss its characteristics.

One of its characteristics is that it attaches to all the objects of power; and by the objects of power I mean all possible things. It is clear that the possible things are infinite; hence the objects of power are also infinite. We mean by saying that the possible things are infinite simply that the successive creation of one occurrent after another does not reach a limit beyond which the intellect cannot conceive of the occurrence of another occurrent. Possibility continues forever, and the divine power encompasses all of that.[10]

The demonstration of this claim, which is that the divine power is all-encompassing, is this. It has been shown that the Maker of the world is one. But, on the one hand, if He has a distinct power for every object of power, then given that the objects of power are infinite, it follows that there are infinitely many powers. This is impossible on the basis of our previous demonstration for the impossibility of there being infinitely many celestial revolutions.[11] On the other hand, if the divine power is one, its attachment

6. This is a translation of the sentence in the Ankara edition. In the Jeddah edition the sentence reads: "We call the attribute that is additional to His essence through which the act becomes ready to come into existence 'power'."

7. The exclusive disjunction to which al-Ghazālī refers here is the one he asserts at the beginning of the current proof—namely, that God's being powerful means that the act He performs must proceed from Him either through His essence or through something additional to His essence.

8. *Fiʿl* (act) is the reading in the Jeddah edition. The reading in the Ankara edition is *maqdūr* (object of power, that is, an object that can be produced by power).

9. The Jeddah edition adds 'through which an act comes into fruition'.

10. The notion of the infinite described here is that of potential infinity. The possible things, and hence the objects of divine power, are infinite in the sense that they can be actualized successively forever, that is, without a limit. We encountered al-Ghazālī's rejection of actual infinity in the Fourth Introduction, p. 16, and the First Treatise, pp. 37–38.

11. This is a rather liberal translation. A literal translation is: 'This is impossible on the basis of the previous refutation of revolutions that have no end.' For this refutation, see the Fourth Introduction, p. 16, and the First Treatise, pp. 37–38.

to its objects among the different substances and modes must be due to a characteristic common to these objects. The only characteristic they share is possibility. It follows from this that every possible thing is inevitably an object of the divine power and can be actualized through it.

In general, if the substances and modes are produced by God, it is impossible that things like them cannot be produced by Him. For the power to produce a thing is also a power to produce its like if it is possible to have multiple objects of power. The divine power relates to all the motions and all the colors in the same manner. It is suitable for creating in perpetuity one motion after another, one color after another, one substance after another, and so on. This is what we meant by saying that the power of God (Exalted is He) attaches to all possible things. Possibility is not restricted to a certain number of things. The essence of the divine power does not relate to a specific number of things as opposed to any other. Thus it is not possible to point to a motion and claim that it is outside the reach of power, whereas a similar thing is an object of this power, since we know with certainty that what is necessarily true of a thing is necessarily true of its like. Three questions[12] arise from this characteristic of divine power.[13]

## FIRST QUESTION

One might ask: "Do you say that the contrary of what is known is an object of divine power?"

We reply:

There is disagreement about this issue. However, no disagreement about it is imaginable if the matter is verified and the complexities of the expressions are eliminated. Here is an elucidation of the issue. It has been established that whatever is possible is an object of the divine power and what is impossible is not an object of power. So let us reflect: Is the contrary of what is known impossible or possible? You will not know the answer unless you understand the meanings of 'impossible' and 'possible' and comprehend their true nature. If you are not careful in your reflection, it might follow both that the contrary of what is known is impossible and that it is possible, that is, not impossible. It would then follow that it is both impossible and not impossible; yet the contradictories cannot both be true.

Know, then, that there is an ambiguity within the scope of these terms.[14] This should become obvious for you when I tell you, for example, that it is true of the world that it is necessary, that it is impossible, and that it is

12. Literally, branches.

13. The characteristic under discussion is that the objects of divine power are precisely all the possible objects.

14. The terms under discussion are 'possible' and 'impossible'.

contingent. As for its being necessary, the case is such that if the will of the Eternal is assumed to exist necessarily, what is willed would inevitably be necessary and not contingent. For it is impossible for what is willed to fail to exist while the will exists eternally. As for its being impossible, if the will is assumed not to attach to the world's existence, the world's occurrence would definitely be impossible, since there would be an occurrent that occurred without a cause; and it is known that this is impossible.[15] As for its being contingent, this is so when one reflects solely on the world's essence without taking into consideration the existence or nonexistence of the will. It is then described as contingent.

There are then three perspectives. The first requires the existence of the will and its attachment to the world; from this perspective it is necessary.[16]

15. There is good reason to believe that the notions of *necessity* and *impossibility* al-Ghazālī employs here are not metaphysical. It is clear that al-Ghazālī is speaking not about divine will in general but about the particular will to create the world. Al-Ghazālī accepts the following two conditionals: (C1) if God's will to create the world exists, then the world exists *necessarily*; and (C2) if God's will to create the world had not existed, it would be *impossible* for the world to exist. He surely rejects the conditional (C3) had God not willed to create the world, God could not have willed to create it. As is clear from this and the next treatise, al-Ghazālī believes that divine freedom is absolute and that it is constrained only by what is logically impossible, such as making the even odd. Perhaps, the clearest way to see the difference between these conditionals is by using the framework of possible worlds. C3 implies that if there is a possible world in which God does not will to create the world, then there is no possible world in which such a will exists. For al-Ghazālī, this amounts to a denial of divine freedom. The notions of necessity and impossibility that occur in C1 and C2 could be interpreted in a way that allows one to affirm C1 and C2 while rejecting C3. One could say that a sufficient condition for the truth of C1 and C2 is that there is no possible world in which the will to create the world exists yet the world fails to exist and there is no possible world in which the will to create the world does not exist yet the world exists. In other words, the existence of God's will to create the world necessitates the existence of the world and the nonexistence of the world necessitates the nonexistence of God's will to create the world. To say that God's will to create the world could exist without the world's existing is to deny God's omnipotence, and to say that the world could exist without the existence of God's will to create the world (assuming that only God can create the world) is to posit the existence of an occurrent that has no cause. The notion of necessity in al-Ghazālī's statement that God's will to create the world exists necessarily should be understood in a similar fashion: if such a will was not realized in some possible world, then it can never be realized in *that* world. This is so, because in order for this will to be realized after being nonexistent, something must occur in God, but God, al-Ghazālī believes, is not a receptacle of occurrents.

16. It is clear that in order for the world to exist necessarily it is not enough that it be the object of just any will. As al-Ghazālī states earlier, the will must exist necessarily if the world is to exist necessarily. (See the previous note for an interpretation of this notion of necessity.) The Islamic philosophers were troubled, however, by the notion of an occurrent (i.e., something that has a beginning) being created through a necessary and eternal will. They believed that willing an act implies two things: (1) once the will is activated and all the requirements for the act are in place, the act must occur, and (2) the will can operate

The second is to posit the nonexistence of the will; from this perspective it is impossible. The third is to withdraw any consideration of will and cause, and hence not to take into consideration the existence or nonexistence of the will; rather we reflect merely on the essence of the world. From this third perspective only one option remains for the world, namely, contingency. We mean by this that by virtue of its essence alone it is contingent; that is, if no condition is posited other than its essence, it is contingent. This shows that it is possible for a thing to be both possible and impossible, in the sense that it is possible by virtue of its essence and impossible by virtue of something other than itself. However, it is not possible for a thing to be possible owing to its essence and also impossible owing to its essence, for these are contradictories.

Let us return to the issue of the contrary to what is known. We say: "If it is part of God's knowledge that Zayd shall die on Saturday morning, then we ask whether the creation of life for Zayd on Saturday morning is possible or not possible." The truth of the matter is that it is both possible and impossible. It is possible by virtue of its own essence without taking into consideration anything other than itself. And it is impossible owing to something other than itself, when the attachment of knowledge to Zayd's death is taken into consideration, and not by virtue of its own essence. What is impossible owing to its own essence is that whose existence is prevented because of its essence, such as a combining of blackness and whiteness, and not because of an impossibility necessitated by something other than its essence. The existence of Zayd's life, if it is supposed, is not prevented by virtue of the essence of life. However, its impossibility is necessitated by virtue of something other than its essence—namely, the essence of knowledge, because otherwise knowledge would turn into ignorance, and it is impossible for knowledge to turn into ignorance.

It has become clear that it is possible by virtue of its essence and impossible because of an impossibility necessitated by something other than

---

only when there is a real choice to be made; it cannot choose when there is no qualitative difference between alternatives. If one adds to these two conditions the suppositions (which al-Ghazālī also accepts) that God is eternal, that He is not a receptacle of occurrents, that His power is all-encompassing, and that His states are indiscernible, one can see why the philosophers concluded that the world proceeded from God by necessity and hence it coexists with God eternally. Al-Ghazālī in *Tahāfut al-Falāsifa* presents the philosophers' arguments for the eternity of the world and argues that God created the world through a necessary and eternal will that designated a certain "moment" to bring the world into existence. It should be noted, however, that positing a time before the creation of the world is problematic, since al-Ghazālī believes that space and time were created with the world. (See al-Ghazālī, *Tahāfut al-Falāsifa*, pp. 88–102, and the rebuttal by Ibn Rushd (Averroës) in *Tahāfut al-Tahāfut*, pp. 7–16.)

itself. If we say that Zayd's life at this time is an object of power, we intend by this only that life, insofar as it is life, is not impossible, as combining blackness and whiteness is. The power of God (Exalted is He), insofar as it is power, is suited to attach to the creation of life, and it does not fall short due to languor, weakness, or any cause within the essence of power. Those are two matters whose denial is impossible: I mean negating the shortcoming of the divine power's essence and affirming the possibility of the essence of life inasmuch as it is only life, and without considering anything other than it.[17]

If our opponent says that [the contrary of what is known] is not an object of power, meaning that its existence leads to an impossibility, then he is truthful according to this meaning; and we do not deny it. There remains to investigate the term: Is it correct from a linguistic viewpoint to use this term in this case or not?[18] It is not hard to see that the correct answer is that the term may be used. For people say that so-and-so is capable of movement and rest, that is, if he wishes, he can move, and if he wishes, he can stay still. They also say that at all times he has the ability to do each of the opposites; yet they know that according to God's knowledge only one of them will take place. Thus linguistic practice confirms what we mentioned. That the term may mean this is a necessary fact, which cannot be denied.

## SECOND QUESTION

One might say:

You claim that the divine power is universally attached to all possible things.[19] What do you say, then, about the objects of the powers of the animals and the rest of the created living beings? Are they also objects of God's power or not? If you say that they are not objects of divine power, you have contradicted your statement that the divine power is all-encompassing.

17. The point here is this. There are two undeniable aspects of the relation between the divine power and the creation of Zayd's life. The first is that the divine power is not too weak to create this life on Saturday morning. The second is that the creation of this life is an object of the divine power when this life is considered *only* in terms of its essence. Given the earlier claim that the objects of the divine power are precisely those things that are possible, the second matter could be expressed as follows: the creation of life in terms of its essence solely is possible. This is al-Ghazālī's formulation.

18. The term under discussion is 'object of power' (*maqdūr*), or equivalently, 'possible' (*mumkin*).

19. This is a restatement of the first characteristic of divine power—namely, that whatever is possible is an object of divine power (*al-mumkināt maqdūrāt*). The converse is obviously true, since what is impossible cannot be an object of any power, that is, whatever is an object of power (any power) is possible (*al-maqdūrāt mumkināt*).

And if you say that they are objects of divine power, it becomes necessary for you to posit an object that is related to two possessors of power; yet this is absurd. Alternatively you must deny that man and the other animals have power. Yet this is a denial of what is necessary and is a repudiation of the demands of the law, since it is impossible to make demands with respect to that over which one has no power, and it is impossible that God (Exalted is He) would say to His servant: "It is incumbent upon you to do that which is within my power and over which I exclusively have power while you have none."

We respond, somewhat expansively, that people are divided into disparate parties regarding this matter. The Mujbirites take the position of denying that man has power; hence they are forced to deny the necessary distinction between tremor and voluntary movement, and to deem impossible the obligations set forth in the revelation.[20] The Muʿtazilites take the position of denying that the power of God (Exalted is He) attaches to the acts of people, animals, angels, jinn, and devils. They claim that whatever proceeds from them is created and originated by them, and that God has no power over it: He can neither prevent it nor originate it.[21]

Two extremely repugnant consequences follow [from their position].

20. The term 'Mujbira' (or more commonly, 'Jabriyya') is used to describe several Islamic theological schools that affirm that no being has power or will save God. Hence there is only one power, which is the divine power, and only one will, which is the divine will. The oldest and most famous of these schools was the Jahmiyya, which was founded by Jahm ibn Ṣafwān (d. AH 128/745 CE). According to them, there is no difference between a tremor and what appears to be a voluntary movement of the hand. Simply put, there is no volition besides God's will and power. Actions and the powers to produce them are attributed to the created living beings only metaphorically. (See al-Shahrastānī, *al-Milal wa-l-Niḥal*, vol. 1, pp. 97–99; al-Baghdādī, *al-Farq bayn al-Firaq*, pp. 146–147; and Amīn, *Fajr al-Islām*, pp. 272–273.)

21. See Religious Preface, note 6, for a brief description of the Muʿtazila school. The position al-Ghazālī attributes here to the Muʿtazilites was not universally accepted by them. This position belonged specifically to many of the Muʿtazilite subschools in Baghdad. The majority of the Muʿtazilite subschools in Basra rejected this position and asserted that *all* possible things are objects of God's power. In particular, all the acts of the created living beings, whether they can be described as good or evil, are within God's power. Hence, according to them, it is within God's power to commit evil and injustice, but because He is all-good, He does not do so. A relatively small group of Basra Muʿtazilites, who followed Abū Isḥāq Ibrāhīm al-Naẓẓām (d. c. AH 231/845 CE), disagreed with their colleagues and asserted that God's goodness is such that evil cannot be an object of His power, that is, He *cannot* commit evil or unjust acts. While the followers of al-Naẓẓām also agreed that the good and virtuous acts of God's servants are objects of His power, they differed, however, regarding whether God can prevent evil acts or not. Some claimed that God can prevent evil acts but refrains from interfering with His servants' expression of free will. Some said that God cannot prevent them, because if He could, He would since He is all-good. In general, the Muʿtazilites share a common core with respect to this issue but they differ greatly in the details. Here is what al-Shahrastānī says about this common core.

One of them is the denial of the consensus of the early Muslims (may God be pleased with them) that there is no creator or originator except God.[22]

---

> They agreed that the servant [of God] is powerful and a creator of his acts, good and evil. He deserves for what he does reward or punishment in the hereafter. The Lord (Exalted is He) is too sanctified to relate evil or injustice to Him, or any act that is unbelief or disobedience. For if He were to create injustice, He would be unjust, just as if He creates justice, He is just. And they agreed that God (Exalted is He) does not do anything that is not virtuous and good. (*Al-Milal wa-l-Niḥal*, vol. 1, p. 57)

Note that this consensus is consistent with the various positions described above. They all agree that created living beings *really* create and originate their acts (for them, an involuntary movement is not a *true* act), and that created living beings create and originate these acts through powers with which God endowed them (in other words, God does not create these acts, but He empowers the individuals to create them). And they all argue that since God is all-good, He would not create evil or injustice. They disagree, however, on many things regarding this issue, but mostly on the answers to the following questions: Does God have the power to create evil and injustice? Does He have the power to prevent evil and unjust acts? Does He have the power to create or prevent what His servants create?

22. The claim that *all* early Muslims (*al-salaf*) accepted the doctrine of occasionalism is central to Ashʿarism. (See note 34 below for a brief description of the Ashaʿriyya school of Islamic theology.) This doctrine asserts that all things, including all causes, all effects, and all acts of living beings are *directly* created by God. The Ashʿariyya school was founded in the tenth century CE (the fourth century AH) by Abū al-Ḥasan ʿAlī al-Ashʿarī, who broke from the Muʿtazilites and became a severe critic of their school. By the second half of the twelfth century CE (the sixth century AH) Ashʿarism became the dominant Islamic theology and an integral part of Sunni orthodoxy. Almost all schools of Islamic jurisprudence, including schools as divergent as the Shāfiʿiyya and the Wahābiyya, adopted Ashʿarism as their official theology (the Ḥanafī school of Islamic jurisprudence, which arguably has the greatest number of followers, adopted the Māturīdiyya school of Islamic theology, which is also considered part of Sunni orthodoxy; this school was founded by Abū Manṣūr Muḥammad al-Māturīdī (d. AH 333/944 CE)). The success of Ashʿarism may be traced in large measure to four things: (1) the tireless efforts of al-Ashʿarī and many of his distinguished followers such as al-Ghazālī and his teacher al-Juwaynī; (2) their vocal opposition to the Muʿtazilites, whose brand of Islamic theology flourished during the ninth century CE (the third century AH) and was adopted by the ʿAbbāsid caliph al-M'mūn (who established the great Bayt al-Ḥikma library in AH 217/832 CE) and was "enforced" as the official theology of the state, earning the Muʿtazilites many influential enemies; (3) their ability to convince the principal Sunni scholars that their doctrines of occasionalism and of acquisition (which is discussed below) were the consensus of the early Muslims; and (4) the establishment in the eleventh century CE (the fifth century AH) of the prestigious Niẓāmiyya schools, which focused on teaching Shāfiʿite jurisprudence and Ashʿarite theology, and which were founded by the powerful vizier Niẓām al-Mulk, who was viewed at the time as the primary defender of Sunni Islam against the propaganda of several Shīʿa groups. The Ashʿarites relied on literal interpretations of many religious texts (Qur'ānic verses, *ḥadīth*s, and reports attributed to some of the Prophet's companions) that appear to support their views, and equally on nonliteral interpretations of all texts that appear to conflict with their views. Many scholars who opposed Ashʿarism and resented its rise to dominance argued that this claim of consensus among the early Muslims was an Ashʿarite dogma that was based on partial textual evidence and questionable interpretations of it. In truth, there is little evidence that the doctrine of occa-

The second is their attributing origination and creation to the power of those who do not know what they create. For if man and the other animals were asked about the numbers, details, and magnitudes of the movements that proceed from them, they would have no information about them. In fact, an infant, taken from his cradle, seeks by his choice[23] his mother's breast and suckles. A kitten after its birth crawls to its mother's nipple with its eyes still shut. A spider weaves webs of strange shapes. The geometer is baffled by their roundness, by the parallelism of their sides, and by the symmetry of their organizations. It is necessarily known that the spiders have no knowledge of what the geometers are unable to know.

The bees structure their honeycombs as hexagons. No honeycomb is square, circular, heptagon, or any other shape. That is because the hexagonal shape is distinguished by a feature, which is demonstrated by geometrical proofs and is not found in other shapes. This feature is founded on several principles. One of them is that the shape that is most spacious and encloses the greatest area is the circular shape, which contains no angles other than the straight angle. The second is that if circular regions are arranged next to each other, useless gaps are inevitably formed between them. The third is that the shape with but a few sides that is closest to the circular shape in spaciousness is the hexagonal shape. The fourth is that if regions whose shape is close to the circular shape, such as a heptagon, an octagon, or a pentagon, are pressed against each other, there would remain useless gaps between them and they would not be contiguous to each other. Although squares may be contiguous to each other, they are much less spacious than circles because their angles are too far from their centers. Since bees need a shape close to a circle to contain their bodies, for [the body of a bee] is close to being round; since, because of the limitation of their space and the greatness of their number, they must not waste any space as gaps between the honeycombs—gaps, which are not big enough to house their bodies; and since among the shapes, in spite of their endless variety, there is only one shape that is close to the circle and has this feature—namely, the ability to be contiguous and not form gaps in between—which is the hexagonal

sionalism and its accompanying doctrine of acquisition (*kasb*) were part of Sunni orthodoxy before Ash'arism became the dominant theology. In fact, the infinitive *kasb* never occurs in the Qur'ān, but several verbs derived from it occur in numerous Qur'ānic verses. Many commentators on the Qur'ān, especially those before al-Ash'arī's time, did not interpret those verses according to the Ash'arite doctrine of acquisition.

23. The expression 'by his choice' is a literal translation of *bi-khtiyārih*. This sounds odd, since al-Ghazālī's point seems to be that the infant seeks his mother's breast instinctively. I think al-Ghazālī intended by this expression that the infant "on his own" seeks his mother's breast.

shape, God (Exalted is He) directed the bees to select the hexagonal shape in constructing their honeycombs.

I wish I knew, Do the bees know these subtleties, which most intelligent men fail to apprehend? Or does the Creator, who is the sole possessor of omnipotence, direct the bees to acquire that for which they have a necessary need? They are carriers of God's plan: His plan is carried out for them and through them. They neither know it nor have the power to abstain from it. In the behavior of animals there are many wonders of this sort. If I were to discuss part of them, hearts would be filled with awe for the greatness and sublimity of God (Exalted is He).

Woe to those who deviate from the path of God, who are deluded by their limited power and weak ability, and who think that they are party to God's creating, originating, and inventing such wonders and marvels. Far from it! The kingdom and the dominion exclusively belong to the Almighty in heaven and earth.

These are the types of repugnant matters that necessarily follow from the Muʿtazilites' doctrine. See now how the followers of the Sunna were guided to what is right and were favored with moderation in belief. They say: "The doctrine of determination is a rejected absurdity and the doctrine of origination is an outrageous presumption,[24] but the truth lies in positing two powers that relate to one act and in asserting that one object of power is related to two possessors of power." There remains only the difficulty of having two powers that relate to one act. The difficulty arises only if the two powers attach to the act in the same manner. If the two powers, however, are different and the manners in which they attach to the act are different, then it is not impossible for there to be multiple attachments to *one* thing, as we will show.

It might be asked: "What made you posit an object of power that is related to two possessors of power?"

We reply:

A conclusive proof[25] rests on the fact that a voluntary movement is different from a tremor. If it is supposed that a tremor is willed by the one

24. The doctrine of "determinism" is the doctrine of the Mujbirites, who assert that no being has power or will except God. The doctrine of "origination" is the doctrine of the Muʿtazilites, who assert that created living beings are originators of their acts. As we have seen, al-Ghazālī attributes to the Muʿtazilites the further belief that the acts originated by these beings are not objects of God's power: He can neither create nor prevent them (but see note 21 above).

25. In the original, it is *burhān*, which is standardly translated as 'demonstration'. I elected to use 'proof', however, for two reasons: (1) al-Ghazālī will later refer to this argument as *dalīl* (proof), and (2) to call a demonstration "conclusive" is redundant.

who experiences it[26] and is intended by him as well, then the only thing that distinguishes it from a voluntary movement is the absence of power.[27] The conclusive proof rests further on the fact that God's power attaches to every possible thing. Every occurrent is possible; a servant's act is an occurrent; therefore, a servant's act is possible. It would therefore be impossible for God's power not to attach to the servant's act. We say that a voluntary movement, inasmuch as it is an occurrent and possible movement, is similar to a tremor. So it is impossible for the power of God (Exalted is He) to attach to one of them and fail to attach to the other, which is similar to it.[28]

In fact, another absurdity follows from this supposition.[29] If God (Exalted is He) wants to stop His servant's hand from moving while the servant wants to move it, then inevitably either motion and rest exist together or neither of them exists. This leads either to the combining of motion and rest or to their absence. Their absence, in addition to being contradictory, necessitates the nullification of both powers, since power is that through which an object of power is brought about once the will is activated and a receptacle is available. It would be absurd for our opponent to think that the object of God' power is preponderant because His power is stronger. For the attachment of one power to a single movement is not superior to the attachment of the other power to that movement if the function of each

26. The expression 'the one who experiences it' is my translation of a single Arabic word *al-murtaʿid* (literally, "the one who shakes").

27. Literally, there would be no distinction except through power. The hypothetical situation is this. Suppose that one wills, wants, and intends to have a tremor. Now suppose that the subject performs a voluntary movement that he wills, wants, and intends. The only difference there is between the tremor and the voluntary movement is that in the case of a tremor power is absent but it is present in the case of a voluntary movement. Al-Ghazālī concludes that power is the distinguishing feature of voluntary action.

28. To recapitulate, the "conclusive proof" is based on two premises: (1) there is a fundamental difference between a tremor and a voluntary movement, and (2) whatever is possible is within God's power. An elucidation of (1) shows that the difference between a man's moving his hand voluntarily and his having a tremor is that he has power in the former case but not in the latter. (See the preceding note.) Al-Ghazālī presents a subargument invoking (2) to show that both voluntary movement and tremor are objects of God's power. Since each of the movements is an act of the man, a man's act is occurrent, and whatever is occurrent is possible, each of the movements is possible. Given premise (2), it follows that each of the movements is an object of God's power. Thus the voluntary movement is attached to two powers: the man's power and God's power. It is also related to two possessors of power: the man and God. Hence the "conclusive proof" presents a response to the original question about the reason for positing an object of power that is related to two possessors of power. However, as we will see later, God's power is "creative," in the sense that it is the one that creates the act, and man's power is "inert," in the sense that it never creates any act to which it attaches.

29. The supposition in question is that for each object of power there is but one possessor of power, which is the position of many Muʿtazilites.

power is to originate. His strength lies in His having power over additional acts, but His power over other acts does not give it preponderance with respect to the one movement in question. The relation of the movement to each of the two powers is that of being originated by it; and since origination is uniform, there is no stronger or weaker and hence no preponderance. Therefore, the conclusive proof for affirming two powers has led us to affirm one object of power that is related to two possessors of power.[30]

If it is said, "A proof should not lead to an incomprehensible absurdity, and what you have mentioned is incomprehensible," then we say, "We must make it comprehensible." Thus we say that God's origination of a movement in His servant's hand is intelligible without the movement's being an object of the servant's power. So long as He creates the movement and the power for it, He is the exclusive originator of both the power and the object of power. It follows that He is the exclusive originator, that the movement exists, and that the one who moves has the power to move. And because he has this power, his state is not the same as the state of having a tremor. So all difficulties are resolved.

In sum, the Powerful, whose power is vast,[31] is capable of originating both the power and its object. Since the terms 'creator' and 'originator' are used to describe the one who, through his power, brings a thing into existence, and since both the power and its object are [brought into existence] through God's power, He is called "Creator" and "Originator." The object of power is not due to the servant's power, although they are concurrent; hence he is not called "creator" or "originator." A different term must be sought for this type of relation. The term that is sought is 'acquisition', fol-

30. The absurd consequence that al-Ghazālī sees following from the supposition that for each object of power there can be only one possessor of power is captured in his example of two possessors of power—God and His servant—and their presumed two distinct objects of power: (1) the stopping of the motion of the human being's (the servant's) hand, and (2) the moving of his hand. On the assumption that God and His servant can respectively cause opposing acts, there would be no act at all: either the resultant act would contain both motion and rest, which is impossible, or it would contain neither as they would negate each other. Moreover, if one contends that there are indeed two opposing intentions but that one of them, God's, overpowers the other, al-Ghazālī replies that, insofar as each intention has a distinct source of origination, the two are equal in power and one cannot overtake the other. The conclusion, then, that one object of power is related to two possessors of power stands, since the opposite supposition resulted in the absurdity that no act occurs. Al-Ghazālī explains below that although the object of power is related to both possessors of power, only one of them, God, is its originator. Indeed, God is the originator even of the power of the other possessor of power. Yet the second possessor of power, the human being who is God's servant, retains the power to move even as God is the originator of his power. The servant's having the power to move preserves the distinction between a voluntary movement and a tremor.

31. This is the reading in the Ankara edition. In the Jeddah edition it is 'the Powerful has vast power'.

lowing the example of the Book of God (Exalted is He), for the term is found in the Qur'ān to describe the doings of God's servants.[32] As for the term 'act', they use it alternately.[33] However, there should be no dispute over names once the meanings are understood.[34]

32. The Arabic term is *kasb,* which is usually translated, in this context, as 'acquisition'. The term also means "gain," "earning," and a host of similar concepts. In this form the term does not occur in the Qur'ān, but several of its derivatives (thirteen, to be exact) occur in many verses to describe the acts of people. All of these derivatives are conjugations of the verb *kasab,* which means (among other things) "to gain," "to acquire," or to "earn." Here is an example of these verses: *And fear the day when you return to God, and then every soul will be paid what it has earned* [*kasabat*], *and they will not be wronged* (Qur'ān, 2:281).

33. The pronoun 'they' refers to the followers of the Sunna. The Arabic term that is usually translated as 'act' is *fiʿl.* In addition to act it can mean "deed," "doing," "effect," "action," and other similar concepts. In linguistics it means verb. In this form (*fiʿl*) the term occurs once in the Qur'ān. Its feminine counterpart also occurs once. About twenty-eight derivatives of this term occur numerous times in the Qur'ān. Some of these occurrences describe the acts of God and some of them describe the acts of people. This is what al-Ghazālī means by saying that they use the term alternately. Here is part of a verse in which the term *fiʿl* occurs: *And We inspired in them the doing* [*fiʿl*] *of good deeds* (Qur'ān, 21:73).

34. The last two paragraphs describe the famous doctrine of *acquisition* (*kasb*), which distinguishes the Ashʿariyya school of Islamic theology. The founder of this school is Abū al-Ḥasan ʿAlī al-Ashʿarī. He was born in Basra in AH 260/873 CE and died in Baghdad in AH 324/935 CE. During the first part of his life, He was a Muʿtazilite who studied under the head of the Muʿtazilites in Bara, Abū ʿAlī Muḥammad al-Jubbāʾī. Whether authentic or not, a story is commonly related about a debate that took place in AH 300/912 CE between al-Ashʿarī and his teacher, which resulted in the former's having serious doubts about the Muʿtazilite doctrine that man is the creator of his deeds and that he will be rewarded or punished in the hereafter in accordance with these deeds. The story runs as follows. Al-Ashʿarī asked al-Jubbāʾī about the fate of three brothers: the eldest died as a righteous man, the middle died as a sinner, and the youngest died in his childhood. The master answered that the eldest will be admitted into paradise, the middle will be condemned to hell, and the youngest will be consigned to an intermediate position in which he experiences none of the bliss of paradise and none of the of torment of hell. Al-Ashʿarī asked what God's answer would be if the youngest brother inquired why he was not admitted into paradise. Al-Jubbāʾī said that God would answer that the youngest brother did not live long enough to perform righteous deeds in order to earn his place in paradise. At this point al-Ashʿarī said that the youngest brother might object that if God had allowed him to live to an old age, he, like his eldest brother, would have performed righteous deeds and would have been worthy of paradise. To this al-Jubbāʾī said that God would respond that He knew if the youngest brother were allowed to live to an old age, he would be a sinner and would end up in hell, so he was better off dying young. Al-Ashʿarī's critical question was, What would God say to the middle brother if he asked why God did not let him die, like his younger brother, when he was a child, so he, too, would be consigned to the intermediate position instead of hell? The story concludes that the master had no response to this question. We should note that al-Ghazālī invokes a similar example in the Third Treatise to argue that it is not incumbent upon God to care for the well-being of His servants. (See note 75 of the Third Treatise for further elaboration.)

According to the tradition, shortly after this debate, al-Ashʿarī had three vivid dreams in which he saw the Prophet instructing him to study the Qur'ān and Ḥadīth, to use reason to establish the fundamental principles of the religion, and to show that in general revelation is superior to reason. He went to the mosque of Basra and ascended the pulpit, where he publically recanted his Muʿtazilism and announced his determination to expose the Muʿtazilites' "scandals and repugnancies."

The doctrine of acquisition is subject to different interpretations. There is a core about which all interpretations agree. This is the core that al-Ghazālī describes in the passage above. Man does not create his act. God creates the act directly. So God is the creator and originator of the act, and the man is neither. However, it *appears* to the man that he has created the act, because at the moment of creating the act, God creates in the man a power that attaches to the same act. Thus there are two powers: God's power and the man's power; and there is one act, which is the common object of both powers. It is the object of both powers not in the sense that each power creates the act, but in the sense that each power "attaches to" the act. In actuality, only one power creates the act, which is God's power. God's power is creative; man's power is inert.

This is the common core. The different interpretations have to do with the relation between man's will (or intention) and the power created in him by God. We know that the relation between the created act and the created power is that the created power attaches to the act. The Ashʿarite doctrine of acquisition is meant to be *fundamentally* different from the Mujbirites' position that man has no power. One of al-Ghazālī's objections to this position is that it trivializes the demands of the divine law, for how can something be obligatory if men have no power over it? But the same objection applies to the doctrine of acquisition if there is divergence between one's intentions and one's acts. If one ends up committing a sin even though one wants to do a good deed because that is the path one's power takes, or if one ends up performing a good deed even though one wants to commit a sin because that is the path one's power takes, then it is extremely difficult to make sense of the demands of the divine law. There are Ashʿarites who suggest that this divergence between intention and act is consistent with occasionalism. Others suggest that there is no divergence between intention and act, because intentions are also created by God. It is hard to see how these interpretations differ in spirit from the Mujbirite doctrine or how they succeed in making better sense of divine obligations. It seems that the only interpretation that does not trivialize divine obligation while maintaining the core of the acquisition doctrine is the one that asserts that God creates an act and creates in the subject the power to perform the act upon the subject's forming the intention to do the act—provided that God, in His wisdom, sees no reason to prevent the realization of this intention. This interpretation also assumes that God's wisdom allows for a sufficient number of intentions to be realized in order to produce a fair judgment concerning the subject's moral status.

Al-Ashʿarī's writings indicate a strong inclination towards a total-providence interpretation that leaves little room, if any, for human free will. Here is a typical passage of al-Ashʿarī's.

> God guided the believers to obey Him, blessed them, took care of them, made them righteous, and guided them [to the truth]. And He guided the unbelievers to the wrong path, not to the truth, did not bless them with evidence [for the truth] . . . Had He blessed them and made them righteous, they would have been righteous, and had He guided them to the right path, they would have been rightly guided. And God is able to make the unbelievers righteous and bless them, so that they would be believers; but He wanted them to be unbelievers, as He knew, did not help them, and closed their hearts [to the truth]. (Al-Ashʿarī, *al-Ibāna ʿan Uṣūl al-Diyāna*, p. 17)

Al-Ghazālī's discussion in this book oscillates between the two interpretations. In this treatise he could be read as being sympathetic to an interpretation that accommodates a mean-

It might be said:

What matters is understanding the meaning, and what you have said is incomprehensible, since if the created, occurrent power[35] does not attach to the object of power, it cannot be understood. For a power that has no object is absurd, just as a cognition that has no cognized object is. And if a power does attach to an object, then it is inconceivable that it would attach to the object in any manner other than being efficacious and causing the object and bringing it into existence. The relation of the object to the power is the same as the relation of an effect to a cause, which is to come into existence through it. If it does not come into existence through it, there would be no relation between them; and hence it would not be a power. What attaches to nothing is not a power, since power is one of the attributes that attach to objects.

We say:

Power does attach to objects. But your statement that attachment is confined to bringing its object into existence is refuted by the manner in which knowledge and will attach to objects. If you say that only the attachment of power is confined to bringing its object into existence, then this is false too. Power, for you, persists from the time before the act occurs. So did it attach then or not? If you say "No," then this is absurd. And if you say "Yes," you cannot mean by attachment that the object of power came into existence through the power,[36] since the object of power has not yet come to be. Thus a kind of attachment must be posited other than that of coming into existence through the power. The attachment at the occurrence is described as coming into existence through the power, but any attachment prior to that time would be different from this. It is a different kind of attachment. So your statement that power attaches to the object in a uniform way is wrong. According to them,[37] the possession of eternal power is analogous to this. For it attaches to the world since eternity, prior to the creation of the world. To say that it attaches then to the world is true, but to say that the world is

---

ingful notion of human free will. However, in the Third Treatise, parts of his discussion entail a position that is incompatible with standard views about fair consequences and desert, and which to a large extent relieves divine will of much of its moral force. (See al-Shahrastānī, *al-Milal wa-l-Niḥal*, vol. I, pp. 106–118; Badawī, *Madhāhib al-Islāmiyyīn*, pp. 487–748; and Amīn, *Ẓuhr al-Islām*, vol. IV, pp. 57–86. Badawī draws two seemingly contradictory implications from al-Ashʿarī's doctrine of acquisition: (1) "Acquisition is the attachment of the servant's power *and will* to the act, which is in reality created by God" (p. 555), and (2) "al-Ashʿarī's doctrine leads to God's being the one who determined and predestined the sinful acts, in the sense that He created them, assigned them, and told about them" (pp. 556–557). I think the first implication is an overly charitable reading of al-Ashʿarī's actual doctrine.)

35. In the Ankara edition it is 'since if the power that is created in a person'.

36. Literally, what is meant by it cannot be that the object of power occurs through it.

37. The pronoun 'them' refers to the Muʿtazilites.

brought into existence through it is false, since the world had not come into existence yet. If these propositions express the same meaning, one of them would be true precisely when the other is true.

If it is said that the meaning of the attachment of power prior to its object's coming into existence is that if the object of this power were to come into existence, it would come into existence through this power, then we say that the attachment is not present but anticipated.[38] Hence it must be said that power is present and it is an attribute that is unattached but it is waiting to be attached when the object of power comes into existence through it. The same applies to the possession of power. An absurdity follows from this, which is that an attribute that was not attached to objects becomes attached. This is clearly absurd.

If it is said that the meaning is that the power is prepared for its object's coming into existence through it,[39] we say that preparedness has no meaning other than that of awaiting its object's coming into existence through it, and this does not entail the presence of attachment. Just as you find it intelligible that a power is present and attaches to an object without the object's coming into existence through this power, we too find it intelligible that there is a power without its object's coming into existence through it; rather, it comes into existence through the power of God (Exalted is He). So our position is not different from your position except in our saying that the object of power is produced by God's power. If it is not a necessary condition for the existence of power and its attachment to an object that the object come into existence through it, then why should it be a requirement that its object not be produced by God's power? The existence of the object

38. Notice that if this counterfactual definition (namely, if the object of the power were to come into existence, it would come into existence through this power) is correct, the doctrine of acquisition would be meaningless, for there would be no meaning for a created human power, which attaches to an object that comes into existence through a *different* power—that is, the divine power. According to this definition, if the object to which the created human power attaches comes into existence, it must have done so through the created human power itself. In other words, if a created human power attaches to objects, then it cannot be inert. The important point, however, is that al-Ghazālī's arguments in this and the following passages are presented from the opponent's point of view. The opponent wants the attachment of power to its object to be the production of this object by this power. But then he faces a problem. Surely there is a sense of a power being attached to its object before the production of this object. After all, we say, for instance, that Zayd is not moving his hand now but is capable (now) of moving his hand (later). So al-Ghazālī's remark that the proposed definition reduces to waiting for attachment rather than having an attachment is meant to show that the opponent is not entitled to his definition. Said differently, al-Ghazālī argues that if the opponent thinks that a power's attachment to an object entails that this power produces the object, then to define attachment in terms of delayed production is really a definition of delayed attachment.

39. As above, the proposed definition is of the meaning of the claim that a power, divine or human, is attached to an object prior to the object's coming into existence.

of power through God's power no more prevents the object from having a relation to the occurrent power than its nonexistence; for if this relation is not prevented by the nonexistence of the object of power, then why would it be prevented by the existence of this object? Whether the object of power is assumed to be existent or nonexistent, there must be a power that attaches to it and that has no object existing at the present time.[40]

It might be said: "A power through which no object of power comes into existence is no different from impotence.'

We say:

If you mean that the state the person apprehends when he has this power is similar to what he apprehends when he is impotent, as when he has a tremor, then this is a denial of what is known necessarily. However, if you mean that [having such power] is no different from being impotent in the sense that the object of power does not come into existence through it, then this is true; but calling it "impotence" is wrong, although when this power's deficiency is considered in relation to the power of God (Exalted is He), it is thought of as being similar to impotence. This would be analogous to saying that power prior to [the occurrence of] the act is, according to their position, identical with impotence in that the object of power has not yet come into existence through it. In this case the use of the term 'impotence' would be precluded on the grounds that power is an apprehended state whose apprehension in the soul is different from the apprehension of impotence. Our case, thus, is no different from this.

In summation, there must be affirmed two different powers. One of them is higher and the other is like impotence when compared to the higher power. You have a choice between affirming for God's servant a power that is imagined to be similar to impotence in some respect and affirming such a power for God (Exalted is He). Do not have any doubt, if you are fair-minded, that a state akin to deficiency and impotence is more proper for the created beings. Indeed, it is not only "more proper', because such a state is impossible for God (Exalted is He). This is the most elaboration that is appropriate for a brief discussion of this question.

## THIRD QUESTION

Someone might ask:

How could you claim that the divine power attaches to the totality of the occurrents, when most of the movements and the other things in the

40. Whether the object of power would be actualized or remain merely possible, there is a power (the divine power, for instance) that attaches to it prior to its actualization. So power at that time is attached to the object but its object does not exist.

world are generated? They are generated from each other by necessity. For the movement of a hand, for example, generates necessarily the movement of the ring and the movement of a hand in water generates the movement of the water. This is observable and reason proves it too. If the movements of the water and of the ring are created by God (Exalted is He), it would be possible for Him to create the movement of the hand without the movement of the ring, and the movement of the hand without the movement of the water; and this is impossible. The same applies to all generated things with all their interconnections.

We say:

What is incomprehensible cannot be dealt with in terms of refutation or acceptance. For in order for a doctrine to be refuted or accepted, it must first be intelligible. What we understand by the expression 'generation' is a body's emerging from the inside of another body; just as the fetus emerges from the belly of the mother and the plant from the earth.[41] This is impossible with respect to the modes, since the movement of the hand has no inside such that the movement of the ring may emerge from it, and it is not something that contains other things so that some of its contents may come out of it. Thus if the movement of the ring is not latent in the essence of the movement of the hand, then what is the meaning of its being generated from it? This must be made comprehensible.

If this is incomprehensible, your statement that it is observable is ignorance and foolishness.[42] For the only thing observed is that the second movement is concurrent with the first, but that it is generated from it is not observable. Your statement that if it is created by God (Exalted is He), He would be able to create the movement of the hand without the movement of the ring and the movement of the hand without the movement of the water is madness. This is analogous to one's statement that if knowledge is not generated from will, God would be able to create will without knowledge or knowledge without life.[43] Rather we say that what is impossible is

41. The Arabic word that is usually translated as 'generation' is *tawallud*. It is derived from the root *walada*, which means to give birth to.

42. 'Ignorance' (*jahl*) is dropped from the Jeddah edition.

43. The target of al-Ghazālī's argument is the claim that so long as *y* is not generated from *x*, God can create *x* without creating *y*. To refute this claim he appeals to the example of will and knowledge. Even though knowledge is not generated from will, he argues, God still could not create will without knowledge. Since knowledge is a necessary condition for will, it is logically impossible for will to exist without knowledge, and God cannot do anything that is logically impossible. Al-Ghazālī's point that knowledge is a necessary condition for will functions as a premise for one standard argument for the doctrine of occasionalism. Occasionalists, whether Islamic or Western, assume that an agent must have comprehensive knowledge of a given act *x*, as well as of its function and consequences, if he is to be able to

not an object of power, and the existence of what is conditioned without its condition is inconceivable. The condition for will is knowledge, and the condition for knowledge is life. Similarly, the condition for a substance's occupying a spatial region is that the region must be vacant. Thus if God (Exalted is He) moves a person's hand, He must make it occupy a region neighboring the region it used to occupy. If the neighboring region is not vacated, how could the hand occupy it? Hence its vacancy is a condition for its being occupied by the hand, since if the hand moves and the region is not made vacant by the disappearance or the movement of the water, two bodies would occupy the same region, and this is absurd. The removal of one of them is a condition for the movement of the other; hence they are concomitant with each other. So it is thought that one of them is generated from the other; but this is wrong.

As for that which is a concomitant but not a condition, it is possible, from our perspective, for its conjunction with its concomitant to be broken. Rather, its concomitance is due to the habitual course of things, such as the burning of cotton when it is near fire and the feeling of cold in a hand when it touches ice. All of this is constant through the execution of God's plan. Otherwise, the divine power, in terms of its essence, is not incapable of creating coldness in the ice along with a sense of touch in the hand while at the same time creating in the hand the feeling of heat instead of cold [when it touches the ice]. Therefore, what our opponent sees as generated is of two types: one of them is a condition, for which the lack of conjunction is inconceivable, and the second is not a condition, for which the lack of conjunction is conceivable if the habitual course of things is broken.[44]

---

will it. Since only God can have complete knowledge of any occurrent *x*, God alone can be the true willer of *x*. Occasionalists further assume that only agents who are true willers are true causes. Given that for any occurrent *x*, only God can be the true willer of *x*, it follows that only God can be the true cause of *x*. Al-Ghazālī argued, as we saw, that since animals lack knowledge of the acts that proceed from them, they cannot be the true causes of these acts. In the West, Arnold Geulincx and Nicolas Malebranche argued for occasionalism along similar lines. (See Nadler, *Occasionalism*, pp. 82–87.)

44. Al-Ghazālī's position on causation is remarkably similar to Hume's. Both men think that one is led to assume that there is a "necessary connection" between cause and effect not due to an inference of reason but due to the influence of "custom," as Hume puts it, or "habit" (*ʿāda*), in al-Ghazālī's term. We are so "habituated" in observing a constant conjunction between two types of events that our imagination cannot envision an event of the first type without envisioning an event of the second as succeeding or being concomitant with the first. Thus Hume writes:

> When I examine with the utmost accuracy those objects, which are commonly denominated causes and effects, I find, in considering a single instance, that the one object is precedent and contiguous to the other; and in inlarging my view to consider

It might be said:

You did not prove that there is no generation, but you denied that it is comprehensible, yet it is comprehensible. We do not intend by generation that a movement comes out of another movement by emerging from its inside, or that coldness is generated from the coldness of the ice by its emerging from the ice and its transfer or by its emerging from that cold-

---

> several instances, I find only, that like objects are constantly plac'd in like relations of succession and contiguity. Again, when I consider the influence of this constant conjunction, I perceive, that such a relation can never be an object of reasoning, and can never operate upon the mind, but by means of custom, which determines the imagination to make a transition from the idea of one object to that of its usual attendant, and from the impression of one to a more lively idea of the other. (*A Treatise of Human Nature*, p. 170)

Of course, there are significant differences between al-Ghazālī and Hume regarding the implications of this doctrine. Al-Ghazālī wants the world to have a place for miracles. If causation is simply the habitual course of things and there is no *real* causal necessity, then there is no reason to think that cause and effect are in the essence of things. But given the observable fact that the world is dominated by natural regularities, the source of these regularities must be located elsewhere—in the will of God. It can easily be seen that if God wills otherwise, the habitual course of things can be broken and a miracle can occur. God is thus the *real* cause of all the effects in the world and we are thus brought closer to occasionalism. As al-Ghazālī states in the First Treatise, every occurrent must have a cause, and since "natural causes" are not really causes, God must be the *direct* cause of all occurrents. If we add to this the conclusion of his "conclusive proof," namely, that the acts of the created living beings and their powers with respect to these acts are created by God, we obtain the doctrines of occasionalism and of acquisition.

Hume, however, argues against miracles. Although he holds that "the necessity of a cause to every beginning of existence is not founded on any arguments either demonstrative or intuitive" (*A Treatise of Human Nature*, p. 172), he nevertheless maintains that when a "wise man" is presented with a report that a miraculous event occurred (that is, that a constant conjunction of events was broken), he "proportions his belief to the evidence . . . and regards his past experience as a *full proof* of the future existence of that event" (*An Enquiry Concerning Human Understanding*, p. 73). The wise man, therefore, compares the likelihood of the report being false to the likelihood of the constant conjunction being broken and concludes that it is far more probable that the report is false than that the constant conjunction is broken. Hume thus mocks those who believe in miracles: "Whoever is moved by *Faith* to assent to it, is conscious of a continued miracle in his own person, which subverts all the principles of his understanding, and gives him a determination to believe what is most contrary to custom and experience" (*An Enquiry Concerning Human Understanding*, p. 90). However, one may justly ask, Why should past experience constitute a "full proof" of future events if, according to Hume, a man's past experience only shows which two events happened to have been conjoined? On what grounds should the wise man reject the report of a divergent event as totally improbable, if "natural causation" does not present us with a necessary connection? Whereas al-Ghazālī takes quite seriously that "natural causation" is merely the habitual course of things, Hume takes it seriously only until he is confronted with the possibility of miracles; then, suddenly, what was merely custom becomes unassailable truth.

ness.[45] Rather, we mean by 'generation' the presence of an existent following another existent and its being existent or occurrent through it. We call the occurrent 'generated' and that through which occurrence takes place 'generating'. This naming is comprehensible. What proves it to be false?

We say:

If this is your explanation, then what proves its falsehood is exactly what proves that an occurrent power cannot originate. For if we deem it impossible to say that an object of power comes into existence through an occurrent power, how could we not deem it impossible that something should come into existence without divine power? The impossibility [of generation without divine power] is based on the universal attachment of divine power. Its being beyond the reach of divine power would annul the universal attachment; and this is impossible. Furthermore, this necessitates impotence and prevention, as previously explained.[46]

Indeed, the Mu'tazilites, who affirm the doctrine of generation, fall into innumerable contradictions when they elaborate on this doctrine. For example, they say theoretical reflection generates knowledge but recollecting the reflection does not generate knowledge,[47] and other similar matters, which will take too long to mention. There is no point in elaborating on that for which there is no need.

You have gathered from the sum of this discussion that *all* the occurrents—their substances and their modes, and those that occur in the animate or inanimate beings—come into existence through the power of God (Glorious and Exalted is He), who is their exclusive originator. It is not true that some created things come into existence through other created things, but all of them come into existence through the divine power. This is what we set out to show in establishing the attribute of power for God (Exalted is He), the universality of its applicability, and the related matters that arise or necessarily follow from it.

45. 'That coldness' (*dhālik al-brūda*) is the reading in the Cairo edition. In the Ankara and Jeddah editions, it is 'the essence of coldness' (*dhāt al-burūda*).

46. The sentence is rather elliptical. It should be understood according to al-Ghazālī's previous discussion in the section on power. Al-Ghazālī claims that it is within God's power to create one of two concomitant things without creating the other so long as one of them is not the condition for the other (as knowledge for will). To say that God cannot create the one without the other is either to attribute *impotence* to God or to claim that the essence of the concomitant things is such that the nonexistence of one of them *prevents* the existence of the other. Al-Ghazālī says that both are false: God's power attaches to all possible things, and the conjunction of concomitant things is not necessary (unless one is the condition for the other).

47. Literally, recollecting it does not generate it. Thus one could interpret the original as saying: "recollecting knowledge does not generate knowledge."

# Second Attribute: Knowledge

We claim that God (Exalted is He) knows all that is knowable, whether existing or nonexisting. The existents are divided into the anteriorly eternal and the occurrent. What is anteriorly eternal is His essence and attributes. Whoever knows something other than himself is even more knowledgeable of his own essence and attributes. Therefore, if it is proved that He knows that which is other than Himself, it is necessary that He also knows His essence and attributes. It is known that He knows that which is other than Himself, since that which is called "the other" is His well-designed handiwork and His exquisite and well-ordered act; and this proves the knowledge of the Maker as well as it proves His power, as previously shown. For if one sees well-arranged lines that proceed with precision from a scribe,[48] and then doubts that the scribe is knowledgeable of the art of writing, he would be foolish to have such doubts. It has thus been established that God knows Himself and what is other than Himself.

It might be asked: "Is there an end to what He knows?" We say "No," For although the existents at the present time are finite, the possible existents in the future are infinite. He knows with respect to all the possible things that do not exist now whether He will bring them into existence or not.[49] Therefore, what He knows is infinite. In fact, if we want to multiply the aspects of a single object by considering different relations and magnitudes, these aspects would exceed any finite limit; and God knows all of these. For example, we say that the double of two is four, the double of four is eight, the double of eight is sixteen, and thus we double the double of two and the double of the double without end. Man knows of these orders only what he is capable of reaching with his mind; and his life will terminate while there still remain an infinity of multiples. Knowing the multiples of the multiples of two, which is only one number, exceeds any confines. The same applies to every number. Hence, what would be the case for other relations and magnitudes? This knowledge, in spite of its attachment to infinitely many knowables, is one, as will be explained when all the attributes are considered collectively.

48. Al-Ghazālī is usually careful to avoid expressions that attribute causal powers to created beings. Thus he says 'proceed from' (*taṣdur ʿalā*) instead of 'are produced by' or 'are generated by'. This is in keeping with the Ashʿarite doctrine of acquisition.

49. This is propositional knowledge: for any given possible thing, God knows that He will bring it into existence or that He will not bring it into existence. Since the number of possible things is infinite, the number of these propositions is also infinite. Below al-Ghazālī will give an example to show that God also has infinite object-knowledge, that is, He knows infinitely many objects.

# Third Attribute: Life

We claim that God (Exalted is He) is living. This is known by necessity. No one who accepts that He is a knower and powerful denies this. It is necessary that whoever is a knower and powerful is also living, since we do not mean by 'living' anything other than someone who is aware of himself and knows his essence and that which is other than himself. How can the one who knows all the knowables and has power over all the objects of power not be living? This is clear. Theoretical reflection on the attribute of life need not be elaborate.

# Fourth Attribute: Will

We claim that God (Exalted is He) is a willer of His acts.

The proof of this is that an act produced by Him is subject to various possibilities none of which can be distinguished from the others without something giving preponderance to one of them. His essence is not sufficient to give preponderance, since its relation to each of two opposites is the same. What is it, then, that specifies one of two opposites to become actual in certain states and not in others? In the same way, power is not sufficient; for its relation to each of two opposites is the same. Similarly, knowledge is not sufficient, contrary to al-Ka'bī, who deemed knowledge to be sufficient on its own without will.[50] For knowledge depends on what is known, attaches to it as is, and does not affect it or change it. Thus if a thing is possible in itself and is equivalent to another possible thing that corresponds to it, then knowledge attaches to it as is. We thus do not assume that one of these two possible things is preponderant over the other; rather we conceive of both of them as possible and as equivalent.

God (Exalted is He) knows that the existence of the world at the time it was brought into existence is possible, and that its existence before or after that time is equivalent to it in possibility, for all these possibilities are equivalent. Hence knowledge ought to attach to them as they are. If the attribute of will decrees that the world should come into existence at a specific time, knowledge would attach to this specification—namely, that it

50. Abū al-Qāsim 'Abd Allāh al-Ka'bī (AH 252/886 CE–AH 319/931 CE) was a master Mu'tazilite and founded a branch of Mu'tazilism, the Ka'biyya, which was one of the Mu'tazilite subschools in Baghdad. He authored many works in theology, logic, Qur'ānic commentary, and other fields. He is most famous for denying that God has an attribute of will. (See al-Shahrastānī, *al-Milal wa-l-Niḥal*, vol. 1, pp. 89–90, and al-Baghdādī, *al-Farq bayn al-Firaq*, pp. 82–83).

should exist at that time—because the will attaches to this specification. So the will is the cause of the specification; and knowledge attaches to this specification, is dependent on it, and does not affect it. If it were possible for knowledge to be sufficient on its own without the need for will, it would be sufficient on its own without the need for power. In fact, knowledge would be sufficient for our acts so that we would not need will, for one of the two possibilities would become preponderant through the attachment of God's knowledge to it; and that is absurd.

It might be said:

This turns against you regarding the will itself. Just as the eternal power does not relate to *only* one of two opposites, the eternal will is not specific to *only* one of two opposites. Its specification of one of two requires a determinant; and this would regress ad infinitum. It is said that the essence is not sufficient for the occurrence of the world. For if it were to occur by virtue of the essence, it would have to coexist with the essence without any delay. Thus there must be power. But power is not sufficient either; for if it were, then why is it this specific time, when any time before it or after it is equally suitable for the possibility of the power's being attached to it? What is it that determines this time? Hence it needs will. Now it would be said that will is also not sufficient; for the eternal will is universal in its attachment just as the eternal power is. Its relation to all the times is the same and its relation to each of two opposites is also the same. For instance, if motion comes into existence instead of rest, then that is because the will attaches to motion, not to rest. It would be asked: "Was it possible for the will to attach to rest?" If it is said "No," then this is absurd. And if it is said "Yes," then they are equivalent—I mean motion and rest in their relation to the eternal will. What was it, then, that made it necessary for the eternal will to specify motion rather than rest? Hence a determinant is needed. The same question would entail a determinant for the determinant; and this would regress ad infinitum.

We say: "This question perplexed the minds of all the sects. None was successfully guided to the truth except the followers of the Sunna. Regarding this question, people are divided into four groups."

The first group says that the world is brought into existence through the essence of God (Exalted is He), and that there is no attribute that is additional to the essence at all. Since the essence is eternal, the world is eternal, and the relation of the world to the divine essence is as the relation of an effect to its cause, as the relation of light to the sun, and as the relation of a shadow to a person. Those are the philosophers.

The second group says that the world is an occurrent. It occurred at the time at which it occurred and neither before nor after through an occurrent will, which occurred not in any receptacle, and which necessitated the occurrence of the world. Those are the Muʿtazilites.[51]

The third group says that the world occurred through an occurrent will that occurred in God's essence. Those are the ones who assert that God is a receptacle of occurrents.[52]

The fourth group says that the world occurred at the time at which the eternal will attached to its occurrence, without the occurrence of the will itself and without any change in the state of the Eternal.

So examine these groups and compare the position of each group to the others'. No group's position is free from a difficulty that cannot be resolved, except the difficulty of the followers of the Sunna, for it is easily resolved.

Regarding the philosophers, they affirm the anterior eternity of the world; this is absurd. For it is impossible for an act to be anteriorly eternal. The meaning of its being an act is that it was not and then it is. Thus if the world has coexisted with God since eternity, how could it be an act? In fact, from this it necessarily follows that there are infinitely many celestial revolutions, as previously discussed; and this is impossible on several grounds.[53] Furthermore, in spite of their plunging into this difficulty, they did not escape the spirit of the question, which is, Why did the will attach to the occurrence of the world at a specific time and neither before nor after, although all times are equivalent in their relation to the will? Even if they manage to avoid the specification of time, they do not manage to avoid the specification of qualities. The world is specified with a particular magnitude and a particular orientation; their contraries are possible according

51. The reason the Muʿtazilites assert that the occurrent divine will does not occur in any receptacle is to maintain the conception of God as immutable, which is by far the dominant conception in Islamic theology and philosophy. According to this conception, God is devoid of any occurrents because God is unchangeable. Thus if God wills to create the world, that will cannot occur *in* God because He is devoid of all occurrents, yet because it is a *divine* will it cannot occur in something other than God; hence it does not occur in any receptacle. In other words, the divine will to create the world is itself created but it occurs literally nowhere. The Muʿtazilites find this strange position inescapable because, for them as for the philosophers, if an eternal will creates the world, the world, too, is eternal—a conclusion they reject. On the other hand, they are strongly committed to the immutability of God. They must also find it obvious that a divine will cannot subsist in a subject other than God. Hence they conclude that the divine will to create the world must occur but not in any receptacle.

52. This is the Karrāmiyya school. It was founded by Abū ʿAbd Allāh Muḥammad ibn Karrām (d. AH 256/869 CE). The Karrāmites were among the few who attributed change to God. In fact, they were extreme literalists: they attributed to God all sorts of attributes, including corporeal ones.

53. Al-Ghazālī is referring to his arguments against actual infinity in the Fourth Introduction, p. 16, and the First Treatise, pp. 37–38.

to reason. The eternal essence does not relate to some possible things to the exclusion of others. There are two grave consequences to their position, for which there is no resolution. We mentioned these in our book *The Incoherence of the Philosophers*, and they have no escape from them at all.[54]

One of them is that some of the celestial movements are westward, that is, from the east to the west, and some are eastward, that is, from the west to the east. The opposite of that is equivalent to it in possibility, since the directions are equivalent for motions. How then is it necessitated by the eternal essence, or by the essences of the angels, which are also eternal according to them, that a certain direction is determined instead of an opposite direction that is equivalent to it in all respects? There is no response to this question.

The second is that the outermost celestial sphere, which is the ninth celestial sphere, and which, according to them, is the mover that coerces all the heavens to move once during a day and a night, rotates on two poles, northern and southern. A pole is nothing but one of two points that are opposite to each other on the surface of the sphere and that remain stationary when the sphere rotates, and the equator is a great circle at the middle of the sphere that is equidistant from the two poles. We say that the body of the outermost sphere is symmetric and uniform, and every point on it could be imagined to serve as a pole. So what is that which necessitates the specification of two points among, according to them, infinitely many points? There must be an attribute that is additional to the essence and whose function is to specify a thing among its counterparts. This attribute is nothing but the will. We gave a complete analysis of these two consequences in the book *The Incoherence of the Philosophers*.

The Mu'tazilites, on the other hand, also plunge into two repugnant errors. One of them is that the Creator (Exalted is He) is a willer through an occurrent will that is not in any receptacle. If the will does not subsist in God, then saying that He has this will is an incoherent statement. It is similar to saying that He is a willer through a will that subsists in something other than Himself.

The second concerns why the will occurred at this specific time. If this is because of another will, the question is necessarily asked about the second will, and this would regress ad infinitum. If this is not because of another will, then let the world occur at this specific time without a will. An occurrent requires a will because of its being possible, not because of its being a body, heaven,[55] a will, or a cognition, and all occurrents are equivalent in

54. See al-Ghazālī, *Tahāfut al-Falāsifa*, pp. 104–7.

55. In the Ankara edition, it is 'a name' (*ism*) instead of 'heaven' (*samā'*), which is in the Jeddah edition.

this regard. Moreover, they do not escape the difficulty, since it would be said to them: "Why did the will occur at this specific time? And why was what occurred the will to move instead of the will to stay still?" For according to them, for every occurrent, there is a will that occurs and attaches to that occurrent; so why did not the will that attaches to its opposite occur?

As for those who opt for affirming the occurrence of the will in God's essence, they manage to eliminate one of the two difficulties, which is that He is a willer through a will that is not in His essence. However, they introduce a new difficulty, which is that God would be a receptacle of occurrents, and this would necessitate His occurrence. Moreover, there remains against them the other difficulty, and hence they do not escape the question.[56]

The followers of the truth, on the other hand, say that the occurrents occur through an eternal will that attaches to them and hence distinguishes them from their opposites that are equivalent to them. One's question, Why does the will attach to this occurrent when its opposite is equivalent to it in possibility?, is the wrong question, since the will is nothing but an attribute whose function is to distinguish one thing among its counterparts. The question, Why does the will distinguish a thing from its counterparts?, is similar to the question, Why does knowledge necessarily reveal its object? It would be said: "The only meaning of knowledge is that it is what necessarily reveals its object." One's question, Why does it necessarily reveal its object?, is similar to his question, Why is knowledge knowledge?, and, Why is the possible possible?, and, Why is the necessary necessary? This is absurd, because knowledge is knowledge by virtue of its essence and so are the possible, the necessary, and the rest of the essences. The same is true of the will: its true nature is to distinguish a thing from its counterparts. Someone's question, Why does it distinguish a thing from its counterparts?, is similar to his question, Why is the will will and the power power? This is absurd.

Every group needs to affirm the existence of an attribute whose function is to distinguish a thing from its counterparts. This attribute is nothing but the will. Thus the group with the most plausible position and the most correct path is the one that affirms this attribute and does not render it occurrent; rather it asserts that it is eternal and attaches to the occurrents at specific times. Hence because of this, an occurrence takes place at that specific time. No group can dispense with [positing such an attribute], and with it the regress necessitated by this question terminates.[57]

Now, given this exposition of the basis of the divine will, you ought to know that, according to us, it attaches to *all* the occurrents. It has become

56. The question is this: "Why did the will occur at this specific time?"
57. See the preceding note for a statement of this question.

apparent that every occurrent is originated by God's power, and whatever that power originates requires a will to direct the power to the object and to assign it to it. Hence every object of power is willed, and every occurrent is an object of power, therefore every occurrent is willed.[58] Evil, unbelief, and sin are all occurrents; therefore they are inevitably willed by God. Whatever God wills is and whatever He does not will is not. This is the doctrine of the righteous early Muslims and the universal belief of the followers of the Sunna—a belief for which demonstrations are given.

As for the Muʿtazilites, they say that all of the sins and all of the evil deeds are committed against God's will; in fact, He is averse to them. It is known that most of what takes place in this world is sin.[59] Therefore, that to which He is averse is more than what He wills. So, according to their claim, He is closer to impotence and deficiency. May the Lord of the worlds be exalted over what the unjust men say.

It might be asked: "How can He command that which He does not will? And how can He will something that He forbids? And how can He will dissoluteness, sins, injustice, and what is bad? And the one who wills what is bad is obscene." We say: "If we uncover the true nature of the matter and explain that it is contrary to the divine will, and if we uncover the natures of the notions of bad and good and explain that they are based on being in accordance with or being contrary to one's needs—and God is too exalted to have needs—then all the difficulties are eliminated." God willing, we will discuss this at the appropriate place.[60]

# Fifth and Sixth Attributes: Hearing and Sight

We claim that the Maker of the world is a hearer and seer. We prove this through the revelation and through reason.

Regarding the revelation, numerous Qurʾānic verses indicate this—

58. Strictly speaking, the first premise—namely that every object of power is willed—is false as stated. Recall that according to al-Ghazālī all possible things are objects of the divine power. But it is clear that not every possible thing is willed by God. It seems that what al-Ghazālī meant to say was: every object originated by God's power is willed; every occurrent is originated by God's power; therefore every occurrent is willed. The premise that every occurrent is originated by God's power is part of the Ashʿarite doctrine of occasionalism.

59. It is clear that what al-Ghazālī means is that most human deeds are sins.

60. See the introductory section of the Third Treatise.

verses such as the Exalted's statement: *And He is the Hearer, the Seer,*[61] and Abraham's statement: *Why do you worship that which can neither hear nor see, and can profit you nothing?*[62] And we know that Abraham's argument does not turn against him with respect to the deity he worships; hence he worships a hearer and seer, otherwise he would be subject to the argument's implication. If it is said, "What is intended by [hearing and sight] is knowledge," we say, "The terms used in the revelation should not be given interpretations different from what is understood from their connotations as they are apparent to the understanding, unless it is impossible to posit such connotations for them; and there is no impossibility in God's being a hearer and seer." Indeed, this must be the case, since it is senseless to deny arbitrarily what the followers of the consensus understand from the Qur'ān.

It might be said:

The reason it is impossible is that if His hearing and sight are occurrent, He would be a receptacle of occurrents; and this is absurd. And if they are eternal, then how could He hear a nonexistent sound, and how could He see the world during the anterior eternity in which the world was nonexistent, when the nonexistent cannot be seen?

We say that this is a question that might be asked by a Mu'tazilite or a philosopher. As for a Mu'tazilite, his argument can be rebutted easily. He accepts that the Exalted knows the occurrents. So we say: "God knows *now* that the world has existed since before the present, how then did He know during anterior eternity, when the world did not yet exist, that the world has existed [before the present]?" If it is possible to affirm an attribute in anterior eternity, which is, during the existence of the world, the knowledge that the world exists, before its existence, the knowledge that the world will exist, and after [the end of] its existence, the knowledge that the world had existed, though this attribute does not change and is expressed as knowledge and the possession of knowledge, then the same is possible for hearing and the possession of hearing and for sight and the possession of sight.

If the question is asked by a philosopher, he denies that God knows the specific occurrents that happen in the past, present, and future. Thus our approach is to transfer the discussion to the case of knowledge and prove to him the possibility of an eternal knowledge that attaches to occurrents, as we will show.[63] Then after proving this with respect to knowledge, we make an inference by analogy regarding hearing and sight.

61. Qur'ān, 17:11.

62. Qur'ān, 19:42. Here is the complete verse: *When he said to his father: "O my father! Why do you worship that which can neither hear nor see, and can profit you nothing?"*

63. See the discussion of the First Characteristic in the Second Part of this treatise.

The rational approach is that we say: "It is known that the Creator is more perfect than any created being, and it is known that the one who has sight is more perfect than the one who cannot see and the one who has hearing is more perfect than the one who cannot hear; hence it is impossible to affirm a description of perfection for a created being and not to affirm it for the Creator." These two principles necessitate an admission that our claim is correct. Which one of them might be disputed?

If it is said, "The dispute is regarding your statement that the Creator is necessarily more perfect than any created being," then we say that this must be conceded on the basis of the revelation and reason. The Muslim community and all rational people are in agreement about it. This question is not raised by a believer. If one's mind can accommodate the possibility of a powerful agent who is capable of inventing something higher and more sublime than one's self, then he is divorced from human instinct and his tongue utters what his heart refuses to accept if he understands what he says. Thus we never see a rational person who actually believes in this possibility.

It might be said: "The dispute is about the second principle, which is your statement that a seer is more perfect than one who does not see and that hearing and sight are perfections." We say that this is apprehended by the intellect as self-evident. For knowledge is perfection and hearing and sight are additional perfections for knowledge. We have shown that they are a form of completion to knowledge and the imagination. Whoever knows something without seeing it and then sees it would benefit from increased revelation and knowledge. Thus how could it be said that this [form of perfection] is true of that which is created but not of the Creator? Or how could it be said that these attributes are not perfections? If they are not perfections, then they are deficiencies, or they are neither deficiencies nor perfections. All of these options are absurd. Hence it has become evident that the truth is what we said.

It might be said:

Your conclusion necessarily applies to the perceptions obtained through the senses of smell, taste, and touch, since to be deprived of them is deficiency and to have them is perfection with respect to apprehension. The cognition of the one who knows a smell is not as perfect as the cognition of someone who perceives it through the sense of smell. Similarly regarding the sense of taste, for knowing a type of food cannot compare to actually perceiving it through the sense of taste.

We reply that the scrupulous men of knowledge explicitly affirmed the existence of perceptions, among which are hearing and sight, and cognition[64] that are perfections with respect to apprehension, so long as the causes, such as touch and contact, that are usually associated with these perceptions are excluded; for such causes are impossible with respect to God (Exalted is He). They, for instance, deem it possible to perceive through sight without the seer and the seen being across from each other. In a similar fashion we reply to the objection. There is nothing to prevent [other types of perception]. However, since the revelation only uses the terms 'hearing', 'sight', and 'cognition', it is not permissible to use other terms.[65] As for that in which there is a deficiency with respect to apprehension, it is not possible at all with respect to God (Exalted is He).

It might be said:

This leads to affirming the sensations of pleasure and pain for God. For the numb man, who feels no pain when beaten, is deficient, and the impotent, who cannot feel the pleasure of intercourse, is deficient. Similarly the loss of desire is a deficiency. So we should affirm desire for God.

We say:

These matters indicate occurrence. They are in themselves, if they are examined carefully, deficiencies and require matters that necessitate their occurrence. Pain, for example, is a deficiency; furthermore it requires a cause, such as beating, and beating is a contact that takes place between bodies. If [its conditions] are examined, pleasure results from the cessation of pain or from the attainment of that which one needs or for which one longs. Need and longing are deficiencies. Whatever depends on a deficiency is itself a deficiency. The meaning of desire is the seeking of something that is agreeable. There is no seeking except when what is sought is not readily available, and there is no pleasure except when something that was not available is attained. Everything that is possible to exist for God already exists. He does not lack anything, which He might desire to seek or upon whose attainment he might feel pleasure. Thus these sensations are inconceivable with respect to God. If it is said that the lack of sensing pain or feeling a beating are deficiencies for the numb man, and to be deprived of the desire for food is a deficiency, and to have them is a perfection, then

64. 'And cognition' (*wa-l-ʿilm*) is the reading in the Ankara edition. In the Jeddah edition it is 'to the extent' (*wa-l-qadr*).

65. So according to al-Ghazālī, there is no impossibility in attributing other perceptions, such as smell and taste, to God so long as their corporeal causes of physical contact are excluded. The reason that one would refrain from attributing such perceptions to God is that the revelation does not mention them. It is worth noting that there is disagreement among those who subscribe to Sunni orthodoxy regarding whether it is possible for God to have other perceptions, such as smell and taste.

what is intended by it is that it is a perfection in relation to its opposite, which is detrimental for the person. Hence it is a perfection when it is related to what is destructive, for deficiency is better than destruction. [Having these sensations], therefore, is not a perfection in itself, unlike knowledge and those perceptions.[66] So understand these matters.

# Seventh Attribute: Speech

We claim that the Maker of the world is a sayer, as the consensus of Muslims affirms.

Be advised that if one attempts to prove divine speech by asserting that reason deems it possible that the creation frequently receives commands and prohibitions, and that every quality that is possible for the creation is founded on a necessary quality of the Creator, then he has transgressed reason. It would be said to him: "If you mean that it is possible for created beings to be commanded by other created beings, for whom speech is conceivable, then that would be conceded. But if you mean that it is possible in general, whether for the creation or for the Creator, then you have presupposed in this argument what is being disputed, and that would not be conceded."[67]

On the other hand, if someone attempts to prove divine speech by relying on the consensus of believers or on a statement of a messenger, then he will have saddled himself with a devastating problem. The consensus of believers is founded on a statement of a messenger. And whoever denies that the Creator is a sayer necessarily denies that it is conceivable to be a messenger of God. For the concept of a messenger is that of one who conveys the speech of the sender; hence if speech is inconceivable with respect to the sender, how could it be possible to conceive of someone's being his messenger? If one says that he is the messenger of the earth or the messenger of the mountain, no one would pay attention to him, because we believe that it is impossible for the earth or the mountain to have speech

66. 'Those perceptions' refers to hearing and sight.

67. Al-Ghazālī's charge is that the argument is question-begging. In order to prove that God has speech, the arguer points out that people receive commands and prohibitions from God and assumes that all giving of commands and prohibitions takes the form of speech. But this is to presuppose the very thing that is in question, namely, that there is divine speech. As we will see, the term 'speech' (*kalām*) covers, for al-Ghazālī, "inner speech," which is pure thought without imagining letters, shapes, or sounds. As an illustration, al-Ghazālī takes what we might call "inner dialogue" and calls it "inner speech" if it is performed without any sounds or shapes. The Arabic expression is *kalām al-nafs*, which literally means "the speech of the soul." Al-Ghazālī argues below that this is a form of speech.

and to send messengers. God is exalted above any comparison. But if someone believes that speech is impossible with respect to God (Exalted is He), then it would be impossible for him to believe a messenger. For he who denies the existence of speech inevitably denies the conveying of speech, yet a message is merely a conveyance of speech and a messenger is merely a conveyer of speech.

Perhaps the best approach is the third approach, which is the one we followed in proving hearing and sight for God. We assert that speech for any living being is a perfection, a deficiency, or neither a deficiency nor a perfection. It is false to say that it is a deficiency or that it is neither a deficiency nor a perfection; hence it is established by necessity that it is a perfection. Every perfection that exists for a created being must necessarily exist for the Creator, since this is more proper, as we previously explained.

It might be said:

The speech, which you made the starting point for your reflection, is the speech of mankind. By speech what is intended is either the sounds and letters themselves or the power of the agent to produce sounds and letters in himself,[68] or a third meaning other than these two. If by speech what is intended is the sounds and letters, these are occurrents. There are occurrents that are perfections for us, but it is inconceivable that they would subsist in God's essence. If the speech subsists in something other than God, then God would not be the sayer of that speech; rather the sayer of that speech would be the receptacle in which the speech subsists. If by speech what is intended is the power to create sounds, then it is, indeed, a perfection. A sayer, however, is not considered a sayer solely by virtue of his power to create sounds, but rather by virtue of his creating speech in himself. God (Exalted is He) has the power to create sounds; so He has the perfection of power. But He would not be a sayer of this speech unless He creates sounds in Himself; and this is impossible, because He would then become a receptacle of occurrents. Therefore, it is impossible for God to be a sayer. If by speech is intended a third meaning, it is incomprehensible; and it is impossible to establish what is incomprehensible.

We say that this division is correct, and that it is accepted as valid to raise objections against all the cases of this division, except the denial of the third

68. The reason for saying 'in himself' is that the power to produce the sounds in something other than himself does not make the agent a sayer of this speech. Al-Ghazālī has in mind the notion that God creates speech for us, since, according to the Ashʿarite doctrine of occasionalism, God literally creates the sounds and letters we utter. This counts as creating speech in *us* and not in Himself. The possession of a power to create speech in others does not make God a sayer. He must be able to create the sounds in Himself, which, al-Ghazālī says, is impossible for God.

case.[69] We concede that it is impossible for sounds to subsist in the essence of God and for Him to be a sayer in this sense. We assert, however, that man is called "a sayer" in two senses. One of them is by virtue of sounds and letters, and the other is by virtue of *inner speech*, which is neither sound nor letter; and this is a perfection. Inner speech is not impossible for God and it does not imply occurrence. The form of speech we affirm for God is inner speech. Inner speech, which is additional to sound and the power to speak, cannot be denied with respect to man. In fact, one may say: "I composed eloquent speech in my mind yesterday." And it may be said that there is speech in so-and-so's mind and he wants to articulate it aloud. The poet says:

> Do not be impressed by the beauty of one's penmanship
> Until it is married to eloquent speech
> For speech is truly in the heart
> But the tongue is made to articulate what is in the heart.

If a notion is uttered by poets, it is an indication that it is an obvious notion that all mankind apprehends. Hence, how could inner speech be denied?

It might be said:

Inner speech, as understood above, is acknowledged. However, it is not outside the domain of cognition and perception, and it is not a distinct genus by itself at all. Rather, what people call "inner speech" and "inner dialogue" is knowledge of the arrangement of terms and expressions and the composition of known and understood meanings according to a specific form. What is in the heart is only known meanings, which are cognitions, and heard expressions, which are known through hearing. Inner speech is also knowledge of the denotations of terms[70] as well as the composition of meanings and terms in a certain order. That is an act, which is called "thinking," and the power from which the act proceeds is called "the faculty of thought." Thus if you posit in the soul something other than the act of thinking, which is the arrangement and composition of terms and mean-

69. The first case of the division is that speech is sounds and letters; the second is that speech is one's ability to produce sounds in oneself; and the third is a meaning that is different from these two meanings. The previous argument denies that there is a third meaning of speech. Al-Ghazālī rejects this denial and asserts that there is a third meaning—namely, inner speech, which is pure thought and has nothing to do with sounds and letters.

70. I followed the Ankara edition in reading *ʿilm maʿlūm al-lafẓ* (literally, "knowledge of what is known by a term") instead of *ʿilm maʿlūmuh al-lafẓ* (literally, "knowledge whose object is a term"), which is the reading in the Jeddah edition.

ings, and other than the faculty of thought, which is the power over this act, and other than knowledge of individual meanings and their combinations, and other than knowledge of individual terms—which are arrangements of letters—and their combinations, then you have posited a queer notion that is unknown to us.

To make our position clear, [we observe that] speech is either command, prohibition, declarative statement, or interrogative statement. A declarative statement is an expression indicative of a cognition in the mind of the sayer, that one knows a thing and knows the term that is used to denote this thing. For example, if someone knows beating, which is a meaning that can be apprehended through sensations, and knows the term for beating, which is composed of the letters *ḍād*, *rā'*, and *bā'*,[71] and which the Arabs use to denote this sensible meaning (this is additional knowledge); and if he has the power to acquire these sounds by means of his tongue and has the will to refer to beating and the will to acquire the term; then the utterance 'This is beating' would proceed from him without the need for anything in addition to these conditions.[72] So for any additional condition

71. The Arabic term for beating is *ḍarb*. Al-Ghazālī lists only the consonants *ḍ* (*ḍād*), *r* (*rā'*), and *b* (*bā'*) and ignores the short vowel *a*. In Arabic grammar, the short vowels are not considered letters.

72. The antecedent of the conditional is remarkable. In addition to its being fairly complex, it is expressed in the language of "acquisition" (*kasb*), which is the Ash'arite doctrine introduced in the chapter on the attribute of power. It also indicates al-Ghazālī's inclination to attribute will, and not only power, to the person "acquiring" the act. The conditions al-Ghazālī lists as sufficient for one's uttering the words 'This is beating' may be grouped into three main conditions, which affirm, respectively, the possession of knowledge, power, and will. Here are the three conditions.

1. The knowledge condition: the person knows what beating is and that the term 'beating' designates beating.
2. The power condition: the person has the power to utter ("acquire") the appropriate sounds that constitute the expression 'This is beating'.
3. The will condition: the person has the will to utter ("acquire") the expression 'This is beating' to refer to beating.

The passage asserts that if these conditions are fulfilled, the utterance 'This is beating' would proceed from the person (without the need for any other condition to obtain). The doctrine of acquisition clearly implies that the human power to acquire the sounds, and the sounds themselves, are directly created by God. If the human will to produce the utterance is metaphysically free, that is, it is an uncaused event that occurs in the agent, then it seems that God has acted on behalf of the human will by creating for the agent the appropriate power and act. On the other hand, if it is assumed that the human will, just like human power, is also created by God, then the notion of human free will would lose its metaphysical force. However, positing a human will that is metaphysically free, in the sense that it implies uncaused events occurring in the agent, contradicts a central tenet of the Ash'arite doctrine

you may posit, we can assume that it does not obtain, yet his utterance 'This is beating' still proceeds; and this would be a declarative statement and speech. As for interrogative statement, this indicates that there is in the soul a request for knowledge. A command indicates that there is in the soul of the commander a request for an act to be performed by the one commanded. A prohibition and other aspects of speech are understood by analogy to these cases. It is inconceivable that there is something beyond these. In general, some of these things, such as sounds, are impossible for God, and some of them, such as will, knowledge, and power, do belong to Him. Whatever is other than these is incomprehensible.

The response is that the notion of speech we seek is a meaning distinct from these forms of speech. In order to avoid lengthy discussion, let us discuss this notion as it pertains to only one aspect of speech—namely, command. We say: "A master's command 'Stand up' to his slave boy is an expression that contains a meaning; this contained meaning in the mind of the master is speech, but it does not belong to anything you mentioned. So there is no need to give an elaborate division." It might be thought that [the meaning of the command] can be identified with the will to attain what is commanded or with the will to convey meaning. It is absurd to say that it is the will to convey meaning; for the conveying of meaning requires something that is meant, and this is distinct from the expression that conveys it and from the will to convey it. It is also absurd to say that it is the will to attain what is commanded; for one might utter a command yet not want the command to be fulfilled; rather, he is averse to its fulfillment. For example, a man might present an excuse to a sultan who intends to kill him as a retribution for the man's spanking his slave boy, where the master's excuse is that he has spanked the slave boy because of his disobedience. As a demonstration, he proposes to command the boy in front of the king and show that the boy would disobey him. Thus if he wants to make his point by saying to the boy before the king "Stand up; I am determined to give you a task from which you cannot be excused," yet he does not want the boy to stand up,[73] then he is at the same time definitely commanding the boy to stand up and definitely not wanting him to stand up. The request that is present in his mind, and which the words of the command designate, is speech, and it

---

of occasionalism—namely, that God is the direct cause of *all* occurrents. It should not be surprising, therefore, that the Mu'tazilites and the philosophers accuse the Ash'arites of denying human free will altogether.

73. *Wlā yurīd an yaqūm* ("and he does not want him to stand up") is the reading in the Ankara edition. In the Jeddah edition it is *walā ta'wīl an taqūm* (roughly, "do not reinterpret my command").

is distinct from the will to have the boy stand up.[74] This should be clear to anyone who is fair-minded.

If it is said that this man is not really making a command, but only the appearance of a command, we say that this is false for two reasons. One of them is that if he is not really making a command, his excuse to the king would not be effective. And it would be said to him: "At this time it is inconceivable that you would make a real command, since a command is a request for the fulfillment of what is commanded, and it is impossible that you want your command to be fulfilled, for its fulfillment is a cause of your ruin. Hence how could you hope to defend yourself with the boy's disobeying your command, while you are unable to make a real command, since you cannot will that in which lies your ruin?" There is no doubt that the man can offer an argument, that his argument would stand and would be a demonstration of his excuse, and that his argument would consist in the disobedience of his command. If it is inconceivable for there to be a command when there is an aversion to the fulfillment of the command, it would not be conceivable at all that the master would offer such an argument. This on its own is conclusive for whoever ponders the matter carefully.

The second reason is that if the man tells the jurists about what has happened, and swears three times that he would divorce his wife if it is false that he commanded the slave to stand up before the king after the king made his threat, and that the slave disobeyed, every jurist would decree that the divorce does not take place. It is not permissible for a jurist to say: "I know it is impossible for you to will at that time that the boy fulfill the command, when this would be a cause for your ruin; for a command is the will to have what is commanded fulfilled; therefore, you made no real command." If a jurist were to say such a thing, it would be denied by consensus.

The matter then has become clear, and it is shown that there is a meaning that is a connotation of the term 'speech' and is distinct from the other meanings. We call this meaning 'speech'; it is a genus that is different from cognition, will, and belief. This is not impossible for God to have; on the contrary, it must be affirmed for God, since it is a form of perfection. It is, therefore, what is intended by eternal speech.[75]

Concerning the letters, they are occurrents, and they are indicative of

74. The request is clearly distinct from the will to have the boy stand up, for this will does not exist (the master does not really want the boy to stand up), while the request that the boy stand up does exist in the mind of the master.

75. The previous two sentences are the reading given in the Jeddah edition. The reading in the Ankara edition may be translated as follows: "Since it is a form of speech, it is, therefore, what is intended by eternal speech."

speech. An indicator, however, is distinct from what it indicates and does not have its attributes even if its indication is essential. For instance, the world is an occurrent and it is indicative of an eternal maker. So why would it be objectionable that occurrent letters should be indicative of an eternal attribute, although this indication is based on terminological convention.[76]

Since inner speech is a subtle notion, it eludes the understanding of most of the weak-minded. They only affirm letters and sounds. They raise, on the basis of their doctrine, questions and objections. We mention some of them in order to show how to respond to the rest of them.

## FIRST OBJECTION

One might say:

How did Moses (peace be upon him) hear the speech of God (Exalted is He)? Did he hear sound and letter? If you say that he did, then, according to you, he did not hear the speech of God, since God's speech is not sound and letter. On the other hand, if he did not hear sound and letter, then how did he hear that which is neither sound nor letter?

We say that he did hear God's speech, which is an eternal attribute subsisting in the essence of God (Exalted is He) but neither sound nor letter. Your question, How did he hear God's speech?, is the question of someone who does not understand the object of a *how*-question, what is sought by it, and what sort of answer is possible for it. Let us explain these matters, so that it will be known that it is impossible to answer this question.

We say:

Hearing is a form of perception. One's question, How does he hear?, is similar to his asking, How do you perceive the sweetness of sugar through the sense of taste? This question can be answered only in one of two ways. The first is to hand sugar to the inquirer, so that he may taste it and perceive its flavor and sweetness, and then say to him: "We perceive its sweetness exactly as you perceive it now." This is a satisfying answer and a full acquaintance. The second is when the first is not possible due either to the unavailability of sugar or to the inquirer's inability to taste sugar. We may say: "We perceive the taste of sugar as you now perceive the sweetness of honey." This answer is correct in a certain respect and wrong in another. The respect in which it is correct is that it defines the object of the question

76. There is nothing conventional about the world. Its presence indicates that it has an eternal maker. The presence of letters, however, is indicative of speech on the basis of a convention (*iṣṭilāḥ*). It is a convention that designates certain shapes and sounds to stand for certain meanings. Nevertheless, the presence of these conventional designators indicates the existence of eternal speech, which is articulated by these designators.

in terms of something similar to it in some respect, which is the source of sweetness. However, it is not similar to it in all respects, since the flavor of sugar is different from the flavor of honey, even though it is comparable to it in some respect, which is the source of sweetness. This is the most that can be attained. If the inquirer has never tasted anything sweet, it would be impossible to answer him and explain to him that about which he asks. He would be like someone impotent asking about the pleasure of sexual intercourse, although he can never experience it. It would be impossible to explain to him except to compare it to the pleasure of eating. This would be wrong in certain respect, since the pleasure of intercourse and the state attained by the one who is engaged in intercourse are not identical to the state attained by the eater, save that the term 'pleasure' is applied to both of them. If he has never experienced pleasure, there would be no possible basis for an answer.

Similarly, if one asks, How did Moses hear God's speech?,[77] the only way to answer his question satisfactorily is to make him hear God's eternal speech, which is not available to us, for that is a privilege of Moses (peace be upon him).[78] Thus we cannot make him hear it and we cannot compare it to anything that he has heard; for nothing among the things he hears is similar to the speech of God (Exalted is He). All the familiar things he has ever heard are sounds; and a sound is not similar to what is not a sound; hence it is impossible to explain to him.

Indeed, if a deaf man asks, How do you hear sound?, and he has never heard a sound, we would be unable to answer him. If we were to say: "It is as you perceive visible objects; for hearing is a perception through the ear just as vision is a perception through the eye," this would be wrong, since the perception of sounds is not similar to the perception of colors. This shows that the question is impossible to answer. Also, if someone asks, How is the Lord of lords seen in the hereafter?, the answer would be impossible, because he is asking about the modality of that which has no modality. For the meaning of one's question, How is it?, is: what sort of thing of which we know is it like? If that about which he asks is unlike anything known to him, the answer would be impossible. This, however, does not show that God's essence is nonexistent. Similarly, the lack of an answer does not show that God's speech is nonexistent. Rather, we ought to believe that His speech is an eternal attribute to which nothing is similar, just as His essence is an eternal essence to which nothing is similar. God's speech is heard in a way

77. This is the reading in the Ankara edition; in the Jeddah edition, 'how can God's speech be heard?'

78. Literally, "a privilege of the Speaker." The 'Speaker to God' (*kalīm Allah*) is an epithet of Moses.

that is different from and unlike the way letters and sounds are heard, just as His essence is seen in a way that is different from and unlike the way bodies and modes are seen.

## SECOND OBJECTION

It might be said:

Either the speech of God (Exalted is He) resides in copies of the Qur'ān or it does not. If it does reside, how could the eternal reside in an occurrent? If you say it does not, then this would be contrary to the consensus, for it is agreed that every copy of the Qur'ān must be respected to the point that touching it is deemed forbidden for anyone who is ritually impure. That can only be so because a copy of the Qur'ān contains God's speech.

We say:

The speech of God (Exalted is He) is written in books, memorized by hearts, and recited by tongues. The paper, ink, script, letters, and sounds are all occurrents, since they are bodies and modes [subsisting] in bodies, and all of these are occurrents. If we say that it—I mean the attribute of the Eternal (Glorified is He)—is written in the books, it does not follow that the eternal speech resides in the books. Just as if we say that fire is written in a book, it does not follow from this that fire itself resides in the book. If fire resides in the book, it would be burned; and if fire itself resides in the tongue of someone who says "fire," his tongue would be burned. Fire is a hot body, which is designated by sounds consisting of parts that generate the letters *nūn*, *alif*, and *rā'*.[79] The burning, hot body is what is designated and it is distinct from the designator. Similarly, eternal speech, which subsists in the essence of God (Exalted is He), is what is indicated and not the indicator. The letters are indicators, and the indicators are not to be violated, because the divine law made them inviolable. Thus respecting the copies of the Qur'ān is obligatory, since they contain indicators of an attribute of God.

## THIRD OBJECTION

It might be said:

The Qur'ān is either God's speech or not. If you say "No," then you have breached the consensus. If you say "Yes," then the speech is nothing but letters and sounds. It is acknowledged that the recitation of a reciter consists of letters and sounds.

79. The Arabic word for fire is *nār*, which consists of the letters *n* (*nūn*), *ā* (*alif*), and *r* (*rā'*).

We say:

Here are three terms: 'recitation', 'what is recited', and 'Qur'ān'. As for that which is recited, it is the speech of God (Exalted is He)—I mean His eternal attribute, which subsists in His essence. As for the recitation, it is the reciter's act that is present on his tongue, and which the reciter has initiated after he abstained from it. The concept of an occurrent is that of a thing that is initiated after it was nonexistent. If our opponent does not understand the term 'occurrent' to mean this, then let us abandon the use of the terms 'occurrent' and 'created' and say, instead, that a recitation is an act that the reciter has initiated after he was not engaged in it, and which is sensible. As for the term 'Qur'ān', it may be used to designate what is recited. If that is what is intended by it, then it is eternal and not created. This is what the early Muslims meant by their saying that the Qur'ān, which is what is recited by the tongues, is God's speech, and it is not created. On the other hand, if what is intended by it is the recitation, which is the reciter's act, then the reciter's act is not prior to the existence of the reciter; and whatever is not prior to the existence of an occurrent is itself an occurrent.

In sum, he who says "The sounds that are divided into letters and which I originated by my choice after being silent are eternal" should not be engaged in discussion and should not be assigned obligations.[80] Rather, this poor man should be told that he does not comprehend what he says, does not understand the meaning of 'letter', and does not know the meaning of 'occurrent'. If he were to understand these matters, he would know that if he is created, then whatever proceeds from him is also created, and that something eternal does not transfer to an occurrent essence. So let us refrain from elaborating what is obvious. In the expression 'In the name of God', if the letter *sīn* is not after the letter *bā'*,[81] then it would not be the Qur'ān; rather, it would be an error. If, however, the letter *sīn* must come after and follow something else, then how could it be eternal, if by 'eternal' we intend that which does not follow anything at all?[82]

80. 'Assigned obligations' (*yukallaf*) is the reading in the Ankara edition. In the Jeddah edition, it is 'spoken to' (*yukallam*). He should not be assigned obligations because, according to Islamic law, a person who is not in possession of normal mental faculties are not subject to religious obligations.

81. All but one of the chapters of the Qur'ān begin with the Arabic phrase *bism Allāh al-Raḥmān al-Raḥīm*, which means "in the name of God, the Compassionate, the Merciful." In the word *bism* the letter *s* (*sīn*) comes after the letter *b* (*bā'*).

82. The final argument may require some clarification because its conclusion is not stated in the paragraph. There are two observations to be made about the Qur'ān: (1) if one changes the order of letters (or, words) in a Qur'ānic verse, the result might not be part of the Qur'ān; (2) letters that exhibit a certain order cannot be the eternal speech of God because the presence of order implies that certain letters come after other letters, and what is eternal cannot come after anything. Observation 2 implies that the written text of the Qur'ān and the recita-

## FOURTH OBJECTION

It might be said:

The Muslims all agree that the Qurʾān is the miracle of God's Messenger (may God bless him and grant him peace), that it is the speech of God (Exalted is He), and that it consists of chapters and verses, which have stops and beginnings. How could something eternal have stops and beginnings? How could it be divided into chapters and verses? And how could something eternal be the Messenger's miracle, when a miracle is an act that is contrary to the habitual course of things, and every act is created? Thus, how could the speech of God be eternal?

We say:

Do you deny that the term 'Qurʾān' is ambiguous, designating both recitation and what is recited? If you concede that it is ambiguous, then when the Muslims affirm of the Qurʾān all the descriptions that follow from its being eternal, such as their statement that the Qurʾān is God's speech and is not created, they intend by 'Qurʾān' that which is recited; and when they affirm of it descriptions that cannot be predicated of something eternal, such as its being composed of chapters and verses that have stops and beginnings, they intend by 'Qurʾān' the expressions that constitute a recitation and that indicate an eternal attribute.[83] If the term is understood as ambiguous, all contradictions are prevented. The consensus asserts that there is no eternal [*qadīm*] save God (Exalted is He); yet God says: *Till it returns like an old* [*qadīm*] *shriveled palm-leaf*.[84] Thus we say that the term *qadīm* is ambiguous, having two meanings.[85] If one of them is affirmed, it is not

---

tion of the Qurʾān are not God's eternal speech. Hence, if the Qurʾān is God's speech, it cannot be identified with the copies of the Qurʾān (*muṣḥaf*s) or with a recitation of the Qurʾān. Al-Ghazālī said earlier that the Qurʾān, in this case, is what is *indicated* by the written text of the Qurʾān and by the recitation. Observation 1 implies that the term 'Qurʾān' may be used to designate the recitation of the Qurʾān. Thus, as al-Ghazālī previously mentioned, the term 'Qurʾān' is ambiguous; it has two meanings: it may signify a Qurʾānic recitation or what is recited.

83. This is the translation of the reading in the Ankara edition. The reading in the Jeddah edition may be translated as follows: "they intend by 'Qurʾān' the expressions that indicate an eternal attribute, which is the Qurʾān." This reading is problematic because the term 'Qurʾān' means two different things in this sentence: the first occurrence implies that the term 'Qurʾān' designates the recitation itself, which is not eternal, and the second occurrence implies that the Qurʾān is the eternal attribute of speech.

84. The verse is about the moon. Here is the complete verse: *And for the moon, We have appointed mansions till it returns like an old shriveled palm-leaf* (Qurʾān, 36:39). The English translation does not reveal what is relevant about the verse. The Arabic word *qadīm* can mean old, ancient, anteriorly eternal, or eternal.

85. It is impossible to use an English translation of the word *qadīm* while preserving the meaning of the Arabic sentence. As mentioned in the previous note, *qadīm* means old as

impossible to negate the other; the same applies to the term 'Qur'ān'. This is a response that applies to all that they mention about the contradictory employments of the term.[86]

On the other hand, if they deny that the term 'Qur'ān' is ambiguous, then we say that as for using the term to designate that which is recited,[87] it is evident from the statements of the early Muslims that the Qur'ān is God's speech and is not created, in spite of their knowledge that they, their voices, their recitations, and their acts are all created. As for using the term to designate the recitation itself, the poet says:

> They sacrificed a grey-haired man who bears the mark of prostration
> And who spends the night being occupied with praising God and with the Qur'ān.[88]

He means reciting the Qur'ān. God's Messenger (may God bless him and grant him peace) says, "There is nothing God loves to hear more than a prophet intoning the Qur'ān beautifully,"[89] and intonation requires recitation. The early Muslims all say that the Qur'ān is God's speech and is not created, and that the Qur'ān is a miracle, which is an act of God (Exalted is He). They, however, know that what is eternal cannot be a miracle. Hence it is clear that the term 'Qur'ān' is ambiguous. He who does not understand this ambiguity thinks that there is a contradiction between these employments of the term.

## FIFTH OBJECTION

It might be said:

It is acknowledged that whatever is presently heard is sounds, and the speech of God is presently heard as is evident from the consensus and from

---

well as anteriorly eternal. Hence it is ambiguous, designating that which has no beginning as well as that whose beginning is in the relatively distant past. If I were to substitute 'anteriorly eternal' or 'old' for *qadīm*, the sentence would most likely turn out false.

86. Al-Ghazālī gives several examples of such employments. For instance, 'the Qur'ān is not created' and 'the Qur'ān is the Messenger's miracle'.

87. This is a translation of the reading in the Cairo edition. The reading in the Ankara and Jeddah editions may be translated as "then it is conclusively known that it is used to designate that which is recited."

88. The poet is most likely Ḥassān ibn Thābit, a companion of the Prophet. The verse is part of a poem that is a eulogy for the third caliph, 'Uthmān ibn 'Affān, who was assassinated in his home while reading the Qur'ān.

89. Reported by Abū Dawūd, *Sunan*, II.355, no. 1473; Aḥmad ibn Ḥanbal, *Musnad*, II.271, no. 7653; Bukhārī, *Ṣaḥīḥ*, LXIX.19, nos. 5023, 5024; Dāramī, *Sunan*, II.171, no. 1488; Muslim, *Ṣaḥīḥ*, VI.34, no. 792; and Nasā'ī, *Sunan*, XI.83, nos. 1017, 1018.

God's statement: *If one of the pagans ask you for asylum, grant it to him, so that he may hear the words of God.*[90]

We say:

If the sound heard by the pagan, when he is granted asylum, is God's eternal speech, which subsists in God's essence, then what privilege does Moses (peace be upon him) have over the pagans in his being distinguished as the one to whom God spoke, since they hear God as Moses did? The only conceivable answer to this is to say that what Moses heard was an eternal attribute that subsists in God's essence, and what the pagan hears is sounds that are indicative of that attribute. This conclusively shows that there is ambiguity either in the term 'speech' or in the expression 'what is heard'. [In the case of 'speech',] the indicators are designated by the name that truly designates what is indicated. For speech is truly inner speech, but the expressions, because they are indicative of it, are also called "speech," as they are called "knowledge," since it may be said that he heard so-and-so's knowledge, where he heard his words, which are indicative of his knowledge. [In the case of 'what is heard',] that which is understood and known through hearing something else may also be described as being heard. For instance, it may be said that he heard the speech of the prince from the tongue of his messenger, when it is acknowledged that the speech of the prince does not subsist in the tongue of his messenger. Rather, what is heard is the speech of the messenger that indicates the speech of the prince.

This is the extent of what we want to mention in explaining the doctrine of the followers of the Sunna concerning inner speech, which is considered mysterious. The rest of the characteristics of divine speech will be discussed, God willing, when we consider the characteristics of the attributes in the second part of this treatise.

90. Here is the complete verse: *If one of the pagans asks you for asylum, grant it to him, so that he may hear the words of God; and then escort him to where he can be secure; that is because they are men without knowledge* (Qur'ān, 9:6). The Arabic expression that is translated into 'the words of God' is *kalām Allāh*, which literally means "the speech of God." In the context of the verse above the translation 'the words of God' is more natural.

# SECOND PART

## *On the general characteristics of the divine attributes, concerning that which they share and that in which they differ*

THERE ARE FOUR CHARACTERISTICS.

# First Characteristic

*[The attributes are additional to the essence]*

The seven attributes,[91] which we established, are not the essence. Rather, they are additional to the essence. According to us, the Maker of the world (Exalted is He) is a knower with knowledge, living with life, powerful with power, and so on with respect to all the attributes.

The Mu'tazilites and the philosophers deny this. They say: "The Eternal is one essence, and it is not possible to posit several eternal essences. The proof for these attributes establishes only that He is a knower, powerful, and living, and not [that there are attributes of] knowledge, life, and power." Let us focus on the attribute of knowledge, so that we do not have to repeat the discussion for all the attributes. They maintain that being a knower is a *state* of the essence and is not an attribute. The Mu'tazilites, however, make an exception for two attributes. They say that God is a willer with will that is additional to the essence, and He is a sayer with speech that is additional to the essence, that He creates will not in any receptacle, and that He creates speech in a corporeal body, and hence He is considered a sayer through this speech.[92]

The philosophers, on the other hand, extend their inference to the case of the will.[93] As for speech, they say He is a sayer in the sense that He creates in the soul of the prophet a hearing of arranged sounds, either while he is asleep or while he is awake. These sounds have no existence outside the soul, but only in the hearing of the prophet. This is similar to the one who sees people in his sleep who do not exist but whose images occur in his brain; and who hears sounds that do not exist. A person present near the one who is asleep hears nothing while the one who is asleep does hear and is so troubled and bothered by a frightful sound that he wakes

91. These are the divine attributes discussed in the First Part—namely, will, power, knowledge, speech, sight, hearing, and life.

92. Literally, He would be its sayer.

93. This is the inference from the oneness of the eternal essence of God to the conclusion that the attributes are not additional to the divine essence. The philosophers, therefore, assert that God is a willer by virtue of His essence alone, and not because He possesses an eternal attribute that is additional to His essence and which is called 'will'.

up frightened and terrified. They also maintain that if a prophet attains a high rank of prophethood, his soul would be so pure that while he is awake he would see wondrous images and hear well-composed sounds that he commits to memory, when all those around him hear and see nothing. According to them, this is the meaning of seeing the angels and hearing the Qurʾān. He who is not at this high rank of prophethood does not see such things except in sleep. This is the essence of the doctrine of those who are misguided.

The goal is to establish the attributes.[94] The conclusive proof is that if one is committed to the claim that God is a knower, then he is committed to the claim that He has knowledge. For what is understood by our saying that He is a knower and that He has knowledge is one and the same, since an intelligent person comprehends an essence and then comprehends that it has a certain state and attribute; hence he comprehends an attribute and [he comprehends] that who has the attribute. The attribute of knowledge, for example, is expressed in two ways. One of them is long, which is to say that this essence is such that knowledge subsists in it. The other is made concise by linguistic declension and derivation, which is to say that the essence is knowing. This is similar to a man who sees a person, a shoe, and the man's placing his foot in the shoe. He may utter a long expression by saying that this person's foot is inside his shoe, or he may simply say he is shod. The only meaning of being shod is that he has a shoe on. The Muʿtazilites'[95] assumption that the subsisting of knowledge in the essence necessitates a state for the essence called 'being knowing' is sheer illusion. Rather, knowledge is *itself* the state. The only meaning for His being a knower is that the essence has a certain state and attribute. That state and attribute is just knowledge.

If one borrows concepts from terms, then, when multiple terms are generated by derivations, one would inevitably fall into error. For instance, deriving the quality of being a knower from the term 'knowledge' produces this error. So one should not be deceived by it. [Making this clear] refutes all that is said and elaborated about cause and effect. This refutation is a priori clear for anyone who has not repeatedly heard these terms. However, if such a concept is impressed on the understanding, it can only be removed by lengthy discussion, which is unsuitable for this brief chapter.

In conclusion we say to the philosophers and the Muʿtazilites: "Is what is understood by our saying 'knower' the same as[96] what is understood by our

94. Al-Ghazālī gave arguments in the First Part for the existence of the attributes. The proof he seeks in this part is to establish that these attributes are additional to essence.

95. The Jeddah edition omits 'Muʿtazilites'.

96. The reading in the Jeddah edition is *ʿayn* (the same as) and in the Ankara edition is *ghayr* (different from).

saying 'existent' or does it point to the existence of an addition?" If they say "No,"[97] then for someone to say that God is an existent knower would be like his saying that God is an existent existent, which is obviously absurd. If, according to its concept, there is an addition, then is this addition specific to the essence of the existent or not? If they say "No," then this is absurd, because it would fail to be a description of God. On the other hand, if it is specific to His essence, then we do not mean by 'knowledge' anything other than this, which is the addition that is specific to the existent essence—an addition that is beyond mere existence and because of which it is correct to derive the name 'knower' for the existent. Thus you are committed to the same concept, and the dispute is merely about terminology.

If I want to bring the same objection against the philosophers, I would say: "Is what is understood by our saying 'powerful' the same as what is understood by our saying 'knower' or is it different from it?" If it is exactly the same, then it would be as if we said that God is powerful powerful, which is sheer redundancy.[98] If it is different, then that is what is desired. Hence, you have affirmed two concepts: one of them is expressed as power and the other as knowledge. Dispute, therefore, is limited to terminology.

It might be said:

Is what is understood by your saying "command" the same as what is understood by your saying "commanding,[99] prohibiting, and reporting" or is it different from it? If it is exactly the same, then it is sheer redundancy.[100] If it is different, then let it be that God has one speech that is a command, another speech that is a prohibition, and yet another speech that is a report. And let it be that His addressing a prophet is different from His addressing another prophet. Similarly, is what is understood by your saying that he knows the modes the same as what is understood by your saying that he knows the substances, or is it different from it? If it is exactly the same, let it be that a man who knows the substances also knows the modes through exactly the same cognition, so that one cognition would have infinitely many objects. If it is different, let it be that God (Exalted is He) has infinitely many different cognitions; and the same applies to speech, power, and will. Similarly, every attribute whose objects are infinite must have infinitely many instantiations; this is impossible. Now if it is possible

97. There are two questions. The *no*-answer pertains to the second questions, that is, saying 'knower' does *not* point to the existence of something different from mere existence.

98. Al-Ghazālī clearly presupposes that someone has said that God is a powerful knower. Since this answer asserts that being powerful and being a knower are the same concept, the statement would reduce to 'God is powerful powerful'.

99. The Jeddah edition omits 'commanding'.

100. The redundancy results from asserting, for example, that He is commanding a command.

for one attribute to be itself a command, a prohibition, and a report, and to replace these various things, then it is possible for one attribute to replace knowledge, power, life, and the rest of the attributes. And if this is possible, then it is possible for the essence itself to be sufficient and to entail power, knowledge, and the rest of the attributes without there being an addition. From this the doctrine of the Muʿtazilites and the philosophers follows.

The response is to say: "This question stirs a major issue concerning difficulties related to the divine attributes—difficulties whose solution is not suitable for a brief discussion. However, since the question has already been mentioned, let us indicate the starting point of the path to its solution." Most thinkers were intimidated by it, and they simply clung to the Qurʾān and the consensus. They said: "These attributes are mentioned in the revelation. For the revelation affirms the existence of knowledge, where it is understood that it is definitely one knowledge; no multiplicity of knowledge is reported in the revelation;[101] hence we do not believe it." This is hardly satisfying, since commands, prohibitions, and reports are all revealed, as well as the Torah, Gospel, and Qurʾān. What prevents us from saying that a command is distinct from a prohibition, and the Qurʾān is distinct from the Torah? It is also revealed that the Exalted knows what is concealed and what is exposed, what is exoteric and what is esoteric, what is wet and what is dry, and so on of what is included in the Qurʾān.

Perhaps the correct response is what we indicate as the starting point of our examination of this issue, which is to assert that every group of intelligent people is required to concede that the proof has led to something that is additional to the existence of the Maker's essence, and which is expressed as His being a knower, powerful, and the other descriptions. There are three possible positions: two endpoints and a middle. Moderation is closest to the right doctrine. As for the two endpoints, one of them is deficiency, which is to restrict existence to one essence that entails all these things and is a substitute for them. This what the philosophers assert. The second endpoint is excess, which is to affirm an attribute that has infinitely many instantiations, such as cognitions, powers, and speeches, which correspond to the objects of these attributes. This is an extreme position, which only some of the Muʿtazilites and the Karrāmites uphold.[102]

The third position is moderation and the middle. It is to say:

Distinct things have with respect to each other degrees of differentiation that are small or great. Two things might be different in their essences,

101. Literally, what is additional to one is not reported.

102. See note 52 above for a brief description of the Karrāmites.

such as the distinction between motion and rest, power and knowledge, and substance and mode. Two things might share a definition and one nature and hence not differ in terms of their essence; rather the difference between them is due to the objects to which they attach. For instance, the difference between power and knowledge is not similar to the difference between knowing a black thing and knowing another black thing or knowing a white thing. Thus if knowledge is characterized by a definition, then the knowledge of all known things is subsumed under this definition. We say: "Moderation in belief is to maintain that every distinction is due to a distinction between the essences themselves. No one of the differentiated things can be sufficient and stand for the other things." Therefore it is necessary that knowledge be other than power, and so is life and the rest of the seven attributes, and that the attributes not be the essence, since the distinction between an attribute and the essence, of which the attribute is predicated,[103] is more pronounced than the distinction between two attributes. As for knowledge of a thing, it is not distinct from knowledge of another thing except in the object to which it attaches. It is not unlikely that an eternal attribute is distinguished by this characteristic, which is that a distinction between the objects to which it attaches does not necessitate in it a distinction between and a multiplicity of instantiations.

It might be said: "This does not eliminate the difficulty, for if you concede that there is any form of difference due to a difference between the objects to which an attribute attaches,[104] then the difficulty persists. What purpose does it serve to examine the reason for the difference, once the difference is present?" I say that the aim of the proponent of a certain doctrine is to show conclusively the superiority of his position over the other's position, and this has been attained decidedly. For there can be only one correct position among these three, or a fourth position should be invented, which is unintelligible. The superiority of the one we advocate, when compared to the two endpoints that oppose it, is known decisively. If a position must be adopted, and there are only these three, and this one is the closest to the truth, then it must be adopted. There may remain some troubling difficulty that follows from this position, but those that follow from the others are far more troubling. It is possible to give some resolution to the one difficulty, but to eliminate it completely—given that the object of our reflection is the eternal attributes, which transcend the understanding of mankind—is un-

103. Literally, since the distinction between the described essence (*al-dhāt al-mawṣūfa*) and the attribute (*al-ṣifa*) . . . .

104. Throughout this treatise, I translate the Arabic expression *muta'alliq al-ṣifa* as "an object to which the attribute attaches," with variations when necessary.

achievable without a long elaboration that is unsuitable for this book. This is the general discussion.

As for the Muʿtazilites, we specifically ask them to explain the difference between power and will. We say that if it is possible for God to be powerful without power, it is possible for Him to be a willer without a will, and there would be no difference between them.[105] It might be said: "He is powerful in Himself, and hence He is powerful over all objects of power. On the other hand, if He were a willer in Himself, He would be a willer of all objects of will collectively, which is absurd, since the contradictory objects of will can be willed alternately but not collectively, while power does attach simultaneously to two contradictory objects of power."[106] The response is to say: "You can say that He is a willer in Himself, but He acts on selected occurrent objects of will, just as you say that He is powerful in Himself, even though His power attaches only to certain objects of power, since according to you the acts of animals and what they generate are outside the reach of both His power and will." If that is possible with respect to power, then it is also possible with respect to will.

As for the philosophers, they fall into contradiction regarding divine speech. Their position is invalid in two respects. One of them is their statement that God (Exalted is He) is a sayer, although they do not posit inner speech and they do not posit sounds in existence; rather they posit the hearing of sound through the creation of hearing in a prophet's ear without external sound.[107] If it is permissible to describe God as a sayer because of

105. Recall that the Muʿtazilites' position regarding the divine attributes is that all attributes other than will and speech are reducible to God's essence. So for them God is powerful and living without the presence of power and life as attributes that are additional to the essence. According to them, will and speech are exceptions. God is a willer and a sayer because He has will and speech that are additional to His essence. Al-Ghazālī challenges the Muʿtazilites on the grounds that they are unable to maintain a distinction between the case of will and the case of power.

106. Al-Ghazālī's argument on behalf of the Muʿtazilites is that the difference between divine power and divine will is that divine power attaches to all possible objects of power, including objects that contradict each other. Of course, power cannot actualize two contradictory objects simultaneously but can do so only alternately. Nevertheless, it attaches to them, because for power to attach to an object $x$ simply means that the power can actualize $x$ under the right circumstances. The divine will, on the other hand, *can* attach to all possible things, including objects that contradict each other. But not all objects *are* objects of the will; when the divine will attaches to an object, that entails that the object will come into existence. Thus, no two contradictory objects *are* objects of the divine will.

107. It is well known that the Islamic philosophers do not affirm the existence of divine attributes that are additional to the divine essence. So, according to them, God is a sayer, not because He has an attribute called "speech" that is additional to His essence, but solely by virtue of His essence. Al-Ghazālī says that God is called "sayer," according to the philoso-

what occurs in another's brain, it would be permissible to describe Him as making sounds and as moving because sound and motion exist in another, which is absurd.[108]

The second is that what they state constitutes a rejection of the revelation in its entirety. For what the one who is asleep perceives is chimeras, which have no reality, and hence if a prophet's apprehension of God's speech is the result of imaginations that are similar to confused dreams, the prophet would have no trust in them and they would not be knowledge. In sum, those philosophers are not believers in a religion or in Islam, but they merely utter agreeable statements to avoid the punishment of the sword. The real dispute with them is with respect to the source of the act, the occurrence of the world, and the attribute of power;[109] thus we do not engage them regarding these details.

It might be said: "Do you say that God's attributes are other than God?" We say that this is a mistake. For if we say "God, the Exalted," then we have referred to the divine essence together with the divine attributes, and not to the essence alone. The name of God does not designate an essence that is assumed to be devoid of the divine attributes, just as it is not said that jurisprudence is other than the jurist, that Zayd's hand is other than Zayd,

---

phers, because He creates the *hearing* of sound in the ear of a prophet, though without the prophet's experiencing inner speech and without the existence of external sounds. As we have seen, al-Ghazālī's explanation of this claim is that the prophets experience God's speech as inner speech without the presence of sounds or letters.

108. Al-Ghazālī argues that the philosophers' describing God as a sayer because of His creating the hearing of sound in a prophet's brain is not essentially different from one's describing God as moving because of His creating movement in someone's leg. The fact that the prophet's hearing is obtained without external sound could be matched by the saying that the leg's movement is obtained without a worldly cause, whether external, such as a push, or internal, such as an act of human will.

109. Al-Ghazālī's main points of contention with the Islamic philosophers include the nature of causation, the eternity of the world, and the attribute of divine will. While the philosophers maintain that causation is the *necessary* natural course of events, al-Ghazālī, as an Ashʿarite, holds the position that all events, including all human acts, are the *direct* creation of God. The philosophers also maintain that the world is the eternal effect of God, which emanates from God by necessity and not through *free* will. Al-Ghazālī, as indicated in the First Treatise, believes that the world is not eternal; it has a beginning and is created by God through a free will that existed eternally. Interestingly enough, he does not mention will in the passage above, rather he mentions power. He might be referring to the question of the relation of God's power to the powers of the created beings. This interpretation makes the issue of power part of the general issue of causation. In *Tahāfut al-Falāsifa*, al-Ghazālī imputes infidelity to the Islamic philosophers on the basis of three of their views: that the world is eternal, that God knows the universals but not the particulars, and that resurrection is spiritual and not physical. (See al-Ghazālī, *Tahāfut al-Falāsifa*, First, Second, Thirteenth, and Twentieth Discussions, and the Conclusion.)

and that the carpenter's hand is other than the carpenter.[110] For any part of what is designated by a name is not other than what is designated by the name. Thus Zayd's hand is not Zayd and is not other than Zayd; rather both expressions are absurd.[111] Similarly every part is not other than the whole, nor is it the same as the whole. If it is said that jurisprudence is other than a man, then this is permissible since being a man does not entail the presence of the attribute of jurisprudence; but it is not permissible to say that jurisprudence is other than the jurist. Thus it is possible that an attribute is other than the essence in which the attribute subsists. This is similar to saying that a mode, which subsists in a substance, is other than the substance, in the sense that the concept connoted by its name is other than the concept connoted by the other's name. This is permissible on two conditions. One of them is that the law does not prevent its use; this is specific to God (Exalted is He). The second is that it must *not* be understood by the term 'other' that which may exist independently of what is *other* in relation to it.[112] For if it is so understood, it would not be possible to say that Zayd's blackness is other than Zayd, because it does not exist independently of Zayd. Therefore, it has become clear what the role of the concept is and what the role of the term is. It is senseless to elaborate what is obvious.

## Second Characteristic

*[The attributes subsist in the essence]*

We claim that all of these attributes subsist in God's essence, that none of them could subsist in something other than His essence, whether the attribute is in a receptacle or not.

The Muʿtazilites contend that the will does not subsist in God's essence because it is an occurrent and He is not a receptacle of occurrents, and that it does not subsist in another receptacle because this would make that

110. The way I understand this argument is that just as the terms 'jurist', 'Zayd', and 'carpenter' do not designate essences that are devoid, respectively, of jurisprudence, Zayd's hand, and the carpenter's hand, so, too, the name 'God' does not designate an essence that is devoid of attributes.

111. It should be clear from the context that the absurd expressions are the negations of the expressions that preceded this sentence. Hence what is absurd is 'It is not the case that Zayd's hand is not Zayd' and 'It is not the case that Zayd's hand is not other than Zayd'.

112. It is permissible, for instance, to say that God's power is other than God's essence provided that (1) the divine law does not prevent it and (2) we do not understand by the expression 'other than God's essence' that God's power can exist independently of God's essence.

receptacle the willer; hence the divine will does not exist in a receptacle. They also maintain that speech does not subsist in His essence because it is an occurrent, but it subsists in an inanimate body, though this body would not be the sayer, rather the sayer is God (Glorified is He).[113]

The demonstration that the attributes must subsist in the essence is dispensable for anyone who understood what we already advanced. Since the proof indicates the existence of the Maker, it then indicates that the maker is of such-and-such attribute. We mean by saying that He is of such-and-such attribute only that He is of *that* attribute. There is no difference between His being of that attribute and the attribute's subsisting in His essence. We have shown that the meanings of our saying "knower" and "there is knowledge in His essence" are one and the same. Similarly, the meanings of our saying "willer" and "will subsists in His essence" are one and the same. Also, the meanings of our saying "no will subsists in His essence" and "not a willer" are one and the same. Describing an essence as a willer through will that does not subsist in it is like describing it as moving through a motion that does not subsist in it. Thus if the will does not subsist in God, then it makes no difference whether it exists or not. So one's statement "He is a willer" would be an erroneous expression that has no meaning.

Similarly for a sayer, God is a sayer by virtue of His being a receptacle for speech, since there is no difference between our saying "He is a sayer" and our saying "speech subsists in Him." And there is no difference between our saying "not a sayer" and our saying "no speech subsists in His essence." The same applies to "someone's making a sound" and "someone's being in

113. The first Muʿtazilite to address the attributes of divine will and speech is Abū al-Hudhayl Muḥammad al-ʿAllāf (AH 135/752 CE–AH 235/849 CE), the leader of the Basra Muʿtazilites during his time. Al-ʿAllāf indeed affirms that God's will is occurrent and it occurs neither in the essence of God (for God's essence is not a receptacle of occurrents) nor in any other receptacle (otherwise that receptacle would be the willer and not God). However, his views about God's speech are more complex than what al-Ghazālī describes. Al-ʿAllāf divides God's speech into two types: that which occurs not in a receptacle and that which occurs in bodies. Neither type subsists in God's essence, because God's speech is an occurrent and God's essence is not a receptacle of occurrents. The first type is God's speech that brings into existence an occurrent, or annihilates an existent, or re-creates something. This speech is His command 'Be'. Since this command initiates, re-creates, or annihilates an occurrent, it requires no receptacle for its existence. All other divine commands, prohibitions, and reports require receptacles, and hence they are created in bodies. Al-Ghazālī says that, according to the Muʿtazilites, the bodies in which God's speech is created are inanimate bodies. Those receiving the command need not be inanimate (for example, God creates a revelation on the tongue of a prophet), but the body in which the speech is created must not have the power to create *this* divine speech; if it does, then the speech would be its speech and not God's speech. Most Muʿtazilites who came after al-ʿAllāf adopted his views on the divine will and speech. (See al-Shahrastānī, *al-Milal wa-l-Niḥal*, vol. 1, pp. 64–67; al-Baghdādī, *al-Farq bayn al-Firaq*, pp. 86–92; Badawī, *Madhāhib al-Islāmiyyīn*, pp. 121–197.)

motion." If our statement "speech does not subsist in His essence" is true of God (Exalted is He), then our statement "He is not a sayer" would be true as well, because they express the same meaning.

What is astonishing is their statement that the will does not exist in a receptacle. If it is possible for an attribute not to exist in a receptacle, then let it be possible for knowledge, power, blackness, motion, and even speech not to exist in a receptacle. So why do they say that He creates the sounds in a receptacle?[114] Let them also not be created in a receptacle. If a sound can be conceived as being in a receptacle only because it is a mode and an attribute, then so can the will. If this is reversed by saying that He does not create speech in a receptacle but He does create will in a receptacle, then the converse would be no worse than the original.

However, since will was required to create the first created being, and since a receptacle is something to be created, the Muʿtazilites could not posit for the will a receptacle that existed prior to the will, for there is no receptacle prior to the will except the essence of God (Exalted is He). Moreover, they do not suppose God to be a receptacle of occurrents.[115] The one who supposes God to be a receptacle of occurrents is more sensible than they are. For the impossibility of the existence of a will that is not in a receptacle, the impossibility of God's being a willer through a will that does not subsist in Him, and the impossibility of the occurrence of a will that is originated by Him without a prior will are apprehended through the intellect as self-evident or theoretically transparent.[116] As for the impossi-

114. As mentioned in the previous endnote, most Muʿtazilites believe that some of God's speech is, in fact, created not in a receptacle.

115. This is *one* of the arguments the Muʿtazilites use. They use the same type of argument to conclude that God's speech when used to create something does not occur in a receptacle. This is the command 'Be', which God says in order to bring something into existence. Since the thing to be created has not yet come into existence, God cannot create the command 'Be' in it; and He equally cannot create the command in Himself, since He is not a receptacle of occurrents; therefore, He creates the command 'Be' not in a receptacle. It should be noted that there is a subtle reason why, for the Muʿtazilites, God can be a sayer through speech he creates in bodies but He cannot be a willer through will He creates in others. The divine speech is created in bodies that do not have the power to create this divine speech, but once the will is created in a body, it makes no sense to say that the body does not have the power to create this will in itself. Will requires no power; it is, in fact, prior to the power. So if a will is created in a body, then that body is a willer through that will and not God. In other words, according to the Muʿtazilites, God can give His speech to another yet it would still be His speech, but He cannot give His will to another without it becoming the other's will.

116. The third impossibility generates an infinite regress, which al-Ghazālī discusses in an earlier chapter. If one maintains that a will is originated by God to create the world, then one may ask whether this will occurred as an act of prior will or not. If one allows for this will to occur without there being an act of prior will, then it would be possible for an occurrent to occur without there being an act of prior will; but then one would no longer have grounds

bility of God's being a receptacle of occurrents, it can be apprehended only through subtle theoretical reflection, as we will mention.

# Third Characteristic

*[The attributes are eternal]*

All the divine attributes are eternal. If they were occurrents, the Eternal would be a receptacle of occurrents, which is absurd, or He would be described with an attribute that does not subsist in Him, which is more clearly absurd, as previously stated. No one affirms the occurrence of life and power, but some think that this is the case with respect to knowledge of occurrents,[117] will, and speech. We prove the impossibility of His being a receptacle of occurrents in three ways.

*The first proof.* Every occurrent is a contingent existent. The eternal posteriorly and anteriorly is a necessary existent. If contingency touches His attributes, that would be contrary to the necessity of His existence, since contingency and necessity are contradictory. Therefore, it is impossible for one whose essence is necessary to have contingent attributes. This is obvious in itself.

*The second proof,* which is the strongest. If an occurrent takes place in God's essence, then there is no alternative other than either that the imagination can conceive of an occurrent prior to which it is impossible for an occurrent to be, or that the imagination cannot conceive of such an occurrent but rather it is possible for every occurrent to have an occurrent prior to it. If the imagination cannot conceive of such an occurrent, then it necessarily follows that it is possible for God to be described as having

---

for insisting that the world must be the act of a prior will. On the other hand, if a prior will, which is required for the occurrence of the first will, is posited, the same question would be reiterated regarding the second will. A third will would be posited, and so on.

117. Some Islamic theologians distinguish between God's knowledge of occurrents and His knowledge of eternals. For instance, His knowledge that He is living is knowledge of something eternal, and hence it is itself eternal and not occurrent. However, His knowledge that an object *x* came into existence is occurrent, because the knowledge that *x* was not and that *x* is are two different cognitions, which depend on the status of *x*; hence they cannot be eternal. It is worth noting that the Islamic philosophers give a similar argument to conclude that God knows the universals but not the particulars, or, as Ibn Sīnā maintains, He knows the particulars in a universal way. They argued that given that knowledge of particular occurrents requires, as the previous argument shows, multiple different cognitions, that God's knowledge is reducible to his essence (the philosophers believe all divine attributes are reducible to the divine essence), and that God's essence is immutable, it follows that God cannot know the constantly changing particulars.

occurrents forever,[118] and this necessitates [the existence of a series of] occurrents that has no beginning; the proof of its impossibility has been constructed. No rational person affirmed this option. On the other hand, if the imagination can conceive of an occurrent prior to which it is impossible for an occurrent to take place, then the impossibility of God's receiving a prior occurrent in His essence is inevitably either by virtue of His essence or by virtue of something additional to Him. It is false that it is by virtue of something additional to Him, since it is possible to suppose the nonexistence of every additional thing that is posited. This necessitates the continuation of occurrents forever,[119] which is absurd. Hence the only option that remains is that it is impossible because He who is a necessary existent has a quality according to which it is impossible, by virtue of His essence, to receive prior occurrents. If that is impossible due to His essence for anterior eternity, then it is impossible for what is impossible to become possible.[120] This is of the same order as the anteriorly eternal impossibility of His receiving color, for this impossibility remains perpetually, because He, by virtue of His essence, does not receive colors, according to the consensus of all rational people. It is not possible that this impossibility turns into a possibility. The same applies to the rest of the occurrents.

It might be said:

This is shown to be false by the occurrence of the world. For it was possible prior to its occurrence and the imagination cannot conceive of a time prior to which the occurrence of the world was impossible; yet it is impossible for the world to have existed for anterior eternity; nevertheless, its occurrence was not impossible.

We say:

This inference is invalid. We affirm the impossibility of positing an essence that is incapable of receiving an occurrent, because it is a necessary existent, but then changes into becoming capable of receiving occurrents. The world, prior to its occurrence, had no essence that could be described either as receptive of occurrence or as unreceptive of occurrence. [If there were such an essence], it would have to change into becoming receptive of the possibility of occurrence; and in this case this objection would follow

118. Al-Ghazālī should have said "since eternity." The Arabic word is *abadan*, which, like 'forever', designates posterior eternity.

119. Similar to the preceding note, al-Ghazālī should have said "since eternity" instead of "forever," since he is referring to an infinite regress of occurrents.

120. The point here is that if by virtue of God's essence no occurrent could occur prior to a certain occurrent *x*, then there was an anteriorly eternal impossibility (i.e., the impossibility for having an occurrent in God's essence) that turned into possibility once *x* occurred. This is absurd; for according to the demonstration of the Third Proposition of the First Treatise whatever is eternal anteriorly is also eternal posteriorly.

in the course of our proof.[121] Yes, this objection necessarily follows from the Muʿtazilites' assertion that the world, when it was nonexistent, had an essence that was anteriorly eternal and receptive of occurrence, and was such that its occurrence took place after there had been no occurrence. However, this objection does not follow from our position. What we assert about the world is that it is an act, and an eternal act is impossible, since what is eternal cannot be an act.

*The third proof.* It is that we say:

If we suppose that an occurrent subsists in God's essence, then prior to that He is described either as having the opposite of that occurrent or as lacking that occurrent. If the having of the opposite occurrent or the lacking of that occurrent is anteriorly eternal,[122] then its cessation or removal is impossible, because the anteriorly eternal cannot be annihilated. On the other hand, if it is occurrent, then there is inevitably an occurrent prior to it, and likewise there must be one prior to this occurrent. This leads to occurrents that have no first occurrent, which is absurd.

The point becomes clear when the supposition is applied to a specific attribute such as speech, for example.[123] The Karrāmites say: "God is a sayer in

121. Al-Ghazālī is saying that the objection leveled against his previous proof would, indeed, be a valid consequence of his reasoning, *if* an anteriorly eternal essence is posited for the world prior to its occurrence and it is assumed that this essence was unreceptive of occurrence before the world actually came into existence. In such a case, this anteriorly eternal essence would have to change from being unreceptive of occurrence to being receptive of occurrence. Given that 'receptive of occurrence' means "capable of occurring," the conclusion of the previous objection is that at the moment of the world's coming into existence, the anteriorly eternal essence of the world would have to change from being incapable of occurring to being capable of occurring. A more complete reconstruction of al-Ghazālī's argument against the objection is this. (1) If the proof that al-Ghazālī gives to show that the eternal essence of God cannot change from being incapable of receiving an occurrent to being capable of receiving an occurrent is valid, and if one posits for the world prior to its occurrence an anteriorly eternal essence, then it would follow that either the world would never come into existence or it would exist for anterior eternity. This is so because, as al-Ghazālī's proof shows, an anteriorly eternal essence cannot change from being incapable of occurring to being capable of occurring. Hence if the world's anteriorly eternal essence were incapable of occurring, it would remain forever incapable of occurring, and consequently the world would never come into existence; and if it were capable of occurring, it would have occurred since eternity. (2) The occurrence of the world shows that both options are false. (3) Al-Ghazālī's original proof is valid. (4) Therefore, the world did not have an anteriorly eternal essence prior to its occurrence. Many (but not all) Muʿtazilites subscribe to the position that the world prior to its occurrence had an anteriorly eternal essence that was always capable of occurring, but it occurred when it did because a divine will to create the world occurred at that moment.

122. Literally, if that opposite or that lack is anteriorly eternal.

123. The supposition is the one stated at the outset of the previous paragraph—namely, that an occurrent subsists in God's essence. When it is applied to speech, we obtain the supposition that speech occurs in God's essence.

eternity, in the sense that He has the power to create speech in His essence. Whenever He originates something not in His essence, He originates in His essence His statement 'Be.'"[124] Thus certainly He was silent prior to the origination of this statement and this silence was anteriorly eternal. Also when Jahm says that knowledge occurs in God's essence, then surely He was heedless prior to that and His heedlessness was anteriorly eternal.[125] We say that cessation of anteriorly eternal silence or of anteriorly eternal heedlessness is impossible, according to the earlier proof for the impossibility of annihilating the anteriorly eternal.[126]

It may be said:

Silence is not a thing; rather, it consists in the absence of speech, and heedlessness consists in the absence of knowledge, ignorance, and its other opposites. Hence if speech is originated, nothing has ceased, for there was nothing but the anteriorly eternal essence, and it persists while other existents, which are speech and knowledge, are added to it. But to say that a *thing* has ceased is incorrect. Similar to this is the existence of the world, for it negates the anteriorly eternal nonexistence. Nonexistence, however,

124. This claim is based on a literal interpretation of several Qur'ānic verses that seem to say that when God wants to create something, He merely says "Be" and it comes into existence. Here is one of these verses: *His command, when He wills something, is to say to it "Be" and it is* (36:82). Some translators drop the phrase 'to it' to avoid the contradictory suggestion that the thing already exists. One might argue, however, that the caution is unwarranted, since the phrase 'to it' could be explained as addressing the representation of the thing in God's thought, rather than the thing itself. At any rate, dropping the phrase 'to it' from the translation is unfaithful to the original, since the verse says *yaqūl lah*. It should be noted that even on this interpretation the problem of God's addressing a representation requires a metaphorical reading in order to maintain that God is devoid of occurrents. Al-Ghazālī will advance such a metaphorical reading later in this treatise. He says that God's saying "Be" is a metaphor for the completion and execution of power. Some commentators on the Qur'ān offer a similar reading.

125. Jahm ibn Ṣafwān (d. AH 128/745 CE) is the founder of the Jahmiyya school of Islamic theology. He was considered by most of the Islamic schools a heretic and even an infidel. The Jahmites are fatalists: they deny human free will and power. Like the Mu'tazilites, the Jahmites believe that God's attributes are reducible to His essence, and hence they are not additional to the essence. Also like the Mu'tazilites, they believe that the Qur'ān is not eternal but is created by God. They maintain that to be a believer is simply to know God and to be an unbeliever is simply to be ignorant of God. Based on an extremely literal interpretation of certain Qur'ānic verses that speak of God as the First and the Last and of the destruction of all things, save God, at the end of time, they contend, contrary to the traditional Islamic belief, that paradise and hell will ultimately be destroyed. Jahm was killed for his beliefs. (See al-Shahrastānī, *al-Milal wa-l-Niḥal*, vol. 1, pp. 97–99; al-Baghdādī, *al-Farq bayn al-Firaq*, pp. 146–147; Amīn, *Fajr al-Islām*, pp. 272–273.)

126. The demonstration of this claim is given in al-Ghazālī's discussion of the Third Proposition of the First Treatise.

is not a thing that might be described as anteriorly eternal and whose cessation may be posited.

The answer may be given in two ways. One of them is that one's statement that silence is the absence of speech and is not an attribute, and that heedlessness is the absence of knowledge and is not an attribute is similar to one's statement that whiteness is the absence of blackness and the rest of the colors and is not a color and that rest is the absence of motion and is not a mode. This is absurd. The very proof that shows the impossibility of the one shows the impossibility of the other.

Our opponents in this matter must concede that rest is a quality that is additional to the mere absence of motion. For anyone who claims that rest is merely the absence of motion is incapable of proving the occurrence of the world. If the appearance of motion after rest indicates the occurrence of that which moves, then similarly the appearance of speech after silence indicates the occurrence of that which speaks, without there being a difference between the two cases.[127] By the very reasoning by which it is established that rest is a thing that is opposite to motion it is also established that silence is a thing that is opposite to speech, and that heedlessness is a thing

127. The conditional sentence supplies the reason why an opponent who claims that rest is merely the absence of motion would be incapable of establishing the occurrence of the world. The argument is this. Since he is an opponent, he also believes that silence is merely the absence of speech and that speech occurs in God's essence. Earlier al-Ghazālī said that the occurrence of speech in God's essence entails that God was silent for anterior eternity. Presumably, if speech is an occurrent, then there must be a first time for the occurrence of speech, because otherwise there would be an infinite regress of occurrents. Hence prior to this first occurrence of speech in God's essence, God must have been silent for anterior eternity. Now since rest, according to this particular opponent, is not an attribute but merely the absence of an attribute (motion), he cannot claim that rest entails the existence of that which is at rest. So he can account for the existence of the world either by assuming, like the philosophers, that motion is anteriorly eternal, and hence the world is also anteriorly eternal, or by insisting that the occurrence of motion entails the occurrence of that which moves (i.e., the world). But if he affirms the second option, he must be willing to affirm that the occurrence of speech entails the occurrence of the sayer (i.e., God). Al-Ghazālī says that the two cases are parallel. In each case there is an attribute (motion, speech) that occurred, and prior to its occurrence there was an anteriorly eternal absence (rest, silence) of that attribute. So if the occurrence of the attribute in one case entails the occurrence of the holder of the attribute, then the second case must follow the same logic. But the second case concerns God and His occurrent speech, and it is absurd to claim that God, who is the holder of speech, occurred when speech occurred (all parties accept that God is eternal). If the occurrence of speech does not entail the occurrence of God, then similarly the occurrence of motion does not entail the occurrence of the world. Thus the opponent who also believes that rest is merely the absence of motion must choose between two options: (1) admit that motion is anteriorly eternal, and hence the world, too, is anteriorly eternal and not occurrent, or (2) admit that the occurrence of motion does not entail the occurrence of the world. Either way this opponent cannot prove the occurrence of the world.

that is opposite to knowledge.[128] This reasoning is that if we apprehend the distinction between the two states of an entity being at rest and being in motion, then the entity is apprehended in both states, the distinction between the two states is apprehended, and this distinction consists merely in the removal of one state of affairs and the occurrence of another state of affairs; for a thing does not depart from itself. This shows that whatever is receptive of something must encompass it or its opposite. The same reasoning applies to speech and knowledge.

This reasoning is not applicable to the distinction between the existence of the world and its nonexistence, since in this case what is apprehended in both states is not a single essence to which existence happens. Yet this reasoning also does not entail two essences, for the world has no essence prior to its occurrence.[129] On the other hand, the eternal has, prior to the occurrence of speech, an essence apprehended in a state that is different from the state in which the essence is apprehended after the occurrence of speech. The one state is designated as silence and the other state as speech. These are two different states; in them a single essence is apprehended, which persists through both states. In its being silent, the essence has a condition, a quality, and a state, and it has a condition and a quality in its being a sayer, as it has a condition in its being at rest and in motion, and white and black. It is inescapable that the contrasting states are congruent.

The second way, which concerns detachment,[130] is to accept, as well, that

128. This is not the first time that al-Ghazālī uses *ma'nā* (literally, "meaning," "sense," "notion," or "concept") to designate a mode, an attribute, or an entity. Of course, al-Ghazālī does not intend by this usage to suggest that these modes and attributes are meanings or concepts. I translated *ma'nā* in this context as 'thing'.

129. If one maintains, as some Mu'tazilites do, that the world has an anteriorly eternal essence to which existence happens, then it is reasonable to assume that the world acquired a different essence when it came into existence. The reason for this duality is that existence, if it is considered an attribute, is unlike any other attribute. For instance, if motion happens to an object in a state of rest, the object becomes a moving object. In this case, what comes into existence is a mode. But if existence happens to an "object," what comes into existence is the object itself—not just a new state of an already existing object. In this case a nonexistent object is transformed into a second, existent object. It is worth noting that many Islamic philosophers and theologians use the term *māhiyya* (usually translated as 'quiddity') to describe a *dhāt* (usually translated as 'essence') without the attribution of existence.

130. The Arabic word is *infiṣāl*, which literally means "separation" or "detachment." Al-Ghazālī most likely refers to the second answer as one that "concerns detachment" (*al-wajh al-thānī fī al-infiṣāl*) because this answer accepts that silence is an essence's lack of speech. He uses the expression *infikāk 'an al-kalām* to mean "lack of speech." But *infikāk* means, among other things, "separation" and "detachment." Translating *infikāk 'an al-kalām* as "detachment from speech" instead of "lack of speech" brings an unwanted connotation—namely, that God and speech were joined and then they became separated, while speech continued to exist. I must mention, however, that my interpretation of al-Ghazālī's expres-

silence is not an [independent] thing but rather consists in an essence's lack of speech. The lack of speech is inevitably a state of that which lacks it—a state that ceases by the occurrence of speech. The state of lacking speech, whether it is called nonexistence, existence, a quality, or a condition, ceases by the occurrence of speech. However, what ceases is anteriorly eternal, yet we have stated that what is anteriorly eternal does not cease, whether it is an essence, a state, or a quality.[131] The impossibility is not due merely to its being an essence, but is due to its being anteriorly eternal. This does not apply to the existence of the world, for its nonexistence, together with its[132] being anteriorly eternal, is negated,[133] since nonexistence is not an essence, and it does not result in a state of an essence—a state, whose change and alteration in an essence may be posited. The difference is evident.[134]

It might be said:

The modes are many, and your opponent does not claim that the Creator is a receptacle of the occurrences of just any of the modes such as colors, pains, pleasures, and so on. Rather, the discussion concerns the seven attributes that you mentioned. There is no quarrel about the attributes of life and power; the quarrel concerns three attributes: speech, will, and knowledge; and it also concerns the meaning of the attributes of hearing and sight[135] for the one who posits them. These three attributes must be occurrents. Furthermore, it is impossible that they would subsist in something other than God; otherwise He would not be described as having them. Hence, they must occur in His essence. It follows that He is a receptacle of occurrents.

As for knowledge of occurrents, Jahm contends that it is an occurrent knowledge. That is because God (Exalted is He) now knows that the world came into existence prior to the present. If He knew in anterior eternity that the world came into existence, then this would be ignorance and not knowledge. On the other hand, if He did not know that it came into existence and now He knows, then it is shown that the knowledge that the world came into existence has occurred. The same applies to knowledge of any occurrent.

---

sion is not shared by all commentators on the text. For instance, al-Sharafāwī, the editor of the Jeddah edition, interprets al-Ghazālī's expression *al-wajh al-thānī fī al-infiṣāl* as saying "the second way of *rebuttal*."

131. As explained above, if the divine speech is occurrent, then there must have been a first occurrence of speech, which entails that there was an anteriorly eternal silence.

132. The pronoun 'its' refers to the nonexistence of the world.

133. That is, the anteriorly eternal nonexistence is negated when the world came into existence.

134. The difference here is between the case of God's anteriorly eternal lack of speech and the case of the world's anteriorly eternal nonexistence.

135. The Jeddah and Ankara editions add 'knowledge' to 'hearing and sight'.

Regarding the will, its occurrence is definite. For if it were anteriorly eternal, its object would have coexisted with it, since if power and will are fully available and all obstacles are removed, the object of the will necessarily takes place. How could the object of the will lag behind the will when power is unobstructed? It is because of this that the Muʿtazilites affirm the occurrence of the will not in a receptacle and the Karrāmites affirm its occurrence in God's essence. They might express this as His creating an origination in His essence whenever an object comes into existence, this being due to the will.

With respect to speech, how could it be anteriorly eternal yet contain information about what has passed? How could God have said in anterior eternity: *We sent Noah to his people,*[136] when He had not yet created Noah? How could He have said in anterior eternity to Moses: *So take off your shoes; you are in the sacred valley,*[137] when He had not yet created Moses? How could He have commanded and forbidden without there being anyone to be commanded and forbidden? If this is impossible, and it is necessarily known that He is a commander and a forbidder, and that it is impossible for Him to be so from eternity, then it is known decidedly that He became a commander and a forbidder after He was neither. This is the only meaning of His being a receptacle of occurrents.

The response is that we say: "If we resolve this doubt concerning these three attributes, an independent proof arises refuting the claim that God is a receptacle of occurrents. For no one affirmed this claim except by reason of this doubt. If it is cleared up, then any assertion based on it would be as false as asserting that God is a receptacle of colors and other matters, which no proof has ever indicated that He might be described as having."

Thus we say:

The Creator (Exalted is He) has known since eternity that the world comes into existence at the time of its origination. This knowledge is a single cognition that entails in anterior eternity the knowledge that the world would later be, at the time of its occurrence that it is, and after that that it was. These states of the world follow each other, while this cognition remains evident to God and unchanging. Rather, what changes is the states of the world.

We demonstrate this with an example. We assume that one of us has knowledge of Zayd's arriving at sunrise, that he attained this knowledge prior to sunrise, that his knowledge has not ceased but persists, and that

136. Qurʾān, 71:1.
137. Qurʾān, 20:12.

no other knowledge has been created for him at sunrise. What is the state of that person at sunrise? Is he a knower of Zayd's arrival or not a knower? It is impossible that he is not a knower, since the knowledge of Zayd's arrival is assumed to persist through sunrise, and he now knows that the sun is rising; hence it follows that he is necessarily a knower of Zayd's arrival. If this knowledge persists after the elapsing of sunrise, then he must know that Zayd has arrived. One cognition has encompassed that the arrival will be, that it is, and that it was. This is how God's eternal knowledge, which is necessarily inclusive of all occurrents, ought to be understood. By analogy to this the case of divine hearing and sight ought to be inferred. For each one of them is an attribute such that through it an object of sight or an object of hearing is apprehended at the time of the object's origination but without the origination of that attribute or of any matter in it. Rather, the occurrents are the objects of hearing and sight.

The conclusive proof for this is that the difference between the states of a single thing, in accordance with its being classified as something that was [after it exists] and as something that is while it exists, does not exceed the difference between distinct essences. It is understood that knowledge does not multiply by multiplying the essences. Thus how could it multiply by multiplying the states of a single essence? If one knowledge can encompass distinct and dissimilar essences, then why would it be impossible for one knowledge to encompass the states of a single essence in relation to the past and the future?

There is no doubt that Jahm denies that the objects of God's knowledge are finite. Moreover, he does not posit infinite cognitions. Hence it follows that he must admit that one knowledge attaches to numerous distinct objects of knowledge. How could he then deem this unlikely with respect to the states of a single object of knowledge? Its proof is that if the cognition of each occurrent originates in God, then that cognition would itself inevitably be either known or unknown. If it is unknown, then it is impossible, because it itself is an occurrent. If it is possible that God does not know this sort of occurrent, then, considering that its occurring in His essence makes it more proper for it to be evident to Him, His not knowing those occurrents that are distinct from His essence is even more likely. On the other hand, if it is known, then either it requires another cognition and this cognition requires infinitely many other cognitions, which is absurd, or He knows both the occurrents and His knowledge of those occurrents with the same knowledge. Thus the essence of knowledge is one and it has two objects of knowledge, one of which is this essence itself and the other is the essence of the occurrent. The possibility of one knowledge that attaches to distinct objects of knowledge inevitably follows from this. How could it then be impossible for one knowledge to attach to the states of a single object of knowledge, while the knowledge is unified and free from change?[138]

With respect to the will, we have mentioned that its occurrence without another will is impossible, that its occurrence through another will leads to an infinite regress, and that the attachment of the eternal will to occurrents is not impossible. It is impossible for the will to attach to something eternal. The world is not eternal, because the will is attached to its origination and not to its existence in eternity. This has been explained earlier.

Similarly, a Karrāmite says that God creates in His essence an origination when the world occurs. Through this origination the world's occurrence takes place at that time. It is said to him: "What was that which determined the origination that occurred in God's essence at that time?" It requires another determinant. Therefore, they are committed with respect to origination to that to which the Muʿtazilites are committed with respect to the occurrent will.

Some people say that this origination is God's saying "Be," which is a sound. This is absurd in three ways. One of them is the impossibility of a sound's subsisting in His essence. The second is that His saying "Be" is an occurrent too. If it occurs without His saying "Be" to "Be," then let the world occur without God's saying "Be" to it. On the other hand, if His saying "Be" requires, in order for it to occur, another saying, then the second saying would require a third, and the third a fourth, and so it regresses infinitely. Furthermore, the one whose mind's achievement is to assert that

138. Al-Ghazālī says that if God's knowledge of an occurrent is itself an occurrent, then either this occurrent cognition is known to God or it is unknown to Him. He argues that it cannot be unknown to God, because if God knows all the occurrents that do not occur in His essence, then He surely knows all the occurrents that do. On the other hand, if God's knowledge of an occurrent is known to Him, then He has a second-order knowledge whose object is the first-order knowledge of that specific occurrent. Now these two cognitions, first-order and second-order, are either two distinct cognitions or identical. If they are distinct, then the same reasoning applies to the second-order cognition, generating a third-order cognition that is distinct from its object, which is the second-order cognition. The reasoning may be repeated ad infinitum, yielding an infinite hierarchy of cognitions. Al-Ghazālī, of course, rejects infinite hierarchies and infinite regressions. This leaves only the current option—namely, that the second-order knowledge is identical with the first-order knowledge. Thus we have a knowledge that is a knowledge of itself and of the specific occurrent (in al-Ghazālī's terms, a knowledge with one essence and two objects: the knowledge's essence itself and the occurrent's essence). This establishes al-Ghazālī's point that it is possible to have one knowledge that attaches to many distinct objects. He finally says that if such knowledge is possible, then it is equally possible that there is one knowledge that encompasses the different states of a single essence. He needs this conclusion in order to show that God's knowledge of the various temporal states of the world's existence is one, eternal knowledge.

God's saying "Be" occurs in His essence as many times as there are occurrents at any moment of time ought not be engaged in debate. Thus, there would accumulate thousands of thousands of sounds at each moment. It is clear that the *nūn* and *kāf* cannot be uttered simultaneously; rather the *nūn* ought to be uttered after the *kāf*,[139] since the superimposition of the letters is impossible, and even if they are superimposed and are not ordered, they would not be speech or a comprehensible utterance. Just as it is impossible to superimpose two different letters, it is also impossible to superimpose two similar letters. It is inconceivable that there are at a single moment a thousand thousand *kāf*s, just as it is inconceivable that there are *kāf*s and *nūn*s. It is incumbent upon those people to ask God to provide them with an intellect, for that is more important for them than busying themselves with theoretical reflection.

The third is that God's saying "Be" addresses the world in the state of nonexistence or in the state of existence. If it is in the state of nonexistence, then the nonexistent cannot comprehend the address. So how could it obey His saying "Be" by coming into existence? And if it is in the state of existence, then how could "Be" be said to that which has being? Observe what God (Exalted is He) does to the one who goes astray from His path. Because of the feebleness of his mind, he does not attain an understanding of the Exalted's statement, *His command, when He wills something, is to say to it "Be" and it is*,[140] and he does not understand that it is a metaphor for the execution and completion of divine power, so that he is led to these embarrassments.

We seek refuge in God from shame and scandal on the day of the greatest fright, the day when the contents of the hearts are revealed and the hidden thoughts are examined. On that day God's veil is removed, exposing the corrupt beliefs of those who are ignorant. It will be said to the ignorant who believes about God (Exalted is He) and His attributes an erroneous opinion: *You were heedless of this. Now We have removed your veil, and piercing is your sight today.*[141]

As for speech, it is eternal. What they ruled out because of the Exalted's statement, *take off your shoes*, and His statement, *We sent Noah to his people*, is based on their supposing divine speech to be sound, which is impossible to reside in God. It is not impossible if it is understood to be inner speech. We say that there subsists in God's essence a tiding about the sending of Noah. Before sending him, it is expressed as 'We will send him', and after sending him as 'We sent him'. The expression varies with the variation of

139. The Arabic word for 'Be' is *kun*. It consists of two consonants *kāf* (*k*) and *nūn* (*n*) and a short vowel *u*.

140. Qur'ān, 36:82.

141. Qur'ān, 50:22.

the states, but the meaning that subsists in God's essence does not vary. Its reality is that it is a tiding that attaches to an informer; this tiding is the sending of Noah at the determined time. This does not vary with the variation of the states, as previously stated regarding knowledge.

Similarly, the Exalted's statement, *take off your shoes*, is an expression that indicates a command. A command is a demand and a request subsisting in the self of the commander. It is not a necessary condition for its subsistence that the one who is commanded should exist. It is possible for it to subsist in the commander's self prior to the existence of the one who is commanded. If the one who is commanded exists, he becomes commanded by virtue of that very demand, without another demand made anew

How many a person who has no son is such that there subsists in his self a demand of his son to seek knowledge if he were to exist; for he may say in his mind to his son: "Seek knowledge." This demand is made efficacious in his mind through the possibility of existence,[142] since if the son were to exist, and if intelligence were created for him as well as the knowledge of what is in the father's mind without assuming the formation of an audible expression, and if the demand is assumed to persist through his existence, then the son would know that he is commanded by the father to seek knowledge, without the commencement anew of a demand in the self. Rather, the same demand persists.

Indeed, the customary course is that the son would only have knowledge through an expression that indicates the inner demand. Thus the father's verbal statement "Seek knowledge" is an indication of the demand that is in his self, whether the demand occurs at that time or it subsists in his self prior to the existence of his son. This is how the subsistence of a command in God's essence ought to be understood. The expressions that indicate it are occurrents, and what is indicated is eternal. The existence of what is

142. Shortly it will be clear that the existence referred to here is the possible existence of the son. The Arabic phrase that I translated as 'through the possibility of existence' is *'alā taqdīr al-wujūd*. The word *taqdīr* has many meanings, such as "estimation," "appraisal," "supposition," "presumption," "anticipation," "respect," and "worth." In Islamic theology the word has a very specific and technical meaning. It is the assignment of a defining term to each existent. It is almost certain that al-Ghazālī does not intend this technical meaning here. It can be claimed, with justice, that the context strongly suggests interpreting *taqdīr al-wujūd* as the possibility of existence. 'Possibility' is not a farfetched meaning of *taqdīr*, for the word implies (among other things) the presumption of existence. Of course, one can presume something to exist without its being possible. (One might simply make an incorrect presumption.) However, the conditional that follows the expression *taqdīr al-wujūd* (i.e., the 'since' clause) makes it clear that the implication is that the existence of the son is possible and not only presumed.

indicated does not require the existence of the one who is commanded; rather his existence is imagined so long as it is possible for the one who is commanded to exist.[143] If it is impossible for him to exist, then the existence of a demand aimed at one whose existence is known to be impossible might be unimaginable. Thus we do not say that there subsists in God's essence a demand for an act by one whose existence is impossible, but by one whose existence is possible; and that is not impossible.

It might be said:

Do you say that God is a commander and a forbidder since eternity? If you say, "He is a commander," then how could He be a commander if He has no one to command? On the other hand, if you say "No," then He has become a commander after He was not.

We say that our associates disagree in their response to this question.[144] The chosen response is that we say that this is an investigation one of whose endpoints concerns the concept and the other, the linguistic usage of the term. So far as the concept is concerned, it has become evident. It is that an eternal command is intelligible, even if it is prior to the existence of the one who is commanded, as with the case of the son.

It remains to say:[145] "Is the name 'commander' used to designate God after the existence of the one who is commanded and his comprehension? Or may it be used to designate Him before that?" This is a terminological matter; a theoretical investigator should not be occupied with such matters. However, the truth is that it is permissible to be used to designate Him, just as it is permissible to call God "powerful" before the existence of the object of power. They do not rule out a powerful agent for whom no object of power exists. Rather, they say that a powerful agent requires an object of power that is known but not [necessarily] existent.[146] Similarly, a commander requires someone to be commanded who is known but not [neces-

143. Again we encounter a derivative of the root *qadara*. The first was *taqdīr* (see the previous note), which I translated as 'possibility'. Now we have *muqaddar* in the expression *muqaddar al-wujūd*. For similar reasons, I translated *muqaddar* as 'possible' rather than as 'presumed'. The textual evidence is strong. The sentence that follows considers the case when the existence of the one commanded is *impossible*.

144. The 'associates' (*aṣḥāb*) here refers to al-Ghazālī's fellow Ashʿarites.

145. 'It remains to say' is the reading in Jeddah edition. The reading in the Ankara edition is 'It ought to be said'.

146. Al-Ghazālī uses the word *maʿlūm* (known) in a sense that does not imply existence. So '$x$ is *maʿlūm*' means "it is known that $x$'s existence is possible." Hence the sentence says that for an agent to be called "powerful" (i.e., "one who has power") there must be possible objects that are known to be within the reach of the agent's power. In this sense the existence of power requires known objects of power and it does not require existent objects of power.

sarily] existent. The existence of that which is nonexistent is known prior to its existence.[147] Indeed, a command requires an act that is commanded as it requires one who is commanded, and it also requires a commander, while the act that is commanded may be nonexistent.[148] It should not be asked, How could he be a commander without there being an act that is commanded? Rather, it should be said that he has commanded an act that is known; it is not a condition that the act exist, but it is a condition that it be known.[149] In fact, if someone, in the course of advising his son, commands him to do something and then he dies, yet the son fulfills what he was advised to do, it would be said that he complied with his father's command, while the commander[150] is nonexistent and the command in his self is also nonexistent. In spite of this, we apply the expression 'compliance with the command'. Thus if it is not required for one's compliance with a command that the commander or the command exist, and for a command to be a

147. The Arabic sentence is *wa-l-maʿdūm maʿlūm al-wujūd qabl al-wujūd*. A very literal translation would be: "And the nonexistent has known existence prior to the existence." Given the sense of *maʿlūm* (known) with which al-Ghazālī is operating here (see the previous note), the meaning of the sentence is that what is nonexistent is known to be possible prior to its actual existence.

148. The Arabic sentence is elliptical. My translation is literal and so preserves this quality. Al-Ghazālī uses four derivatives of the root *amara*: *amr*, *maʾmūr bih*, *maʾmūr*, and *āmir*. *Amr* is the actual command, such as 'Seek knowledge'. *Maʾmūr bih* is the act whose performance is solicited by the command (i.e., the act that is commanded); for instance, the seeking of knowledge. *Maʾmūr* is the one who receives the command (i.e., the one who is commanded). And *āmir* is the one who issues the command (i.e., the commander). On the surface the sentence seems to be at odds with itself and with the rest of the passage. It seems that it asserts that a command (*amr*) requires an act that is commanded (*maʾmūr bih*), one who is commanded (*maʾmūr*), and a commander (*āmir*). Yet the sentence also says that, whereas a command requires a commander, the act that is commanded need not actually exist. There is a simple interpretation of this sentence that removes the apparent inconsistencies. The sentence has two components. (1) A command requires an act that is commanded as it requires one who is commanded; these two requirements are on a par, that is, the command requires the first as much as it requires the second. Since al-Ghazālī earlier suggested that a command does not require the actual presence, but only the possible existence, of the one who is commanded, his now saying that the two requirements are on a par indicates that a command similarly does not require the actual presence of the act that is commanded. (2) A command does require the actual existence of a commander even though the act that is commanded may be absent. Statements (1) and (2) are thus fully consistent. However, al-Ghazālī later says that even the actual existence of the commander is not required in order for there to be a command. Thus al-Ghazālī gradually reduces the number of aspects of a command that have to have actual existence in the present to zero.

149. Reading *maʿlūm* (known) instead of *maʿdūm* (nonexistent), which is the reading in the original. As explained in note 145 above, the sense of *maʿlūm* here is that 'whose possible existence is known'.

150. *Āmir* (commander) is the reading in the Jeddah edition. In the Ankara edition it is *amr* (command).

genuine command it is not required that the act that is commanded exist, then why should the existence of the one who is commanded be required?

Both the role of the concept and the role of the term have become evident from this discussion. The investigation concerns only them. That is what we wanted to discuss in general and in detail with respect to the impossibility of God's being a receptacle of occurrents.

# Fourth Characteristic

*[The names that are derived from these divine attributes are true of God eternally]*

The names that are derived for God (Exalted is He) from these attributes are true of Him eternally—anteriorly and posteriorly. He is eternally living, a knower, powerful, a hearer, seer, and sayer.[151] As for the names that are derived for Him from acts, such as 'the Provider', 'the Creator', 'the Exalter', and 'the Debaser', there is disagreement whether they are true of him for anterior eternity or not.[152] However, if this matter is made clear, it will be evident that no disagreement about it is possible.

The comprehensive statement is that the names by which God are called are of four categories. In the first [category are those names that] designate only his essence, such as 'the Existent'. These are true of Him for anterior and posterior eternity.

In the second [category are those names that] designate the essence with the addition of a negation. For instance, 'the Anteriorly Eternal' designates an existence that is not preceded by nothingness for anterior eternity; 'the Posteriorly Eternal' designates an existence with the negation of its being succeeded by nothingness for posterior eternity; 'the One' designates an existence with the negation of a partner; and 'the Self-Sufficient' designates an existence with the negation of need. These too are true of Him for anterior and posterior eternity, since what is negated of Him is negated by virtue of His essence; hence it accompanies the essence perpetually.

In the third [category are those names that] designate existence together with an attribute that is additional to it and that has implied meaning,[153]

151. Al-Ghazālī does not mention the seventh attribute, will (so God is a willer).

152. The question concerns their application in *anterior eternity* because once the world was created and God actually provided for its inhabitants, it is true of Him that He is the Provider. It is a matter of dispute among the Islamic theologians whether descriptions, such as 'the Provider', are true of Him before the relevant acts were performed.

153. 'An attribute that has implied meaning' is my translation of *ṣifa min ṣifāt al-maʿnā*. A very literal translation would be "one of the attributes of the meaning," which makes little

such as 'the Living', 'the Powerful', 'the Sayer', 'the Knower', 'the Willer', 'the Hearer', and 'the Seer', and what is based on these seven attributes, such as 'the Commander', 'the Forbidder', 'the Aware', and others like them. These, for the one who believes in the eternity of all the attributes, are also true of God for anterior and posterior eternity.[154]

In the fourth [category are those names that] designate existence in relation to one of His acts, such as 'the Bountiful', 'the Provider', 'the Creator', 'the Exalter', 'the Debaser', and others like them. These are subject to disagreement. One group says that they are true of Him for anterior eternity, since if they were not, then His having such attributes would necessitate change. Others say that they are not true of Him for anterior eternity, since there was no anteriorly eternal creation; ḥence how could He be a creator for anterior eternity?

What clarifies the matter is that a sword in a sheath is called "a cutter," and when it cuts—during the state of actual contact—it is also called "a cutter." They have two different meanings. The sword in the sheath is a cutter *in potentiality*, and when the cutting takes place, it is a cutter *in actuality*. Similarly, the water in a jug is called "thirst-quenching" and at the time of drinking is also called "thirst-quenching." These are two different usages. The sense in which a sword in a sheath is called "a cutter" is that the quality through which cutting takes place is present in the sword. The absence of cutting at present is not due to a deficiency in the sword's essence, its sharpness, or its readiness; rather it is due to another matter that is beyond its essence.

In the same sense in which a sword in a sheath is called "a cutter" the name 'the Creator' is true of God (Exalted is He) in anterior eternity. For if

---

sense. The intended idea is that although these attributes are additional to the essence of God, they are derived from what God's essence means. Al-Ghazālī argued in the first part of this treatise that these seven attributes are established by reflecting on what it means to be the God of the world, that is, the necessary existent who initiates all occurrents.

154. This sentence must be qualified. Al-Ghazālī intends by 'all the attributes' the seven divine attributes of life, will, knowledge, power, speech, hearing, and sight. If one interprets 'all the attributes' unrestrictedly, the sentence would be a tautology: of course if one believes in the eternity of all the attributes, the seven principal ones and the derived ones, then he would believe that every name that is based on any of these attributes is true of God eternally. However, the point is more complex than my remark suggests. An Ash'arite theologian, such as al-Ghazālī, might claim that God has only seven real attributes. These are part of what God is. While it is possible to suppose that there might have been no creation, it is not possible to suppose that God might have no knowledge. On this view, it could be claimed that there are divine *attributes* (i.e., the seven principal ones) and divine *names*, the latter of which designate God's essence, His essence with a negation, His essence with a real attribute, or His essence as related to one of His acts. Al-Ghazālī's position in his discussion of the Fourth Characteristic is rather similar to the one stated here.

the creation takes place in actuality, this would not be due to a matter that was at first not in God's essence and then happened anew. Indeed, everything that is required to bring about the act of creation exists in anterior eternity. On the other hand, the Creator' is not true of God in anterior eternity in the sense in which a sword in the state of cutting is called "a cutter." This is what concerns the meaning [of these names]. It has become evident that he who says that this name is not true of God in anterior eternity is correct and intends the second sense; and he who says that it is true of God in anterior eternity is also correct and intends the first sense. Once the matter is clarified, disagreement ceases.

This is the sum of what we want to state in the treatise on the divine attributes. It comprises seven articles; and the chapter on power branched into three questions, and the one on speech into five objections; and four characteristics that are common to the attributes were covered. Thus the total is close to twenty articles. But the seven are the principal articles, although every article is founded on other articles through which it is established. Let us busy ourselves now with the Third Treatise of the book.

# THIRD TREATISE

∴

## *On the Acts of God (Exalted is He)*

THE ENTIRETY OF THE ACTS OF GOD (EXALTED IS HE) ARE CONTINGENT,[1] AND NONE OF THEM MAY BE DESCRIBED AS OBLIGATORY.

WE STATE IN THIS TREATISE SEVEN PROPOSITIONS.

We claim that it is possible for God (Exalted is He) not to assign obligations to His servants, that it is possible for Him to assign obligations to them beyond their ability, that it is possible for Him to bring suffering upon them without compensating them and through no fault of theirs,[2] that it is not obligatory for Him to care for their well-being, that it is not obligatory for Him to reward obedience and punish disobedience, that nothing is made obligatory for a person by virtue of reason but only by virtue of the revelation, and that it is not obligatory for God to send messengers,[3] and if He

1. I translated *jā'iza* (or *yajūz*) here as 'contingent' and below as 'possible'. The context suggests this variation. The first occurrence of *jā'z* indicates that none of the acts of God is necessary, that is, it is possible for Him to perform an act and it is possible for Him to refrain from the act. This is the sense of contingent. Below, in his list of the seven propositions, he indicates that God might have performed an alternative act. This is the sense of possible.

2. My translation of the Third Proposition is somewhat liberal. A literal translation would be elliptical. Here is a literal translation of the original: "it is possible for Him to bring suffering upon the servants without compensation or fault."

3. The list of the seven propositions ends here. The last sentence is complementary to the last proposition.

does send messengers, it is neither bad nor absurd, and furthermore it is possible to confirm their truthfulness by means of miracles.

The totality of these propositions is based on an investigation into the meanings of 'obligatory', 'good', and 'bad'. The investigators waded into this matter and elaborated at length on whether the intellect could deem something good or bad and whether it could obligate. There is much confusion because they did not gather the correct meanings of these terms and because their terminology varies. How can two opponents discuss whether the intellect could obligate or not,[4] while they have not yet attained an understanding of the meaning of 'obligatory'—an understanding that is final and agreed upon among themselves?

Thus let us begin by investigating the terms. It is essential to be clear about the meanings of six terms: 'obligatory', 'good', 'bad', 'frivolity', 'foolishness', and 'wisdom';[5] for these terms are related, and their vagueness is the source of mistakes. The appropriate course in such investigations is to set aside the terms and acquire the meanings by the intellect using different expressions, and then pay attention to the terms that are being investigated and look into the variation in terminology.

We say regarding the term 'obligatory' [*wājib*] that it is undoubtedly used to describe an act. The [alternative] usage by which the Eternal and the setting of the sun are called 'necessary' [*wājib*] is not our concern here.[6] It is apparent that if performing an act is not preponderant over refraining from it, so that it is not more likely for an agent to perform it than to refrain from it, then it is not called "obligatory." If its performance is preponderant and more likely, then here too is not called "obligatory" due to just any type of preponderance, but the preponderance must be of a specific type.[7]

It is a given that an act might be such that it is known or imagined that

4. *Al-ʿaql yūjib am lā* (the intellect obligates or not) is the reading in the Ankara edition. In the Jeddah edition, it is *al-fiʿl wājib am lā* (the act is obligatory or not).

5. These terms in Arabic are, respectively, *al-wājib*, *al-ḥasan*, *al-qabīḥ*, *al-ʿabath*, *al-safah*, and *al-ḥikma*.

6. The English does not capture the meaning of the original. The source of the difficulty is that in Arabic there is one word that means necessary, obligatory, and one's duty, which is *wājib*. Al-Ghazālī is making clear that he is not discussing the sense of *wājib* as necessary. The sense of necessary is intended when we describe the Eternal or the setting of the sun as *wājib*. The intended sense of *wājib* in this treatise is "obligatory" or "a matter of duty." In Islamic law the word *farḍ* is also used to describe an act or a ritual that is religiously obligatory (or equivalently, a religious duty). Although most schools of Islamic law treat *wājib* and *farḍ* synonymously, there are Islamic jurists (mostly Ḥanafites) who distinguish between *wājib* and *farḍ*.

7. The Ankara edition reads "there must be a specific preponderance to its performance." I adopted the reading in the Jeddah edition.

refraining from it would lead to harm—a harm that would either come soon in this worldly life or far in the future in the next life, and would be either moderate and tolerable or so great as to be intolerable. The classification of an act and the types of its preponderance into these divisions is established by the intellect without [the need for] express terminology.

So let us return to the term and say:

It is a given that what prevents[8] moderate, tolerable harm is not called "obligatory." For a thirsty person who does not immediately drink water will be harmed a little, but it is not said that drinking is obligatory for him. It is also a given that what does not occasion harm at all and the performing of which leads to benefit is not called "obligatory." For trade, earning money, and supererogatory rituals all lead to benefits, but they are not called "obligatory." Indeed, what is specifically called "obligatory" is that act the refraining from which leads to definite harm. If this harm obtains in the next life—I mean the hereafter—and is known through the revelation, we call the act "obligatory," and if the harm obtains in this worldly life and is known through reason, in this case too the act might be called "obligatory." The one who does not affirm the revelation might say that it is obligatory for a hungry person who is dying of hunger to eat if he finds bread. He means by 'eating is obligatory' that performing it is preponderant over refraining from it because of the harm that is caused by refraining from it. We do not forbid this convention according to the law.[9] The terms are open to all and there are no restrictions on them either due to the revelation or

8. In the original it is *mā fīh*, which may be translated as 'what contains' or 'what involves'. I substituted 'prevents', since the context clearly implies that if *refraining from* an act leads to little harm, then it is not considered obligatory.

9. The Sixth Proposition, stated at the beginning of this treatise, asserts that nothing is made obligatory for a person by virtue of reason but only by virtue of the revelation. In this passage al-Ghazālī permits an act to be described as obligatory if refraining from it leads to a definite harm in this life and this harm is known through reason. He does not say that such an act is definitely obligatory but that it *might be* described as obligatory. I think there is an interpretation that renders the two statements consistent with one another. One can maintain that although, strictly speaking, an act is made obligatory solely by virtue of the revelation, nevertheless, an act may be conventionally described as obligatory by virtue of reason, if refraining from it leads to a definite harm in this life, where such harm is known by reason. I think al-Ghazālī could be alluding here to a standard problem with consequentialism: what are the criteria by which a bad consequence is judged to be bad? Thus if refraining from an act leads to definite harm in this life, why is this harm deemed "bad," and hence the act deemed "obligatory"? What if a person is willing to experience this type of "harm" believing, say, that it cleanses his soul; is he still obligated to perform the act? On the other hand, if the harm is in the hereafter and the revelation identifies it as definite harm, then what prevents this harm is obligatory. I am not claiming that this is certainly al-Ghazālī's underlying doctrine. But it does explain away the apparent inconsistency.

due to reason. Linguistic practice would bar a usage of a term if it fails to describe the subject matter as it is known.[10]

We have arrived at two meanings for 'obligatory', both of which are based on encountering harm. One of them, however, is more general, because it is not specific to the hereafter;[11] the second is more specific and it is our usage.[12] 'Necessary' [*wājib*] may be used in a third sense,[13] which is that whose non-occurrence leads to an absurdity; for example, when it is said that if the occurrence of something is known, then its occurrence is necessary. Its meaning is that if it were not to occur, then knowledge would become ignorance, and that is impossible.[14] Thus the meaning of its being necessary is that its opposite is absurd. Let this third sense be called 'necessary' [*wājib*].

As for the term 'good', the basis of its meaning is that the act in relation to the agent divides into three categories. One of them is that it is in accordance with him, that is, it serves his purpose; the second is that it is contrary to his purpose; and the third is that there is no purpose in performing it or refraining from it. This division is established by the intellect. The act that is in accordance with the agent is called "good" for him; there is no meaning to its being good other than its accord with his purpose. The act that is contrary to his purpose is called "bad"; there is no meaning to its being bad other than its contrariety to his purpose. The act that is neither contrary to nor in accordance with his purpose is called "frivolity," that is, there is no benefit in it to begin with; and the one who does frivolities is called "frivolous" and might be called "foolish." The one who does bad

10. Literally, linguistic practice would bar it if it is not according to the known subject matter.

11. *Al-ākhira* (the hereafter) is the reading in the Jeddah edition. In the Ankara edition, it is *al-ākhar* (the other).

12. I followed the Cairo edition in reading *wa-huwa iṣṭilāḥunā* (and it is our usage) instead of *wa-huwa iṣṭilāḥī* (and it is conventional), which is the reading in the Jeddah and Ankara editions. The general sense of 'obligatory' concerns acts the refraining from which results in definite harm, and the specific sense concerns acts the refraining from which results in definite harm that is experienced in the hereafter and is known through the revelation. It is the second sense that al-Ghazālī intends by 'obligatory' in this treatise.

13. Again, the oddity of this expression is because what is necessary and what is obligatory are denoted by one term in Arabic, which is *wājib*. Thus al-Ghazālī here is describing yet another sense of *wājib*. This sense corresponds to 'necessary' in English and not to 'obligatory'. Although there is an Arabic word—namely, *ḍarūrī*—that means necessary but not obligatory, this is not the term al-Ghazālī uses here.

14. The concept of knowledge al-Ghazālī employs is similar to what is supposed in Western philosophy—namely, that knowledge entails truth. So if S knows that *x* occurred, then it must be true that *x* occurred. If it turns out that *x* did not occur, then S believes something false (al-Ghazālī calls believing what is false "ignorance"). But if S believes something false, then he does not know it, which contradicts the assumption that S knows that *x* occurred.

things—I mean an act that is harmful to him—is called "foolish." The name 'foolish' is more applicable to him than to the frivolous.

All of this is true when attention is paid only to the agent and when the act relates only to the agent's purpose. If it relates to someone other than the agent and it is in accordance with this other person's purpose, then it is called "good" for the one with whose purpose it accords; and if it is contrary [to that person's purpose], it is called "bad."[15] If it is in accordance with one person's purpose but not another's,[16] it is called "good" for the first and "bad" for the other. For the terms 'good' and 'bad' are based on whether there is accord or contrariety, and these are relational matters that vary with people. They even vary with the states of a single person, and they vary with the purposes attached to a single state. An act might be in accordance with a person in one way and contrary to him in another way; hence it would be good for him in one way and bad for him in another way.

He who has no religion may deem it good to commit adultery with the wife of another and consider winning her a blessing; and he would deem bad the act of the one who exposes his secret and would call him "a slanderous person who has done a bad deed." The devout, on the other hand, would call him "a righteous person who has done a good deed." Each one of them uses the terms 'good' and 'bad' according to his purpose. Indeed, a king might be killed; all of his enemies would deem the act of the killer good, and all of his supporters would deem it bad.

Such variation is even present with respect to the sensible good. There are those who are created with a pleasant, natural complexion that is a shade of brown. A person with such a complexion loves this brown shade of skin and deems it good. While a person who is created with a fair, reddish complexion dislikes brown skin, deems it bad, and considers those who love it and think it good to be foolish.

This conclusively shows that good and bad, for all mankind, are descriptions of two relational qualities that vary with that to which they relate, and not of qualities of essences, which do not vary with relations. It is surely possible that a thing is good for Zayd and bad for ʿAmr, but it is not possible that a thing is black for Zayd and white for ʿAmr, since colors are not relational qualities.

If you understood the meaning,[17] then know there are also three usages for the term 'good'. One speaker uses it for whatever serves a purpose, whether the purpose is near at hand or far in the future. Another speaker

15. That is, it is bad for the one whose purpose was thwarted by the act.

16. Literally, if it is in accordance with one person but not another. Al-Ghazālī intends that it is harmful to another.

17. That is, the meaning of 'good' and 'bad'.

uses it specifically for what serves a purpose in the hereafter; and this is what the revelation deems good, that is, it exhorts its performance and promises a reward for it; and it is the usage of our peers.[18]

The bad, for every group of people, is what opposes good. Thus the former is more general and the latter is more specific.[19] According to this convention some people who do not fear God may describe the acts of God (Exalted is He) as bad if they are not in accordance with their purposes. For this reason, you see them cursing the celestial sphere and the eternal duration;[20] they say: "The celestial sphere has become senile;[21] how bad its acts are." And they know that the Agent is the creator of the celestial sphere. This is why God's Messenger (may God bless him and grant him peace) says: "Do not curse the eternal duration, for God is the eternal duration."[22]

There is a third usage of 'good', as when it is said: "An act of God is good no matter what it is, although God has no needs."[23] The meaning of this is that there are no repercussions to God or blame of Him because of the act, for He is the agent in His kingdom, in which no one else has a share.

18. By 'our peers' he refers to the jurists and theologians who subscribe to Sunni orthodoxy. In what follows al-Ghazālī interrupts the list of the three usages of 'good' to introduce the convention for using 'bad'. After that he returns to the third usage of 'good'. It is interesting that what al-Ghazālī is defending here is a form of ethical egoism. The good with respect to *all* people is that for which they will be rewarded in the hereafter. On the other hand, what is called 'good' in this worldly life is what serves a person's purpose; hence it is relative to that person's specific purpose. Since what is good in this life may be bad in the hereafter, and since the good of the hereafter is the *true* good (for it serves our best interest in the long run), the good in this life, which is known by reason rather than by the revelation, is merely an appearance of the good. It follows that what is truly good, like what is truly obligatory, is known only through the revelation, and not through reason.

19. The term 'bad' is more general because it is an umbrella term that designates whatever is not good, unlike the term 'good', which has well-delimited usages—namely, the three conventions discussed here.

20. 'Eternal duration' is the translation I prefer for *dahr*. Some translators use 'eternity' and 'eternal time'. 'Eternity' is defensible, but 'eternal time' is somewhat problematic in philosophical and theological contexts. Although in ordinary discourse *dahr* means a long (possibly, infinite) period of time, in theology *dahr* is equated with the "duration" in which God exists. Therefore this "duration" is eternal and atemporal. Of course, the term 'duration' itself has temporal connotations. This is unavoidable even in Arabic, since the term *dahr* has temporal connotations as well.

21. The Ankara edition adds 'and the eternal duration turned backwards'.

22. Reported by Aḥmad ibn Ḥanbal, *Musnad*, II.491, no. 10346; Bukhārī, *Ṣaḥīḥ*, LXV.45, no. 4826; LXXVIII.101, no. 6181; and Muslim, *Ṣaḥīḥ*, XL.1, no. 2246.

23. Since God has no needs, it cannot be said that an act is in accordance with or contrary to His purposes of fulfilling certain needs. Al-Ghazālī implies that when one speaks of an act as serving a person's purpose, it should be understood that this purpose is the fulfillment of a certain need or desire, whereas no such purpose can be attributed to God. It should be noted that al-Ghazālī uses the same word, *gharaḍ* (purpose or intention), in relation to people and to God.

As for the term 'wisdom', it is used in two senses. One of them is the absolute, comprehensive knowledge of the orders of things in their minute as well as grand aspects, and the determination of how they should be in order to fulfill the functions required of them. The second sense adds to this knowledge[24] the power to originate these orders and arrangements and make them excellent and exact. Thus it is said that 'wise' derives from 'wisdom', which is a kind of knowledge, and it is said that 'wise' derives from 'perfecting',[25] which is a kind of act.

The original meanings of these terms have now become clear to you.[26] There are, however, three mistakes that the estimative faculty may make. Discussing them is beneficial for avoiding difficulties that have plagued many groups of people.

*The first mistake.* A person might use the term 'bad' for what is contrary to his purpose, even though it is in accordance with the purpose of another; but he does not pay attention to the other—since everyone by nature is consumed with himself and belittles the others—and hence he judges the act to be absolutely bad. He might say that it is bad by virtue of itself, whereas it is bad with respect to him, in the sense that it is contrary to his purpose. As if his purposes were the whole world for him. Thus he "estimates"[27] that what is contrary to his purpose is contrary in itself; accordingly he relates badness to the essence of the thing and makes an absolute judgment. He is originally right in deeming it bad, but he is wrong in his judgment that it is absolutely bad and in relating badness to the essence of the thing. The source of this mistake is his heedlessness in not paying attention to others—indeed, in not paying attention even to his own states; for what he deems good in some of his states might be exactly the same as what he, [in other states], deemed bad but which changed and became congenial to his purpose.

*The second mistake.* Something could be contrary to one's purposes in all but rare cases, and hence the person might judge it to be absolutely bad, because of his heedlessness regarding the rare cases and because of the en-

24. I replaced 'it' with 'this knowledge' for clarity. However, it is possible to interpret the 'it' as referring to the first sense of 'wisdom'. In this case, the meaning would be that the second sense adds to the first sense the presence of the power to create and prefect these systems.

25. 'Wisdom' in Arabic is *ḥikma* and 'perfecting' (or 'making perfect', or 'making exact') is *iḥkām*. Both of these words, as well as *ḥakīm* (wise), are derived from the same root.

26. These are the six terms mentioned at the beginning of this treatise.

27. The Arabic verb is *yatawahham*, which, in ordinary discourse, could be translated as 'imagine'. However, it is almost certain that al-Ghazālī is using the word in its technical philosophical sense, since the agent is making a value judgment and it is the estimative faculty, not the imaginative faculty, that adds value judgments to representations.

trenchment of the majority of cases and their dominance in his mind. For example, he might deem that lying is absolutely bad in all cases, and that its badness is due to its essence alone as lying, and not due to an additional notion. The reason [for this judgment] is his unawareness of how many beneficial matters depend on lying under certain circumstances. Even if such circumstances take place, he might be, by nature, averse to considering lying good because he is fully accustomed to considering it bad. For his nature, since early youth, is averse to lying due to discipline and good upbringing; he is taught that lying is bad in itself and that he should never lie. Lying is bad, indeed, under a certain condition, which always accompanies lying except in rare cases; because of this he has not been made aware of that condition.[28] Thus the badness of lying and his absolute aversion to it become rooted in his nature.

*The third mistake*. The estimative faculty asserts the converse. It thinks that if one thing is observed to be associated with another, then the latter is inevitably always associated with the former as well. A person might not know that although the specific is always associated with the general, it is not necessary that the general be associated with the specific. For example, it is said that a snakebite victim—I mean one who was bitten by a snake—fears a multicolored rope; and it is said that the reason is that the victim perceived what is harmful as appearing like a multicolored rope, so when he perceives the rope, his estimative faculty, before his intellect judges, asserts the converse and judges that it is harmful. Thus the victim, by nature, feels aversion following the "estimation" and the imagination,[29] even though the intellect denies it.[30]

In fact, a person might be averse to eating a mushy, yellow dessert[31] because it looks like excrement. He might even feel the urge to vomit if someone says that it looks like excrement. He would not be able to eat it although the intellect denies [the judgment that it is filth], because the "es-

28. Judging by his earlier remarks about 'good' and 'bad', causing harm is the condition under which lying is bad. For example, lying to make peace between enemies would be permissible according to al-Ghazālī's criterion for the good. Indeed, making peace between people is one of the cases in which Islamic law permits lying. Al-Ghazālī says that because this condition is almost always satisfied, a person is not made aware of it; hence he does not know that lying is bad *only* under this condition and presupposes that lying is bad always. If he were to be made aware of the condition, then he would know that when the condition is not satisfied, lying is not bad; thus he would not assert that lying is bad absolutely and by virtue of its essence alone.

29. Literally, the nature is averse following the "estimation" and imagination. The term 'estimation' is used here in the technical sense described in note 21 of the First Treatise.

30. That is, the intellect denies the judgment of the estimative faculty, which is that the rope is harmful.

31. The dessert is *khabīṣ*, which is a cooked dessert made by mixing thoroughly date and fat; it is usually yellowish and mushy.

timation" was quick to assert the converse. He perceived the filth as mushy and yellow; thus if he sees something mushy and yellow, he judges that it is filth.

Indeed, in our nature there are matters much greater than this. The names that are used to name Indians and Negroes are associated with the ugliness of the bearers of these names. This association might influence one's nature to the extent that if the most beautiful Turks and Romans were given these names, one by nature would feel aversion to them. This is because the estimative faculty perceives ugliness associated with these names, and it asserts the converse; hence if it perceives a name, it judges the bearer of the name to be ugly; thus one's nature feels aversion.[32]

Although the matter is clear to the intellect, it should not be ignored; for mankind's eagerness and its reluctance to say, believe, and do certain things are based on such "estimations." As for following pure intellect,[33] it can be undertaken only by God's devout servants to whom God (Exalted is He) has shown the truth as it is and has given the strength to follow it. If you want to see this regarding matters of belief,[34] then present to the understanding of a common Muʿtazilite a doctrine that is plausible and clear. He would be quick to accept it. If you say to him, however, that it is a doctrine of al-Ashʿarī, he would be averse to it and refuse to accept it. He would recant and reject exactly what he had accepted earlier, so long as he has a bad opinion of al-Ashʿarī. For he has been made averse to [Ashʿarism] since his early youth. Also, were we to state a doctrine that a common Ashʿarite would deem plausible, and then tell him that this is a doctrine of a Muʿtazilite, he would be averse to it after having believed it and would recant and reject it.[35]

I do not say that this is characteristic of only the common people, but rather that it is characteristic of most of those I have seen who claim to have knowledge. They are no different from the common people in their

32. These examples make clear what al-Ghazālī means by the estimative faculty's asserting the converse. The original apprehension is that A's are B's (i.e., A's are associated with B's), and the converse judgment is that B's are A's (i.e., B's are associated with A's). For example, in the case of the snakebite victim, the estimative faculty apprehends that a harmful snake is multicolored and long, but it asserts the converse—namely, that a multicolored, long object is a harmful snake. Hence a person whose estimative faculty made the converse assertion would associate a multicolored rope with the value judgment "being harmful," which would result in his fearing the rope. Note that the presence of the value judgment is the reason al-Ghazālī speaks of the "estimation" rather than simply the imagination.

33. Alternatively, pure reason (*al-ʿaql al-ṣirf*).

34. That is, to see that most people do not follow pure intellect in matters of belief.

35. See note 6 of the Religious Preface for a brief description of the Muʿtazila school of Islamic theology, and note 34 of the Second Treatise for a brief discussion of some of the Ashʿarite doctrines.

conformism; in fact, they add conformity to proofs to their conformity to doctrines. In their theorizing, they do not seek the truth, but they seek tricky proofs to support what they believe to be true through conformism and hearsay. If they encounter in their theorizing something that confirms their belief, they say: "We have obtained proof." On the other hand, if they encounter something that disconfirms their belief, they say: "We have encountered a dubious matter." Thus they maintain the belief that they acquired originally through conformism, declaring everything that opposes it dubious and everything that agrees with it a proof. However, correct practice is the opposite of this: they should not believe anything at first; they should look at the proof and call what follows from it true and what is contrary to it false.

The source of all of this is being accustomed to approving or disapproving [of certain things] and acquiring certain morals since early youth.[36] If you become aware of these causes for error, then it will be easy for you to avoid many difficulties.

It might be said:

Your discussion is founded on the claim that being good or bad reduces to being in accordance with or contrary to purposes; but we see that a reasonable person deems good that in which there is no benefit for him and deems bad that in which there is benefit for him. Regarding deeming something good: a person may see a human being or an animal about to die, and would deem it good to save him, even with a drink of water, although he does not believe in the revelation and does not expect a reward for it in this life, and it is not performed in view of people, so that he cannot expect praise for it. Indeed, the absence of all purposes may be supposed, and still he would prefer saving him over ignoring him, because he deems the former good and the latter bad. Regarding that which can be deemed bad in spite of its serving a purpose: for example, a person may be threatened with a sword to renounce his belief in God, and the law permits him to do so; but he might deem it good to be steadfast in the face of [death by] the sword and refuse to make such declaration. Also, a person who does not believe in the revelation may be threatened by the sword to breach a covenant, and no harm would come to him as a result of breaching it, yet he would die as a result of maintaining it; still he would deem it good to maintain the covenant and not to breach it. This shows that there is a meaning for 'good' and 'bad' other than what you have mentioned.

36. The Arabic words that I translated as 'approving' and 'disapproving' are, respectively, *istiḥsān* and *istiqbāḥ*, which literally mean "to deem good" and "to deem bad." The literal meaning shows the relation between this passage and the previous discussion about the meaning of 'good' and 'bad'.

The answer lies in a reconsideration of the mistakes we mentioned, which would satisfy the desire for an answer. As for the person who does not believe in the revelation and yet prefers to save rather than to ignore a victim: the elimination of harm that befalls a human being is part of human empathy; it is a nature from which it is impossible to detach oneself. A person imagines himself to be in the same calamity, and assumes that another is able to save him but refrains from that, and realizes that he would deem this bad; then he imagines himself to be in the place of the person who is about to die; by nature he feels aversion to what the person who is about to die would think of him;[37] and thus he eliminates this aversion from his soul by saving the victim.

The same case may be supposed with an animal, which cannot be "estimated" to deem something bad,[38] or with a person who has no empathy or mercy, which is impossible to imagine since a human being cannot be detached from empathy and mercy. If it is, nevertheless, assumed to be the case in spite of its impossibility, then something else remains—namely, the praise for having good character and mercy for the creation.[39] If it is further supposed that no one knows about the act, then it is possible that it would become known. On the other hand, if it is assumed that it is impossible to be known, then there might still remain in his soul a preference [for the act] and an inclination analogous to the snakebite victim's natural aversion to that rope. For if he sees that praise is always associated with such an act, and he enjoys praise, then he will enjoy doing that with which praise is associated; even though he knows through his intellect that there will be no praise. Similarly, if he sees that harm is associated with what looks like a rope, and he naturally is averse to harm, then he will be averse to that with

37. The sentence does not express the thought completely. The meaning is that he, by nature, feels aversion to what the person who is about to die would think of him *if he were not to save him*. The translation follows the reading in the Ankara edition. The reading in the Jeddah edition may be translated loosely as follows: "he feels, by nature, revulsion by what he believes of the victim's disapproval of his act [if he were not to save him]."

38. That is, which the estimative faculty cannot regard as being capable of deeming anything bad.

39. Given the generality of the consequent, it is reasonable to suppose that al-Ghazālī intends to include in the antecedent the case of the victim being a nonhuman animal. If one supposes that the person is *not* detached from human nature, and hence he feels empathy, then it can be argued, along Ghazālian lines, that the person will save the animal, even though he cannot imagine that the animal approves or disapproves of his act, because he can imagine the pain of the animal and its desire to stay alive. Hence through empathy he can "feel" the animal's pain and desire to live, so he acts by saving the animal. This type of analysis may be found in some ethical theories in Western philosophy as well.

which harm is associated; even though he knows through his intellect that there will be no harm.[40]

In fact, if a person has seen his beloved in a certain place and has socialized with her there frequently, then, by nature, he feels in his soul that this place, together with its walls, is unique among all other places. This is why the poet says:

I pass by the dwellings—the dwellings of Laylā,
I kiss this wall and that wall.
It is not the love for the dwellings that enamors my heart,
But it is the love for the one who inhabited these dwellings.[41]

And Ibn al-Rūmī says—and how wonderful what he says—by way of explaining to people the love for one's country:

The countries of men are made beloved to them,
All the things they did there during their youth.
The mention of their countries reminds them
Of the years of their youth; hence they long for them.[42]

If a person studies habits and morals, he sees instances of this beyond enumeration. [Ignorance of habits and morals] is the reason that leads some to make mistakes—those who are impressed by the appearances of things, are headless of the secrets of the souls' morals, and do not know that such inclinations are produced by the soul's being influenced, due to disposition and nature, by mere "estimation" and imagination, which are erroneous and not according to the judgment of the intellect.[43] For the faculties of

40. One way to make the analogy between the case of the snakebite victim and the person who saves another more perspicuous is to see that what the latter desires is the pleasant feeling of being praised for his merciful character—even if he is not really merciful. Just as the snakebite victim, having observed that a snake is always multicolored and long, makes the converse judgment that every multicolored long object is a snake and is frightened when he sees a multicolored long object, so the person who saves another, having constantly observed that people who are praised for their merciful character had performed altruistic acts, makes the converse judgment that whoever performs an altruistic act is praised for his merciful character and anticipates the pleasure of that praise. Of course, he knows that no one will know about his heroic deed, but the mere thought of being praised gives him a pleasant feeling as if he were actually praised for his merciful character.

41. The poet is Qays ibn al-Mulawwaḥ, who is popularly known as Majnūn Laylā. These verses are mentioned in his *Collected Poems.*

42. These verses are mentioned in his *Collected Poems.*

43. I followed the Ankara edition in reading *ghalaṭ, lā bi-ḥukm al-ʿaql* (erroneous and *not* according to the judgment of the intellect) instead of *ghalaṭ bi-ḥukm al-ʿaql* (erroneous according to the judgment of the intellect), which is the reading in the Jeddah edition.

the soul are created [in such a way that they become] obedient, through the course of habits, to the "estimations" and imaginations. For instance, if a person imagines delicious food either by remembering or seeing it, he immediately salivates and his mouth drools. This is due to the obedience of the faculty that God has dedicated to the secretion of saliva, which assists in the chewing of food, to the imagination and the "estimation." Its function is connected to the "estimation," even though the person knows that he does not want to start eating either due to fasting or to some other reason. Also, he might imagine a beautiful picture of someone with whom he desires to have sexual relation. If this picture persists in the imagination, the faculty responsible for extending the instrument of the act comes into effect, and moves the vapor into the hollows of the nerves and fills them with it, and the faculty responsible for exuding the lubricating pre-seminal fluid, which assists in having intercourse, comes to action. All of this takes place despite the assurance of the intellect's judgment [that one ought] to refrain from the act at that time. But God (Exalted is He) has created these faculties so that, due to the course of habit, they would be obedient to and controlled by the rule of the imagination and the "estimation," whether the intellect supports the "estimation" or not. [Ignorance of] such matters is the source of making mistakes regarding the cause of preferring one act to another.[44] All of this is based on purposes.[45]

Regarding renouncing one's belief in God: although it is deemed bad, the intellect does not deem it bad when it is under the threat of the sword; indeed, it might even deem standing one's ground to be bad. If, on the other hand, it does deem it good to stand one's ground, then there are two reasons for this. One of them is a man's belief that the reward for being steadfast and surrendering to death is greater. The other is that he expects praise for his holding firm to his religion. How many brave men rode the back of danger and attacked a large group, which they knew that they could not overtake, yet they belittled what might have happened to them, because of their being recompensed by the pleasure of being praised and glorified after their death.

Similarly, the reason for one's refusal to breach a covenant is the praise of mankind for those who maintain their covenants and their constant advisement to each other [to maintain the covenants], since they advance people's interests. If it is supposed that he does not expect praise, then the reason for his behavior is the estimative faculty's judgment that this behavior is always associated with praise, which is pleasurable, and that whatever

44. Literally, of preferring one side of the act to the other.

45. Al-Ghazālī's point is that all of our preferences have to do with purposes, even though we may not see it and think that we act—and should act—without purposes.

the pleasurable is associated with is itself pleasurable, just as whatever is associated with what is disliked is itself disliked, as was mentioned in the previous examples.

This is what is appropriate for this brief discussion, which unlocks the secrets of this treatise. The one who appreciates the value of this discussion is the one who has theorized about the intelligibles for a long time. We have benefited from this introduction in preparing our discussion of the propositions. So let us turn to them.

## First Proposition

*It is possible for God not to create; and if He creates, it is not obligatory for Him to do so; and if He creates people, He might not assign obligations to them; and if He does assign obligations, it is not obligatory for Him to do so.*

A sect among the Muʿtazilites says that it is incumbent upon Him to create and to assign obligations after He creates.

The proof of its truth is that we say: "One's statement that creating and assigning obligations are obligatory is not comprehensible; for we have explained that what we understand by the term 'obligatory' is that which results in an immediate or delayed harm for the one who refrains from it, or that whose contrary is impossible."[46] Being harmed is impossible with respect to God (Glorified is He). Also, there is no impossibility that is necessitated by refraining from creating or assigning obligations; except when it is said: "This would lead to something contrary to what has been known and willed since eternity." This is true, and according to this interpretation it is necessary, since if the will is supposed to exist or knowledge is supposed to attach to a thing, then the occurrence of the object of will and of the object of knowledge is necessary without doubt.[47]

It might be said: "It is incumbent upon Him for the benefit of the creation, not for a benefit obtained by the Creator."

46. As explained previously, the third sense (i.e., that whose contrary is impossible) must be translated as 'necessary'; in Arabic the term *wājib* means obligatory and necessary.

47. Al-Ghazālī argues that it is necessary that God create and obligate people *if* the knowledge that these acts will be performed or the will to perform them exists in advance. Consider the case of knowledge. We assume that it has been eternally part of God's knowledge that God will create people and will assign obligations to them. Thus to suppose that it is possible for God not to create and obligate while He has knowledge that He will do so is to suppose that it is possible for something not to occur while it was known that it would occur. Knowledge, however, entails truth; it follows that if it is known that $x$ will occur at time $t$, then $x$ will occur at time $t$. Note that if knowledge is not held fixed, it is possible for God not to create.

We say:

Your statement that it is for the benefit of the creation is a causal explanation, yet the judgment to be explained is the act's being obligatory; so we request that you explain the meaning of the judgment; for it is not sufficient to mention a cause. What is the meaning of your saying that it is obligatory because it is beneficial for the creation? And what is the meaning of 'obligatory', when we understand by 'obligatory' only these three senses, which are absent here?[48] If you intend a fourth sense, explain it first and then state its cause. We might not deny that mankind derives benefit from being created and, also, from being obligated. However, what benefits someone other than himself is not obligatory for him if benefiting the other has no benefit for him. This conclusion is absolutely inescapable.

We further say:

This explanation is applicable with respect to creating but not with respect to assigning obligations; and it is not applicable for those in the existing creation, though it would be applicable if God were to create them in paradise—with felicity, and without grief, sorrow, or pain. As for this existing creation: all the rational people have wished to be nonexistent. One of them has said: "I wish I were gone and forgotten." Another has said: "I wish I were nothing." Yet another has said: "I wish I were this straw," as he picked it from the ground. Another has said while pointing at a bird: "I wish I were this bird."[49] These are the sayings of prophets and saints, and they are the rational ones. Some of them wish never to have been created and some, by wishing to be an inanimate object or a bird, wish not to have been obligated.

I wish I knew how a reasonable person finds it acceptable to say that there is benefit for mankind in being obligated. The very meaning of benefit negates hardship; and to obligate is precisely to require hardship,[50] which is pain. It is the reward, to which one looks forward, that is the

48. Recall that the three senses are (1) that which results in a harm in this life for the one who refrains from it, (2) that which results in a harm in the hereafter for the one who refrains from it, and (3) that whose contrary is impossible (this is the sense of necessary).

49. There are several traditions that contain these assertions. There is a Qur'ānic verse in which Maryam, the mother of Jesus, says during childbirth: *I wish I had died before this and were gone and forgotten* (19:23). It was also reported that the wife of the Prophet 'Ā'isha said: "I wish I were gone and forgotten," that the Prophet's companion 'Umar ibn al-Khaṭṭāb, the second caliph, picked a straw from the ground and said: "I wish I were this straw; I wish I were not a thing to be remembered; I wish I were gone and forgotten; I wish I were never born," and that the Prophet's companion Abū Bakr, the first caliph, said to a bird: "I wish I were like you, O bird, and were not born human." (See, for example, al-Ghazālī, *Iḥyā' 'Ulūm al-Dīn*, vol. VI, p. 2782.)

50. The word I translated as 'hardship' is *kulfa*. To assign obligations (or, to obligate) is *taklīf*. These two Arabic words derive from the same root.

benefit. And God is able to bring this benefit to people without assigning obligations.

It might be said: "If a reward is obtained with desert, it is more pleasurable and more sublime than what is given immediately and by favor." The response to this is that it is more proper to seek refuge in God from having a mind that leads to being arrogant towards God (Great and Glorious is He), to being too proud to accept His favors, and to positing pleasure in rejecting His grace than to seek refuge in God from the accursed devil. I wish I knew how one who entertains such thoughts could be considered rational. He who is troubled by an eternal residence in paradise because it was not preceded by toiling and fulfilling obligations is too insignificant to be addressed or debated; and this is so even if it is conceded that reward is deserved by fulfilling obligations—we will show the contrary of this claim.

Furthermore, I would ask, Where does a servant of God find the obedience for which he deserves reward? Is it not caused by his existence, power, and will, the health of his organs, and the presence of its causes? Is there a source for all of this other than God's favor and grace?

We seek refuge in God from being totally detached from the rational instinct. For this statement[51] is of that type.[52] It is more proper to ask God to bestow rationality upon the one who makes such a statement than to be occupied with debating him.

# Second Proposition

*We claim that it is up to God to assign to His servants obligations, whether within their ability or beyond their ability.*

The Mu'tazilites assert that this is false. However, the belief of the followers of the Sunna is that the true nature of obligating is that it is a form of speaking; that it has a source, namely, the obligator, whose sole condition is his being a sayer; that it has a receiver, namely, the one who is obligated, whose condition is his being able to comprehend the speech (thus speaking to an inanimate object or to an insane person is not called 'addressing' or 'obligating', obligating being a type of addressing); and that it has an object, namely, what is obligatory, whose sole condition is that it is comprehensible—as for its being possible, this is not a condition for the existence

51. The current statement is the claim attributed to the opponent earlier, namely: "If a reward is earned, it is more pleasurable and more sublime than if it is given immediately and as a favor."

52. That is, it is totally detached from the rational instinct.

of the thing spoken.[53] Obligating, therefore, is a form of speaking. If the speaking proceeds from one who can make what is spoken comprehensible, is directed to one who can comprehend it, and is about something comprehensible, and if, in addition, the addressee is lower in rank than the addresser, then it is called 'obligating'. If, however, the addressee is of the same rank as the addresser, then it is called 'soliciting'. And if the addressee is higher in rank than the addresser, then it is called 'supplicating' and 'asking'. The basic requirements are the same, but the names differ due to the different relations.

The demonstration that this is possible[54] is that [if it were impossible], its impossibility would be inescapably due either to the inconceivability of its essence, such as a conjunction of whiteness and blackness, or to its being deemed bad.[55] It is false that it is impossible due to its essence; for whiteness and blackness *cannot* be supposed to be conjoined, but it *is* possible to suppose this. It is inevitable that assigning obligation either is expressed verbally—this is the position of our opponent—yet it is not impossible for a man to say to his disabled slave "Stand up," something that is clearly fea-

53. The point of the last clause is that it is not a condition for the existence of the obligation (which is the thing spoken) that it is possible to be fulfilled by the one who is obligated. This is al-Ghazālī's central claim—namely, that God may assign to His servants an obligation that exceeds their ability, and hence it is not possible for them to fulfill.

54. That is, it is possible for God to assign obligations that are beyond people's ability.

55. What al-Ghazālī is demonstrating is that it is possible for God to assign an obligation to His servants that is beyond their ability. The consequent of the conditional posits two senses in which it may be said that it is impossible for God to assign obligations that exceed the ability of the one who is obligated. The first sense is metaphysical impossibility, which would result from a contradiction inherent in the essence of such an obligation. Many Islamic theologians, including almost all the Muʿtazilites, argue that assigning such an obligation is against God's justice (for, presumably, He will hold people accountable for not fulfilling their obligation), and since God *cannot* be unjust, it is self-contradictory for such an obligation to exist. The second sense is that assigning such an obligation is bad; and although there is nothing logically impossible about God's choosing to perform a bad act (since God is absolutely free and powerful), He is too good to make such a choice. There are many Islamic theologians who hold this position. They even invoke two Qurʾānic statements to justify their view. The first is a supplication in which the believers ask: *Our Lord do not burden us with what we have no ability to bear* (2:286), and the second is: *God does not assign to a soul an obligation that is beyond its ability* (2:286). They interpret the first verse as showing that it is indeed possible for God to assign obligations that exceed the ability of His servants; for if this were not possible, it would make little sense for His servants to ask Him not to do so. (It should be noted that there are different interpretations of this verse.) They interpret the second verse as showing that God, owing to His goodness, does not assign such obligations. As we will see, al-Ghazālī rejects both arguments. Following al-Ashʿarī, he believes that being unjust and being bad are properties that are inapplicable to God's acts. (See, e.g., Badawī, *Madhāhib al-Islāmiyyīn*, pp. 563–564; al-Shahrastānī, *al-Milal wa-l-Niḥal*, vol. 1, p. 115; and al-Baghdādī, *al-Farq bayn al-Firaq*, pp. 239–240.)

sible even according to our opponent's position; or, as we believe, it is a requirement that resides in the mind,[56] and just as it is imaginable that one might in his mind require an able person to stand, it is also imaginable that this might apply to a disabled person. Indeed, he might in his mind require this of an able person, and the requirement would persist even as a disability occurs without the master's knowledge. The requirement would reside in the master's mind,[57] and it demands of the disabled person to stand, with God (Exalted is He) knowing that he is disabled, even though this is unknown to the one who is imposing the requirement. Even if he were to know this, it would not be impossible for the requirement to continue along with the knowledge that it cannot be fulfilled.

It is also false to say that such an obligation could not exist on the basis of what is deemed bad;[58] for our discussion concerns God (Exalted is He), and that is inapplicable to Him, since He is free from needs and that is based on needs.[59] As for the rational person, who is bound by the demands of purposes,[60] this might be deemed bad coming from him. But what is deemed bad coming from a servant of God is not deemed bad coming from God.

It might be said: 'There is no benefit in it,[61] and what is without benefit is a frivolity, and it is impossible for God (Exalted is He) to act frivolously.[62]

We say:

There are three claims here. The first is that there is no benefit in it. We do not concede this. It might have benefit for God's servants—benefit that God sees. The benefit might not be the observance of the obligations and the reward for it. There might be benefit in making clear what is being commanded and the ensuing belief in the obligation. A command might be rescinded before it is fulfilled, as when God commanded Abraham (peace be upon him) to sacrifice his son and then He rescinded the command be-

56. Literally, resides in the soul (or, in the self, *nafs*). 'The mind' is more appropriate here than 'the soul', since it is problematic to say that a religious obligation is a requirement that resides in God's soul.

57. Literally, reside is his self (*dhāt*).

58. The reading in the Jeddah edition is *istiḥsān* (deeming something good) and in the Ankara edition *istiḥālāt* (impossibilities). My reading is *istiqbāḥ* (deeming something bad) since the context clearly calls for it.

59. As al-Ghazālī explains in the introduction to this treatise, deeming something good or bad is based on needs (or, purposes), and hence it is inapplicable to God.

60. Literally, bound by the mold of purposes (*al-maḍbūṭ bi-qālib al-aghrāḍ*). This is in the Jeddah edition. In the Ankara edition, it is "bound by the dominance of purposes" (*al-maḍbūṭ bi-ghālib al-aghrāḍ*).

61. That is, there is no benefit in assigning obligations that are beyond the ability of the one obligated.

62. Literally, frivolity is impossible for God (Exalted is He).

fore it was fulfilled. He also ordered Abū Jahl to be a believer yet related that he would never be a believer—and it is impossible to negate what He relates.[63]

The second claim is that what has no benefit is a frivolity. This is a redundant expression; for we have explained that what is intended by 'frivolity' is only that in which there is no benefit. If something else is intended by it, then it is incomprehensible.

The third claim is that it is impossible for God to act frivolously. There is a misconception in this. Frivolity is nothing but an act in which there is no benefit; it is an act that relates to benefits. If an act does not relate to benefits, it can only be called 'a frivolity' as a sheer metaphor with no truth to it. This is analogous to one's statement that the wind is frivolous when it rustles the trees, since there is no benefit in this. It is also analogous to one's statement that the wall is oblivious, that is, it lacks knowledge and ignorance. This is false, since 'oblivious' is used to describe what is receptive of knowledge and ignorance but lacks both of them. To use it to describe

63. Abū Jahl was one of the nobility of the tribe of Quraysh, to which the Prophet Muḥammad belonged. He was a sworn enemy of Muḥammad and his followers. He fought the Muslims vehemently and brutally. He was asked by the Prophet to change his ways and convert to Islam, but it is believed that there are Qur'ānic indications that he would never be a believer. Al-Ghazālī could have used a better example, which is the case of the Prophet's uncle Abū Lahab. Abū Lahab was also extreme in his opposition to Islam and used torture and violence against the early Muslims. There are Qur'ānic verses that explicitly state that Abū Lahab and his wife will be condemned to hellfire in the hereafter: *Perish the hands of Abū Lahab and perish he. All his wealth and all that he gains will not profit him. He will burn in a fire of blazing flames. His wife shall carry the firewood. A rope of palm fiber shall be wrapped around her neck* (111:1–5). The point here is that since God said that Abū Lahab would never be a believer, it is impossible for him to fulfill God's command to the people of Quraysh to embrace Islam. The value of assigning an obligation that cannot be fulfilled lies in that it makes clear what is being commanded and that there is a duty to fulfill it. The impossibility here is conditioned on God's knowledge, that is, given God's knowledge that Abū Lahab will refuse to believe, it is impossible for him to believe. However, this impossibility need not exclude Abū Lahab's free choice; for one might maintain that Abū Lahab had free will and rational capacity; hence he could have chosen to become a Muslim; but had this been the case, God, of course, would not have known that Abū Lahab would not be a believer, but rather He would have known the contrary. What is impossible is the conjunction of God's knowledge that Abū Lahab would never be a believer and Abū Lahab's becoming one. It is important to note, however, that al-Ash'arī argued at length against the claim that an unbeliever chose freely unbelief over faith and that God has known the outcome of his free choice since eternity. Here is one of his many arguments: "It might be said to [the Mu'tazilites] that if the unbelievers are able to choose faith, you cannot then deny that they might actually succeed in becoming believers; and if they might actually succeed and achieve [faith], then they might be praiseworthy; yet [the latter] is not possible; hence it is not possible that they are able to achieve faith; it necessarily follows that God (Great and Glorious is He) assigned the ability to achieve faith *only* to the believers." (See al-Ash'arī, *al-Ibāna 'an Uṣūl al-Diyāna*, pp. 67–79; the quoted passage is on p. 68.)

what is not receptive of knowledge and ignorance is a metaphor that has no foundation. The same applies to using the term 'frivolous' to describe God (Great and Glorious is He) and calling His acts 'frivolities'.

The second proof regarding this issue—a proof that no one can escape—is that God (Exalted is He) obligated Abū Jahl to become a believer, though He knew that he would not believe, and related that he would not believe. It is as if He commanded him to believe that he would not believe. For part of what God's Messenger (may God bless him and grant him peace) related is that Abū Jahl would not believe, and he was commanded to believe the Messenger. Thus it was said to him: "Believe that you will not believe." And this is impossible.

The explanation of this proof is that it is impossible for something that is contrary to what is known to take place. It is not impossible by virtue of itself, but by virtue of something other than itself. What is impossible to take place by virtue of another is similar to what is impossible by virtue of itself. He who says that the infidels, who did not believe, were not required to believe has denied the revelation. And he who says that their belief in God is imaginable together with God's knowledge that it will never take place has disavowed reason. Thus every party is committed to saying that a command is imaginable while its fulfillment is unimaginable.[64]

It does not help to say that it is an object of power and the infidel had the power to do it.[65] According to us, there is no power prior to the act; the infidels had only the power to disbelieve, which is what proceeded from them. As for the Mu'tazilites, they believe that the power is not prevented from existing, but the power is not sufficient for the object of power to occur; rather it requires other conditions such as will. However, one of these conditions is that God's knowledge would not change into ignorance. Power is never sought for its own sake but for producing an act; yet how could an act be produced that would result in transforming knowledge into ignorance?

It has become clear that there can actually exist an act of obligating whose object is impossible by virtue of something other than itself. By analogy we

64. This is the desired conclusion, if one equates 'imaginable' with 'possible'. It asserts that it is possible for God to command something (i.e., to assign an obligation) whose fulfillment is impossible.

65. The 'it' here refers to God's command whose fulfillment is unimaginable. This statement says that regardless of what is known by God, in principle the unbeliever has the power to obey the command, even if he does not actually obey the command. In this sense God's knowledge that Abū Jahl will never become a believer does not negate Abū Jahl's power to become a believer. It is only that Abū Jahl will never exercise this power to become a believer, and hence nothing contrary to God's knowledge will ever take place. This is supposed to establish the opponent's view that God's command to Abū Jahl to become a believer is not beyond the power of Abū Jahl.

infer that there can be an act of obligating whose object is impossible by virtue of itself;[66] for there is no difference between the two obligations with respect to their being expressed, their being imagined to be required, or their being deemed good or bad.[67]

## Third Proposition

*We claim that God is able to bring suffering upon an animal that is innocent of any crime, and that He is not required to reward it.*

The Muʿtazilites say that this is impossible because it is bad. Hence, they are necessarily led to assert that if a bug or a flea is harmed by being smashed or swatted, then God (Exalted is He) is obligated to resurrect it and compensate it for it. Others affirm that their spirits would return through incarnation into other bodies, and would attain pleasure then that is equivalent to their previous pain. This is a doctrine whose corruption is clear. We, however, say that bringing suffering upon those who are innocent of crimes, such as animals, children, and the insane, is feasible; indeed, it has been witnessed and perceived.

There remains our opponent's statement, which is that God is obligated to resurrect the creature that is harmed and compensate it after that harm.[68] We return to the meaning of 'obligatory'. It has been shown that being obligated is impossible with respect to God (Exalted is He). If they explain this by intending a fourth sense of 'obligatory', then it is incomprehensible.

66. Literally, by analogy we infer what is impossible in itself.

67. The cases that al-Ghazālī considers in this section all concern divine commands whose fulfillment is impossible by virtue of conditions extraneous to the commands themselves. For instance, God requires an unbeliever to believe in Muḥammad's message while He knows that he will never believe, or God requires one to perform an act, and then rescinds His command before the act can be performed. Al-Ghazālī says that there might be divine commands that are impossible to fulfill by virtue of *their own essence*. The two types of commands are analogous in many ways. They both can be spoken by God, they are both requirements, and they both can be deemed good or bad, from our point of view. Recall that, according to al-Ghazālī, an obligation is a type of speech that is a requirement residing in one's mind and is addressed to someone who is lower in rank than the addresser. Whether the obligation cannot be fulfilled by virtue of itself or by virtue of another is irrelevant to this definition. Thus if God can assign an obligation whose fulfillment is impossible by virtue of a condition extraneous to it, then He can equally assign an obligation whose fulfillment is impossible by virtue of something intrinsic to it. It is worth noting that the latter assertion is denied by almost all Islamic theologians, including most of the Ashʿarites.

68. Literally, this obligates Him to resurrect and reward after that.

If they claim that refraining from [this compensatory act][69] is contrary to His being wise, then we say that if by 'wisdom' it is intended, as previously stated, the knowledge of the order of things and the power to produce this order, then there is nothing in [refraining from this act] that is contrary to wisdom. If another sense is intended, then the only form of wisdom that is due to God is what we mentioned; anything other than that is a meaningless expression.

It might be said that this leads to His being unjust, whereas God says: *Your Lord is never unjust to His servants.*[70] We say that injustice is inapplicable to God due to pure negation, just as being oblivious is inapplicable to a wall and being frivolous to the wind. For injustice is imaginable on the part of someone whose act might affect what belongs to another, yet this is unimaginable with respect to God (Exalted is He), or on the part of someone who is under the command of another and acts in a way that is to contrary to this command. A man is not imagined to be unjust in whatever he does regarding his own property, so long as he does not contradict the commands of the revelation; [if he did], he would be unjust in this sense. Thus injustice is inapplicable to someone who cannot be imagined to infringe upon the property of another or to be under the command of another. This is because the necessary condition for injustice is absent; it is not because such a one lacks something in himself.[71]

Let this subtle point be understood, because it is the cause of the misunderstanding.[72] If injustice is given a meaning other than this, then it is incomprehensible; and hence no affirmation or negation applies to it.

# Fourth Proposition

*We claim that it is not obligatory for God to care for the well-being of His servants, but He may do whatever He wills and decree whatever He wants.*

Thus we contradict the Mu'tazilites, who placed restrictions on the acts of God (Great and Glorious is He) and made it obligatory for Him to care for

69. The expression 'this compensatory act' refers to the act of resurrecting and compensating the innocent creature for the harm that was inflicted on it during its life.

70. Qur'ān, 41:46.

71. The point is that God cannot be unjust—not because he lacks power or free will, but because everything belongs to God (hence God's acts do not affect the property of another) and everything is subservient to God (hence God cannot be under the command of another).

72. The original is an idiomatic expression: 'it is the cause for the slippage of the foot' (*mazallat al-qadam*).

the well-being [of His servants]. As previously stated, the same thing that proves that nothing is obligatory for God (Exalted is He) also proves the falsity of this view. In addition, observation and reality prove its falsity; for we will show them acts of God (Glorious is He) that will force them to concede that they do not serve the interests of His servants.

Let us suppose that there are three children: one of them died a Muslim in his youth, another reached maturity, became a Muslim, and died a Muslim in his maturity, and the third became an infidel in his maturity and died while in the state of infidelity. Justice, for them,[73] would require that the mature infidel reside forever in hellfire, and that the mature Muslim have a higher rank in paradise than the Muslim youth.

The Muslim youth might say: "O Lord, why did You give me a rank lower than his?" God might say: "Because he reached maturity and obeyed me, and you did not obey me by performing acts of worship, since you did not reach maturity."[74] He might say: "O Lord, You made me die before reaching maturity; my best interest would have been for my life to have been extended until I reached maturity, so that I might have obeyed you and attained his rank; why did You deny me this rank forever, when You were able to make me qualified for it?" God would have no answer but to say: "I knew that if you had reached maturity, you would have sinned rather than obeyed me, and then you would be subject to My punishment and wrath; so I saw that this low rank in paradise was more proper and better for you than punishment." The infidel might then call from the abyss and say: "O Lord, did You not know that if I reached maturity, I would be an infidel? Had you made me die in my youth and placed me at that low rank in paradise, I would have loved that and it would have been better for me than Your condemning me forever to hellfire; so why did You make me live when death was better for me?" There would be no answer available for God at all.[75]

73. The pronoun 'them' refers to the Muʿtazilites.

74. Literally, after reaching maturity.

75. This example is based on the "problem of the three brothers," with which, according to the tradition, Abū al-Ḥasan ʿAlī al-Ashʿarī—the founder of the Ashʿariyya school of Islamic theology—challenged the Muʿtazilite master Abū ʿAlī Muḥammad al-Jubbāʾī (see note 34 of the Second Treatise for further elaboration). As mentioned previously, al-Ghazālī is an Ashʿarite, and for him this example serves, therefore, as a conclusive refutation of the Muʿtazilites' doctrine that divine justice is based on desert. (Since al-Ghazālī thinks that the three cases described in the example are not only possible but actual, he uses it to show that God does not care about the well-being of all people and that such caring is not incumbent upon Him.) A Muʿtazilite, however, could deny that this example presents events that could actually happen. A Muʿtazilite might say, for example, that when the Muslim youth inquired about the reason for his having been assigned a rank in paradise lower than that of the mature Muslim, God could have responded that He knew that had He extended the youth's life and allowed him to reach maturity, the youth would indeed have obeyed God and performed

It is common knowledge that these three divisions exist, and this example shows conclusively that serving the best interest of all God's servants is not obligatory for God, nor does it happen.

## Fifth Proposition

*We claim that if God (Exalted is He) assigns obligations to His servants and they obey Him, then it is not obligatory for Him to reward them; rather if He wants to, He may reward them, punish them, or even annihilate them and never resurrect them; that He does not care whether He forgives all the infidels and punishes all the believers; and that this is not impossible in itself, nor does it contradict any of the divine attributes.*

This is so because for God to assign obligations is for Him to deal with His slaves and possessions [as He wants].[76] As for rewarding, this is another, independent act. To say that it is obligatory in any of the three senses is incomprehensible. Also, it is meaningless to speak of it as being good or

---

acts of worship, but even so, he would have been deserving of exactly the same rank that he now occupies in paradise and not that of the mature Muslim, since the latter is still more righteous than the youth would have been. The Mu'tazilite could conclude, in other words, that in all three cases, the people received what they deserved. Nevertheless, the Mu'tazilite would now have to grant that children who die in their youth might be given ranks in paradise higher than the ranks of observant and righteous Muslims who die in maturity, in the event that God determines that, had they lived to maturity, they would have become more observant and righteous than the Muslims who lived to maturity. (This implication, we note, constitutes a revision of certain strains of Mu'tazilism, but it is *not* a revision of their common doctrine of the intermediary position, for the intermediary position, the state of being neither believer nor infidel, is the position of a Muslim who commits a major sin and not that of a child who dies in his youth.) The Mu'tazilite would also have to deny that the Muslim youth as described in al-Ghazālī's example, that is, one who, had he lived to maturity, would have been a sinner or an infidel deserving of eternal damnation, could actually exist. Only thus would a Mu'tazilite be able to maintain that reward and punishment are always dispensed on the basis of desert. Since not all parts of the Islamic tradition support such a conclusion, a Mu'tazilite would have to offer nonliteral interpretations of texts that support the contrary conclusion. An Ash'arite, however, faces the same problem and would have to resolve it the same way. In reality, all Islamic legal, theological, and philosophical schools (including literalist schools, such as the Ẓāhiriyya) have relied on nonliteral interpretations to reconcile their doctrines with texts that appear on their face to contradict them.

76. The original is *taṣarruf*, which is a noun meaning, among other things, "conduct," "behavior," and "dealing." In this context, however, the word carries with it the connotation of "acting freely as one wishes." Thus I believe that what al-Ghazālī intends is that God's assigning obligations (*taklīf*) to mankind is an exercise of His right to deal (*taṣarruf*) with His slaves and possessions (*'abīdih wa-mamālīkih*) in any way He pleases.

bad.[77] If another meaning is intended, then this too is incomprehensible, unless it is said that this would make His promise false, yet this is impossible. We believe that it is necessary in this sense and we do not deny it.[78]

It might be said: "It is bad to assign obligations and yet refrain from rewarding when one is able to reward."

We say:

If you mean by 'bad' that which is contrary to the needs of the one who obligates, then the Obligator is too exalted and sanctified to have needs. However, if you mean by it that it is contrary to the needs of the one who is obligated, then this would be acceptable. But God is not prevented from performing an act that is bad for the one who is obligated; for what is bad and what is good for the one obligated are on a par with respect to God.[79]

Moreover, if we press their corrupt belief, we do not concede that he who employs his slave is usually obligated to reward him, because a reward is compensation for a service; this would annul the benefit of having slaves.

77. Literally, and there is no meaning for good or bad.

78. The Arabic word I translated as 'necessary' is *wājib*. As was indicated previously, *wājib* means both "obligatory" and "necessary." So al-Ghazālī is saying here that since God promised to reward those who fulfill their religious obligations, it would be necessary for Him to reward them; otherwise, His promise would be false and that is impossible. It is tempting to read *wājib* here as 'obligatory', and argue that because of God's promise, He is "obligated" to fulfill His promise and reward His obedient servants. Al-Ghazālī, however, argued repeatedly that no act of God is obligatory, for an obligatory act, by definition, is an act such that if one refrains from performing it, a definite harm in this life or in the hereafter would befall him. It is clear that this definition is inapplicable to any act of God. Al-Ghazālī seems to think that the fulfillment of a promise, or at least the intention to fulfill one's promise, is part of the definition of a promise. Hence it would be logically impossible for one to make a promise with the intention to break it (in this case, one did not make a promise even if he thought that he did). God's promises, therefore, must be made with the intention of being fulfilled, and since God realizes all His intentions (for He is all-powerful and immutable), it is logically necessary (but not obligatory) that God fulfill all his promises. In this sense, God's rewarding His obedient servants is necessary, though not obligatory. Al-Ghazālī will return to this issue in the Seventh Proposition of this treatise and offer a different argument for the impossibility of God's promise to be false. He will argue that it is impossible for God's speech to contain lies; and since His promise is made through speech, it cannot be a false promise.

79. There are two points here; both have been addressed previously. Al-Ghazālī believes that whether an act is good or bad has to do with whether it is in accordance with or contrary to one's needs and desires (purposes). The first point is that, since God has no needs, the two notions are inapplicable to His acts. (Al-Ghazālī does say, however, that it is correct to say that whatever God does is good, because this usage of 'good' has nothing to do with needs; the statement simply means that there are no repercussions or blame for whatever God does in His kingdom.) The second point is that although, according to this definition, it is indeed bad for the one who is obligated not to be rewarded for fulfilling the obligation, it is not incumbent upon God to serve the interest of His servants.

A slave is obligated to serve his master simply because he is his slave; if he serves in order to be compensated, then this is not a service.

Among their startling statements is their saying that it is incumbent upon God's servants, because they are His servants, to be grateful as a fulfillment for their obligation for receiving His blessings, and that it is incumbent upon Him to reward them for their gratefulness. This is absurd. For the one whose right is fulfilled has no obligation to compensate. If that were the case, then the reward would require a new gratefulness, and this gratefulness would require a new reward, and there would be an infinite regress. Hence, the servant and the Lord would each be bound by the other's right forever, which is absurd.

More repugnant than this is their statement that God (Exalted is He) is obligated to punish eternally and to condemn to hellfire forever whoever disbelieves in Him, and that, indeed, whoever commits a major sin and dies before atoning would be condemned to hellfire forever.[80] This shows ignorance of generosity and magnanimity, and of reason, habit, revelation, and all matters. We say that habit dictates and reason indicates that to overlook and forgive is better than to punish and avenge. People's praise for the forgiver is greater than their praise for the avenger, and to pardon is deemed good by them more assuredly. How is it, then, that to pardon and be gracious are deemed bad and a prolonged retribution is deemed good?

Furthermore, this is true with respect to someone who is harmed by being sinned against and whose rank is lowered by being disobeyed. But unbelief and faith, and obedience and disobedience, are on a par with respect to God (Exalted is He). Insofar as His divinity and loftiness are concerned, they are equivalent.[81] Moreover, even if one follows the path of retribution and deems it good, how could he deem good an eternal and everlasting punishment as retribution for a single word uttered in one moment?[82]

80. The second clause is a partial statement of one of the five principles that constitute the common core of Mu'tazilism. It is the doctrine of the intermediary position. According to the tradition, this was the doctrine that inaugurated the Mu'tazila as a distinct school of Islamic theology. As explained previously, the doctrine concerns the status of a Muslim who commits a major sin and dies without atoning for his sin. There were two views: one held that such a person was an infidel and the second that he was a believer. Wāṣil ibn 'Aṭā' (AH 80/699 CE–AH 131/748 CE), the founder of the Mu'tazila school, decreed that such a person was neither a believer nor an infidel, rather he was a grave sinner (*fāsiq*), which is an intermediary position between that of a believer and that of an infidel; and that a grave sinner will be condemned to hell for eternity, but he will be tormented at a lesser degree than an infidel.

81. The pronoun 'they' refers to unbelief and faith, obedience and disobedience.

82. The "single word" is a declaration of unbelief in God. This is a translation of the reading in the Jeddah edition. The reading in the Ankara edition may be translated as follows: 'Moreover, how could one deem it good to follow the path of retribution and, in addition to

A mental asylum is more suitable than gatherings of scholars for one whose intellect leads him to deem good such an extreme response. Rather we say that if one follows the very opposite of this path, it would be more reasonable and more in accordance with the regularity of deeming things good or bad—the regularity according to which the "estimation" and imagination make their judgments, as previously explained.

We, in fact, say that it is deemed bad for a man to punish someone for an old crime that is difficult to deter, except[83] for two reasons. One of them is that punishment should deter and serve an interest in the future. Punishment is thus deemed good out of concern lest a future purpose go unfulfilled. Therefore if there is no future interest to be served by it, punishment merely for the sake of retribution for what has passed is bad, because there is no benefit in it for the one punished or for any other person. Rather the perpetrator is harmed by it, so that not inflicting harm on him is good. Inflicting harm is deemed good only if it engenders a benefit. Since there is no benefit, and what has passed cannot be corrected, punishment here is the extreme of badness.[84]

The second reason is that we say:

If the victim is harmed and feels resentment and intense rage, then this rage is painful, and extinguishing it relieves the pain. Also, it is more befitting for the perpetrator to be the one to feel pain. When the perpetrator is punished, the pain of the sensation of rage is removed from the victim, but it is now felt by the perpetrator; and this is more proper. Although this too is a reason, it is indicative of a deficiency of the victim's intellect and of his being controlled by anger.

However, making punishment obligatory, when it serves no future interest for anyone known to God (Exalted is He) and does not prevent harm from befalling the victim, is the extreme of badness. This is more reasonable than one's statement that refraining from punishment is extremely bad.

At any rate, the whole discussion is fallacious. For being subject to an obligation posited by the estimative faculty on the basis of imagined needs

---

this, to deem good an eternal and everlasting punishment as a retribution for a single word uttered in one moment?'

83. I followed the Ankara edition in including 'except' (*illā*). The Jeddah edition leaves it out.

84. It is interesting to note that al-Ghazālī's conception of punishment is that of deterrence rather than of retribution. This should not be unexpected after the decidedly consequentialist treatment he gives of 'obligatory', 'good', and 'bad'. In the following paragraph, he will consider a type of a retributive justification for punishment, but he will ultimately reject it as revealing a shortcoming in the intellect of the victim. Even in considering the validity of the "retributivist" case, however, the reasoning al-Ghazālī employs has more to do with consequences than with desert.

is inapplicable to God, who is too sanctified to have needs. But we wanted to refute what is corrupt with what is corrupt to show that what they imagine is fallacious.[85]

# Sixth Proposition

*We claim that if the revelation had not come, it would not be incumbent upon mankind to know God (Exalted is He) and to thank Him for His blessings.*

Thus we contradict the Muʿtazilites, who say that the mere intellect makes this obligatory.

We prove the proposition by saying:

Does the intellect make it obligatory to reflect theoretically and to seek knowledge for the sake of a benefit obtainable from doing so, or in spite of its admitting that God's existence and nonexistence are on a par regarding immediate or later benefits? If you say that the intellect judges that [knowing God] is obligatory in spite of its admitting that there is absolutely no immediate or later benefit in it, then this is the judgment of ignorance, and not of the intellect. For the intellect does not enjoin acting frivolously; and everything that is devoid of all benefits is a frivolity. If, on the other hand, there is benefit in it, then it inevitably relates either to the one who is worshiped or to the worshiper. It is impossible for the benefit to relate to the one who is worshiped, since He is too exalted and sanctified to receive benefits. If it relates to the worshiper, then it must be either in this life or in the hereafter. As for this life, worship is pure toil in which there is no benefit. As for the hereafter, what is expected is a reward, but how does the worshiper know that he will be rewarded for it? Indeed, he might be punished for it. Hence, the judgment that he will be rewarded is foolishness that has no basis.[86]

It might be said:

It occurs to a person that he has a Lord, and if he thanks Him, He will reward him and bestow His blessings upon him, but if he shows ungratefulness for His blessings, He will punish him. It would never occur to him that

85. The point is that al-Ghazālī combats the corrupt Muʿtazilite view that God is obligated to reward and punish in accordance with desert with the corrupt view that God would only punish to fulfill a purpose. Since God is free from all needs and purposes, the view that He would only punish if the punishment fulfilled a purpose is itself "corrupt."

86. It is foolishness because, presumably, without revelation it is not known that there will be a reward for worshiping God. Acts of worship might be uncompensated or even punished. (See Fifth Proposition.)

it is possible to be punished for being grateful. And to guard against harm that is "estimated" by the intellect[87] is comparable to being at guard against a known harm.

We say:

We do not deny that the nature of a rational person makes him inclined to guard against harm, whether it is "estimated" or known. It is not forbidden to call such an inclination "obligatory," for there should be no quarrel over terminology. But our discussion concerns whether it is more proper to perform an act rather than to refrain from it on the grounds that there will be reward or punishment, when it is known that being grateful and being ungrateful are on a par with respect to God (Exalted is He). He is unlike any one of us, for we are comforted by gratefulness and praise, are moved by them, and enjoy them; and we are pained by ungratefulness and hurt by it.

If it becomes clear that both attitudes are on a par with respect to God (Exalted and Blessed is He), then preferring one of the two is impossible. Indeed, the opposite might occur to him, that is, he might [think that he would] be punished for being grateful for two reasons. One of them is that his preoccupation with being grateful subjects his mind and heart to toil and steers them away from pleasure and appetite, though he is a created servant, endowed with appetites and made able to enjoy them. Perhaps, his purpose is to indulge in pleasures and to make use of God's blessings, and not to toil in that in which there is no benefit for God (Exalted is He). This possibility is more likely.

The second is to compare himself to the one who wants to offer thanks to a king; and thus he investigates the king's qualities, manners, residence, the bedroom he shares with his wife, and all his hidden secrets as a repayment for the king's bounties upon him. It will be said to him: "With this type of gratefulness you deserve to have your head severed. What benefit does this nosiness bring you?[88] And who are you to investigate the secrets of the kings, their qualities, their deeds, and their manners? And why do you not busy yourself with what pertains to you?" Hence the one who seeks knowledge of God (Exalted is He) must know[89] the subtleties regarding His attributes and His acts, His wisdom and the purposes of His acts. Only someone of high status is qualified for all of this; how does a servant of God know that he is deserving of such a status?

87. That is, the estimative faculty of the intellect deems it harmful.

88. Alternatively, why are you consumed with this nosiness? Both translations are liberal. The literal translation is 'What have you with this nosiness?'

89. The expression 'must know' is the translation of the reading in the Jeddah edition. The reading in the Ankara edition may be translated as "is as he must know."

This shows that their contentions are fantasies that took hold of them by virtue of habit—fantasies, which may be inescapably opposed by other fantasies.[90]

It might be said:

If the source of obligation does not derive from the intellect, then this would result in confuting a messenger of God. For if he brings forth a miracle and says, "Reflect upon it," the addressee may say: "If the reflection is not obligatory, then I will not engage in it; and if it is obligatory, then it is impossible that its source is the intellect, since the intellect does not obligate; and it is impossible to be established by the revelation, since the revelation can only be verified by reflecting on a miracle; and the reflection cannot be made obligatory before verifying the revelation." This would result in preventing the truth of the prophecy from ever becoming apparent.

The answer is that the source of this question is ignorance of the nature of the obligatory. We have explained that the meaning of being obligatory is that there is a preponderance in favor of performing a given act over refraining from it in light of the prevention of harm that is "estimated" or known to occur[91] by refraining from the act. If this is what being obligatory means, then that which obligates is what gives preponderance, and that is God (Exalted is He). For if He attaches punishment to refraining from reflecting [on a miracle], then doing so would have preponderance over refraining from it. The meaning of the prophet's statement that it is obligatory is that it is made preponderant by God's attaching punishment to one of the two options. As for apprehension, it is simply the knowledge of the obligation and not [the source of] the obligation itself.[92] It is not a condi-

90. This is the conclusion of al-Ghazālī's argument against the one who says that it occurs to a person that if he is grateful to his Lord, he will be rewarded, and if he is ungrateful, he will be punished, and that it never occurs to a person that he might be punished for being grateful. Al-Ghazālī's point is that these beliefs and expectations are based on the human habit (or disposition) of being pleased when one is grateful to us, and being hurt when one is ungrateful to us. To assume that God acts in a manner similar to our habitual behavior is a fantasy, which can be opposed by equally possible fantasies, such as rewarding indulgence in pleasures and punishing preoccupation with worship.

91. That is, it is known to occur or deemed by the estimative faculty to occur. Although it is acceptable to translate *wahm* occasionally as imagination (or, even, fantasy), I think al-Ghazālī here intends the Avicennan technical sense of *wahm* (i.e., "estimation"), because he is talking about believing that harm will occur; and as we indicated previously, evaluative judgment with respect to such things as whether something is harmful is the domain of the estimative faculty.

92. This sentence is somewhat elliptical. Al-Ghazālī means that the intellect does not render something obligatory by apprehending it. The intellect simply apprehends an act to be obligatory once it was made obligatory by an independent cause. Performance of an act is made obligatory by being preponderant over refraining from it because refraining from the act would result in harm.

tion for something's being obligatory that its being obligatory be known; rather this knowledge should be available for the one who seeks it.

A prophet may say:

Infidelity is a deadly poison and faith is a healing that is a source of happiness, because God made one of them a source of happiness and the other deadly. I do not assign any obligation to you. For to obligate is to give preponderance, and the giver of preponderance is God (Exalted is He). I merely relate that it is a poison, and I guide you to a path in which you know my truthfulness and which is the reflection on a miracle. If you follow this path, you will know [my truthfulness] and be saved, and if you stray from it, you will be ruined.

This is analogous to a physician attending to a patient who is undecided between two medicines at his disposal.[93] The physician says to him: "Do not take this medicine, for it is fatal to a living being. You are able to know this by feeding it to this cat, which will die instantaneously; this proves what I told you. As for the other medicine, your recovery is in it. You are able to know this through experimentation: if you drink it, you will recover. It does not matter to me or to my teacher whether you die or recover; for my teacher is in no need of your existence, and neither am I." If the patient says to this, "Is this made obligatory upon me by the intellect or by your statement?, and so long as this is unclear to me, I will not engage in experimentation," he will cause his death; yet this will not harm the physician.

Similarly, God tells a prophet that obedience is recovery while disobedience is illness, and that faith is a source of happiness while infidelity is ruinous. He also tells him that He has no need for mankind, whether they become happy or miserable. The business of a messenger is to relate and to guide to the path of knowledge, and then to move on. He who reflects does so for his own sake and he who neglects to reflect does so against his own interest. This is clear.

It might be said: "The matter reverts to the intellect being the source of the obligation, since the addressee, when he hears the speech of the prophet and his preaching, anticipates punishment. Thus his intellect causes him to be cautious; and this can be attained only through reflection. Hence reflection becomes obligatory upon him."

We say:

The truth that dissolves this difficulty[94] without following imagination[95] or conforming to a decree is that what is obligatory, as explained, is simply a kind of preponderance with respect to an act. The obligator is

93. Literally, placed between his hands.

94. Literally, the truth that removes the cover of this.

95. In the Cairo edition it is *wahm* (imagination, or "estimation" in the technical sense), and in the Ankara and Jeddah editions it is *rasm*, which means, in the technical sense, a

God, because He is the giver of preponderance. A messenger relates what is preponderant. A miracle is a proof of his truthfulness in what he relates. Reflection is the cause of knowing the messenger's truthfulness. The intellect is the tool for reflection and for understanding the meaning of what is related. Human nature is disposed to being cautious as a result of the intellect's understanding of the warning. There has to be a nature that finds a promised punishment disagreeable and a promised reward agreeable if it is to be disposed to being cautious. Indeed, any one who cannot understand a warning and cannot appreciate it through belief or knowledge is incapable of being disposed to being cautious. Understanding can come only through the intellect. The intellect does not understand by itself that there is preponderance; rather it must hear this from a messenger. The messenger does not give preponderance to performing an act over refraining from it; but God is the giver of preponderance; and the messenger is an informer. The truthfulness of a messenger is not made evident through itself but through a miracle. The miracle proves nothing without reflection; and reflection is attained through the intellect.

The meanings have now been uncovered. The correct statement about these expressions is that what is obligatory is what is preponderant, the obligator is God (Exalted is He), the informer is the messenger, the apprehender of the warning and the truthfulness of the messenger is the intellect, and what is disposed to seek the path of salvation is the human nature. This is how the truth of this issue must be understood. No attention should be paid to the familiar statements that neither satisfy the desire nor clear an obscurity.

# Seventh Proposition

*We claim that sending prophets is contingent;*
*it is neither impossible nor obligatory.*

The Muʿtazilites say it is obligatory. The manner in which one can respond to them has already been explained.[96] The Barāhimites say that it is impossible.[97]

---

definition that is based on the extrinsic qualities of a thing. It is contrasted with *ḥadd*, which means a definition that is based on the intrinsic qualities of a thing.

96. Al-Ghazālī is referring to his explication of the notion of obligatory. Since an act is obligatory for someone when performing it will prevent a harm that would befall him if he were to refrain from it, no act is obligatory for God since nothing could benefit or harm Him.

97. The Barāhimites (*al-barāhima*) comprise many religious sects, including the Sabians, the worshipers of Brahma, and other religious sects that subscribe to the doctrine of

A demonstration of its possibility is that since it is proved that God (Exalted is He) is a sayer and it is also proved that He is powerful and so capable of representing inner speech by creating expressions, sounds, scripts, and other indications, it is proved that sending messengers is possible. We do not mean by it[98] anything other than that a tiding regarding what leads to benefit in the hereafter and what leads to harm—benefit and harm being understood according to the habitual course of things— subsists in God's essence, that an act proceeds from Him that conveys this tiding through a person, that He commands [that person] to relate the tiding, and that an act proceeds from Him that transcends the ordinary and accompanies that person's claim to having a message. None of this is impossible in itself. It is founded on [the possibility of] inner speech and the creation of that which represents speech and that which proves the truthfulness of a messenger.

If it is judged to be impossible from the point of view of deeming something good or bad, then we will have uprooted this principle with respect to God (Exalted is He). Furthermore, it cannot be deemed bad to send a messenger, in light of the canon for deeming something bad.[99] The Muʿtazilites, in spite of allowing this,[100] do not deem [the sending of a messenger] bad.

Since neither conceiving it as bad nor conceiving it as impossible is in itself necessary, we should mention the Barāhimites' skeptical arguments. The utmost doubt they offer is three skeptical arguments.

The first skeptical argument is their saying: "If a prophet is sent to relate something that agrees with the intellect, then it is dispensable for the intellect.[101] In this case the sending of the prophet is a frivolity; and this is impossible for God (Exalted is He). If he is sent to relate something that

---

reincarnation. Since the Sabians believe in the prophethood of John the Baptist, not all the Barāhimites deny the possibility of prophecy. Al-Ghazālī may have in mind a theistic sect that al-Shahrastānī, among others, describes as the followers of an Indian man called Barāhim who denies the possibility of prophecy on the grounds that reason is sufficient for attaining belief in and knowledge of God. Al-Shahrastānī attributes the following argument to Barāhim, which is, as will be seen, the first skeptical argument discussed by al-Ghazālī. Whatever a messenger relates is inevitably one of two types: it is either intelligible or unintelligible. If it is intelligible, then it can be known on the basis of the intellect alone; if it is unintelligible, then it should be rejected as unbefitting human rationality. Either way there is no need for the messenger. (See al-Shahrastānī, *al-Milal wa-l-Niḥal*, vol. II, pp. 601–606.)

98. The pronoun 'it' refers to God's sending a messenger.

99. According to al-Ghazālī, something is deemed bad, as we learned at the beginning of this treatise, if it is contrary to one's purpose (or need). Hence nothing could be deemed bad in relation to God, since He has no needs; and sending messengers cannot be deemed bad in relation to mankind, since it accords with their purpose of attaining eternal happiness and avoiding eternal misery.

100. That is, allowing the canon for deeming things good or bad to apply to the acts of God.

101. What is dispensable for the intellect is the prophet's relating of the tiding.

does not agree with the intellect, then it would be impossible to believe and accept it."

The second skeptical argument is that it is impossible to send a messenger because it is impossible to establish his truthfulness. For if God (Exalted is He) asked mankind in words to believe him and spoke to them loudly, there would be no need for the messenger. On the other hand, if He does not speak to them in words, then He aims to prove the messenger's truthfulness by an act that transcends the ordinary. This cannot be distinguished from sorcery, talismans, and wondrous anomalies, which, for someone who has no knowledge of them, transcend the ordinary. And if these things are on a par in their transcending the ordinary, the miracle cannot be trusted, and no knowledge of the truthfulness of the messenger is attained.

The third skeptical argument is that if the miracle is distinguished from sorcery, talismans, and illusions, how do we know the truth? Perhaps God wants to misguide and mislead us by making us believe the prophet. Perhaps whatever the prophet says leads to happiness actually leads to misery, and whatever he says leads to misery actually leads to happiness; but God (Exalted is He) wants to lead us to ruin and to mislead us by the statements of the prophet. For misguiding and misleading are not impossible for God, according to you, since the intellect does not deem things good or bad.

This is the strongest skeptical argument that a Muʿtazilite should use to achieve his purpose of proving the necessity of asserting that the intellect can deem a thing bad. He should say that if misleading is not bad, then the truthfulness of a messenger can never be known, and it cannot be known if his message contains misinformation.[102]

The response is that we say:

As for the first skeptical argument, it is weak. For the Prophet (may God bless him and grant him peace) came to relate tidings that intellects cannot know independently but that they understand independently once they

102. Al-Ghazālī's point is that the third skeptical argument offers a Muʿtazilite his strongest argument for the claim that the intellect on its own is capable of deeming something bad. Al-Ghazālī presents the argument in a compact form. Here is an expanded version of the argument. The third skeptical argument can be employed as a reductio ad absurdum against the supposition that the intellect on its own can never deem something bad. For if we assume that this supposition is true, then the third skeptical argument would go through, and we would have to conclude that the truthfulness of a messenger can never be ascertained, since the intellect cannot deem it bad that God might be misguiding and misleading us by this message. A Muʿtazilite considers this a disastrously absurd conclusion, for he thinks that it is beneficial for mankind to be able to ascertain the truthfulness of a messenger, and, indeed, that it is possible for them to do so. This would seem to establish the truth of the Muʿtazilite doctrine that the intellect on its own can make judgments about what is good and bad.

know. The intellect does not guide one to what is beneficial and what is harmful among the acts, statements, morals, and beliefs; and it does not distinguish between the one who is miserable and the one who is happy; just as it cannot independently apprehend the qualities of medicines and drugs. But if it knows, then it understands, believes, and benefits from hearing the tidings; hence it avoids what leads to ruin and aims at what leads to happiness.[103] This is similar to its benefitting from the statements of a physician in its knowing the illness and the remedy. The intellect knows the truthfulness of the physician from circumstantial evidence and other matters. Similarly, it infers the truthfulness of the messenger from miracles and circumstantial evidence. There is no difference [between the two cases].

As for the second skeptical argument, which is about a miracle's not being distinguished from sorcery and illusions, this is not so. No rational person thinks that sorcery might result in bringing the dead to life, turning a stick into a serpent, splitting the moon, parting the sea, healing the blind and the leper, and similar matters. Briefly stated, if the one who says this claims that every object of God's power could be obtained through sorcery, then he makes a claim that is necessarily known to be impossible. And if he differentiates certain acts from others,[104] then it is conceivable that a messenger may be believed on the basis of a thing that is known not to be sorcery. It remains next to reflect on the individual messengers and their specific miracles: whether what they perform is the sort of thing that can be achieved through sorcery or not. When there is doubt about something, it will not be believed if either the prophet does not challenge a group of the

103. It might be thought that the passage is not asserting the impossibility of the intellect's knowing independently what leads to benefit or harm and who will be happy or miserable in this worldly life but only in the hereafter. Yet it seems that the passage is denying the possibility of such knowledge concerning both. Al-Ghazālī argues that the intellect *on its own* cannot make such value judgments without the aid of other resources, such as emotions, dispositions, sense experiences, and revelation. For instance, the intellect *on its own* cannot determine whether a certain bitter drink is beneficial or harmful without certain external and internal experiences, such as hearing a physician telling him that the drink is poisonous or that it is a medicine that will cure his illness. And even after he is being told that his cure is in this medicine, the intellect on its own cannot determine that this is a good thing. It can only make such a determination if the person has a desire for (or, an interest in) attaining health. Furthermore, as al-Ghazālī argued earlier, the intellect needs revelation in order to know which course of action is ruinous and which is beneficial. It might be interesting to note that the doctrine that the intellect on its own cannot deem something good or bad anticipates Hume's similar doctrine that the rules of morality cannot be derived from reason alone.

104. That is, if he is willing to admit that at least some acts, unlike others, cannot be produced by sorcery.

greatest sorcerers with it[105] or he does not allow them enough time to meet the challenge, or[106] they are able to meet the challenge. However, it is not our purpose now to examine specific miracles.

As for the third skeptical argument, which is based on imagining God's misleading us and thus generating skepticism [about the message], we say that so long as the manner in which the miracle proves the truthfulness of the prophet is known, it is known that he can be trusted. This is so when we know the message and its meaning and we know the manner of the proof.

We say:

Suppose a person proclaims to a king's soldiers in the presence of the king that he is a messenger from the king to them and that the king requires that they obey him when he distributes provision and land to them, and they ask him for a demonstration while the king remains silent. He says: "O king, if I told the truth in what I have claimed, then rise from your bed three times successively and then sit down, which is contrary to your habit." After the person has made his request, the king rises three times successively and then sits down. The people who are present would acquire a necessary knowledge that he is indeed a messenger of the king, before it occurs to them to ask whether this king is accustomed to misleading others or whether this is impossible for him.

In fact, if the king says, "You told the truth; I have made you a messenger and a representative," it would be known that he is a messenger and a representative. By the same token, if the king performs an act that is contrary to his habit,[107] then that would be as if he said: "You are my messenger." This would constitute the initiation of an investiture, appointment, and delegation of authority. It is inconceivable that a delegation of authority is a lie though this is conceivable in relating news. The knowledge that the delegation of authority is indeed a true delegation is necessary.[108]

105. Reading *idhā lam yataḥaddā bih al-nabiyy* (if the prophet does not challenge with it) instead of *mā lam yataḥaddā bih al-nabiyy* (unless the prophet challenges with it), which is the reading in the original.

106. *Aw* (or) is the reading in the Ankara edition. In the Jeddah edition, it is *wa* (and).

107. That is, he performs an act that is contrary to his habit as confirmation that the messenger is being truthful in claiming that he is appointed by the king. The act that is contrary to the king's habit is analogous to the miracle that proceeds from God as confirmation of the truthfulness of a prophet. Recall that, according to the Ash'arites, a miracle is simply an act that is contrary to the "habitual" manner in which God causes occurrents.

108. Al-Ghazālī's point is very interesting. He is discussing a type of utterance that contemporary analytic philosophers call "speech act" (or "performative utterance"). When a king says to a person "I hereby make you my representative," the person immediately becomes a representative of the king. The king performs an action by making this utterance: it is the action of initiating "an investiture, appointment, and delegation of authority" (to use al-Ghazālī's expression). This is analogous to a justice of the peace's saying to a man and a

This is why no one denied the truthfulness of the prophets on this basis, but they denied that what the prophets brought forth transcends the ordinary, and they attributed it to sorcery and illusions, and they denied the existence of a Lord, who is a sayer, who commands and forbids, and who proves the truthfulness of the messengers. Whoever admits all of this attains a necessary knowledge of the truthfulness of the prophets.

It might be said:

Suppose that people saw God (Great and Glorious is He) with their eyes and heard Him with their ears, when He said: "This is my messenger, telling you the path of your happiness and of your misery." What assures you that He did not mislead the messenger and those to whom he is sent, and did not say of the one who would be miserable [in the hereafter] that he would be happy and of the one who would be happy that he would be miserable? For this is not impossible, since you do not believe that the intellect can deem a thing bad. In fact, if we suppose that there was no messenger but

---

woman, who just exchanged marriage vows, "I hereby pronounce you husband and wife"; the justice of the peace, by making this utterance, performs the action of making the man and woman a married couple. There is a great deal of contemporary literature about speech acts, and, as a result, a good deal is known about their nature, types, and conditions. A point that is relevant to al-Ghazālī's discussion is that, as widely believed, speech acts are of two types: conventional and nonconventional. Nonconventional speech acts require a complex set of intentions to be realized by the performer of a speech act. For instance, if one says to another "I agree with you" while he has no intention of agreeing with the other, no agreement would be enacted. Conventional speech acts, on the other hand, require no relevant intention, but they require a convention that bestows an appropriate authority. For instance, if the justice of the peace, in our previous example, utters his words ("I hereby pronounce you husband and wife") while he lacks the intention of enacting the marriage, the action would still be preformed, and the marriage would be enacted. However, if someone who lacks the appropriate authority pronounces a couple to be husband and wife, while he has all the relevant intentions, the intended action would not be performed, and the marriage would not be enacted. The king's pronouncement in al-Ghazālī's example is of the conventional type. Once the king utters the appropriate words before his army, the man becomes his representative, unless the king withdraws the authority by performing another speech act. Al-Ghazālī's point about miracles is that the king can perform the same act without making a speech act; he can perform "a miracle" that confirms the statement "The king made me his representative and my proof that he did is the performance of this miracle" when uttered by a certain person. Al-Ghazālī says that the complex action that consists of the man's making this utterance and the king's performing this "miracle" is equivalent to the king's performing the speech act of saying "I hereby make you my representative." Since a speech act is not subject to truth or falsity—but rather, it is subject to success or failure—and since the king has the appropriate conventional authority, the complex act of the man's making his utterance and the king's performing his "miracle" cannot fail; and hence the man must be the representative of the king. This is analogous to the complex act that consists of a man's saying that he is the messenger of God and that the performance of a certain miracle is his proof for his truthfulness and of the successful performance of the miracle. (For contemporary discussion of speech acts, see Austin 1962 and 1970, Searle 1969, and Strawson 1964.)

God (Exalted is He) told us in words "Your salvation is in fasting, praying, and almsgiving, and your ruin is in refraining from them," how do we know that He is truthful? He might be deceiving us in order to lead us astray and ruin us. For, according to you, lying is not bad in itself; and if it is bad, doing what is bad and unjust is not impossible for God (Exalted is He), neither is what leads to the ruin of all mankind.

The response is that we can trust that God does not lie, since lying pertains to speech, and God's speech is not sounds or letters, through which deceit could occur. It is, however, a meaning that subsists in the self of the Exalted. For each thing a man knows, there subsists in himself a tiding that represents what he knows in a manner appropriate to his knowledge. It is inconceivable that there should be lies in these tidings;[109] similarly it is inconceivable with respect to God (Exalted is He).

In sum, lying in inner speech is impossible; this validates our trust,[110] which they deny. It has become clear that so long as the act is known to be an act of God (Exalted is He), and to exceed the ability of the humans, and so long as it accompanies the claim to prophethood, necessary knowledge of the truthfulness [of the prophet] is attained. Any doubt would be about whether the act is within the ability of humans or not. Hence, once it is known that it is an act of God, no room for doubt remains at all.

It might be said: "Do you deem charismata[111] possible?" We say: "People have different opinions about these, but the truth is that they are possible." This is based on God's departing from what is habitual in response to a supplication of a human being or due to a need of his. This is not impossible in itself, because it is possible, and it does not lead to some other impossibility. Furthermore, it does not lead to invalidating miracles,[112] since a charisma is simply brought forth without a challenge associated with it. If it is associated with a challenge, we call it "miracle" and it necessarily proves

109. There can be no lie in these tidings because there can be no lie in the inner-speech representations of what one knows. The next passage makes this point explicit.

110. That is, it ensures trusting that God does not send a messenger with a false message in order to mislead us.

111. The Arabic word is *karāmāt* (plural of *karāma*). *Karāma* is a power possessed or an act performed typically by a religiously devout person (a saint) that transcends what is humanly possible and that is a gift from God. It is distinguished from *muʿjiza* (miracle), which only a prophet may perform. There is no English word other than 'charisma' that comes close to capturing the meaning of *karāma*. 'Charisma' is, however, a term of Christian theology, and has decidedly Christian connotation. I am using this word here, divorced from its Christian connotation, to mean simply "a miracle performed by a person who is not a prophet." I reserve the word 'miracle' for *muʿjiza*.

112. It might be thought that the existence of charismata invalidates the prophets' miracles, since if someone who is not a prophet can perform something miraculous, then performing a miracle is not the exclusive mark of a prophet.

the truthfulness of the challenger. And if it is not [in response to] a supplication, it might even be brought forth at the hands of a sinner, because it is in itself an object of divine power.

It might be said: "Is it an object of power to bring forth a miracle at the hands of a liar?"

We say:

A miracle that is associated with a challenge has the same role as God's saying: "You are truthful and you are My messenger." To demonstrate the truthfulness of a liar is impossible in itself. And every one to whom it is said "You are My messenger" becomes a messenger and is prevented from being a liar. The conjunction of someone's being a liar and his being told what is equivalent to God's saying "You are My messenger" is impossible, because his being a liar means he is not told "You are My messenger," and the meaning of a miracle is that he is told "You are My messenger." The act of the king, in our previous example, is necessarily equivalent to his saying "You are my messenger." Hence it has become clear that this is not an object of power because it is impossible; and what is impossible is not within the reach of power.

This is the completion of this treatise. So let us now undertake to prove the prophethood of our prophet, Muḥammad (may God bless him and grant him peace), and to prove [the truth of] what he relates. And God knows best.

# FOURTH TREATISE

∴

IT CONSISTS OF FOUR CHAPTERS.

THE FIRST CHAPTER: ON ESTABLISHING THE PROPHETHOOD OF OUR PROPHET, MUḤAMMAD (MAY GOD BLESS HIM AND GRANT HIM PEACE).

THE SECOND CHAPTER: ON SHOWING THAT WHAT HE RELATES REGARDING THE RESURRECTION AND CONGREGATION, THE PATH, THE BALANCE, AND THE TORMENT OF THE GRAVE IS TRUE. IT CONSISTS OF AN INTRODUCTION AND TWO SECTIONS.

THE THIRD CHAPTER: ON THE IMAMATE. IT CONTAINS AN INVESTIGATION INTO THREE ISSUES.

THE FOURTH CHAPTER: ON EXPLAINING WHICH AMONG THE SECTS MUST BE CHARGED WITH INFIDELITY AND WHICH MUST NOT, AND ON ENUMERATING THE CANONS ON WHICH ONE MUST RELY FOR IMPUTING INFIDELITY. WITH THIS WE CONCLUDE THE BOOK.

# FIRST CHAPTER

## *On establishing the prophethood of our prophet, Muḥammad (may God bless him and grant him peace)*

We need to establish his prophethood specifically in response to three sects. The first sect is the ʿAysawites.[1] They assert that he is a messenger to the Arabs only and not to others. This is clearly false. For they admit that he is truly a messenger, and it is known that a messenger does not lie, and he claimed that he was a messenger to both worlds,[2] and he sent his emissaries to Khosru, Caesar, and the rest of the kings of the non-Arabs. This was widely reported about him. Hence what they assert is impossible and contradictory.

The second sect is the Jews. They deny his truthfulness, not due to reflection on him and his miracles, but because they claim that there is no prophet after Moses (peace be upon him). Thus they deny the prophethood of Jesus (peace be upon him). We must, therefore, establish for them the prophethood of Jesus; for their understanding might fall short of apprehending the miraculousness of the Qurʾān, but it would not fall short of apprehending the miraculousness of bringing the dead to life and healing the blind and the leper. We say to them: "What leads you to differentiate

1. According to al-Shahrastānī, al-ʿAysawiyya was a sect that broke away from mainstream Judaism. Its members were the followers of Abū ʿĪsā Isḥāq ibn Yaʿqūb al-Aṣfahānī, who was active during the reign of the second ʿAbbāsid caliph, Abū Jaʿfar al-Manṣūr (r. AH 137/754 CE–AH 159/775 CE). He claimed that he was a prophet and the first of five emissaries of the awaited Messiah, all of whom would precede the coming of the Messiah, and that God spoke to him directly and commanded him to liberate the Israelites from the sinful nations and unjust kings. Al-Shahrastānī also mentions that Abū ʿĪsā forbade his followers to eat the flesh of all animals, commanded them to pray ten times a day, and imposed many laws that conflicted with Jewish law. (See al-Shahrastānī, *al-Milal wa-l-Niḥal*, vol. 1, pp. 257–258.)

2. The Arabic word is *thaqalayn* (literally, two weighty things). They stand here for the world of humans and the world of jinns. The word is borrowed from the Qurʾānic verse: *We shall settle your affairs, O both worlds* [*thaqalān*] (55:31).

between the one who proves his truthfulness by bringing the dead to life and the one who proves it by turning the stick into a serpent?" They have no way out of this at all; but they are misled by two dubious doctrines. One of them is their saying that supersession[3] is impossible in itself, because it implies initiation and then alteration, and this is impossible with respect to God (Exalted is He).[4] The second is that some atheists instructed them[5] to say that Moses (peace be upon him) said "Uphold my religion so far as there are heavens and earth," and that he said "I am the seal of the prophets."

As for the first dubious doctrine, it is refuted by a proper understanding of supersession, which is nothing but a pronouncement indicating the invalidation of an established decree whose continuation was conditional on not being followed by a pronouncement that invalidated it. It is not impossible for a master to say to his slave "Stand up" in absolute terms, without indicating to him the intended duration of his standing, and the slave knows that standing is required of him for as long as the master's interest in his standing persists. The master knows the duration of his interest but he does not make it known to the slave. The slave understands that he is commanded to stand up absolutely, and that his duty is to continue to stand up indefinitely until the master tells him to sit down. If he tells him to sit down, he would sit down without imagining that the master has become aware of or has perceived an interest that he did not previously know of and just now has come to know. It is possible that the master knows the duration of his interest in having the slave stand up and knows that it is best if he does not make it known to the slave but, rather, commands him in absolute terms, so that he may continue to obey; and then when his interest changes, he commands him to sit down.

The differences between the decrees of the divine laws must be understood in a similar fashion. The coming of a prophet is not by itself an invalidation of the divine laws of those before him, not even in most of the decrees. Only some of the decrees are invalidated, such as changing the kiblah or removing a prohibition, and so forth. These are interests that vary with

3. This is a literal translation of the Arabic word *naskh* (in this context, 'supersession', 'supplantation', 'abrogation', 'nullification', or 'invalidation'). Al-Ghazālī uses this term to refer to one law's superseding another law. In particular, he is referring to the Islamic belief that certain Islamic laws superseded certain Jewish laws.

4. This is because, according to a common theological doctrine of the monotheistic traditions, God is not susceptible to change, and supersession seems to imply change in God's decrees.

5. The reading in the Jeddah edition is *laqqanahum* (instructed them, or prompted them), and in the Ankara edition *li-fihm* (according to the understanding of), which renders the English as follows: "The second is that according to the understanding of some of the atheists, they say . . .".

the eras and the states. There is nothing in them that indicates a change, an awareness following ignorance, or a contradiction.

Moreover, the Jews could maintain this doctrine only if they believed that there was no divine law from the time of Adam (peace be upon him) until the time of Moses (peace be upon him), and they denied the existence of Noah and Abraham (may God bless them and grant them peace) and their divine laws. In this way they would be no different from those who deny the prophethood of Moses and his divine law. [To maintain] all of this is to deny what is known with certainty through widely transmitted reports.

As for the second dubious doctrine, it is silly for two reasons. One of them is that if what they say about Moses were true, then no miracle would have appeared at the hands of Jesus. Miracles are necessarily a proof of one's truthfulness. Thus how can God demonstrate the truthfulness of someone who shows the untruthfulness of Moses, when He also demonstrated the truthfulness of Moses?[6] Hence, will they deny the existence of Jesus' miracle or will they deny that bringing the dead to life is a proof of the truthfulness of the challenger?[7] If they deny any part of this, it becomes necessary for them to do the same with respect to Moses' revelation—a necessity from which they have no escape. Yet if they concede it, it becomes necessary for them to assert the untruthfulness of those who relayed to them that Moses (peace be upon him) said: "I am the seal of the prophets."

The second is that this dubious doctrine was taught to them after the coming of our prophet, Muḥammad (may God bless him and grant him peace), indeed after his death. If it were true, the Jews would have used it as an argument [against him], given that they had fought Islam with the sword. Our prophet affirmed the truthfulness of Moses, and arbitrated among the Jews according to the Torah, as regarding the judgment of stoning and others. Why was this doctrine, then, not shown to him in the Torah? And what dissuaded them from doing so? It is known with certainty that the Jews did not use this argument; for if it were the case that they had, it would have

6. The reading in the Jeddah edition is *wa-huwa ayḍan muṣaddaqun* (and his truthfulness has also been demonstrated [by God]) and in the Ankara edition is *wa-huwa ayḍan muṣaddiqun lahu* (and he [Jesus] also believes in his [Moses'] truthfulness). The argument is a reductio ad absurdum. Suppose what they say about Moses—namely, that he said that he was the seal of the prophets—is true and that Jesus indeed performed miracles. God, by giving Jesus miracles, demonstrates the truthfulness of Jesus—namely, that he is a prophet. But this means that God has demonstrated the falsity of Moses' claim that he was the seal of the prophets. This is contradictory, since God previously demonstrated the truthfulness of Moses by giving him miracles. Therefore, one must deny that Moses said that he was the seal of the prophets or deny the miracles (and hence the prophesy) of Jesus.

7. The challenger here is Jesus, who challenged people with his miracles.

been decisive and irrefutable, and it would have been reported widely. It is also known that they did not forsake this argument while they were able to use it; for they were keen on attacking Muḥammad's revelation with all possible means in order to protect their lives, wealth, and women.

If the prophethood of Jesus (peace be upon him) is established for the Jews, then we establish the prophethood of our prophet (may God bless him and grant him peace) using [the same proofs] with which we establish his prophethood for the Christians.[8]

The third sect is the Christians.[9] They permit supersession, but they deny the prophethood of our prophet, Muḥammad (may God bless him and grant him peace), for they deny his miracles. There are two ways to prove his prophethood by means of miracles.

### [THE FIRST WAY OF PROVING THE PROPHETHOOD OF MUḤAMMAD BY MEANS OF MIRACLES: THE MIRACLE OF THE QURʾĀN]

The first is to focus on the Qurʾān. We say: "A miracle has no meaning except when it is combined with a prophet's making a challenge in order to confirm his truthfulness with a challenge that mankind cannot meet." Muḥammad's challenge to the Arabs,[10] given their obsession and occupation with literary eloquence, is widely reported. The lack of an imitation[11] of the Qurʾān is well known. For if there were one, it would have been widely known. When even the worst poets challenged others with their poetry and their challenge was met, the competitions and the exchanges between them were widely known. Therefore it cannot be denied that he challenged the Arabs with the Qurʾān; it cannot be denied that the Arabs were masters of literary eloquence; it cannot be denied that they were eager to refute his prophecy with all possible means in order to protect their religion, lives, and wealth, and to rid themselves of the domination and subdual of the Muslims; and it cannot be denied that they were incapable [of meeting the challenge]. For if they were capable, they would have done so, since habit

8. Al-Ghazālī's point is that if the Jews can be convinced of Jesus' prophethood, then they can also be convinced of Muḥammad's prophethood using the same arguments that would convince the Christians of Muḥammad's prophethood.

9. The expression 'the Christians' (*al-naṣārā*) is omitted in the Ankara edition.

10. Al-Ghazālī is referring to Muḥammad's challenge to the Arabs to produce a piece of literature that is of the same literary eloquence as the Qurʾān's (that is, to produce an *imitation* of the Qurʾān). The challenge is declared in the Qurʾān in several verses.

11. The Arabic word, which al-Ghazālī uses frequently in this section, is *muʿāraḍa*. It has several meanings, including "opposition," "meeting a challenge," "counterpart," and "imitation." I use different translations of this word, depending on the context.

requires by necessity that whoever is able to prevent destruction from befalling him must engage in such prevention. Had they done so, that would have been well known and relayed.

These are premises, some of which are known through widely transmitted reports and some through the course of habits. All of this induces certainty. So there is no need for elaboration.

In a similar fashion, the prophethood of Jesus (peace be upon him) may be established. A Christian cannot deny any part of this. It is possible for him to tell about Jesus and to be faced[12] with a denial of Jesus' claim to prophethood, of his proof of bringing the dead to life, of the reality of bringing the dead to life, or of the failure of others to meet his challenge. Or it might be said that his challenge was met but it was not reported. All of these are denials that are not available to the one who accepts prophecy in principle.

It might be asked: "In what way is the Qur'ān miraculous?" We say: "Literary excellence and eloquence, together with marvelous constructions and a style that is beyond the style of the Arabs in their speeches, poems, and the rest of their literary genres." Combining these constructions with such eloquence is miraculous beyond the ability of mankind.

Indeed, it might be observed[13] that the Arabs have poems and speeches that are judged to be eloquent,[14] and it might be related about some of those who attempted to produce imitations of the Qur'ān that they followed Qur'ānic constructions after they learned them from [hearing] the Qur'ān, but their imitations lacked eloquence and were feeble, as was reported about the fraudulent verses of Musaylima the Liar,[15] when he said: "The

12. Literally, it is possible that he would be opposed regarding Jesus.

13. *Yarā* (see or observe) is the reading in the Jeddah edition. In the Ankara edition, it is *yarid* (relate).

14. The thought is incomplete. The point is that those eloquent speeches and poems lack the distinctive Qur'ānic constructions.

15. Musaylima ibn Ḥābīb al-Ḥanīfī, who is famously known in Islamic history as 'Musaylima the Liar' (*al-kadhdhāb*), claimed to be a messenger of God and attempted to establish contact with the Prophet Muḥammad, who rebuffed his efforts and ridiculed his claims. Musaylima had many followers, and his movement continued until the reign of the first caliph, Abū Bakr, who extinguished his movement in a bloody battle referred to as 'the Battle of Yamāma' (AH 11/632 CE). Many of the Prophet's companions were killed in that battle—a matter that greatly worried 'Umar ibn al-Khaṭṭāb, a close companion of the Prophet who would become the second caliph. So he impressed upon Abū Bakr the urgent need to officially collect and record the Qur'ān before the companions who memorized the whole Qur'ān (the *ḥāfiẓ*s) died out. Parts of the Qur'ān had been transcribed during the life of the Prophet by several appointed companions, the whole Qur'ān was committed to memory by many companions, and every companion memorized at least some parts of the Qur'ān (they had to in order to perform the daily prayers). But there was as yet no complete ver-

elephant. What do you know about the elephant? It has a tail like a hemp rope. And a long trunk."[16] It might be possible to produce this and others like it, but they are so inferior that those who have literary eloquence find them repulsive and ridiculous.

As for the literary eloquence of the Qur'ān, all the Arabs judged it to be marvelous, and it is never relayed that any one of them insisted that there is a fault with its style. Therefore, it is miraculous and beyond the ability of mankind in these two aspects; I mean, in the combination of these two aspects.[17]

It might be said: "Perhaps the Arabs were occupied with warring and fighting, so that they did not attempt to produce an imitation of the Qur'ān; had they aimed at it, they would have been able to do so. Or perhaps other obstacles prevented them from busying themselves with it." The reply is that what they state is madness. For repelling the challenge of a challenger by means of a literary composition is much easier than repelling it by means of the sword, considering what befell the Arabs at the hands of the Muslims in terms of capture, killing, captivity, and the waging of battles.

Furthermore, what they mention does not refute our conclusion. The Arabs abstained from meeting the challenge only because God (Exalted is He) made them abstain. To prevent someone from doing what is in his power and what is habitual is one of the greatest miracles. For if a prophet says "The proof of my truthfulness is that I today can move my finger and no human can do the same," and if no one is able to meet his challenge on that day, his truthfulness is established. The loss of their ability to move, in the light of the fact that their organs are healthy, is one of the greatest miracles. Hence if it is assumed that the ability [to produce an imitation of the Qur'ān] exists, then their not having anyone to represent them and their abstention from meeting the challenge is one of the greatest miracles,

---

sion of the Qur'ān that was deemed to be the authoritative one. There was therefore a need to examine the written and oral traditions, collect all the verses and chapters of the Qur'ān, and reach an agreement about which elements culled from these various sources constitute the most authentic version of the Qur'ān. The process was concluded during the reign of the third caliph, 'Uthmān ibn 'Affān, with the production of five to seven official and identical written copies of the Qur'ān. The copies were distributed to the main provinces (*amṣār*) of the Islamic state along with the directive that all future copies of the Qur'ān were to be produced in accordance with these official copies. It is worth noting that not all the Prophet's companions who had extensive knowledge of the scripture were consulted in the process of determining the official version; some of them were angered at having been excluded.

16. The construction follows in part a common Qur'ānic construction, such as the verses: *Indeed, We have revealed it in the Night of Power. And what do you know about the Night of Power? The Night of Power is better than a thousand months* (97:1–3).

17. The two combined aspects are the ones al-Ghazālī mentioned earlier: literary eloquence and marvelous constructions.

considering their dire need to rid themselves of the Prophet's control over their lives and wealth. All of this is known by necessity.

This is the way to prove Muḥammad's prophethood to the Christians. If they insist on denying any of these clear matters, then we should only engage them by displaying a similar opposition with respect to Jesus' miracles.

### [THE SECOND WAY OF PROVING THE PROPHETHOOD OF MUḤAMMAD BY MEANS OF MIRACLES: OTHER MIRACLES]

The second way is to establish his prophethood by means of a collection of events that occurred for him and that transcended the ordinary, such as the splitting of the moon, the speech of the mute brute, the gushing of the water from between his fingers, the stones' glorification of God when they were held in his hand, little food turning into much, and other events that transcend the ordinary. All of this is a proof of his truthfulness.

If it is said that none of these events is relayed via widely transmitted reports, then we say that even if this is true, it does not refute our conclusions, so long as the *totality* of these events was reported widely. This is analogous to the bravery of ʿAlī (may God be pleased with him)[18] and the generosity of Ḥātim,[19] which are known with certainty through widely transmitted reports, although no one of these events is fully proven through widely transmitted reports.[20] For the establishment of the qualities of bravery and generosity is known with certainty from those events *collectively*. Similarly, the totality of those wondrous affairs is proven through widely transmitted reports. No Muslim would doubt them at all.

If a Christian says, "These matters, neither individually nor collectively, have reached me through widely transmitted reports," then it would be said to him, "If a Jew who has never mixed with Christians moves to a country and claims that the miracles of Jesus (peace be upon him) were never

18. ʿAlī ibn abū Ṭālib was the Prophet's cousin and son-in-law. He was the fourth and the last of the caliphs known in the history of Islam as "the rightly-guided caliphs" (*al-khulafāʾal-rāshidūn*). Those are the first four caliphs to rule immediately after the death of the Prophet. ʿAlī's reign (AH 36/656 CE–AH 40/661 CE) was marked by a severe and bloody division among the Muslims (*al-fitna*), which resulted in his assassination and the rise of the Umayyad dynasty (AH 40/661 CE–AH 133/750 CE). The Shīʿa believe that he was the first of the infallible Imams and that he was divinely entitled to rule the Muslim nation after the death of the Prophet. ʿAlī is widely considered one of the bravest companions of the Prophet.

19. Ḥātim al-Ṭāʾī was a pre-Islamic figure, who was famous among all the Arabs for his generosity and hospitality.

20. The events here are the historical narratives about ʿAlī's bravery and Ḥātim's generosity.

widely reported to him, and even if they were, they were reported by the tongues of Christians, who have a vested interest in the matter,[21] then how are you different from this Jew?" The only way to be different is to say: "You must mix with the people among whom these reports are widely transmitted, so that you too should become aware of them; for someone who is deaf is never aware of widely transmitted reports, and so is the one who behaves like the deaf." This would be our defense when someone denies, in the same manner, the wide transmission of a report. And God knows best.

21. I followed the Ankara edition in reading *muhtammūn bih* (care about it, interested in it, or have a vested interest in it) instead of *muttahamūn bih* (accused of it, or are suspect in it), which is the reading in the Jeddah edition.

# SECOND CHAPTER

## *On showing that it is obligatory to believe in matters reported in the revelation[22] and deemed possible by reason*

IT CONSISTS OF AN INTRODUCTION AND TWO SECTIONS.

22. In the Ankara edition it is *sharʿ* and in the Jeddah edition it is *samʿ*. As explained previously, in this context both mean "revelation." However, *sharʿ* is more precise, since *samʿ* refers to those parts of the revelation, such as the affairs of the hereafter, which cannot be known independently.

# Introduction

What is not known through necessity is divided into: that which is known through a proof of reason but not through the revelation, that which is known through the revelation but not through reason,[23] and that which is known through both.

That which is known through a proof of reason but not through the revelation is the occurrence of the world and the existence[24] of the Originator and His power, knowledge, and will.[25] If any of this is not established, it cannot be established through the revelation. For revelation is founded on speech. Hence if inner speech cannot establish something, then the revelation cannot establish it either. It is impossible for anything that is prior in rank to inner speech to be established by inner speech and what is founded on it. Speech itself, according to our description, also cannot be established through the revelation.[26] However, some of the investigators argued and claimed that it can, as we previously indicated.

Regarding that which is only known through the revelation, it speci-

23. This (second) clause is omitted in the Ankara edition.

24. In the Jeddah edition it is *wujūd* (existence) and in the Ankara edition it is *wujūb* (necessity).

25. This category should be defined as that which is known through a proof of reason but *cannot* be known through the revelation. There are numerous propositions, such as the propositions of geometry, that are known through proofs of reason but not through the revelation. However, there is *no* logical impossibility in their being known through the revelation. They are *in fact* not known thorough the revelation because they are not reported in the revelation, but they *could have been,* had God decided to tell us about them, just as he told us, as many maintain, about historical and natural facts. If we define this category in these terms, then it makes sense that al-Ghazālī restricted this category to knowledge of the occurrence of the world and of the existence of the Creator and His basic attributes. As he will argue below, these propositions *cannot* be established by means of the revelation since knowing that the revelation is true presupposes knowledge of the truth of these propositions. (See the following note.)

26. Al-Ghazālī is concerned here with circular reasoning. As discussed in the Second Treatise, God's speech is inner speech, and since the revelation is God's speech, it is inner speech. To believe that this inner speech is revealed by God, one has to believe first that there is a God who is a sayer. So the existence of God and His attributes is prior in logical order to the belief in the revelation. Furthermore, that a certain speech is God's revelation is also prior in logical order to what is proved on the basis of the revelation. It follows that

fies one of two possibilities as the actual one. This is inaccessible to the intellect independently. It can only be known from God (Exalted is He) through revelation and inspiration, and we know it, through hearing, from the one to whom it is revealed—these are such things as the resurrection and congregation,[27] reward and punishment, and the like.

That which is known through both is everything that is within the bounds of reason, and posterior in rank to God's speech; for instance, the issue of seeing God, and God's being the exclusive creator of all the movements and modes, and whatever is analogous to these. Furthermore, whatever is claimed to be revealed must be examined: if reason deems it possible, then it must be believed conclusively if the testimonial evidence is conclusive and does not permit its content and testimonial chain to be regarded as merely likely; if the evidence is probabilistic, then it must be believed as a likelihood. The obligation to believe with one's tongue and heart is an act, like other acts, that can be founded on probabilistic evidence.

For instance, we know conclusively that the companions rebuffed everyone who claimed that a servant of God might be the creator of anything or any mode. They denied that merely on the basis of God's statement *God is the Creator of everything*.[28] It is known that although this statement is universal, it might be particular. Hence, its being universal is a matter of likelihood. The matter becomes conclusive through an investigation of the rational methods that we have stated. However, we know that they used to deny that before investigating rational methods.[29] Thus it should not be assumed that they allowed probabilistic evidence only in matters of jurisprudence; on the contrary, they also allowed it in affirming matters of belief and testimony.

Regarding what reason deems impossible, if it is reported in the revelation, it must be interpreted metaphorically. It is inconceivable that the revelation contains what is conclusively contrary to reason. Most of the *ḥadīth*s that are literally anthropomorphic are inauthentic; and those of

---

God's existence, His attributes, and the creation of the world cannot be established through the revelation, but only through a proof of reason.

27. 'Resurrection and congregation' is the common translation of *al-ḥashr wa-l-nashr*. Individually, each of *al-ḥashr* and *al-nashr* means, in this context, "resurrection." The literal meaning of the former is "to gather" and of the latter is "to spread." When they are used together as one expression to describe the affairs of the hereafter, they refer to the act of resurrecting the dead and congregating them before God.

28. Qur'ān, 39:62.

29. That is, they used to deny that man is the creator of anything, before investigating any rational method.

them that are authentic are not conclusive but are amenable to metaphorical interpretation.[30]

If reason is neutral regarding a certain thing, not deeming it impossible or possible, then it must be believed because of [the availability of] testimonial evidence. It is sufficient for believing it that reason does not deem it impossible; and it is not required that reason deem it possible.[31] There is a difference between the two cases—a difference that a dull mind might not notice, so that it does not comprehend the difference between one's saying "I know that the matter is possible," and his saying "I don't know whether it is impossible or possible." The difference between them is as great as that between heaven and earth: the first is possible with respect to God (Exalted is He) and the second is not possible.[32] For the first is having knowledge of a thing's possibility and the second is not having knowledge of a thing's impossibility. In both cases affirmation is obligatory.[33] This then is the introduction.

30. As we have seen in previous treatises, al-Ghazālī on the issue of *ta'wīl* (metaphoric interpretation) is closer to the Muʿtazilites than to the Ashʿarites. Al-Ashʿarī, like Aḥmad ibn Ḥanbal and other opponents of *ta'wīl*, rejects metaphorical interpretation of anthropomorphic Qur'ānic verses and *ḥadīths*. They are *almost* literalists. They accept the literal meaning of these verses and *ḥadīths* but they deny that God is like any of His creation. Hence, for example, if a tradition implies that God has a hand, they affirm a hand for God but they deny that it is like any hand created by God. Their motto may be stated as follows: "We affirm for God all the qualities implied by Qur'ānic verses and authentic *ḥadīth*s without specifying their *modalities* (*bilā kayf*) and we affirm that God is unlike anything else." The *true* literalists, on the other hand, affirm for God these qualities together with their anthropomorphic modalities. Al-Ghazālī transcends the influence of al-Ashʿarī in this matter and adopts a rationalist position: all anthropomorphic descriptions of God that are found in the revelation (Qur'ān and Ḥadīth) must be interpreted metaphorically. (See, e.g., First Treatise, Eighth Proposition.)

31. This is an interesting statement about the scope of reason. Al-Ghazālī apparently is not committed to the law of excluded middle regarding what is provable by reason. It seems that he allows for something to be neither provable to be impossible nor provable to be possible. So if there is no proof of reason that something is impossible, it does not necessarily follow that the thing is possible. In contemporary parlance, human reason is incomplete: there might be something impossible for which there is no proof of reason that it is impossible and there might be something possible for which there is no proof of reason that it is possible.

32. The first saying, "I know that the matter is possible," is possible with respect to God and with respect to man. The second saying, "I do not know whether it is impossible or possible," is possible with respect to man, since human reason is incomplete, but it is not possible with respect to God, since God's knowledge is perfect.

33. If the revelation supports a claim that is declared neither possible nor impossible by reason, or that is declared possible by reason, then it is obligatory to believe it. These are the two cases al-Ghazālī refers to.

# First Section

*This concerns showing that reason affirms what is revealed regarding the resurrection and congregation, the torment of the grave, the path, and the balance.*

### [RESURRECTION]

Regarding resurrection, we mean by it the reoccurring of creation. It is proved through conclusive evidence in the revelation, and it is possible on the basis of the first creation.[34] For to re-create is a second creation, which is no different from creating originally. It is called "re-creation" only in relation to the previous origination. He who is capable of creating and originating is capable of re-creating. This is what is intended by the Exalted's statement: *Say "He will give them life who created them for the first time."*[35]

It might be said: "What do you mean? Are the substances and modes annihilated and then all re-created? Or are the modes annihilated but not the substances, and it is the modes that are re-created?" We say that all of this is possible. There is no conclusive proof in the revelation that certifies one of these possibilities.

One of these possibilities is that the modes are annihilated and the body of man remains, having the form of dust, for instance. Thus life, color, moistness, composition, shape, and other modes are removed from it. The meaning of re-creating them would be that those modes themselves are brought back to the body or that it is given again modes similar to them. For us, a mode does not persist.[36] Life is a mode, and the existent is at every hour another mode, and the man is that man by virtue of his body. He is one not by virtue of his modes, for every mode is renewed and is not the previous mode. Hence it is not a necessary condition for re-creation that the same modes be re-created. We mention this because some of our colleagues have concluded that it is impossible to re-create the same modes. This is false. However, the arguments for its falsity are elaborate; there is no need for this, given our purpose here.

The second possibility is that bodies are annihilated as well, and then re-

34. Literally, it is possible as proved by its origination.

35. Qur'ān, 36:79.

36. As al-Ghazālī stated previously (First Treatise, Third Proposition), a mode is continuously created from one moment to the next. Being here and now is part of the essence of a mode.

created by being originated for the second time. It might be said: "In what way is the re-created body distinguished from the first? And what is the meaning of your statement that the re-created body is exactly the same as the first, when what is nonexistent has no continuing identity, which would allow [the same one] to be brought back?"

We reply:

In God's knowledge, the nonexistent is divided into that which had a previous existence and that which had no previous existence, just as an anteriorly eternal nonexistence is divided into that which will have existence and that which God (Exalted is He) knows will have no existence. This division according to God's knowledge cannot be denied; for God's knowledge is comprehensive and His power is all-encompassing. The meaning of *re-creating* [the same thing] is substituting existence for a nonexistence that had previous existence, and of *creating* its counterpart, originating existence for a nonexistence that had no previous existence. This is the meaning of re-creating.

So long as a body is supposed to persist and the issue is reduced to renewing modes that are replicas of the first ones, the revelation has been affirmed, and the problem of re-creating and distinguishing the re-created thing from the first is resolved.

We have discussed this matter with elaboration in the book *The Incoherence of the Philosophers*, and based our refutation of their doctrine on positing the persistence of the soul,[37] which for them is not extended, and positing its return to govern a body, whether this body is the exact same body of the man or another body.[38] This is a necessary consequence that is not in accordance with what we believe; for that book was composed to refute their doctrines, not to establish the true doctrines. Given that they assumed that man is what he is by virtue of his soul and that his occupation with governing a body is accidental to him, and since, according to them, the body is an instrument, we made it necessary for them—since they believe in the persistence of the soul—to affirm the reality of re-creation as the return of the soul to its governing a body—any body.

To give now a theoretical verification of [what we stated in] this chapter would lead us to an investigation into the spirit, the soul, life, and what is true of them. The [fundamental] beliefs should not be burdened with such penetration into these limits of the intelligibles. What we have mentioned is sufficient for explaining the moderation in belief regarding what is reported in the revelation.

37. The pronoun 'their' refers to the Islamic philosophers.

38. See al-Ghazālī, *Tahāfut al-Falāsifa*, 20th Discussion, pp. 282–306.

## [THE TORMENT OF THE GRAVE]

As for the torment of the grave, it is proved conclusively in the revelation. Widely transmitted reports indicate that the Prophet (may God bless him and grant him peace) and his companions (may God be pleased with them) sought refuge from it in their supplications to God. A famous statement of the Prophet, when he passed by two graves, is "They are both being tormented."[39] Another proof for it is God's statement, *And a dreadful torment engulfed the people of Pharaoh. The fire! They are exposed to it morning and evening,*[40] to the end of the verse.

Since it is possible, it is obligatory to believe in it. The manner in which it is possible is apparent. However, the Muʿtazilites deny it, for they say: "We see the dead person visible and he is not being tormented; besides, the dead might be devoured and eaten by lions." This is madness. As for observing a person, this is an outward observation of the body. What experiences the torment, however, is part of the heart or of the inner self, whatever that may be. It is not necessary for being tormented to exhibit an outward bodily movement. The one who observes the appearance of a sleeping person does not see what the sleeping person feels of pleasure when he has a nocturnal emission and the pain when he imagines a beating and the like. If the sleeping person wakes up and relates his visions, pleasures, and pains, someone who never experienced sleep would readily disbelieve him, being deceived by the outward calmness of his body when he observed him. This is similar to the Muʿtazilites' denial of the torment of the grave. Regarding the one whom the lions devoured, the most one needs to say is that the belly of the lion is a grave. Bringing life again to a part that can perceive pain is possible. Not everyone who feels pain feels it in his whole body.

As for Munkar and Nakīr's questioning the dead,[41] it is true, and believing in it is obligatory, because it is reported in the revelation and because it is possible. What is required of them[42] is only to induce understanding ei-

39. Reported by Abū Dawūd, *Sunan*, I.11, no. 20; Aḥmad ibn Ḥanbal, *Musnad*, I.225, nos. 1979, 1980; Bukhārī, *Ṣaḥīḥ*, IV.55, no. 216; XXIII.82, no. 1361; Dāramī, *Sunan*, I.61, no. 739; Ibn Māja, *Sunan*, I.26, no. 347; Muslim, *Ṣaḥīḥ*, II.34, no. 292; Nasāʾī, *Sunan*, I.27, no. 31; and Tirmidhī, *al-Jāmiʿ al-Ṣaḥīḥ*, I.53, no. 70.

40. Qurʾān, 40:45–46. The rest of verse 46 is: *and on the day when the Hour is proclaimed [it will be said] "Admit the people of Pharaoh to the severest torment."* This part indicates that the first part deals with a torment prior to the Day of Judgment. Traditional Islamic belief refers to this type of torment as 'the torment of the grave'.

41. According to the traditional Islamic belief, Munkar and Nakīr are two angels who question the dead about their beliefs and past deeds.

42. The pronoun 'them' refers to the two angels Munkar and Nakīr.

ther with or without sound, and what is required of him[43] is only to understand. Understanding requires nothing but life, and man does not understand through the whole of his body but only through a part of the inside of his heart. Bringing life to a part that understands a question and answers it is possible and within God's power.

There remains someone's statement: "We see the dead but we do not see Munkar and Nakīr, we do not hear their voices when they ask questions, and we do not hear the voice of the deceased when he answers." This would necessarily imply the denial of the Prophet's seeing of Jibrīl (peace be upon him), and his hearing of Jibrīl's speech and Jibrīl's hearing of his answer.[44] He who believes in the revelation cannot deny this;[45] for it only requires that God create in him a hearing of that voice and a seeing of that individual. And these were not created in the ones present near him nor in ʿĀʾisha (may God be pleased with her),[46] though she used to be present near him at the time that he was in the midst of receiving a revelation. Denying this[47] is rooted in atheism and in the denial of the far extent of God's power. We have concluded our refutation of it.

To deny this would also necessarily imply denying the visions of a sleeping person and his hearing of loud, disturbing sounds. If it were not for experience, one would readily disbelieve all those who hear from one who has slept a tale about his affairs.

Woe to the person whose imagination falls short of appreciating that God's power encompasses these matters,[48] which are trivial in relation to the creation of the heavens and the earth and what is between them and the wonders they contain. The reason those who have gone astray turn away from believing in these matters is precisely the reason they would, were it not for observation forcing them to believe this, turn away from believing that man, with all the wonders and marvels that he contains, is created

43. The pronoun 'him' refers to the dead person.

44. Jibrīl, in the Islamic tradition, is the angel who relayed the revelation to the Prophet Muḥammad.

45. That is, he cannot deny the possibility of Munkar and Nakīr's questioning the deceased, since the power that made the Prophet hear and see Jibrīl while no one around him shared his experience can make the deceased hear and answer the questions of Munkar and Nakīr while no one present is made aware of the deceased's experience.

46. ʿĀʾisha bint Abū Bakr was the wife of the Prophet Muḥammad and the daughter of his close companion Abū Bakr, the first caliph after the death of the Prophet. She was one of the principal narrators of Ḥadīth.

47. Again, the demonstrative 'this' refers to Munkar and Nakīr's questioning the dead.

48. *These matters* are the torment of the grave, Munkar and Nakīr's questioning the dead, and the Prophet's seeing and hearing Jibrīl.

from a filthy drop. Therefore, that for which there is no proof that it is impossible must not be denied due to its mere unlikelihood.

## [THE BALANCE]

As for the balance,[49] it, too, is true. It is proved in the revelation conclusively. Since it is possible, it is obligatory to believe in it.

It might be said:

How are the deeds weighed, when they are modes that have ceased to exist and what has ceased to exist cannot be weighed? If it is posited that they are brought back and created in the body of the balance, this would be impossible, since it is impossible to bring back modes. How could the movement of a man's hand, which is an expression of obedience, be created in the body of the balance? Does the balance move with it, so that it would be a movement of the balance and not the movement of a man's hand? Or does the balance not move, and hence the movement would subsist in a body that does not move with it (which is impossible)? Furthermore, if the balance moves, its tilt would vary according to the durations and numbers of movements and not according to the rank of their merits; for a movement of a part might be more sinful, by miles,[50] than the movement of the whole body. This is impossible.

We say that God's Messenger (may God bless him and grant him peace) was asked about this. He said: "The sheets of deeds are weighed; for the noble scribes write down the deeds in sheets, which are bodies. If they are placed in the balance, God (Great and Glorious is He) creates in its pan a tilt that is equivalent to the rank of the good deeds, and He has the power to do what he wishes."[51]

It might be said: "What benefit is there in this? And what is the meaning of this reckoning?" We say that no benefit is to be sought in an act of God (Exalted is He), for [He says]: *He is not questioned about what He does but they are questioned [about what they do]*.[52] We have proved this. Moreover, it is not unlikely that there *is* a benefit in this: the servant of God would see the magnitude of his deeds and he would know that he is being recompensed fairly, or that he is being forgiven by an act of grace. It is not unlikely that he who is intent on punishing his agent for a misdeed regarding his

49. The Arabic term is *al-mīzān*, which means "the scale." I used 'the balance' because it is the standard choice of the translators of the Qur'ān.

50. The unit of length al-Ghazālī uses is *farsakh*, which is an old Arabic unit that is roughly equivalent to three miles.

51. Reported by Qurṭubī, *al-Jāmiʿ li-Aḥkām al-Qurʾān*: VII.135.

52. Qur'ān, 21:23.

property or is intent on forgiving him would make it most clear to his agent the magnitude of his misdeed, so that he may know that the man is being fair in punishing him or that he is being gracious in forgiving him. This is if a benefit is sought in God's acts, and we have refuted this.

### [THE PATH]

Regarding the path, it is also true, and because it is possible, it is obligatory to believe in it. It is a bridge that extends over the surface of hell. All of mankind will walk on this bridge, and when they all arrive there, it will be said to the angels: *And stop them, for they must be questioned.*[53]

It might be said: "How is this possible, when, according to what has been narrated, the path is finer than a hair and sharper than a sword? Thus how is it possible to pass over it?" We say that if this question is asked by someone who denies the power of God (Exalted is He), then our response to him is to establish the all-encompassing nature of His power, and we have already done so. On the other hand, if it is asked by someone who affirms His power, then walking on the path is no more wondrous than walking on air. The Lord (Glorious and Exalted is He) is capable of creating the power to do this. Its meaning is that He creates in the person the power to walk on air, and He neither creates in his essence [a disposition] to fall down nor does He create in the air [a disposition] to part. If this is possible with air, [it is surely possible with] the path, which is, in any case, more solid than air.

## Second Section

This section concerns apologizing for not including sections that could have dealt with matters of belief that I deemed more proper to refrain from discussing, because a brief discussion of beliefs should contain only the important matters that are essential for a description of sound belief. As for matters that there is no need to bring to mind and that, if brought to mind, are such that there would be no harm in not learning about and not knowing their requirements, wading through them to discover the truth of the matter is not suitable to what is required to refine the fundamental beliefs. Such a study consists of three types of subjects: intellectual, semantical,[54] and legal.

53. Qur'ān, 37:24.

54. The Arabic term is *lafẓī* (literally, verbal). However, all the issues that al-Ghazālī discusses under this heading are semantical.

An example of an intellectual subject is an investigation into the occurrent power, into whether it attaches to two opposites or not, whether it attaches to different objects or not, whether it is possible for an occurrent power to attach to an act [occurring in a place] different from the place of the power, and similar matters.

An example of a semantical subject is an investigation into that which is referred to by the term 'sustenance': what is it? And what are the limits and referents[55] of the terms 'success', 'failure', and 'faith'?

An example of a legal subject is an investigation into when it is obligatory to enjoin the good, what the condition of repentance is, and comparable matters.

All of this is not important for religion.[56] What is important is for man to remove any doubts that occur to him regarding the essence of God (Exalted is He) to the extent we discussed in the First Treatise, regarding His attributes and their characteristics as we discussed in the Second Treatise, regarding His acts in order to believe that they are possible and not obligatory as discussed in the Third Treatise, and regarding God's Messenger (may God bless him and grant him peace) in order to know his truthfulness and to believe all that he related as we discussed in this treatise. What is outside these matters is not important. However, we will discuss with respect to each type one of the issues that we ignored, in order to know the issues that are similar to it, and to show that it is outside the important issues, which are sought in matters of belief.

### [AN INTELLECTUAL ISSUE]

As for an intellectual issue, there is, for instance, the disagreement among people regarding one who is killed: is it to be said that he died at his predestined time? And if it is supposed that he was not killed, is it necessary that he die at that time or not? There is no harm in avoiding this subject. But we will describe an approach to its solution.

Hence we say:

If one of two things is not correlated with the other, but they occur together, then to posit the non-occurrence of one of them does not necessitate the non-occurrence of the other. For instance, if Zayd and 'Amr died together, and then we suppose the non-occurrence of Zayd's death, neither the non-occurrence of 'Amr's death nor the occurrence of his death follows

55. I followed the Ankara edition in reading *musammayātuhā* (their referents) instead of *musabbibātuhā* (their causes), which is the reading in the Jeddah edition.

56. The phrase 'for religion' (*fī al-dīn*) is omitted in the Jeddah edition.

from this. Similarly, if Zayd dies during a lunar eclipse, and we suppose the non-occurrence of the death, the non-occurrence of the eclipse does not necessarily follow from this. And if we suppose the non-occurrence of the eclipse, the non-occurrence of the death does not follow; for none of them is correlated with the other.

As for two things between which there is a relation and a correlation, there are three categories. One of them is the relation of equivalence, such as the relation between right and left, and between above and below. It is necessary that one of them would be absent if the other is supposed to be absent, because they are related to each other such that the true nature of one of them can only subsist with the other's subsistence.

The second is that they are not equivalent, but one of them is prior in rank, such as the condition and the conditioned. It is known that the absence of the condition necessitates the absence of the conditioned. Thus, if we see one's knowledge together with his being alive, and his will together with his knowledge, the absence of knowledge necessarily follows from supposing the absence of life, and the absence of will from the absence of knowledge. This is expressed as a condition; it is that which must exist in order for the other thing to exist, while the existence of the other thing is not through it, rather it is with it.[57]

The third is that the relation is between a cause and an effect. The absence of the effect necessarily follows from supposing the absence of the cause if the effect has only one cause. If it is imagined that it has [more than one] cause, the absence of the effect necessarily follows from supposing the absence of *all* the causes. The absence of all effects does not necessarily follow from supposing the absence of a cause, but only the absence of that cause's specific effect follows.

After explaining this meaning we return to the issue of killing and death. Killing is severing the head, and it consists of modes that are the movements of the beheader's hand and of the sword, and of modes that are the separations of parts of the beheaded's neck. Another mode co-occurs with these modes—namely, death. If there is no correlation between the severing and death, the absence of death does not follow from supposing the absence of severing; for they are two things created together, co-occurring in accordance with the habitual course of things, but there is no correlation

57. I believe that al-Ghazālī is describing a *necessary* condition that is not a *cause*. If *C* is a necessary condition for *A*, but not a cause of it, then not-*C* entails not-*A* (that is, *C* must exist in order for *A* to exist) but *A*'s existence is not brought about by *C*. I think this is what he means by saying that it exists "with it" but "not through it." The next case al-Ghazālī considers is a case of causality.

between one and the other. They are similar to co-occurring things that are not co-occurrent according to the habitual course of things.

If the severing of the head is the cause and originator of death, and there is no other cause, the absence of death necessarily follows from its absence. Among those who affirm causation, there is no disagreement regarding death's having causes other than severing the head, such as ailments and internal causes. Hence the absence of death does not follow absolutely from the absence of severing, unless the absence of the rest of the causes is supposed in addition to this.

We return to our purpose. We say that anyone among the followers of the Sunna who believes that God is the exclusive originator, that there is no generation,[58] and that no created thing is the cause of a created thing would say: "The Lord (Exalted is He) is the exclusive originator of [the conjunction of] death and the severing of the head. Hence supposing the absence of severing does not necessitate the absence of death." This is the truth.

He who believes that [the severing of the head] is a cause and adds to this his observation of a sound body and of no other external cause of death believes that if the severing is absent and there is no other cause, then the effect must be absent too, since all causes are absent. This belief is correct, if it is correct to believe in causation and to restrict all causes to what is known to be absent.[59]

Therefore, the dispute over this issue is prolonged. Most of the investigators of it do not appreciate its source. Hence [the solution to] it must be sought in the canon we mentioned regarding the omnipresence of God's power and the annulment of generation. On the basis of this, it must be said about the one who is killed that he died at his predestined time, for this predestined time is the time at which God (Exalted is He) created his death, whether it was accompanied with the severing of the head, a lunar eclipse, the falling of rain, or not. All of these, for us, are co-occurrents and not causes, but some co-occur repeatedly according to the habitual course of things,[60] and some do not.

58. 'Generation' (*tawallud*) is a concept that was introduced earlier. It describes the capacity of one thing to generate another. One might believe that God is the exclusive originator but still believe that certain things that God originates carry within themselves the potentiality for other things, and that when the right circumstances obtain this potentiality is actualized and new things are *generated* from the previous ones. In this sense God remains the originator because he originated the first things *actually* and the second things *potentially*.

59. The "causation" referred to here is the causation between created things, and "the causes" are the causes of death.

60. 'According to the habitual course of things' is my translation of a single expression *bi-l-ʿāda* (literally, due to the habit).

However, some posit a natural cause for death arising from our disposition, and claim that every temper has a designated degree of potentiality: if it is left without interference, it will reach the end of its [natural] duration, and if it is corrupted by way of destruction, there would be a shortening of its duration in relation to its natural requirement. A predestined time is the natural duration. For instance, it might be said that a wall will last one hundred years according to the characteristics of its build, but it might be demolished by an axe immediately. Its predestined time is a way of expressing its duration that is in accordance with its essence and potentiality. Hence it would be necessary to say that if it is demolished by an axe, it is not demolished at its predestined time. And if nothing happens to it externally until it falls apart, it would be said that it fell apart at its predestined time. The expression 'predestined time' is understood according to this principle.[61]

## [A SEMANTICAL ISSUE]

As for the second issue, which is semantical, there is, for instance, the disagreement among people regarding faith: does it increase and decrease or is it always at the same level?

The source of this disagreement is not knowing that the term is ambiguous—I mean the term 'faith'. Once the denotations of this term are distinguished, disagreement is removed. The term has three meanings. It might be used to express certain and demonstrative belief. It might also be used to express a conformist belief when it is unquestionable. It might, further, be used to express belief that is accompanied by deeds in accordance with it.

The proof that it is used to express the first meaning is that he who knows God by means of a proof and dies after having this knowledge is judged to have died a believer. The proof that it is used to express conformist belief is that the populace of the Arabs believed God's Messenger (may God bless him and grant him peace) merely because of his goodness and kindness to them and because of their reflection on the states of his affairs, without reflection on proofs for monotheism and on the implications of his miracles, and the Prophet used to affirm their faith. God (Great and Glorious is He) says, *You will never believe us*,[62] that is, you will not be a believer.[63] God's

61. Literally, this expression is founded on that principle.

62. Qur'ān, 12:17.

63. The verse al-Ghazālī cites occurs in the story of Joseph, when his brothers, after throwing him into an empty well, went to their father, Jacob, and claimed that Joseph was devoured by a wolf. They said: "You will never be *mu'min* (literally, a believer) of us," and by that they meant that you would never be *muṣaddiq* (literally, someone who believes the

Messenger (may God bless him and grant him peace) did not distinguish between different types of belief.[64] The proof that it is used to express deeds is the Prophet's saying "The adulterer does not commit adultery while he is a believer"[65] and his saying "Faith has more than seventy divisions, the least of which is the removal of obstacles from the road."[66]

We return to our purpose, and so we say that if 'faith' is used in the sense of demonstrative belief, it cannot be imagined to increase or decrease. Rather, certainty, if it is achieved with completion, cannot be increased, and if it is achieved without completion, then it is not certainty. Certainty is an all-or-nothing property, in which no increase or decrease is imaginable, unless what is intended is an increase in clarity, that is, an increase in the reassurance of the soul. For the soul, at first, is reassured to some extent regarding theoretical beliefs that are certain; when proofs accumulate regarding a single matter, this accumulation of evidence has the benefit of increasing the reassurance. Everyone who studies a science is aware of a variation in his soul's reassurance regarding necessary knowledge, such as that two is greater than one and that the world is an occurrent and its originator is one. He is also aware of the variation between issues due to the abundance or scarcity of their proofs. The variation in the reassurance of the soul is apparent to anyone through introspection. If 'increase' is explained in this sense, it need not be withheld from believing [with certainty].

If 'faith' is used in the sense of conformist belief, then in no way can one deny variation in it. For we apprehend through observation a variation in the states of a Jew, a Christian, and a Muslim regarding their commitments to their beliefs. One of them might be such that no amount of intimida-

---

truthfulness) of us. Al-Ghazālī invokes the Qur'ānic text to argue that because the Arab masses believed (were *muṣaddiqs* of) the Prophet, they became believers (*mu'mins*) in God; in other words, had they *not* believed the Prophet, they would *not* have become believers. The argument turns on the use of the Arabic terms *mu'min* and *muṣaddiq* (both are typically translated as 'believer'). The former is used usually when the intended sense is "believing in God" or "having faith" and the latter when the intended sense is "believing the truthfulness of someone." Al-Ghazālī is arguing here that the terms *mu'min* and *muṣaddiq* can be interchangeable—more specifically, that *mu'min* is sometimes used in the Qur'ān to mean *muṣaddiq*. The meaning of the original is lost in the translation. Although I added 'you will not' to convey part of the intended meaning, the English sentence is still obscure.

64. Literally, between a belief and a belief.

65. Reported by Bukhārī, *Ṣaḥīḥ*, XLVI.30, no. 2475; Ibn Māja, *Sunan*, XXXVI.3, no. 3936; and Muslim, *Ṣaḥīḥ*, I.24, no. 57.

66. Reported by Abū Dawūd, *Sunan*, XXXIV.15, no. 4676; Aḥmad ibn Ḥanbal, *Musnad*, II.414, no. 9334; Bukhārī, *Ṣaḥīḥ*, II.3, no. 9; Ibn Māja, *Sunan*, INTRODUCTION.9, no. 57; Muslim, *Ṣaḥīḥ*, I.12, no. 35; Nasā'ī, *Sunan*, XLVII.16, nos. 5004, 5005; and Tirmidhī, *al-Jāmi' al-Ṣaḥīḥ*, XLI.6, no. 2617.

tion, frightening, scientific verification, or imaginative convincing would have an effect on him or diminish the hold of dogma on his heart, and, in the case of another, in spite of his being determined in his belief, his heart might be more compliant with respect to accepting what is certain. This is because the dogma in one's heart is like a commitment in which there is none of the relief and comfort of certainty, and a commitment varies in its strength or weakness. No fair-minded person would deny this type of variation. It is only denied by those who have heard the names of sciences and beliefs, but their souls have never perceived their true nature,[67] and they have never taken notice of the variation of their states and the states of others regarding these matters.

If 'faith' is used in the third sense, which includes acting in addition to having belief, it is obvious that variation is applicable to action. However, does persistence in action lead to variation in belief? This requires reflection. It is more proper in this regard to abandon pretense.[68] The truth lies in the best of what is said [about this subject]. So I say that persistence in performing pious deeds has the effect of strengthening the soul's confidence regarding conformist belief and of securing it in the soul. This is a matter that is known only to the one who introspects the states of his soul, monitors them during his persistence in performing pious deeds and during his lack of persistence, and observes a variation in the state of his inner self. His comfort with his beliefs increases because of his persistence in action, and his confidence becomes stronger. In fact, a believer who for long persisted in action in accordance with his belief is much more resistant to being influenced by one who is trying to change him and create doubts in him than a believer who has been persistent for a short time. Indeed, the habitual course of things requires this. For if one who feels in his heart mercy for an orphan pats him on the head and looks after him, he would discover in his heart, when he does acts in accordance with mercy, an increase in the depth of mercy; and if one who feels in his heart humbleness with respect to another acts in accordance with this humbleness by prostrating himself before him and kissing his hand, his veneration of and humbleness with respect to the other increases. It is for this reason that we worship God by persisting in acts that are required by the heart's veneration of Him—acts such as bowing and prostrating, which lead to an increase in the heart's veneration of Him. These are matters that are denied by those who are pe-

67. Literally, they have never perceived their "taste" in their souls.

68. The pretense here, I presume, is to insist that persistence in action has no relation to the strength of belief.

dantic in their speech and who come to know the structure of the sciences by hearing their names without apprehending them through the experience of theoretical reflection.[69] This is the truth regarding this issue.[70]

An issue of this type is people's disagreement regarding the meaning of 'provision'.[71] The Mu'tazilites say that this consists of what a man owns. So they thought it necessary that God (Exalted is He) makes no provisions for animals.[72] They might also say that it is what is gained lawfully. We say to them: "It follows that unjust men would die after living all their lives without ever receiving provisions from God."[73] Our colleagues say that provision consists of whatever one makes use of, and that it is divided into that which is lawful and that which is unlawful. And they elaborate on the definition of provision and the definition of grace. To waste time in such matters is the practice of one who does not distinguish between what is important and what is not, and who does not appreciate the value of the remainder of his life and the insignificance of the issue. One's life must be spent only on that which is important. The theorists face problematic issues, such that investigating them is more important than investigating the conditions of using certain terms and the requirements of that usage. We ask God (Exalted is He) to guide us to occupy ourselves with what is relevant to us.

### [A LEGAL ISSUE]

As for the third issue, which is legal, there is, for instance, the disagreement among people regarding a sinner: May he enjoin the good and forbid evil?[74] This requires a legal reflection. How, then, can it be appropriate to discuss it here, and briefly? At any rate, we say that the truth is that he may enjoin

69. Literally, through the "taste" of theoretical reflection.

70. The issue here is the semantical issue of deciding whether the term 'faith' denotes a quality that permits variation or not, that is, whether faith is a matter of degree or is an all-or-nothing property.

71. The Arabic word is *rizq* (provision, or sustenance). It refers here to the provisions that God makes for the creation.

72. This is because, presumably, it cannot be truly claimed that a nonhuman animal *owns* things.

73. This is meant as a modus tollens argument. It runs as follows. If God's provision for a person is that which the person gains lawfully, then unjust men, given that they never gain anything lawfully, receive no provisions from God. Since the consequent is false (for God makes provisions for all people), the antecedent is false.

74. The Arabic verb is *yaḥtasib*, which is commonly used with a noun describing an act. For example, the statement that so-and-so *yaḥtasib* such-and-such act (or deed) means that so-and-so does this act for the sake of God and His reward. In Islamic law, the term is used in a more restricted sense, which is to enjoin the good and forbid evil (*ya'mur bi-l-ma'rūf wa-yanhā 'an al-munkar*).

the good and forbid evil. The approach is to present the matter in stages. Thus we ask: "Is it a requirement for enjoining the good and forbidding evil that the one who enjoins and forbids be infallible with respect to minor and major sins?" If this were made a requirement, then the consensus would be breached. For the prophets' infallibility with respect to major sins is known through the revelation, but with respect to minor sins is disputable. Where can an infallible person be found in this world?

If, on the other hand, they say that this is not a requirement, since the man who wears silk, for instance, though he is being disobedient to God, may forbid others from committing adultery and drinking alcohol,[75] then we ask: "May the one who drinks alcohol disapprove of an infidel's unbelief, try to prevent him from subscribing to unbelief, and even fight him because of it?" If they say "No," they breach the consensus. For the Muslim armies consistently contain both those who commit sins and those who are obedient to God, yet none is prevented from the fight, neither during the time of God's Messenger (may God bless him and grant him peace) nor during the time of his companions and their followers.

If they say "Yes,"[76] we ask: "May the one who drinks alcohol prohibit murder or not?" If they say "No," we ask: "What is the difference then between this one and the man who wears silk yet prohibits the drinking of alcohol, and the adulterer who prohibits unbelief?" Just as a major sin is greater than a minor sin, major sins also vary.

If they say "Yes,"[77] and confine the one who commits a sin to prohibiting a greater sin but not an equivalent or a lesser one, then this would be arbitrary and without foundation.[78] For adultery is a greater sin than drinking alcohol, yet it is not unlikely that one might commit adultery while prohibiting the consumption of alcohol and refraining from it. In fact, he might even drink alcohol, yet prohibit his servants and friends from drinking and say: "Refraining from drinking is obligatory upon you and me, and to command one to refrain from what is prohibited is obligatory upon me, just as my refraining from it is. I may come closer to God by performing one of these two obligations. My refraining from one of them does not necessitate my refraining from the other." Therefore, just as it is permissible for

75. According to Islamic law, men (but not women) are prohibited from wearing clothes made of silk. Also, as is well known, Muslims are prohibited from drinking, serving, selling, or possessing alcoholic beverages.

76. That is, if they concede that someone who consumes alcohol may fight the infidels.

77. That is, if they concede that someone who drinks alcohol may prohibit murder.

78. *Taḥakkum* (arbitrariness) is the reading in the Jeddah edition. The reading in the Ankara edition is *al-ḥukm* (the decree); hence the sentence would be rendered 'this decree has no basis.'

him not to command another to refrain from drinking, while he himself refrains from drinking, it is permissible for him to command others to refrain from drinking while he does not refrain from drinking.[79] Both of these are obligatory. Not performing the one does not necessitate not performing the other.

It might be said:

Repugnant consequences follow from this. For instance, a man might commit adultery with a woman whom he has coerced; and when she chooses to unveil her face, he might say to her while he is in the act: "Do not unveil your face, for I am not a man whom you are prohibited to marry.[80] Unveiling your face before such a man is forbidden. You are coerced to commit adultery but you *choose* to unveil your face. Hence I forbid you to do so." There is no doubt that this act of forbidding evil is without merit and repugnant, and no sane person would engage in it. Of the same sort is one's statement: "Two things are obligatory for me: to act and to command another to act. I perform one of them, even if I refrain from the other." One might as well say: "It is obligatory for me to perform ablution and to pray; yet I pray even if I leave out ablution." Or: "The law advises me to eat a pre-dawn meal[81] before fasting; I eat a pre-dawn meal even if I do not fast." This is absurd. For eating a pre-dawn meal is for the sake of fasting and performing ablution is for the sake of praying, and each one is a condition for the other; hence it is prior in rank to that for which it is a condition.[82] Similarly,

79. Literally, it is permissible that he drinks and commands [others] to refrain. I took the liberty of reformulating al-Ghazālī's sentence, since the original might suggest that drinking is permissible for him.

80. The phrase 'a man whom you are prohibited to marry' is a translation of *maḥram laki*. A *maḥram* is a man, such as a brother, father, or uncle, whom Islamic law prohibits a woman to marry. (The expression *laki* means "to you.")

81. The Arabic term is *tasaḥḥur*, which means "eating a pre-dawn meal before the day of the fast." It was the practice of the Prophet to eat such a meal.

82. There is a sense of 'condition' in which praying is a condition for performing ablution and fasting is a condition for eating a pre-dawn meal, and there is another sense of 'condition' in which performing ablution is a condition for praying and fasting is a condition for eating a pre-dawn meal. In this passage al-Ghazālī seems to be saying the former since performing ablution is *for the sake* of praying and eating a pre-dawn meal is *for the sake* of fasting. Hence praying and fasting are prior in rank to performing ablution and to eating a pre-dawn meal. Later al-Ghazālī's seems to convey another sense of 'condition'. According to this sense, '*x* is a condition for *y*' means that *x* is a requirement for *y*. Hence performing ablution is a requirement for praying: the prayer is not valid without ablution. And fasting is a requirement for eating a pre-dawn meal: eating a pre-dawn meal is senseless without the intention to fast. Although the law encourages, but does not require, eating a pre-dawn meal (*tasaḥḥur*) before the fast, the concept of *tasaḥḥur* implies that the pre-dawn meal is consumed in preparation for the fast; hence to eat a pre-dawn meal without the intention to fast renders the concept of *tasaḥḥur* vacant.

one's own soul takes priority over the other's. So let one refine his own soul first and then the other's. If he neglects his own soul and occupies himself with the other's, this would be the reverse of the necessary order. On the other hand, if he refines his own soul and refrains from enjoining the good and forbidding evil and from improving the character of others, this would be a sin, but there would be no contradiction in it. In the same vein, an infidel has no business spreading the word of Islam, unless he himself becomes a Muslim. If he says that there are two things obligatory for me, and it is for me to refrain from one of them but not the other, this would not be accepted from him.

We would answer that, according to us, it is permissible for the man who commits adultery with a woman to forbid evil, and hence to forbid her from unveiling her face. You say that this forbidding of evil is without merit and repugnant. The point is not that it is meritorious or without merit, or that it is commendable or repugnant, but the point is that it is lawful or unlawful. How many lawful things are dull and unpleasant and how many unlawful things are attractive and desirable? What is lawful is not the same as what is desirable and what is unlawful is not the same as what is repugnant.

A conclusive proof is that we state:

His saying to her "Do not unveil your face, for it is forbidden" and his action to prevent her from doing so are an utterance and a deed. It may be said that either this utterance and deed are prohibited, or they are obligatory, or they are permissible. If you say that they are obligatory, then this is our position; if you say that they are permissible, then he may do what is permissible; and if you say that they are prohibited, then what is the basis for their prohibition, given that they were obligatory before his committing adultery? How then does that which is obligatory become prohibited simply by his engaging in something forbidden? His utterance that this is forbidden is true according to the law[83] and his deed is only to prevent her from doing what is forbidden. To say that either one of these is prohibited is absurd.

We do not mean by our statement that a sinner may enjoin the good and forbid evil anything but that his utterance is lawful and his deed is not prohibited. This is different from praying and performing ablution, for performing the prayer is ordained and performing ablution is its condition. A prayer without ablution is a sin and not a true prayer—it forfeits its being a prayer. On the other hand, neither does the man's utterance forfeit its being

83. Reading *illā ṣidqun ʿan al-sharʿ* instead of *ṣidqun ʿan al-sharʿ*, which is in the original. According to the original, the sentence may be rendered 'There is no truth, according to the law, in his utterance,' which is the opposite of what is intended.

true nor does his deed forfeit its being a prevention of what is forbidden.[84] Similarly, eating a pre-dawn meal is just [consuming] food in advance to aid with the fast. Seeking aid for something is incomprehensible without the intention to perform that for which one seeks aid.

As for your statement that one's refining his soul is a condition for improving the character of another, this is the issue of our dispute. How do you know that this is so? If one says that his purifying his soul from committing sins is a condition for participating in a war to stop the infidels, and that his purifying his soul from committing minor sins is a condition for his prohibiting major sins, then this statement would be similar to yours, which is a breach of the consensus.

Regarding the infidel, if he, by the sword, converts to Islam another infidel, we do not stop him. Rather we say that he ought to declare that there is no deity but God and that Muḥammad is the Messenger of God, and to command others to do so as well. However, it is not established that his declaration is a condition for his commanding others—he may utter the declaration even if he does not command others, and he may command others even if he does not utter the declaration.

This is the bottom line of this issue. We wanted to mention it so you may know that such issues are not appropriate for the art of theology, especially when beliefs are discussed in brief. And God knows best.

84. Al-Ghazālī's point is that the committing of adultery does not negate the truth of the man's utterance that unveiling her face is forbidden nor does it change the nature of the man's deed of preventing her from doing what is forbidden. This is dissimilar to the case of prayer and ablution: not performing ablution invalidates the prayer and changes its nature from an ordained obligation to a sin.

# THIRD CHAPTER

## *On the imamate*[85]

Know that an investigation into the topic of the imamate is also not among the important matters, and it does not belong to the art of the intelligibles, rather it is one of the legal topics. Furthermore, it excites prejudices. The one who avoids wading into it is safer than the one who wades into it even if he succeeds; how then would it be if he errs? At any rate, since this topic typically concludes a study of beliefs, we wish to follow the usual approach. For hearts are strongly repelled by an approach that departs from what is familiar.[86] However, we will discuss the matter briefly. Thus we say that an investigation into this topic deals with three issues.

## First Issue

*On showing that appointing an imam is obligatory*

We should not think that this obligation derives from the intellect. We have explained that obligations derive from the revelation, except when 'obligatory' is interpreted to designate an act, such that there is benefit in performing it or harm in refraining from it. According to this interpretation, it cannot be denied that appointing an imam is obligatory, since it leads to benefit and prevents harm in this worldly life. However, we present a conclusive legal demonstration that it is obligatory. We will not rely solely on

85. The *imamate* is the office of the imam. An *imam* is either a leader of an Islamic state, a distinguished jurist, or someone who is in charge of a congregation of Muslims and the leader of their congregational prayers. Al-Ghazālī is discussing the office of the imam in the first sense, that is, a leader of an Islamic state.

86. This is a translation of the reading in the Cairo edition. The reading in the Ankara and Jeddah editions may be rendered as 'For the hearts are strongly repelled if they are weaned from following an approach that differs from what is familiar.' It is clear that this reading does not fit the context.

the consensus of the Muslim community; rather we bring attention to the basis of this consensus.

Hence we say:

Well-ordered religious affairs are decidedly a purpose of the man with the revelation (may God bless him and grant him peace). This is an unquestionable premise about which no dispute is imaginable. We add to it another premise, which is that well-ordered religious affairs can only be achieved through an imam who is obeyed. The correctness of the proposition that the appointment of an imam is obligatory follows from these two premises.

If it is said that the last premise, which is that well-ordered religious affairs can be achieved only through an imam, is not conceded, then we say: "Its demonstration is that well-ordered religious affairs can be achieved only through well-ordered worldly affairs and well-ordered worldly affairs can be achieved only through an imam who is obeyed." These are two premises; which one is the subject of dispute?

It might be said: "Why do you say that well-ordered religious affairs can be achieved only through well-ordered worldly affairs? On the contrary, it can be achieved only by the destruction of worldly affairs, for religious affairs and worldly affairs are opposites, and hence to be occupied with making one of them flourish is the ruin of the other."

We say:

This is the argument of someone who does not understand what we intend here by 'worldly affairs'. For it is an ambiguous term that may be used to designate indulgence in luxury and pleasure and being excessive beyond what is needed and necessary, or it may be used to designate all that is required prior to one's death. One of the designations is opposed to religion and the other is its very condition. It is in this way that the one who does not distinguish between the meanings of ambiguous terms errs.

We thus say:

Well-ordered religious affairs are achieved through knowledge and worship. These cannot be achieved without the health of the body, the maintenance of life, the fulfillment of needs—such as those for clothing, shelter, and food—and security from the onset of calamities. How true this is: "When a man wakes up safe among his family, with a healthy body, and in possession of his daily sustenance, it is as if the whole world is made available to him."[87] A man does not achieve security in his life, body, wealth, home, and sustenance under all circumstances but [only] under some. Re-

87. This is a *ḥadīth*. It is reported by Ibn Māja, *Sunan*, XXXVII.9, no. 4141; and Tirmidhī, *al-Jāmiʿ al-Ṣaḥīḥ*, XXXVII.34, no. 2347.

ligious affairs cannot flourish unless security is achieved in these important and necessary matters. Otherwise, if one spends all his time being occupied with protecting himself against the swords of oppressors, and with winning his sustenance from exploiters, when would he find time for working and seeking knowledge, which are his means for achieving happiness in the hereafter? Therefore well-ordered worldly affairs—I mean the fulfillment of needs—are a condition for well-ordered religious affairs.

As for the second premise, which is that worldly affairs and security in life and wealth can be maintained only through an imam who is obeyed, it is confirmed by observing the periods of social upheavals when the sultans and imams die. If these periods are prolonged and not quickly terminated by the appointment of another sultan who is obeyed, the killing would continue and the sword would dominate, famine would spread, livestock would diminish, and industry would collapse; and whoever wins would plunder; and no one who manages to stay alive would have time to worship or seek knowledge; and the majority would die under the shadows of the swords. For this reason it has been said that religion and sultan are twins, and also that religion is a foundation and the sultan is a guard: that which has no foundation collapses and that which has no guard is lost.

In sum, no rational person doubts that if mankind, given their different classes, diverse desires, and disparate opinions, are left to their own devices without decrees that they obey and that unify their factions, they would all end in ruin. This is an epidemic that has no remedy other than a strong sultan who is obeyed and who unifies their disparate opinions. This shows that a sultan is necessary for achieving well-ordered worldly affairs, and well-ordered worldly affairs are necessary for achieving well-ordered religious affairs, and well-ordered religious affairs are necessary for achieving happiness in the hereafter, which is decidedly the purpose of all the prophets. Therefore, the obligation of appointing an imam is among the essential requirements of the law—a requirement that by no means can be ignored.

## Second Issue

*On showing who among mankind may be appointed an imam*

We say:

It is clear that it is not possible to designate someone to be made an imam on the basis of his desire to be one. He must be distinguished by a characteristic in which he differs from the rest of mankind—a characteristic that concerns him and a characteristic that concerns the others.

Regarding the characteristic that concerns him, he must be qualified, in terms of sufficiency, knowledge, and religious devotion to manage people and motivate them to seek what is good for them. In general, the qualities of a judge are required of him, with the addition of his Quraysh lineage.[88] This fourth condition is known through the revelation,[89] for the Prophet (may God bless him and grant him peace) said: "The imams are from Quraysh."[90] These qualities distinguish him from most of mankind. However, a group of Qurayshites might be found to possess all these qualities. Hence there must be another distinguishing characteristic. This can only be investiture and delegation of authority by someone other than himself. For someone is appointed an imam once he alone is specified by investiture.

It remains to investigate the quality of the one who appoints the imam. For this is not a post available to just anyone, but there must be a certain characteristic that he has. Investiture is made through one of three means: either through a designation from the Prophet (may God bless him and grant him peace); or through a designation from the imam of the time, and that is by appointing a specific person among his sons or the members of Quraysh to succeed his reign; or through investiture made by a man with great influence, which makes others follow him and offer their pledge of allegiance [to the designated imam]. This might be available, in certain times, to one person who is highly distinguished and blessed with influence over all others. In such a case, his pledging of allegiance and delegating authority to someone would be sufficient without others also delegating authority. For the purpose is to unify the diverse opinions under one person who is obeyed. The imam would become obeyed when this person who is obeyed pledges his allegiance to him. That might not be available to one person, but to two, three, or more people. They must gather and pledge allegiance to someone and agree to invest him with authority, so obedience may be achieved.

Indeed I say: "If there were, after the death of an imam, only one Qurayshite who was capable of being obeyed and followed, and he assumed the imamate, appointed himself, and occupied himself with [its responsibili-

88. Quraysh is the tribe of the Prophet Muḥammad. Its members were the nobility of Mecca. The requirement that an imam must belong to Quraysh is a matter of dispute among the Islamic jurists.

89. The other three conditions are the ones listed earlier, which are sufficiency, knowledge, and religious devotion. It should be mentioned that Muslims believe that the revelation Muḥammad received was expressed in terms of the Qur'ān and the Ḥadīth.

90. Reported by Aḥmad ibn Ḥanbal, *Musnad*, III.129, no. 12292; Bayhaqī, *al-Sunan al-Kubrā*: III.5298; Bukhārī, *Ṣaḥīḥ*, LXI.2, nos. 3500, 3501; Muslim, *Ṣaḥīḥ*, XXXIII.1, nos. 1820, 1821; and Ṭabarānī, *al-Muʿjam al-Kabīr*: I.725.

ties] and, through his influence and sufficiency, made the people follow him, and he was endowed with the attributes of the imams, then the imamate would be rightfully his and obedience to him would become obligatory." For he would have been appointed by virtue of his influence and sufficiency, and to oppose him would be to incite social upheaval. However, he who has these qualities is not incapable of obtaining the allegiance of the highly distinguished men of his time and of those who are entrusted with great authority. Such allegiance would remove any doubt about his claim to the imamate.[91] Thus, this sort of authority is usually achieved only through pledging of allegiance and investiture.

It may be asked: "What do you see appropriate? If the goal is to have someone whose decree is obeyed and who unifies diverse opinions, prevents people from warring and fighting, and motivates them to seek what is good for them in this worldly life and the hereafter, and if a man has risen to rule who has all these qualities except knowledge but nevertheless consults the scholars and follows their judgments, then what do you see appropriate, must he be deposed and opposed or must he be obeyed?"

We say:

What we see as appropriate and assert is that he must be deposed if it is possible to replace him with someone who fulfills all the conditions without inciting social upheaval and armed conflict. If this is not possible without causing armed conflict, then he must be obeyed and his imamate is judged valid. For what we lose by the difference between his being knowledgeable on his own and his consulting others is less than what we would lose by submitting to someone else if this would incite a social upheaval with unknown consequences. In fact, this might lead to the loss of life and property. The addition of the quality of knowledge is a distinguishing character and a perfection that furthers people's interest; hence it is not permissible to sacrifice the principal interests for the sake of distinguishing characters and perfections.

These are legal issues. The one who is dismayed by what opposes popular belief should calm his dismay, for the matter is far less grave than he thinks. We have fully investigated these notions in the book titled *Al-Mustaẓhirī*, which was composed to refute the Esotericists.[92]

91. Literally, this would make doubts unlikely.

92. The book's complete title is *Al-Mustaẓhirī fī al-Radd ʿalā al-Bāṭiniyya* (*The Mustaẓhirī Book for Refuting the Esotericists*). It was so called because it was written at the request of the ʿAbbāsid caliph Al-Mustaẓhir bi-Allāh (r. AH 487/1094 CE–AH 512/1118 CE). The book consists of an exposition and refutations of the claims and doctrines of a Shīʿa sect known as *al-Ismāʿīliyya* (Ismāʿīlites), *al-Bāṭiniyya* (Esotericists), and *al-Taʿlīmiyya* (Instructionists). They are called 'Ismāʿīlites' because they affirm that Ismāʿīl ibn Jaʿfar al-Ṣādiq is one of the

It might be said: "If you are forgiving regarding the quality of knowledge, then it becomes incumbent upon you to be forgiving regarding the quality of justice, and other qualities."

We say:

This leniency is not a matter of choice; but necessities render prohibitions permissible. For instance, we know that eating dead animals is prohibited,[93] but to die [of hunger] is much worse. I wish I knew how someone who does not accept this [principle][94] could judge that the imamate in our time is invalid insofar as its conditions are not fulfilled, while he is unable to replace the imam with someone who seeks it, for even he cannot find someone who fulfills its conditions. Which of his states is better: to say that the judges are dismissed, appointments are invalid, marriages are annulled, all the decrees of the governors everywhere in the world are unenforceable, and all of mankind are engaged in what is unlawful; or to say that, based on the current state and necessity, the imamate is valid and the decrees and appointments are enforceable? He has three options: either he prevents people from engaging in marriage and in all acts that are related to the affairs of judges—this is impossible, since it leads to the abrogation of all worldly affairs and to the splintering of opinions and is ruinous for the people and an incitement for the vulgar; or he says that people may engage in marriage and other acts but, though they are engaging in something unlawful, he does not declare them corrupt and sinful due the necessity of the situation; or he judges[95] that the imamate, due to the necessity of the situation, is valid despite the lack of the fulfillment of its conditions. It is known that something that is far, when compared with something that is farther, is considered near and that the lesser of two evils is good in relation to the other, so a rational person must choose it.

This is the resolution of this issue, and it, without further elaboration, is sufficient for the one who is attentive. However, he who does not understand the true nature of a thing and its cause and, instead, has an estab-

---

infallible Imams, and they are called 'Esotericists' and 'Instructionists' because they claim that they follow the authoritative *instructions* of infallible hidden imams, who understand the *esoteric* (true) meanings of the Qurʾānic verses. The book is also known as *The Scandals of the Esotericists* (*Faḍāʾiḥ al-Bāṭiniyya*) and *The Refutation of the Esotericists* (*Al-Radd ʿalā al-Bāṭiniyya*). (See al-Shahrastānī, *al-Milal wa-l-Niḥal*, vol. 1, pp. 226–235; and al-Baghdādī, *al-Farq bayn al-Firaq*, pp. 199–218.)

93. The prohibition concerns eating the flesh of dead animals that are not killed for the purpose of consumption—dead animals such as those that are killed by other animals or that died due to natural causes.

94. The principle here is the one mentioned above—namely, that necessity renders prohibitions permissible.

95. I omitted 'we say that'.

lished belief due to a prolonged exposure to it is by nature repelled by its opposite. For to wean the weak-minded from something familiar is a very difficult matter, which even the prophets were unable to achieve. How, then, could others?

It might be said: "Why do you not say that to designate an imam is incumbent upon the Prophet (may God bless him and grant him peace) and upon the caliph, so that no disagreement may ensue, as some of the Imāmites assert,[96] for they claim it is obligatory?"

We say:

If it were obligatory, the Prophet would have made a designation, yet he did not designate [a successor], nor did 'Umar. In fact, the imamate of Abū Bakr, 'Umar, 'Uthmān, and 'Alī (may God be pleased with them) were all established by investiture.[97] Thus do not pay attention to the one who feigns ignorance [of the facts] by claiming that the Prophet (may God bless him and grant him peace) designated 'Alī for the imamate in order to prevent conflict and that the companions denied the designation or did not disclose it. Such a claim can be opposed by an analogous claim, which is to say: "How would you deny someone's statement that the Prophet designated Abū Bakr [for the imamate], and that his companions agreed to uphold and follow this designation?" This would be closer to the truth than assuming that they denied his designation of 'Alī or did not disclose it. Furthermore, an obligation to designate is entertained only when it is not possible to avert disagreement, yet this is not impossible; for pledging allegiance to someone removes the reason for disagreement. The proof of this is that there was no disagreement during the reigns of Abū Bakr and 'Uthmān (may God be pleased with them),[98] yet they were appointed by people's pledging allegiance to them; however, disagreement abounded

96. 'The Imāmites' is another name for the Shī'a, who believe that only the infallible Imams have a divine right to rule the Muslim nation. There are several schools within the Shī'a. Some believe in twelve Imams and some in seven. They agree that these Imams are descendants of 'Alī ibn abū Ṭālib, the Prophet's cousin and son-in-law, who is the first Imam. According to them, 'Alī was designated by the Prophet, in a famous *ḥadīth*, to be his successor, but other companions of the Prophet, especially the first three caliphs, Abū Bakr, 'Umar, and 'Uthmān, did not disclose the truth of the Prophet's designation of 'Alī in order to deprive him of his rightful claim to the caliphate. The Sunnis, on the other hand, deny the authenticity of this *ḥadīth* (and of other *ḥadīth*s similar to it). It is nearly impossible to settle the dispute between the Sunnis and the Shī'a because each group has different authoritative collections of Ḥadīth and some of their criteria for the authenticity of *ḥadīth*s are different too. Al-Ghazālī will allude to some of these issues below.

97. The investiture here was made by the majority of the Prophet's distinguished companions.

98. In fact, there was a major upheaval during the reign of 'Uthmān, which resulted in his assassination. Al-Ghazālī must be referring to the fact that 'Uthmān's appointment to the

during the reign of ʿAlī (may God be pleased with him), yet the Imāmites believe that he was appointed by a designation [from the Prophet].

## Third Issue

*On explaining the belief of the followers of the Sunna regarding the Prophet's companions and the rightly-guided caliphs (may God be pleased with them)*

Know that people are excessive in two directions: some exceed in praise to the extent of attributing infallibility to the Imams, and some attack the Prophet's companions with accusations and hurl insults at them. Do not be one of the two groups; rather follow the path of moderation in belief.

Know that the Book of God (Glorified and Exalted is He) contains praises for the Muhājirūn and the Anṣār.[99] There are many widely transmitted reports about the Prophet's commending them in various terms—reports such as his statement "My companions are like stars; no matter whom you follow, you would be rightly guided,"[100] and his statement "The best of people are the people of my century."[101] Every companion received special praise, which would take too long to relate. Thus you must adopt this belief regarding them, and do not think ill of them on the basis of things related about them that conflict with having a high opinion of them. Most of what has been related is invented due to zealotry and has no foundation. And even what has been authenticated can be interpreted figuratively. And, at any rate, nothing was related in which reason cannot admit a mistake or an oversight. One must assume that the aim of their acts was always the good even if they did not attain it.

Regarding the famous armed conflict between Muʿāwiya and ʿAlī, and

---

imamate was mostly unopposed but ʿAlī's appointment was opposed by Muʿāwiya ibn Abū Sufyān, the governor of Syria at the time, and his followers.

99. The Muhājirūn (literally, emigrants) are the followers of Muḥammad who emigrated from Mecca to Medina in AH 1/622 CE. This emigration is known as the Hegira (*hijra*) and it marks the beginning of the Islamic calendar (*Hijrī*). The Medinan followers of Muḥammad, who granted him refuge after the Hegira, are known as the Anṣār (literally, supporters). The Muhājirūn and Anṣār were the most distinguished among the Prophet's companions. There were many others who joined the ranks of the companions after the Muslims conquered Mecca and most of Arabia during the last years of Muḥammad's life.

100. Reported by Dhahabī, *Mīzān al-Iʿtidāl*: I.1511, I.2299; and Ibn Ḥajar, *Lisān al-Mīzān*: II.488, II.594.

101. The expression 'the people of my century' refers to the Prophet's companions. Reported by Bukhārī, *Ṣaḥīḥ*, LXII.1, nos. 3650, 3651; LII.9, no. 2652; Muslim, *Ṣaḥīḥ*, XLIV.52, no. 2533; and Tirmidhī, *al-Jāmiʿ al-Ṣaḥīḥ*, XXXIV.45, no. 2222.

'Ā'isha's journey to Basra,[102] one must assume that she was seeking to quell the social upheaval, but she lost control of the matter; for the ends of things do not always conform to the initial purpose, but they veer out of control. One should assume that Mu'āwiya was operating on the basis of an interpretation and a likelihood. The things that have been related that differ from this are merely isolated reports. The authentic among them are mixed with falsehoods. Much of the dispute is invented by the Rejectionists,[103] the Secessionists,[104] and those meddlesome people who intrude in these arts.

Hence we ought to maintain our rejection of any report that is not authenticated and to interpret figuratively what has been authenticated. Regarding a report that you cannot so interpret, say: "It might have a figurative interpretation and a rationale, which I am unable to see."

Know that you are in a position either to think ill of a Muslim and attack his integrity and be a liar, or to think well of a Muslim and prevent your tongue from attacking his integrity, even if it happens that you are wrong. To err in thinking well of Muslims is safer than to be correct in attacking their integrity. For instance, if a Muslim avoids cursing Lucifer, Abū Jahl,

102. Mu'āwiya ibn Abū Sufyān was the governor of Syria. He rejected 'Alī's ascension to the caliphate, declared secession from the central imamate, and demanded that 'Alī punish the people who rebelled against 'Alī's predecessor, 'Uthmān ibn 'Affān, who was assassinated in AH 36/656 CE. 'Alī, of course, never doubted that the killing of 'Uthmān was unjustified; but since there was a large group of conspirators who planned the assassination of 'Uthmān, 'Alī decided, for the sake of avoiding a civil war, to let the matter pass. The chasm between Mu'āwiya and 'Alī culminated in the Battle of Ṣiffīn in AH 37/657 CE. When Mu'āwiya's army was about to be defeated, he requested an arbitration to resolve the conflict and determine whether his demand for punishing the killers of 'Uthmān was justified. 'Alī saw in this request a trick by the other army to escape defeat, but he was pressured by many tribal chiefs in his army to accept the arbitration. A group of 'Alī's supporters perceived 'Alī's agreement to arbitrate as an abrogation of his duties as the legitimate caliph of the Islamic state and seceded from his army. They came to be known as *al-Khawārij* (the Secessionists). They declared 'Alī and Mu'āwiya infidels and took up arms against 'Alī, who defeated them in a battle. Later they plotted the dual assassination of both men. Mu'āwiya escaped the assassination but 'Alī was assassinated in AH 41/661 CE. After the assassination of 'Alī, Mu'āwiya declared himself the caliph of the Islamic state and succeeded in obtaining the allegiance of most of the leaders of Muslim communities. This transformation of power marked the end of the reign of the "rightly-guided caliphs" (*al-khulafā' al-rāshidūn*) and the beginning of the Umayyad dynasty, which turned the caliphate into a royal structure.

'Ā'isha bint Abū Bakr was the wife of the Prophet, who, together with two distinguished Prophet's companions Zubayr and Ṭalḥa, also disputed 'Alī's decision not to pursue the killers of 'Uthmān, and fought 'Alī in the Battle of the Camel (*Ma'rakat al-Jamal*)—it was so called because 'Ā'isha rode on a camel during the battle—in AH 36/656 CE. 'Alī's troops defeated the opposing army.

103. 'The Rejectionists' (*al-Rwāfiḍ*) is a derogatory name for the Shī'a.

104. See note 102 above for a brief description of the Secessionists (*al-Khawārij*).

Abū Lahab, or anyone you wish among those who are evil throughout their lives, then he is not harmed by his silence; but if he makes a minute error in accusing a Muslim of something of which God (Exalted is He) knows he is innocent, then he is ruined.

Indeed, most of what is known about people is not permissible to talk about, because the revelation is emphatic in prohibiting malicious gossip, even if what is reported is true of the person. He who understands these chapters and is not inclined by nature to be meddlesome should choose to be silent, to think well of all Muslims, and to voice the praises of all the righteous predecessors.

This is the judgment regarding all the Prophet's companions. As for the rightly-guided caliphs,[105] they are more meritorious than the others. Their order with regard to merit is, according to the followers of the Sunna, similar to their order in assuming the imamate.

This might be taken as similar to our statement that so-and-so is better than so-and-so, meaning that his status, in God's knowledge, is higher in the hereafter. This is hidden knowledge, which only God has, as well as His Messenger if God permits him to know. We cannot claim that there are widely transmitted conclusive reports attributed to the man with the revelation that assert this order of merit. What is actually related is the praise for all of them. To deduce a comparative judgment regarding merit from the subtleties of his praise for them is a mere conjecture and an intrusion into a matter for which God created no need in us.

To determine merit in the eyes of God on the basis of overt behavior is also problematic. Its extent is sheer speculation. For how many people who exhibit questionable behavior have high status in the eyes of God, because of a secret in their hearts or a characteristic that is hidden in their inner selves? And how many people who are renowned for their overt acts of worship are subjects of God's wrath because of malevolence that resides in their inner selves. Only God has knowledge of the secrets of the heart.

However, if it is established that merit is known only through revelation, and that revelation is known only through what the Prophet relates, then those who were most aware of what the Prophet related regarding comparative merit were the companions who were close to the Prophet (may God bless him and grant him peace) in all his states.[106] And they agreed to place

105. Those are the four caliphs who reigned immediately after the death of the Prophet. They are, in order, Abū Bakr (r. AH 11/632 CE–AH 13/634 CE), ʿUmar ibn al-Khaṭṭāb (r. AH 13/634 CE–AH 24/644 CE), ʿUthmān ibn ʿAffān (r. AH 24/644 CE–AH 36/656 CE), and ʿAlī ibn abū Ṭālib (r. AH 36/656 CE–AH 41/661 CE).

106. This is the translation of the reading in the Jeddah edition. The reading in the Ankara edition may be rendered as follows: 'those who were most aware of what the Prophet

Abū Bakr first; Abū Bakr then appointed 'Umar; after that they agreed to appoint 'Uthmān; and after that they agreed to appoint 'Alī (may God be pleased with them all). No one should think that they betrayed the religion of God for any purpose. Hence, their consensus is the best evidence for their merit.[107] The followers of the Sunna based their belief regarding this order of merit on this consensus. Then they searched for reports [from the Prophet] and they found texts that gave them knowledge of how the Prophet's companions, who were the people of the consensus, came to establish this order

These are the conditions of the imamate that we wanted to discuss briefly. And God is more knowledgeable of what is right.

---

related regarding the comparative merits of the companions were those who were close to the Prophet in all his states.'

107. The pronoun 'their' refers to the rightly-guided caliphs.

# FOURTH CHAPTER

## *On explaining which among the sects must be charged with infidelity*

Know that sects, with regard to this issue, are extreme and zealous. Some groups might go so far as to charge with infidelity all the sects save the ones to which they belong. If you want to know the true path regarding this matter, then know before anything that this is a legal issue—I mean the issue of imputing infidelity to someone who made a statement or performed an act. Sometimes this is known through evidence based on the revelation and sometimes this is only determined through independent opinion.[108] There is no room here at all for evidence of reason.

We cannot explain this until we explain our saying that a certain person is an infidel, and make its meaning clear. This implies, regarding his place in the hereafter, that he will be in hellfire forever; and, regarding his status in this worldly life, that it is not obligatory to punish the one who kills him, that he cannot marry a Muslim, that his life and property are not inviolable, and the rest of such judgments. This also indicates that some statement he utters is false, or some belief he has is an ignorant one. It is possible to know through the evidence of reason the falsity of the statement and the ignorance of the belief; but to know that this falsehood or this ignorance is sufficient for imputing infidelity is another matter. That this means that another may spill his blood and take his property and that it is permissible to say that he will reside in hellfire forever is a legal matter. For it is possible, according to us, that the revelation might assert that a liar, an ignorant person, or an unbeliever would reside in paradise forever, that his infidelity would be immaterial, and that his life and property would be inviolable; and it is possible that it might assert the opposite.

Indeed, it is not possible that it would assert that falsity is truth or that

108. 'Independent opinion' is my translation of *ijtihād*. It is customary to translate *ijtihād* as 'independent legal opinion'. However, since *ijtihād* can be in matters of theology, as well as of jurisprudence, I elected to omit the word 'legal'.

ignorance is knowledge. But this is not what we seek in this issue. What is sought is whether the revelation makes this ignorance and this falsehood a cause for annulling his inviolability and decreeing that he will reside in hellfire forever. This is analogous to our question whether a youth who utters the declaration of faith is subsequently an infidel or a Muslim, that is, whether this true utterance which proceeds from him and this correct belief that is found in his heart are decreed by the revelation to be a cause for the inviolability of his life and property. This is within the purview of the revelation. However, describing his utterance as false or his belief as ignorant is not within the purview of the revelation. Therefore, knowing that someone is a liar or is ignorant could be through reason, but knowing that he is an infidel or a Muslim can only be through the revelation.[109]

This is similar to a legal investigation into whether someone is a slave or a freeman. This means whether the cited cause is declared by the law to be sufficient for the annulment of his testimony and investiture, for the elimination of his property, and for not applying the punishment [of death] to his master, who owns him, if he were to kill him.[110] All of this requires legal judgments whose foundation can be sought only from the revelation. It is possible to rule in these matters sometimes conclusively and sometimes with likelihood through independent opinion.

Therefore this principle has been affirmed. For we affirmed in [the study of] the fundamental principles of jurisprudences, as well as of the secondary, that if someone makes a legal judgment, he must know this judgment either through one of the principal sources of the law, such as consensus

109. Al-Ghazālī's point is that determining one's utterance to be false or one's belief to be ignorant is a matter of using reason. Reason compares the content of an utterance or a belief to the known facts, whether these facts are known through the senses, reason, or revelation, and determines accordingly whether this content is false or ignorant. Ordinarily such determination is made by reason and is outside the purview of the revelation. Al-Ghazālī says first that it is not for the revelation to make such a determination; hence one assumes that only reason can so determine. But he later weakens his claim and says that it is *possible* for such a determination to be made through reason. I think that al-Ghazālī is allowing for the possibility that the revelation may declare a certain person to be a liar or ignorant. The definite statement he makes is that it is not for reason but only for the revelation to determine the conditions for being an infidel or a Muslim. This is consistent with al-Ghazālī's belief in absolute divine freedom and its independence of the categories of good and bad. God, if He wishes, may decree that not believing in Him is the condition for being a Muslim and believing in Him is the condition for being an infidel (*kāfir*); also He may award all privileges to the unbeliever and strip all rights from the believer.

110. It is worth noting that the legal decrees al-Ghazālī mentions regarding the non-Muslims and slaves are matters of great dispute among the Muslim jurists. Many jurists believe that some of these and similar decrees are inconsistent with the practices of the Prophet and his companions.

or a transmitted report,[111] or through a legal analogy[112] based on a principal source.

A principle, which is conclusively determined, is that everyone who disbelieves Muḥammad (may God bless him and grant him peace) is an infidel, that is, he will reside in hellfire after death forever and his life and property are not inviolable, to the full extent of such decrees. However, unbelief has ranks.

The first rank is the unbelief of the Jews, the Christians, and all [the rest of] the religious sects, such as the Magi, idolaters, and others. To charge them with infidelity is laid down in the Book,[113] and the Muslim community is in agreement about it. This is the principle; everything else is related to it.[114]

The second rank is the unbelief of the Barāhimites, who deny prophecy in principle,[115] and the atheists who deny the existence of the Maker of the world. These are related to the textual evidence in terms of appropriateness. These—I mean the Barāhimites—disbelieve him and disbelieve the

111. The transmitted report here is meant to be a Qur'ānic verse or a *ḥadīth*.

112. I followed the standard translation of Western scholars of Islamic jurisprudence, by rendering *qiyās* as 'legal analogy'. *Qiyās* in logic is 'inference' or 'syllogism', and I think that one could make the case that occasionally the Muslim jurists mean by *qiyās* 'inference', since some of their legal opinions are inferred from other decrees by modes of reasoning that cannot comfortably be called "analogy."

113. The Book is the Qur'ān.

114. It is surprising that al-Ghazālī places the Jews and the Christians, who along with the Sabians are recognized as People of the Book, in the same rank as the idolaters. Islamic law awards the People of the Book special rights, such as the right of free worship, which are not awarded to the idolaters. The People of the Book have an elevated status in Islamic tradition because they, unlike the idolaters, are followers of divine religions and carriers of divine scriptures. Their lives, properties, and places of worship are all protected under Islamic law, and it is lawful for Muslims to eat their food (except what is forbidden, such as pork) and to marry their women. The permission to marry their women gives the People of the Book a special place in the Muslim community, since allowing women of the People of the Book to be mothers of Muslim children is to accord them a revered status. Mothers in the Islamic tradition, as they are in many other religious traditions, are awarded a status of great respect and reverence. The textual and historical evidence is bountiful. Here are two Qur'ānic verses: *Those who believe [in the Qur'ān] and those who follow the Jewish [scripture], and the Christians, and the Sabians—whoever believes in God and the Last Day and does right—shall have their reward with their Lord, and no fear shall come upon them, nor shall they grieve* (2:62); and *This day [all] things good and pure are made lawful for you. The food of the People of the Book is lawful for you, and your food is lawful for them. And the chaste women of the believers and the chaste women of the People of the Book [are lawful for you], when you give them their marriage dowries and live with them in honor, not in fornication, nor taking them as secret concubines. If anyone rejects faith, fruitless is his work and he will be among the losers in the hereafter* (5:5).

115. See note 97 of the Third Treatise for a brief description of the Barāhimites.

rest of the prophets; hence they are more deserving of the charge of infidelity than the Christians and the Jews. The atheists are even more deserving of the charge of infidelity than the Barāhimites, because they add to their unbelief in the prophets their denial of the existence of the Sender (shining is His power); a necessary consequence of this is to deny prophecy. Whoever makes a statement that denies prophecy in principle or denies the prophethood of our Prophet, Muḥammad, in particular is placed at this rank unless he withdraws his statement.

The third rank is those who believe in the Maker and prophecy, and believe the Prophet, but hold beliefs that conflict with what is asserted in the revelation. They say: "The Prophet is truthful; the purpose of what he said is the welfare of mankind; but he could not be explicit with respect to the truth because the understanding of mankind is unable to apprehend it." Those are the philosophers.[116] They should definitely be charged with infidelity regarding three issues. The first is their denial of bodily resurrection, the torment of hellfire, and the pleasures of paradise, such as the beautiful women with big lustrous eyes,[117] the food, the drink, and the clothes. The second is their saying that God does not know the particulars and the details of events but knows only the universals while the heavenly angels know the particulars. The third is their statement that the world is eternal and that God (Glorious is He) is prior to the world in order just as a cause

116. Al-Fārābī, Ibn Sīna (Avicenna), and Ibn Rushd (Averroës), indeed, hold this view. For example, al-Fārābī writes:

> The process continues until it settles at the same state that obtained during the time of Aristotle. Scientific theorization reaches its end, all the methods are distinguished, theoretical and practical philosophy are perfected in their entirety, and nothing remains in them that requires investigation . . .
>
> After all of this, the need arises to enact laws and teach the public the theoretical matters, which have been deduced, completed, and verified by means of demonstration, and the practical matters, which have been deduced by the power of the intellect. The art of enacting laws consists in the ability to give imaginative representations of the theoretical intelligibles, which the public finds difficult to conceive of; in the ability to deduce the political actions that are beneficial for attaining happiness; and in the ability to persuade the public of the theoretical and practical matters, which [the public] must be taught by all methods of persuasion. If the laws, of both of these types, are enacted, and the methods in which the public is persuaded, taught, and educated are added to them, religion then has been established, through which the public is taught, educated, and given all that it needs to attain happiness. (Al-Fārābī, *Kitāb al-Ḥurūf*, pp. 151–152.)

117. The Arabic phrase is *ḥūr al-ʿayn*. According to the Islamic tradition, *ḥūr al-ʿayn* are the women of paradise.

is prior to the effect, but otherwise they are equal in terms of [the duration of] their existence.[118]

If they are confronted with the Qur'ānic verses,[119] they claim that because people's intellects are inadequate for understanding the intellectual pleasures, these are represented to them metaphorically as sensual pleasures. This is clear unbelief. To assert this claim is to nullify the value of the revelation, and to close the door on [any opportunity] for being guided by the light of the Qur'ān and for attaining right guidance[120] from the sayings of the messengers (may God grant them peace). If it were permissible for the messengers to lie for the sake of people's interest, their statements no longer could be trusted; for any utterance made by them would be supposed to be a lie that they made for the sake of people's interest.

It might be said: "Why did you, in spite of this,[121] say that they are infidels?" We say: "Because it is known with certainty from the revelation that whoever attributes lies to God's Messenger (may God bless him and grant him peace) is an infidel; and they attribute lies to the Messenger. Although they give (unsound) rationalizations for such lies, the Messenger's utterances would remain lies nonetheless."

The fourth rank is the Mu'tazilites, the anthropomorphists,[122] and all the sects other than the philosophers. These profess belief; think it impermissible [for the messengers] to lie, whether it is for the sake of some interest or not; do not posit a rationale for lying; and put forth metaphorical interpretations, but they err in their interpretations. Their status belongs to [those who are engaged in] independent opinion. He who studies independent opinions ought to avoid imputing infidelity [to its practitioners] as much as he can. For rendering violable the lives and properties of those who perform the prayers facing the kiblah and declare that there is no deity

118. The position al-Ghazālī is attributing to the Islamic philosophers is that God and the world coexist. God is the cause of the world but does not precede it in "temporal order"; He is prior to the world in essence, in order, and in the fact that the world "emanated" from Him. This causal relation is analogous, for example, to the sun's being prior in order, not in time, to its light. The problem is more complex than it appears, because al-Ghazālī believes both that God preceded the world—and thus the world has a beginning—and that time is created by God with the world. So, precisely speaking, it does not make sense to say that God is prior to the world in time, since, according to al-Ghazālī, before the creation of the world, there was no time.

119. That is, the Qur'ānic verses that promises all sorts of bodily pleasures in paradise.

120. *Istifādat al-rushd* (attaining right guidance) is the reading in the Jeddah edition, while *istib'ād al-rushd* (to make seeking right guidance fruitless) is the reading in the Ankara edition.

121. That is, in spite of their belief in God and His messengers.

122. *Al-mushabbiha*—those who attribute human qualities to God.

but God and that Muḥammad is God's Messenger is a grave matter. To err in leaving one thousand infidels alive is better than to err in shedding even one cup of a Muslim's blood. The Prophet (may God bless him and grant him peace) says: "I was ordered to fight people until they say that there is no deity but God; if they say it, they make their lives and properties inviolable for me, unless it is rightful to take them."[123]

These sects divide into those that are excessive and extreme and those that are moderate in relation to the former. A practitioner of independent opinion who thinks they should be charged with infidelity might have a more sound opinion regarding certain issues and sects. An elaborate discussion of singular issues would be long, and it would incite divisiveness and spite. Most of those who wade in these matters are moved by zealotry and the dictates of whim rather than by firmness in defending the religion.[124]

The proof that imputing infidelity to them is not permissible is that what is definite, according to us, on the basis of textual evidence, is to charge with infidelity the one who disbelieves the Messenger, and these clearly do not disbelieve. Furthermore, it is not established that an error in interpretation is grounds for the charge of infidelity. Hence a proof for it must be given. On the other hand, it is conclusively established that inviolability is attained by one's statement that there is no deity but God.[125] Therefore there must be a conclusive reason to revoke this inviolability. This is sufficient for showing that the unrestraint of someone who exaggerates in imputing infidelity to others is not justified by any demonstration. A demonstration is either a principle or an analogy based on a principle; and the principle here is unequivocally disbelieving the Prophet. He who does not disbelieve is not described as an unbeliever in the first place; hence he remains sheltered by the general inviolability that is conferred by the declaration of faith.

The fifth rank is the one who refrains from an unequivocal unbelief but denies one of the revealed principles known through reports widely transmitted from God's Messenger (may God bless him and grant him peace), and says: "I do not know whether the attribution of this to God's Messenger has been established." This is analogous to one's statement that the

123. The meaning is that "it is rightful to take them because of a crime they commit that is punishable by death or the loss of property." Reported by Aḥmad ibn Ḥanbal, *Musnad*, I.11, no. 67; Bukhārī, *Ṣaḥīḥ*, II.17, no. 25; Ibn Māja, *Sunan*, XXXVI.1, nos. 3927–3929; Muslim, *Ṣaḥīḥ*, I.8, nos. 20–22; Nisā'ī, *Sunan*, XXV.1, nos. 3090–3095; and Tirmidhī, *al-Jāmiʿ al-Ṣaḥīḥ*, XLI.1, nos. 2609, 2610.

124. I followed the Jeddah edition in reading *al-taṣallub li-l-dīn* (literally, staying firm in the religion) instead of *al-naẓar li-l-dīn* (literally, investigating the religion), which is the reading in the Ankara edition.

125. The 'inviolability' here refers to the inviolability of a person's life and property upon his uttering the declaration of faith.

five prayers are not obligatory; and when the Qur'ān and other reports are read to him, he says: "I do not know whether this really came from God's Messenger; it might be erroneous or even fraudulent." Or it is analogous to someone who says: "I affirm that the hajj is obligatory, but I do not know where Mecca or al-Ka'ba is, and I do not know whether the city that people face in the prayers and to which they make hajj is the same city to which the Prophet made hajj and which the Qur'ān describes."

Such a person also must be judged to be unbeliever, because he disbelieves but he is too cautious to admit this; for both the select and the masses apprehend the widely transmitted reports. The falsity of what he says is not similar to the falsity of the Mu'tazilites' doctrine, since the latter is exclusively apprehended by those who are capable of keen theoretical reflection. However, if this person has only recently converted to Islam and these matters have not yet been widely transmitted to him, we should permit him time until they are transmitted to him. Moreover, we do not charge him with infidelity because he merely denies a matter that is known through widely transmitted reports. For if he denies the occurrence of one of God's Messenger's battles that are widely reported, or denies the Messenger's marrying Ḥafṣa bint 'Umar (may God be pleased with him), or denies the existence of Abū Bakr (may God be pleased with him) and his caliphate, then he should not be charged with infidelity; because it is not a denial of one of the principles of religion in which it is obligatory to believe, unlike [the denial of] the hajj, prayer, and the other pillars of Islam.

We also do not charge him with infidelity if he opposes what has been agreed upon. We have an opinion regarding imputing infidelity to al-Naẓẓām, who rejected the principle of consensus.[126] For there are many doubts about whether consensus is a decisive argument. Consensus is merely the agreement on a theoretical opinion. What we have been discussing is an agreement on a report of a sensible matter. The agreement of a large number of people on reporting a sensible matter, which leads to its being widely transmitted, entails necessary knowledge; while the agreement of the people of influence and expertise on a single theoretical opinion does not make knowledge necessary except regarding what is reported in the revelation. Hence it is not permissible to prove the occurrence of the world through widely transmitted reports about those theoreticians who

126. Abū Isḥāq Ibrāhīm al-Naẓẓām (d. AH 231/845 CE) was a leading Mu'tazilite, who excelled in theology, philosophy, and jurisprudence, and composed many important treatises. He was famous for adopting many unorthodox positions. It is believed that he was the first to reject the consensus of Islamic scholars (or for that matter, of the Prophet's companions) as one of the principal sources of Islamic law and theology. Some Islamic jurists charged him with infidelity. (See the following note for further discussion.)

affirm its occurrence. Widely transmitted reports can only support sensible matters.

The sixth rank is someone who does not affirm unbelief nor does he disbelieve one of the principles of religion that is conclusively known through widely transmitted reports, but he denies something whose correctness is known through pure consensus and *only* through consensus. He does not even affirm what is widely transmitted [about consensus]. For instance, al-Naẓẓām denied that consensus, on its own, is a decisive argument. He said that there is no conclusive rational proof or widely transmitted proof for the impossibility of error on the part of people who reach consensus that cannot be interpreted non-literally. According to him, all the reports and Qurʾānic verses that are presented as proof are subject to non-literal interpretation. In saying this, he has broken away from the consensus of the followers of the Prophet's companions. For we know that they have agreed that the consensus of the Prophet's companions is an established truth that cannot be opposed. Thus he has denied [the validity of] consensus and broken away from the consensus.[127]

This is a matter of independent opinion, on which I have my own theoretical reflection. There are many difficult issues regarding whether consensus is a decisive argument. This fact could be the beginning of a rationale.[128] However, if this door is opened, it would lead to repugnant matters. Someone might say that it is possible for a messenger to be sent after our Prophet, Muḥammad (may God bless him and grant him peace); and he would avert a charge of infidelity. The evidence for the impossibility of this,[129] upon reflection, derives inevitably from consensus; for reason does not deem it impossible. As for the Prophet's reported statement "There will be no prophet after me"[130] and the saying of the Exalted *And the seal of*

127. According to al-Ghazālī, there is a consensus of the followers of the Prophet's companions (*al-tābiʿūn*) that the consensus of the Prophet's companions regarding a certain religious position is a conclusive proof for the truth of that position. So al-Naẓẓām, in denying the validity of consensus as a principal source of law and theology, has not only rejected the principle of consensus but also has broken away from the consensus of the followers of the Prophet's companions. It seems that al-Ghazālī is of the opinion that the charge of infidelity that was leveled against al-Naẓẓām by some Islamic jurists is unjustified. He says below that al-Naẓẓām's view is a matter of independent opinion (*ijtihād*), since there are many difficulties that surround the issue of the conclusiveness of consensus as a religious argument. Al-Ghazālī seems to affirm the conclusiveness of consensus on pragmatic grounds, for denying the principle of consensus "opens the door to many repugnant views."

128. That is, a rationale for rejecting the principle of consensus.

129. 'The impossibility of this' refers to the impossibility of sending a messenger after the Prophet Muḥammad.

130. Reported by Aḥmad ibn Ḥanbal, *Musnad*, v.454, no. 23792; Bukhārī, *Ṣaḥīḥ*, LX.50, no. 3455; Muslim, *Ṣaḥīḥ*, XXXIII.10, no. 1842; and Tirmidhī, *al-Jāmiʿ al-Ṣaḥīḥ*, L.67, no. 3726.

*the prophets*,[131] that person is not unable to interpret them non-literally. He might say "'the seal of the prophets' is intended to designate the messengers of steadfast determination,[132] for God's saying 'the prophets' is a general term, and it is not unlikely to delimit what is general; and the Prophet's statement 'there will be no prophet after me' is not intended to refer to a messenger, for there is a difference between a prophet and a messenger—a prophet has a higher degree than a messenger," and the rest of such sort of babble.

This and similar interpretations cannot be claimed to be impossible merely on the basis of the text, for we, in interpreting apparent anthropomorphic attributions, affirmed possibilities that reach farther than these interpretations, yet this did not nullify the texts. However, the correct response to this person is that the consensus of the Muslim community is to understand from this statement and his other affairs that he implied that there would never be a prophet after him, nor would there be a messenger, and that there is no room for interpretation or for specification. The one who denies this, therefore, only denies this consensus. At this point several interwoven and related issues spring up, each one of which is in need of theoretical reflection. The speculations of the one who engages in independent opinion regarding these matters are judged affirmatively or negatively.

Our purpose here is to elucidate the applications of the principles on which a charge of infidelity may be based. These may belong to those six ranks; and any other posited case may be subsumed under one of those ranks. One might engage in independent opinion insofar as these principles are concerned. The purpose is to examine the principles—not the details.

It might be said: "To prostrate oneself before an idol is infidelity, and it is an act that is not subsumed under these principles; is it another principle?"

We say:

No; for infidelity consists in one's believing that the idol is sublime, and this would be to disbelieve God's Messenger (may God bless him and grant him peace) and the Qur'ān. His belief in the sublimity of the idol is ascer-

131. Qur'ān, 33:40. The complete verse is: *Muḥammad is not the father of any of your men, but he is the Messenger of God and the seal of the prophets; and God is the knower of all things.*

132. The messengers of steadfast determination (*ulū al-ʿazm*) are Noah, Abraham, Moses, Jesus, and Muḥammad. They are so described in the following Qur'ānic verse: *Then patiently persevere as did the messengers of steadfast determination, and do not be in haste about* [*the unbelievers*]; *on the day when they shall see what they have been promised, it will be as if they had not tarried longer than an hour of daylight. Proclaim the message. But shall any be destroyed except those who transgress*? (46:35). For a commentary, which enumerates those messengers, see al-Zuḥaylī, *al-Tafsīr al-Munīr*: *Fī al-ʿAqīda wa-l-Sharīʿa wa-l-Manhaj*, vol. xiii, pp. 391–392.

tained sometimes through an unequivocal expression, sometimes through a gesture if he is mute, and sometimes through an act that conveys his belief conclusively, such as prostrating himself before an idol where it cannot be assumed that the prostration is before God (Exalted is He). For instance, he might prostrate himself while an idol is in front of him serving as a wall, and he is heedless of it or he does not believe in its sublimity. This is known by means of accompanying evidence. It is analogous to our observing an infidel praying with us in a congregation; is he judged to be a Muslim? That is, can this be used as proof for his belief in the truthfulness [of Muḥammad]? Therefore this matter is not outside what we have mentioned.

We restrict ourselves to this extent regarding the identification of the conditions for imputing infidelity. We discussed it because the jurists did not engage in it and the theologians did not investigate it from a legal point of view, for such an investigation is not part of their art. Some of them did not notice that this is a legal issue. To investigate the conditions that are sufficient for imputing infidelity insofar as they are lies and ignorance is an intellectual investigation, but to investigate them insofar as they require the annulment of inviolability and the eternal condemnation to hell is a legal investigation. And this is what has been sought.

Let us conclude the book at this point. We have made clear the moderation in belief. We omitted all unnecessary details and extrapolations, which are beyond the central tenets of belief and their foundations. We restricted the proofs we mentioned to those that are clear and accessible and that most minds can comprehend. We ask God (Exalted is He), in His grace and bountiful generosity, not to make this book result in harm befalling us and to place it in the balance of our good deeds when our acts are returned to us.

# Interpretive Essay

If, on the one hand, proving the existence of God means proving that there is an eternal cause of the world, then al-Ghazālī's proof for the existence of God occupies the first three propositions of the First Treatise of the *Iqtiṣād*. If, on the other hand, proving the existence of God means proving the existence of a being who possesses the nature and attributes and is the agent of the acts attributed to Him by a certain religious tradition, then, with few exceptions, the whole *Iqtiṣād* must be seen as one multifaceted argument for the existence of God, as described in one variety of Sunni orthodoxy.

This interpretive essay approaches the four treatises as primarily an articulation of a single argument for the existence of a transcendent being whose essence, attributes, and acts are those affirmed of Him by orthodox Sunni theology based on the Ash'arite tradition. Although this essay is selective in its treatment, it nevertheless follows the main contours of the argument of the *Iqtiṣād* and explains its central facets. I try to give the readers here something that I do not give them in the notes. I try to give the big picture. The notes mainly deal with the details and background of al-Ghazālī's discussion; this essay deals with the implications of this discussion and the relations between its elements.

Some of what I say here has been argued for in my published works on *Tahāfut al-Falāsifa* and on *al-Iqtiṣād fī al-I'tiqād*: "Al-Ghazālī's Philosophers on the Divine Unity" (*Arabic Sciences and Philosophy* 20 (2010): 281–306); and "Al-Ghazālī's Ethical Egoism and Divine Will" (in *Monotheism and Ethics: Historical and Contemporary Intersections Among Judaism, Christianity and Islam*, edited by Y. Tzvi Langermann, Leiden: Brill, 2012, pp. 163–196).

## I

The First Treatise, which is titled "Theoretical Reflection on the Essence of God," consists of ten propositions and their demonstrations. They are: God exists, God is eternal anteriorly, God is eternal posteriorly, God is not an extended substance, God is not a body, God is not a mode, God is not located in a direction, no anthropomorphic description is true of God, God is seeable, and God is one. Al-Ghazālī's argument for the First Proposition is meant to show only that the world has a cause. He first argues that since the world is occurrent—that is, it has a beginning in time—and since every occurrent has a cause, the world has a cause. He explains that the second premise is a priori: its truth follows from the meaning of 'occurrent' and 'cause'. The central part of the argument is a demonstration of the first premise. Al-Ghazālī argues that it is clear that the world contains occurrents, since it contains motion and change, all of which originate in time; but whatever contains occurrents must itself be an occurrent; therefore the world is occurrent. The pivotal premise here is that whatever contains occurrents must be an occurrent. This premise follows from two principles: the first is that there are no actual infinities, and the second is that what is anteriorly eternal cannot cease to exist. The first principle entails that the world contains a finite number of occurrents, occurrents being objects, events, or processes that originate in time. If one assumes that the world is anteriorly eternal, then, given that it contains only a finite number of occurrents, there must have been a time in the history of the world when there were no occurrents, and this time stretches back to eternity. In other words, for a period of anterior eternity, the world was in a state of rest, without any sort of change or motion. But by the second principle, it would then follow that the world should continue in this state forever. Since, however, as was already concluded, the world is clearly not devoid of occurrents, the assumption that the world is anteriorly eternal is false, and we must conclude that the world itself is occurrent. Al-Ghazālī defends the first principle in his discussion of the First Proposition. His argument is a rehearsal of familiar ancient and medieval complaints about the concept of actual infinity. The second principle is defended in his demonstration of the Third Proposition.

The demonstration of the Second Proposition ("God is eternal anteriorly") is a standard cosmological argument: the world has a cause; if this cause is occurrent, then, by al-Ghazālī's earlier premise that all occurrents have causes, it must have a cause; again if this cause is occurrent, it must also have a cause; and so on, ad infinitum. Since infinite regress is impossible, however, this chain must terminate with an uncaused cause. But an uncaused cause cannot be occurrent (all occurrents have causes). Therefore this uncaused cause is anteriorly eternal, because everything is either occurrent or anteriorly eternal (either it has a beginning in time or it exists since eternity). Al-Ghazālī says that this anteriorly eternal uncaused cause is "what we seek and call 'the Maker of the world.'"

It is interesting to note that al-Ghazālī does not argue here that every anteriorly eternal cause is uncaused. The principle that every occurrent has a cause entails only that an uncaused thing is not occurrent; but it does not ensure that every non-occurrent thing, i.e., every anteriorly eternal thing, has no cause. The Islamic philosophers, for instance, believed that the world is anteriorly eternal, yet caused. Observe that al-Ghazālī's principle that whatever is not devoid of occurrents is itself an occurrent implies that the Maker of the world is devoid of occurrents.

The Third Proposition ("God is eternal posteriorly") is an immediate consequence of the Second Proposition along with the principle that whatever is eternal anteriorly cannot cease to exist. Hence al-Ghazālī demonstrates the Third Proposition by giving a demonstration of this principle. Since this principle plays a central role in the argument of the *Iqtiṣād*, the soundness of its demonstration is essential for al-Ghazālī's overall defense of Ashʿarism. The demonstration is based on a single premise: nonexistence cannot be the *direct* object of any agent's act. This is a standard assumption of medieval Islamic philosophers and theologians. Nonexistence is nothing; but an agent who acts through power must have an object for his act; hence no agent can produce nonexistence as the direct object of an act of power. It follows that nonexistence can be created only indirectly as an outcome of an intermediary. There are two intermediaries that can result in the annihilation of an existent: the creation of its contrary, and the removal of one of its necessary conditions. For example, according to al-Ghazālī, an extended substance can be annihilated by not having motion or rest created in it, since being at motion or rest is a necessary condition for the existence of any extended substance. Now the argument proceeds as follows. If there is an anteriorly eternal thing, then its contrary cannot also be anteriorly eternal, since two contraries cannot coexist from eternity. Hence if its contrary exists, it must be occurrent; but then it is more reasonable to conclude that this occurrent contrary is annihilated by the existence of the anteriorly eternal rather than that the anteriorly eternal is annihilated by the existence of the occurrent contrary. This leaves one option for annulling the existence of the anteriorly eternal—namely, the removal of a condition necessary for its existence. There are two cases regarding this necessary condition: either it is occurrent or it is anteriorly eternal. It cannot be occurrent, since in this case there would be a time when the condition did not exist but the anteriorly eternal did. Thus the necessary condition would have to be anteriorly eternal, having coexisted with the anteriorly eternal thing for which it is a necessary condition. But now we are talking about annulling a necessary condition that is anteriorly eternal. The same reasoning as above applies to this anteriorly eternal condition, resulting in positing a second condition that is anteriorly eternal and whose removal is required for the annihilation of the first condition. This cycle of reasoning generates an infinite regress of anteriorly eternal necessary conditions, all of which must be annulled in order for the first anteriorly eternal thing to be annihilated. Given the nearly universal ban on infinite regress in medieval philosophy and theology, it is concluded that the anteriorly eternal cannot cease to exist.

Note that the premise that nonexistence cannot be the object of any agent's act is not about change but annihilation. Al-Ghazālī does not dispute the obvious fact that a piece of cotton can be transformed into ash and smoke when it is burned. This is not a case of annihilation; it is a case of changing form. Al-Ghazālī argues that in order to make an existent cease to exist, nonexistence must be created in place of the existent; but it is merely a linguistic convention to speak of nonexistence as being created: nonexistence is not a "thing" to be created through an agent's act. The annihilation of an existent must be produced by creating or not creating a certain thing. If a contrary of an existent is created, then it is obvious that the existent would cease to exist, since contraries cannot coexist. On the other hand, if a condition that is necessary for the existence of an existent is removed (by not being created), then the existent cannot continue to exist. According to al-Ghazālī, these are the only conceivable ways of making an existent cease to exist.

The Fourth through Eighth Propositions establish the transcendence of God: God is neither an extended body nor a mode subsisting in a body, and all anthropomorphic descriptions of God are false. An immediate consequence of this is that all anthropomorphic Qur'ānic verses and *ḥadīth*s must be understood metaphorically. This position sets al-Ghazālī apart from a whole group of Ash'arites who follow al-Ash'arī's standard teaching on this matter. Al-Ash'arī, being influenced by Aḥmad ibn Ḥanbal (AH 164/780 CE–AH 241/855 CE), taught that all descriptions of God found in the Qur'ān or Ḥadīth must be interpreted literally, but without attributing any modalities to them (*bilā kayf*)—modalities that might render these descriptions analogous to human descriptions. The reason for the *bilā kayf* doctrine is that part of accepting the literal meaning of the descriptions of God in the scripture is accepting that God is unlike any of His creation, since the Qur'ān explicitly says: *There is nothing whatever like Him, and He is the Hearer, the Seer* (42:11). This doctrine allowed al-Ash'arī to reject the metaphorical interpretation of anthropomorphic Qur'ānic verses and *ḥadīth*s without falling into hard anthropomorphism (*tashbīh*). Thus, for example, since the Qur'ān says regarding God's command to Noah to build an ark: *Construct an ark under Our eyes and Our inspiration* (11:37), God must have eyes, but these eyes are unlike any of the eyes He created or might create.

Al-Ashʿarī argued that the Qur'ān was revealed in the tongue of the Arabs, and since the Qur'ān contains no falsehoods, its verses ought to be understood as the Arabs would ordinarily understand these verses; otherwise, if some of these verses were to be given metaphorical interpretation, they would be false according to the way in which the Arabs ordinarily understand them. For instance, the Arabs understand the command 'Construct an ark under Our eyes' to mean "Build an ark under the watchfulness of Our eyes"; to say that God has no eyes and that this expression really means "Build an ark with Our knowledge" is to say that its literal meaning, according to which the Arabs understand the command, is actually false. If this were the case, then God would have told the Arabs things that are false according to their ordinary understanding of the scripture. Since the scripture contains no falsehoods and is transmitted to ordinary Arabs, no part of the scripture should be given metaphorical interpretation. But given that the Qur'ān says that God is unlike any of His creation, no description of God should be understood in a way that makes God resemble His creation, hence the *bilā kayf* doctrine.

Al-Ghazālī rejects this argument and considers the *bilā kayf* doctrine as rendering meaningful terms nonsensical. For if we ought to understand by the term 'eyes', when applied to God, "eyes that are unlike any eyes that were created or could be created by God," then this term is rendered nonsensical, since it is impossible to call something an "eye" and at the same time assume that it is unlike any eye that is or might be created. He argues that saying that the Qur'ān was revealed in the tongue of the Arabs does not entail that it ought to be interpreted according to the way the populace understand its expressions; for the Qur'ān is linguistically miraculous, and hence its expressions and constructions are the most eloquent and excellent of all Arabic prose and poetry. The Arabs in their eloquent speech frequently use metaphor, and Qur'ānic expressions are no exception. Indeed, it is more likely that metaphor is employed when incommensurate realities, such as God and His attributes, are described. An intelligent person who is versed in the Arabic language readily understands the command 'Construct an ark under Our eyes' to mean "Construct an ark under Our sight," for he understands that God cannot have eyes, and hence the term 'eyes' is a metaphor for sight, since it is a common practice of Arabs to borrow a term indicating a cause to refer to its effect, so the term 'eyes', which indicates the cause of sight, is borrowed to refer to its effect—namely, sight. Al-Ashʿarī's argument, according to al-Ghazālī, confuses the correct way of understanding an expression with the way in which the populace understands it. The verses of the Qur'ān and the prophetic *ḥadīth*s need not be confined to shallow usage; these are the most eloquent of the Arabs' speech, and hence they should be understood according to the dictates of the intellect and of linguistic excellence.

Many Ash'arites followed al-Ghazālī's teaching. Scholars who subscribe to Sunni orthodoxy are divided into those who reject metaphorical interpretation (*ta'wīl*) and accept the *bilā kayf* doctrine and those who believe that when the literal meaning of scripture contradicts the dictates of reason, the expressions of scripture must be understood metaphorically. Scholars in the first of these groups also believe that since scripture is God's word, there is no case in which the literal meaning of scripture's expressions contradicts reason, so that there is no justification for engaging in metaphorical interpretation.

After discussing four propositions affirming the transcendence of God, al-Ghazālī gives a demonstration of the orthodox doctrine that the righteous will see God in the hereafter. Of course, no one can demonstrate a statement of fact, and this doctrine, if true, is a statement of fact. Hence al-Ghazālī divides the proposition into a claim of possibility and a claim of actuality—that is, God is *seeable* and God will be *seen*. He observes that the actuality claim can be established only through revelation, but it entails the possibility claim. Later he says that the evidence of the revelation and of the traditions of the early Muslims is overwhelming, so that it is feasible to claim that there is a consensus of the early Muslims about the fact of God's being seen in the hereafter. Although al-Ghazālī considers the evidence of the revelation, and offers interesting discussions of some Qur'ānic verses, most of his demonstration of the Ninth Proposition is a theoretical reflection aimed at showing that God is seeable. His argument is quite surprising. It might be reconstructed as follows. Since all essences are knowable, and since whatever is knowable is seeable, all essences are seeable. Given al-Ghazālī's essentialism—namely, that every existent has an essence—it follows that every existent is seeable; but God is an existent, albeit a necessary existent; hence God is seeable. This conclusion entails that an existent that can be the object of seeing need not have spatial properties and relations, since God can be the object of seeing and it is clear that God has no spatial properties or relations.

This last conclusion contradicts a standard Mu'tazilite principle that an object of seeing must have spatial relations. The Mu'tazilites employ this principle to argue that since God has no spatial relations, He cannot be the object of seeing, and hence He is not seeable. The Mu'tazilites thus believe that claiming that God will be seen in the hereafter is akin to attributing anthropomorphic qualities to God. This led the Muʿtazilites to offer a metaphorical interpretation of all Qurʾānic verses and *ḥadīths* whose literal meaning implies that God is seeable. The most important of these texts are the verses: *Faces, on that day, will be radiant, looking towards their Lord* (Qurʾān, 75:21–22). The Muʿtazilites interpreted 'looking towards their Lord' as having complete knowledge and awareness of God.

Al-Ghazālī fundamentally disagrees with the Muʿtazilites. Although he agrees with them that God has no spatial properties or relations, and that it is impossible for God to be seen as bodies and colors are seen, he rejects three of their positions: (1) being an object of seeing requires having spatial relations; (2) God is not seeable; and (3) all revealed texts that imply that God is seeable ought to be interpreted metaphorically. Al-Ghazālī thinks that the true nature of seeing is applicable to God and to all essences, including abstract properties such as power and knowledge. Hence al-Ghazālī affirms the general conclusion that all existents can be the objects of seeing. In order to reach this conclusion he presupposes that all essences can be known, and then argues that since the true nature of seeing is a state that is a perfection and completion of a state of apprehension, and since knowing an existent is a state of apprehension, it is possible to see any existent that is knowable; for it is possible to have a state that is a perfection and completion of any state of apprehension.

In order to show that this argument is sound, al-Ghazālī needs to explain and defend three premises: (1) all essences are knowable; (2) all existents have essence; and (3) the true nature of seeing is a state that is a perfection and completion of a state of apprehension. In his demonstration of the Ninth Proposition, al-Ghazālī does not argue for the first two premises. The second premise is a version of essentialism, and al-Ghazālī, like most medieval Islamic theologians and philosophers, is an essentialist. The first premise is borrowed from the Islamic philosophers. An essence is understood to correspond to an intrinsic definition (*ḥad*), and intrinsic definitions are all accessible to the human intellect, since there are no conceivable constraints as to what form might be comprehended and what form might not be comprehended by the intellect.[1]

Al-Ghazālī spends considerable space explaining and arguing for the third premise. He sees the true nature of ordinary seeing as a matter of hav-

1. It might be of interest to note that certain passages in Aristotle's *De Anima* suggest that this position might be traced to Aristotle. On one reading of Aristotle's passages on the intellect in *De Anima*, the passive intellect when it is thinking becomes like the object of its thinking; since the objects of thinking are forms; and since the passive intellect can think of any form, the passive intellect, when it is not thinking, cannot have any form. This reading explains why the passive intellect is assumed to be pure potentiality.

ing a state of apprehension that is a perfection and complete illumination of a state of visualization. The difference between seeing the face of a friend and imagining his face while the eyes are shut is that the former is a form of perfection and completion of the latter. He generalizes this relation to argue that any state of apprehension that is a perfection and completion of another state of apprehension is a form of seeing. He takes this as the true nature of seeing. In the final analysis, then, people will see God in the hereafter not as they see bodies and colors in this life, but by attaining a state of perfect and complete knowledge of His essence not accessible to them in this life. Al-Ghazālī's conception of the true nature of seeing is thus very similar to the Mu'tazilites' metaphorical interpretation of 'seeing God', although the Mu'tazilites would disagree with al-Ghazālī's claim that perfect and complete knowledge is a form of seeing, and would most likely contend that what al-Ghazālī does in effect is offer a metaphorical interpretation of 'seeing God' while pretending not to.

The Tenth Proposition states that God is one. Al-Ghazālī's demonstration of this proposition is the standard account found in the books of theology. The demonstration relies on what is known in Western philosophy as Leibniz's law: the identity of indiscernibles. It has the structure of a reductio ad absurdum of the notion that there is more than one god. If there is a multiplicity of gods, then by the law above, they must be discernible. But if they are all absolutely perfect, how can they differ from one another? The only way in which bearers of the same attributes could differ is in occupying different regions of space or periods of time. But if gods have no spatial or temporal properties or relations, there is no respect in which they could differ from one another. There cannot, therefore, be more than a single god.

Although al-Ghazālī considers several ways of distinguishing gods from one another, each proposal is shown to lead to absurdity. For example, if one supposes that there are two gods in charge of creation, one who creates the substances and the other who creates the modes, then, since there can be no substance that has no modes and there can be no mode without a substance in which it subsists, neither can create without the cooperation of the other. Since cooperation in this sense is necessary, the second god has no choice but to cooperate. But a god with no free choice lacks a condition for perfection. Therefore he is not a god after all.

## II

The Second Treatise, which is titled "On the Divine Attributes," deals with the seven principal attributes, which the Ash'arites affirm of God. These are power, knowledge, life, will, hearing, sight, and speech. The treatise is divided into two main parts. In the first part, al-Ghazālī proves the existence of each principal attribute and discusses its specific characteristics and some of their implications. In the second part, he discusses matters that are common to all the attributes. The first part consists of six sections—each section is devoted to a single attribute, except that hearing and sight are discussed in one section. Every section begins with a standard proposition asserting that God has that specific attribute. I will not summarize and reconstruct al-Ghazālī's central arguments in each of these sections. Most of this task is carried out in the notes. Instead, I will discuss certain aspects of the *attributes of agency*—namely, power, knowledge, will, and life—and certain aspects of the *attributes of apprehension*—namely, hearing, sight, and speech.

Al-Ghazālī presupposes in this treatise one of his central doctrines, which he employs in other works. The doctrine asserts that causal agents must satisfy three conditions: (1) they must have the necessary power to produce their effects; (2) they must have comprehensive knowledge of their effects and of the consequences of these effects; (3) they must have free will to specify these effects among other things that are equivalent to them in possibility. The power condition seems indisputable. Even the philosophers who believe in natural causes attribute natural powers to objects through which they produce their effects.

Al-Ghazālī offers an argument for the free will condition in the Third Discussion of *Tafāfut al-Falāsifa*. The argument is based on the observation that if two "causes" are present, a proximate one that has no volition and a more remote one that has volition, linguistic usage and theoretical reflection attribute causal agency only to the cause with volition. The example al-Ghazālī gives in the *Tahāfut* is of a man who throws another into fire with the result that the second man is killed. Here we have a proximate "cause" for the death, which is the fire, and a more remote cause, which is the man. The fire has no will but the man does. Although we might say that the fire burned the victim, we would not say that the fire is the victim's killer. Linguistically and theoretically, we attribute the act of killing to the cause with volition: we say that the first man is the killer, and that he killed the second man by throwing him into the fire. Al-Ghāzālī's points is that all attributions of causal agency to natural objects that have no volition are metaphorical, and that when a better candidate for causal agency—better in the sense of having volition—is present even if it is farther away in the causal chain, we abandon the metaphor and attribute causal agency to this farther cause. This condition excludes all inanimate objects and nonhuman animals from being true causal agents.

Human beings satisfy the first and third conditions for causal agency, those of power and volition, but they lack the second, the knowledge condition. To the best of my knowledge, al-Ghazālī simply assumes this condition without arguing for it.[2] God is the only being who has comprehensive knowledge of the effects He produces and of their consequences. But how do we know that God has it? Al-Ghazālī derives God's omniscience from His omnipotence. In the First Treatise, al-Ghazālī established that God created the world. Given the great degree of complexity and design the world has, God's power must be vast. Since every possible state of affairs can be in principle actualized (with an appropriate adjustment to the existing world), and since every component of every possible state of affairs is of the same type as some actual states of affairs, and since whoever capable of producing something is capable of producing things of the same type as that thing,[3] God can actualize every possible thing, that is, God can be the causal agent of every possible thing. Given the power condition, God's power must be all-encompassing. But now if God can actualize any possible thing, then, by the knowledge condition, God has comprehensive knowledge of all possible things, as well as of their consequences should they become actual.

Finally, al-Ghazālī argues that God's will can attach to all possible things, that is, anything possible can be willed by God so long as no contradiction ensues (e.g., God can will that my hand be at rest or in motion, though He cannot will simultaneous rest and motion in my hand). Al-Ghazālī reaches this conclusion by affirming that God can create whatever is possible, and that for every possible thing that can be created, there are other equally possible things that also can be created; hence if God were to create any occurrent, He must have a will that specifies this occurrent among its equivalents and direct the power to it in order to make it actual.

This last argument needs some elaboration. Al-Ghazālī believes that everything created by God could have been created under slightly different descriptions. As he puts it, "an act produced by [God] is subject to various possibilities none of which can be distinguished from the others with-

2. Al-Zabīdī in *Itḥāf al-Sāda al-Muttaqīn bi-Sharḥ Iḥyāʾ ʿUlūm al-Dīn* (vol. II, p. 261) offers an argument, which he attributes to al-Ashʿarī, for the knowledge condition that is very similar to al-Ghazālī's argument for the volition condition. He says that those who are ignorant of effects or oblivious to them cannot be considered their causal agents. He does not give an example, but he most likely would say that if someone pushed a person without being aware of the consequences of his action, and this push accidentally resulted in the death of that person, we would find it difficult to say that the first man killed the second, or to attribute causal agency to the first.

3. For example, a winged horse shares the type of being a horse with earthly horses, and shares the type of having wings with earthly birds, and the one who is capable of creating earthly horses and birds must be capable of creating a winged horse.

out something giving preponderance to one of them." Al-Ghazālī's main example is the creation of the world. If we are allowed to speak of time prior to the creation of the world, then it is clear that the world could have been created at a moment of time different from the one at which it was actually created. All moments are indistinguishable in terms of their suitability for the creation of the world. The same applies to everything that is produced by God. Any magnitude that God created could have been created slightly smaller or slightly greater without any violation of the excellence of the world. In order for God to determine a specific effect among its equals, He must have a quality whose sole function is to determine one effect among others that are equivalent to it in terms of possibility. This quality is free will.

God, then, is the only being that has sufficient power, knowledge, and will to create the occurrents in the world. Since no created entity, human beings included, satisfies all these three conditions, none of them can be a causal agent. It follows that God is the sole causal agent in existence, who directly creates all occurrents. This is the doctrine of occasionalism.

Let us consider some of the important consequences of this doctrine. Note first that for al-Ghazālī our knowledge of any occurrent is sufficient for knowing that God has knowledge. For if we know that an occurrent exists, then we know that this occurrent must have a cause (since all occurrents have causes); but given the doctrine of occasionalism, God must be the cause of this occurrent, which entails, by the knowledge condition, that God has comprehensive knowledge of this occurrent and its consequences. Furthermore, God must have life, since being alive is a necessary condition for having knowledge. Al-Ghazālī established in the First Treatise that if a thing has a certain attribute since eternity, then it must continue to have this attribute for eternity. We know that the existence of a single occurrent is sufficient to demonstrate that God has life. If God has life since eternity, then He will continue to be alive for eternity even if all occurrents were to cease to be created. It cannot be the case that God was not living and then acquired life in order to create the occurrents; for, again, if He lacked life since eternity, He would have to continue in this state forever, which means that He would never have knowledge, and hence would never be a causal agent. Since no being other than God can be a causal agent, occurrents exist without having causes—but that is impossible.

Another consequence of the doctrine of occasionalism involves the conception of the difference between voluntary and involuntary acts. A man's moving his hand to scratch his head is fundamentally different from a tremor. Many philosophers would say that the difference between the two movements is that the former is freely willed and intended by the man while the second is not. Many Islamic theologians saw the difference as a difference in power: the man had the power to move his hand when he scratched his head but he lacked this power in the case of tremor. The concept of power, as employed by those Islamic theologians, is a matter of having control over one's acts. Al-Ghazālī, working within this tradition, explains that the fundamental difference between a voluntary and involuntary act must lie in the presence of power, and not in the presence of will or intention, since it is conceivable that a man who is experiencing a tremor might decide to will and intend the tremor of his hand; but this does not make the tremor an act of volition. It is not a voluntary act, because he lacks control over this movement, which means that he lacks the power to move his hand. On the other hand, when he moves his hand voluntarily, he has control over this movement, that is, he has the power to move his hand.

The Muʿtazilites argued that if religious obligations are to have any justification, a man must have control over his acts: how could it be justified for God to command people to do what they lack the power to do? For a variety of reasons having to do with divine justice and goodness, many Muʿtazilites believed that the acts produced freely by people are outside the reach of God's power. There is, however, in addition, one metaphysical reason that convinced many Muʿtazilites that any act an agent, whether human or nonhuman, produces through its power is outside the reach of God's power. Al-Ghazālī discusses this reason in this treatise. In most animals the fundamental distinction between an act that is under the animal's control and an act that is not may also be observed. If this is so, then human and nonhuman animals alike produce acts through powers they possess. If such acts were also under the power of God, there would be single acts that were the objects of two powers. The Muʿtazilites saw this consequence as absurd, since an act's being under the control of an agent seems clearly to exclude its being under the control of a different agent: what would the outcome be if one of the agents wants to perform the act and the other wants to refrain from the act?

Al-Ghazālī agrees with the Muʿtazilites that meaningful obligations entail that human acts must be the objects of powers they possess. He also agrees that the distinction between an act that is under one's control and an act that is not is a fundamental distinction for human and nonhuman animals alike. But al-Ghazālī rejects the Muʿtazilite argument that these facts show that the acts of human beings and animals are beyond the reach of God's power. His rejection of this argument is based on the famous Ashʿarite doctrine of acquisition (*kasb*). This doctrine states that any voluntary act that proceeds from a person is, like everything else, directly created by God, but at the time of creating this act, God also creates in the person a power whose object is that act. Hence it appears to the person that he is creating his act, since he has the necessary power whose object is that act; but in reality his "occurrent" power is causally inert and only God's "eternal" power is creative, in the sense that only it is causally capable of creating the act. An immediate consequence of this doctrine is that any voluntary act is an object of two powers: the eternal power of God and the occurrent power of man. Al-Ghazālī thus sees nothing wrong with positing a single object for two powers.

While many Ash'arites before al-Ghazālī simply affirm the doctrine of acquisition without explaining how it is possible for an act to be the object of two powers, al-Ghazālī may be the only one to mount a brilliant defense of this doctrine, arguing elaborately that it is perfectly meaningful for an act to be the object of two powers. His defense is based on the observation that an act can be an object of two powers if these powers have different causal qualities: one of them creative and the other inert. Most of his discussion is aimed at making sense of the claim that a person's act can be the object of his created power even though it is not this power but God's power that produces the act. I will not reconstruct his argument here; I devote several notes to it. There surely is, however, a conceptual problem here: being the object of a certain power implies that the object is under the control of the agent who possesses this power; it is unclear what exactly it means to say that man's voluntary act is the object of his power if this power is causally inert.

Al-Ghazālī turns next to the divine attributes of apprehension—namely, hearing, sight, and speech. He argues that since these capacities are perfections in created beings and do not require the existence of occurrents, and since every perfection in a created being that does not require the existence of an occurrent is a perfection in the Creator as well, it follows that God, too, has hearing, sight, and speech.[4]

Al-Ghazālī is aware that this argument might be extended inappropriately. For instance, one might argue that since the senses of smell and taste and the ability to feel pain and pleasure are perfections in created beings, God, too, must smell, taste, and feel pain and pleasure. Al-Ghazālī offers two responses to this contention. The first response is as follows. In the case of other perceptions, such as smell and taste, these faculties must be examined in order to determine whether it is true of them that they do not require the existence of occurrents. If it is found that they do not, then in-

4. It is clear that if a human perfection requires the existence of some occurrent, it cannot be attributed to God, since, according to al-Ghazālī, God is devoid of occurrents.

deed there is nothing to prevent God from having these perceptions. Nevertheless, since the revelation affirms hearing and sight, but no other perception, for God, it is not permissible to attribute to God any other types of perception.

Al-Ghazālī remains agnostic as to whether smell and taste require occurrence. It is clear from his discussions of the true nature of sight in the First Treatise and of God's speech in the Second Treatise that he believes that sight and speech do not. Although he does not give an analysis of hearing, his discussion of the manner in which Moses heard the speech of God indicates that there can be hearing without occurrence, even though we might never know, in this life, what this manner is. Moreover, the revelation attributes hearing to God. Since, however, in the case of smell and taste we do not have demonstrative proof that these perceptions require no occurrence, and since the revelation does not affirm them of God, we do not attribute them of God.

The second response concerns the ability to feel pain and pleasure. Al-Ghazālī says that these abilities in reality indicate deficiencies and not perfections. They appear as "perfections" because not having these abilities is destructive to the created being: the ability to feel pain is needed in order to prevent harm and the ability to feel pleasure is needed in order to attain what one needs and longs for. Since, however, a perfect being cannot be harmed and has no needs and longs for nothing—a perfect being lacks nothing—they are not perfections.

Interestingly, al-Ghazālī argues that, like the existence of God, divine speech cannot be established on the basis of revelation. Just as one cannot rely on the authority of revelation to argue for the existence of God, since one must first believe in God before he can accept the authority of revelation, so one cannot argue that since God issued commands and prohibitions and sent messengers, he must be able to speak; for one needs first to believe that God has the power of speech in order to believe that He truly can issue commands and prohibitions and send messengers.

Most of the section on divine speech is devoted to clarifying the nature of divine speech. Since we associate many occurrents with speech—uttering sounds and letters, hearing God's words on a specific occasion, reciting the Qur'ān, writing God's words in a copy of the Qur'ān, and so on—al-Ghazālī must make clear that God's speech is *inner speech* (literally, the speech of the soul, *kalām al-nafs*). Thus all contexts in which we seem to be associating God's speech with occurrence arise because of the ambiguity of certain words, such as 'Qur'ān' and 'recitation'. God's speech is eternal and the Qur'ān, in one sense of the term 'Qur'ān', is the speech of God; hence the Qur'ān is eternal and not created. This is the orthodox doctrine regarding the status of the Qur'ān. The question whether the Qur'ān is anteriorly eternal or created was bitterly debated by the Islamic theologians, with the Muʿtazilites insisting that it is created and the Ashʿarites, among others, affirming its anterior eternity. Al-Ghazālī does not debate this issue in the *Iqtiṣād*; he simply affirms the anterior eternity of the Qur'ān as an immediate consequence of three premises: (1) the Qur'ān is God's speech, (2) God's speech is a divine attribute, and (3) all divine attributes are eternal anteriorly and posteriorly. All (theistic) Islamic sects accept the first premise, but the second and third premises are disputed. Al-Ghazālī argues for the second and third premises in the First and Second Parts of the Second Treatise, respectively. We already presented his argument for the second premise, and will discuss his argument for the third premise below.

The Second Part of the Second Treatise is devoted to four characteristics that the seven divine attributes share. These characteristics are: (1) the attributes are additional to the essence; (2) they subsist in the essence; (3) they are eternal; and (4) all the names that are derived from these attributes are true of God eternally. The first three characteristics entail that God is a composite being. He consists of eight eternal existents: His essence and His seven attributes. Al-Ghazālī does not see in this a challenge to monotheism. For him God is one, since there is only one necessary existent, even though He is composed of an eternal essence, which exists in virtue of itself, and seven eternal attributes, which subsist in this essence. Al-Gazālī is very clear about this. He says that it is a mistake to identify God with the divine essence alone. When we utter the name 'God', "we have referred to the divine essence together with the divine attributes, and not to the essence alone."

This position is in stark opposition to the position of the Islamic philosophers and the Muʿtazilites, who affirm that true monotheism means that there is no plurality, whether external or internal, with respect to God: He is one and simple. The philosophers and the Muʿtazilites argue that God has no eternal attributes that are additional to the essence. The traditional ninety-nine beautiful names of God found in revelation, together with a host of other names such as 'Enjoyer' and 'Enjoyable', are all reducible to His essence, His essence together with a negation, or His essence together with a relation. For instance, 'The Existent' and 'The Necessary Existent' describe His essence, which is pure existence; 'The Anteriorly Eternal' and 'The Posteriorly Eternal' describe His essence with a negation—not being preceded or succeeded by nonexistence; 'The Creator' describes His essence with a relation—all existents emanated from His essence directly or through intermediaries.

An attribute that is attributed to God in some way other than these three is called "a positive attribute." The philosophers affirmed that God has no positive attributes, whether eternal or occurrent. He cannot have occurrent attributes, for if an attribute occurs in the essence of God, He would be a receptacle of occurrents, which contradicts the principle that God is devoid of occurrents. They also argue that if there are positive eternal attributes that are additional to the divine essence, then either these attributes exist in virtue of themselves or in virtue of the essence. But if, on the one hand, they exist in virtue of themselves, then they are necessary existents that are additional to the essence, so that there would be a plurality of necessary existents, which contradicts the divine unity. And if, on the other hand, they exist in virtue of the essence, then, although, they are not necessary existents, nevertheless their subsistence in the essence would be a necessary condition for the existence of the essence, thereby rendering the existence of divine essence dependent on a condition and hence not itself necessary. In other words, the philosophers argue that if one allows for internal plurality within God, then one must either allow for an external plurality of necessary existents or deny that God's essence exists necessarily. Most of the Muʿtazilites make an exception for will and speech. They believe that God has two positive attributes—namely, will and speech. However, they escape the philosophers' arguments by assuming that these two attributes are occurrent and that when they occur, they occur not in God's essence; hence God remains immutable and devoid of occurrents. They assume that an act of divine will occurs not in any receptacle and that divine speech is created in an inanimate object.

Al-Ghazālī in making the case for positive divine attributes that are eternal and subsist in the divine essence has to deal with the philosophers' arguments. He agrees with the philosophers that God's attributes are not occurrents, since God is not a receptacle of occurrents. He in fact gives three proofs for the claim that God is devoid of occurrents. He considers the second proof to be the strongest of the three. It is a reductio ad absurdum demonstration that involves identifying possibility with conceivability. Suppose that God is a receptacle of occurrents. In that case, then, either the imagination can conceive of an occurrent in God prior to which no occurrent is possible or it cannot. If it cannot, then there must exist in God an infinite chain of occurrents that has no beginning. Al-Ghazālī takes this to be an obviously absurd—and hence disqualifying—consequence. This leaves only the other option—namely, that the imagination *can* conceive of an occurrent in God prior to which no other occurrent is possible. Let this occurrent be $x$. Now we ask, Why is it impossible to have occurrents in God prior to $x$? There are only two possible answers: (1) this impossibility is due to God's essence, and (2) it is due to something other than God. It cannot be due to something other than God, for anything other than God can be imagined not to exist, and hence the nonexistence of whatever prevents occurrents prior to $x$ from being possible can be imagined; but if this can be imagined, then occurrents prior to $x$ can be imagined, which contradicts the supposition that no occurrent prior to $x$ is possible (i.e., conceivable). We are left with the last option: the impossibility of occurrents prior to $x$ is due to the essence of God. Since the essence is anteriorly eternal, this impossibility must have lasted for anterior eternity until the moment at which $x$ occurred. So we have a case of an anteriorly eternal impossibility that at some point turned into possibility (when $x$ occurred). But this contradicts the fundamental principle that whatever is eternal anteriorly is also eternal posteriorly. Thus we must reject this option too, which entails that the assumption with which the reductio begins is false. Therefore God cannot be a receptacle of occurrents.

As for the philosophers' second argument that positing positive eternal attributes entails either that there is a multiplicity of necessary existents or that God is not a necessary existent because His existence would be conditioned on the subsistence of the attributes in His essence, al-Ghazālī does not offer a direct rebuttal in the *Iqtiṣād*. He in fact considers this argument and responds to it in the Sixth Discussion of *Tahāfut al-Falāsifa*. But his discussion in the *Iqtiṣād* elaborates further on his response in the *Tahāfut*. Al-Ghazālī says that the correct answer is that God is a necessary existent as a whole, essence and attributes together. Indeed the divine attributes could not exist without subsisting in the divine essence, but it makes no sense to ask whether God could exist without having His attributes, since the term 'God' refers to the composite of essence and attributes. This would be similar to one's question, Is it possible for a jurist to exist without his jurisprudence? It is clear that the man, who is a jurist, may exist without his jurisprudence, since being a man does not entail having jurisprudence, but being a jurist entails having jurisprudence. Thus once we utter the name 'God', we have already referred to the essence including the attributes, and this composite is a necessary existent, who is the only necessary existent in being.

In the *Tahāfut*, al-Ghazālī charges the philosophers' argument with circularity. As we have seen above, the philosophers invoke the oneness of the necessary existent to argue that there can be no positive attributes that exist in virtue of themselves, since in this case they all would be necessary existents. In other words, the philosophers defend the simplicity of God (i.e., that God is not composed of essence and attributes) by invoking the oneness of the necessary existent. In the Fifth Discussion of the *Tahāfut*, al-Ghazālī summarizes the philosophers' main argument for the oneness of the necessary existent as follows: if there were two or more necessary existents, then they would have to be alike in at least one respect such as being necessary existents, and also unlike in some respects (since indiscernibles are identical); but this means that each necessary existent is composed of at least two aspects: one that it shares with the other necessary existents, and one in which it differs from them. On the assumption that a necessary existent admits no composition, it follows that there can be at most one necessary existent. Since the philosophers argue for the existence of a necessary existent, they can now affirm that there is exactly one necessary existent. It is clear that this argument invokes the simplicity of the necessary existent to conclude that the necessary existent is one. But as explained above, the philosophers typically invoke the oneness of the necessary existent to argue that He cannot be a composite of essence and attributes. This is circular reasoning: simplicity is invoked to arrive at oneness, and then oneness is invoked to arrive at simplicity.

## III

The Third Treatise, "On the Acts of God," consists of an introduction in which al-Ghazālī introduces into the canons of Islamic theology an ethical theory, and seven propositions that collectively paint a picture of divine freedom that is not subject to the constraints of reason, justice, or morality as commonly understood. Al-Ghazālī summarizes these seven propositions at the outset of this treatise: "We claim that it is possible for God (Exalted is He) not to assign obligations to His servants, that it is possible for Him to assign obligations to them beyond their ability, that it is possible for Him to bring suffering upon them without compensating them and through no fault of theirs, that it is not obligatory for Him to care for their well-being, that it is not obligatory for Him to reward obedience and punish disobedience, that nothing is made obligatory for a person by virtue of reason but only by virtue of the revelation, and that it is not obligatory for God to send messengers." In the course of proving these propositions, he introduces a deterrence theory of punishment, a response to theodicy that is very different from the theodicy he popularizes in *Iḥyāʾ ʿUlūm al-Dīn*,[5]

5. Al-Ghazālī gives a brief summary of the main sections of the *Iqtiṣād* in the Third Chapter of *Kitāb Qawāʿid al-ʿAqāʾid* (*The Book of the Foundations of Belief*) of the *Iḥyāʾ* (vol. I, pp. 246–269), and so re-describes the response to theodicy he first argues for in the Third Treatise of the *Iqtiṣād*. However, in *Kitāb al-Tawḥīd wa-l-Tawakkul* (*The Book of Monotheism and Reliance on God*) of the *Iḥyāʾ*, al-Ghazālī popularizes (vol. IV, pp. 2931–2933) a form of best-of-all-possible-worlds theodicy, which is at odds with his earlier response to theodicy. It is an open question as to why al-Ghazālī offers two accounts of theodicy, and

novel conceptions of obligating, promise, justice, and revelation, as well as many original arguments.[6] I will not summarize al-Ghazālī's discussion of each proposition. Rather, I will discuss some of the central themes that emerge from this treatise.

Al-Ghazālī, like almost all theologians and philosophers, holds that divine will is constrained by the limits of logical possibility: God cannot will logically impossible states of affairs.[7] Al-Ghazālī places no other constraints on the divine will, no matter how weakly 'constraint' may be interpreted. The Muʿtazilites posit a host of constraints on the divine will. These constraints range from logical, to moral, to counterfactual. For instance, some Muʿtazilites say that it is logically impossible for God to will acts of injustice, because such acts are contrary to His being just, which is a state of His essence. Other Muʿtazilites say that it is possible for God to will acts of injustice, but He is morally obligated not to do so, and since God fulfills all His obligations, He does not will acts of injustice. A third group of Muʿtazilites argue that although God can will acts of injustice and He is under no obligation to refrain from such acts, nevertheless He *would never* will an unjust act because God is all-good. Al-Ghazālī rejects all these arguments, and explains that it is logically impossible for God to will an unjust act because, due to "pure negation," it is logically impossible for any act of God to be unjust: the conditions for the possibility of injustice are absent with respect to God. An act is unjust if and only if it is an improper use of

---

which account is his "true" response to the problem of evil. Surprisingly, Ormsby in his well-regarded study of al-Ghazālī's theodicy (Ormsby 1984) barely takes up this question. He considers (pp. 192–196) only very briefly the *Iqtiṣād*'s more radical approach to theodicy, and he seems to minimize the extent to which it differs from the later, popular account: "Although al-Ghazālī composed *al-Iqtiṣād fī al-Iʿtiqād* as a manual of dogmatic theology and did not himself regard the methods of the kalām as the only, or even the best, approach to higher truth, there is no reason to conclude that his exposition [in the *Iqtiṣād*] conflicts with his later, more complex views" (p. 195).

6. Having said this, I must note that some of al-Ghazālī's arguments in this treatise are standard Ashʿarite arguments.

7. There are notable dissenters in the Islamic and Western traditions. A familiar example is Descartes. Whereas he did not quite say that God can create logical contradictions, he did contend that we cannot affirm that He cannot. In a letter to Mesland, 2 May 1644, he wrote regarding the difficulty of conceiving of God's acting freely by making it possible for contradictories to be true together: "It is easy to dispel this difficulty by considering that the power of God cannot have any limits, and that our mind is finite and so created as to be able to conceive as possible the things which God has wished to be in fact possible, but not be able to conceive as possible things which God could have made possible, but which he has nevertheless wished to make impossible. The first consideration shows us *that God cannot have been determined to make it true that contradictories cannot be true together*. . . . And even if God has willed that some truths should be necessary, this does not mean that He willed them necessarily" (Cottingham et al., vol. III, p. 235; emphasis added).

the property of another or it is against the command of someone who has authority over the person. Since everything belongs to God and everyone is subservient to God, none of God's acts, no matter what sort of act it is, can ever be unjust. It follows that God may will what he wants in His kingdom, including acts that we ordinarily deem "unjust," without ever being properly described as committing injustice. In other words, God's freedom is absolute and cannot be exercised unjustly. As we will see later, the same analysis applies to the cases of obligatory, good, and bad.

Al-Ghazālī, like many others, believes that all objects of divine power (i.e., the things that are within the reach of divine power) are possible (*al-maqdūrāt mumkināt*) and all possible things are objects of divine power (*al-mumkināt maqdūrāt*). Al-Ghazālī does not place any further constraints on divine power. But if one believes that God can will an object just in case it is possible, one should conclude that the objects that God *can* will are precisely those that are within the reach of His power.

Note that it is incorrect to say that the objects of divine will are exactly the objects of divine power. An object of divine power (*maqdūr*) is an object that is within the reach of divine power; it need not be actual. This only means that it is made actual or *can be* made actual by divine power. An object of divine will (*murād*) is an object that is actually willed by God, and hence one that is actual. According to al-Ghazālī, when God wills something, the will specifies that thing and directs power to it, whence the power brings about the willed thing. So God's willing something is sufficient for the thing's becoming actual. But this also shows that every possible object of divine will is an object of divine power: whatever can be willed can be created.

Al-Ghazālī also argues that every object that divine power originates is willed by God. This view depends on al-Ghazālī's conception of will in general. As shown in the Second Treatise, the will is an attribute whose function is to specify an option among equally possible options and to direct power to that option. Power on its own cannot make such specifications. Its sole function is to make the possible actual, but not to specify which possible is to be actualized. To ask why the will specifies a particular option among many equally possible options is to ask the wrong question. Al-Ghazālī seems to imply in his discussion of the divine attribute of will in the Second Treatise that if there is sufficient reason for choosing A over B, knowledge and power would be sufficient for bringing about A, and there would be no need for will. The will is needed to specify an option among equally possible options precisely when there is no good reason to do so.

This view of will, however, presents a problem for al-Ghazālī. If the will is needed only to specify something among things that are alike, then for any act of power for which there is sufficient reason, the will would not be needed; and hence there would be many occurrents in the world that were not willed by God. Al-Ghazālī rejects this conclusion. Since he asserts that every occurrent is willed by God (*kul ḥādith murād*), he must believe that there is never sufficient reason to distinguish just one act from among all possible acts, that is, for any given act, there must be at least one other act that is indistinguishable from the first act with respect to certain conditions.[8] There are several passages in the *Iqtiṣād* and the *Iḥyāʾ* that clearly indicate that al-Ghazālī holds such a view. The will, therefore, is not only sufficient for the power to act but also necessary. In order to conclude that *all occurrents are willed by God*, al-Ghazālī, as an Ashʿarite, invokes the Ashʿarite doctrine of occasionalism: all occurrents, including all acts of living beings, are *directly* created by God. His argument runs as follows: every occurrent is originated through a divine power; and everything that is originated through a divine power requires a divine will that specifies it and directs the power to it; hence every occurrent is willed by God.

Al-Ghazālī's central theme in the Third Treatise is that divine will is not subject to any constraints of reason, justice, or morality. We have already seen from the Second Treatise, that the will acts precisely when there is no sufficient reason to act and that every occurrent requires an act of will. It follows that there is never sufficient reason for any occurrent (other than for logically concomitant occurrents; see note 8). We also previously showed that divine will is not constrained by the demands of justice as commonly understood, since according to al-Ghazālī the concept of injustice is inapplicable to the acts of God. As for moral constraints, al-Ghazālī defends a form of ethical egoism that renders the categories of good and bad inapplicable to God's acts. He also defends a certain conception of obligatoriness, which implies that none of God's acts can be described as obligatory. All of these are conceptual impossibilities, and hence they are logical impos-

8. Strictly speaking, al-Ghazālī could not affirm this principle without certain qualifications. In the chapter on divine power in the Second Treatise of the *Iqtiṣād*, al-Ghazālī discusses cases of acts that are *necessarily* concomitant with each other, in the sense that the occurrence of one of them is a sufficient condition for the occurrence of the other. One such case is the movement of a hand in water and the movement of the water. The movement of a hand in water is a sufficient condition for the movement of the water. So if a hand is moving in water, it cannot be said *in this case* that there is a possible occurrent, which is an alternative to the movement of the water, and which God can will. It is not possible for a hand to move in water without the water moving as well; for if the hand moves to occupy a certain region of space and the water does not move, there would be two physical objects occupying the same region, which is absurd. Thus still water in which a hand moves is not an object of the divine power (it is not a possible object), and hence it is not a possible object of the divine will. Such cases, therefore, place no new constraint on divine will.

sibilities. They therefore conform to the only constraint al-Ghazālī affirms of divine will—namely, logical impossibility.

Al-Ghazālī's ethical theory is sketched in the introductory part of the Third Treatise. The theory is based on an account of the *correct* meanings of three terms: 'obligatory' (*wājib*), 'good' (*ḥasan*), and 'bad' (*qabīḥ*). Although the Arabic term *wājib* means either obligatory or necessary, al-Ghazālī's concern is with *wājib* in its sense of obligatory. An act is described as obligatory for a person if and only if a definite harm will befall the person if he refrains from doing the act. Any act that will lead to a great harm in the hereafter if one refrains from it is one that is *definitely* obligatory for *all* people. Such acts can only be known through revelation. In addition, an act *might be called* "obligatory"—though it is not definitely obligatory—if it is known through reason that refraining from it will lead to significant harm in this life. Al-Ghazālī states at the outset of the Third Treatise that reason does not render an act obligatory for a person; only revelation does.

An act of an agent belongs to one of three categories depending on its relation to the agent's purpose (*gharaḍ*). Either it is in accordance with his purpose, it is contrary to his purpose, or there is no purpose in performing it or refraining from it. An act in the first category is called "good," in the second, "bad," and in the third, "frivolity." It is clear that al-Ghazālī understands by 'being in accordance with his purpose' as "serving his best interest," and by 'being contrary to his purposes' as "being detrimental to his best interest." Thus this ethical theory is a form of ethical egoism.

It is natural for ethical egoism to be relativistic. After all, what serves one person's interest might not serve another's interest, and hence what is good for one might not be good for another. But it is incorrect to conclude that, because of this relativistic feature of ethical egoism, it is really a form of ethical relativism. Ethical relativism typically rejects any objectivity in moral judgment. What is good and what is bad are determined by the belief of some person or persons, some institution, some society, or some culture. Ethical egoism, by contrast, does not hold that what is morally good for someone is what he believes to be good for him but what is *in fact* good for him—even though what is in fact good may differ from one individual to another and indeed, as al-Ghazālī indicates, from one state of an individual to another.

Just like 'obligatory', the term 'good' (and 'bad') has two senses. One agent might use it to describe any act that serves his interest in this life. Another might use it to describe an act that serves his interest in the hereafter. The latter is the good of the revelation; for the revelation enjoins the performance of these acts and promises eternal reward for them. This is the *universal* good, since these acts serve the *real* interest of *everyone* who performs them. The universal good is known only through revelation.

Given that an act that serves a person's purpose in this life might be detrimental to his purpose in the hereafter and that eternal bliss *must* be the purpose of all people, it follows that what serves a worldly purpose is an *appearance* of the good. Saying that something is an appearance of the good need not imply that it is a "false" good, that is, that it appears to be good but is not truly good. It may be truly good in this life and in the hereafter, that is, it serves one's best interest in this worldly life and in the hereafter. However, if it serves an interest in this life but brings harm in the hereafter, then it is a mere appearance of the good and is in fact bad. The same applies mutatis mutandis to what is universally bad and what appears to be bad.

According to al-Ghazālī's theory, God is the source of what is universally good and what is universally bad. To say that something is universally good is to say that it necessarily serves all people's best interests; to say that it is universally bad is to say that it necessarily harms them. The notion of "necessity" here is not logical; it is conditioned on God's will. It is because God willed to reward doing $x$ with eternal bliss, that $x$ is necessarily good for everyone, that is, that doing $x$ necessarily serves the real interest of anyone who does $x$. It cannot happen that doing $x$ fails to serve everyone's real interest because if that were the case, God would have willed something false, which is impossible (recall that whatever God wills is and whatever He does not will is not). Thus God, by willing that certain acts shall be rewarded with eternal bliss and certain acts shall be punished with eternal damnation, determines what is universally good and what is universally bad, that is, what is necessarily good for all people and what is necessarily bad for all people. God's will is the (only) source of what is universally good and what is universally bad.

For al-Ghazālī the most important consequence of these definitions of 'obligatory', 'good', and 'bad' is that an agent who cannot be harmed has no obligations at all, and none of the acts of an agent who has no interests can be good or bad. Since no harm can befall God and since He has no interests, He has no obligations at all and none of His acts can be described as good or bad. Note that the quality of being frivolous is also inapplicable to the acts of God, even though no interest of His is served by His performing an act and no interest of His is harmed by His refraining from an act. This is because God has no interests, yet frivolity presupposes the possibility of having interest.

An act of God surely cannot be said to be good for God since nothing is good for God: no act serves God's interest, for He is too exalted to have interests. Given al-Ghazālī's conclusion that all occurrents are willed by God, and given that many of these occurrents are detrimental for many people, it follows that in this sense too it cannot be said that all the acts of God are good. Surprisingly, al-Ghazālī suggests an interpretation of the principle that all God's acts are good that has nothing to do with the moral good as he defines it. He says that this principle means that there are no repercussions or blame for whatever God does in His kingdom

One aspect of absolute divine freedom that emerges from al-Ghazālī's treatment in this treatise is that God may and does assign obligations that are impossible for human beings to fulfill. In this he opposes the Māturīdites, whose brand of Islamic theology is believed by many to have a claim to Sunni orthodoxy equal to that of Ash'arite theology.[9] The Māturīdites deny on the basis of reason and revelation that God would assign obligations that are beyond the ability of the one who is obligated. They argue that an *essential quality* of a religious obligation is that the one who is obligated is commanded by God to fulfill the obligation, and that it is impossible that God would command us to do something that we could not possibly do.

Most of the Ash'arites reject this argument but agree that it is not possible for God to assign an obligation that is *by virtue of its essence* impossible to fulfill. God cannot obligate a person, for example, simultaneously to move and not move his hand. The Ash'arites, however, all agree that God not only can but also does assign obligations that people cannot fulfill either because the obligations are beyond their ability or because they are impossible by virtue of something *extraneous* to their essence. The standard example of assigning an obligation that is impossible by virtue of something extraneous to its essence is the assigning of an obligation to a person who God knows will not fulfill the obligation. Given God's knowledge, which is extraneous to the essence of the obligation, it is *impossible* for the person to fulfill the obligation; if he did, God would know something false, yet knowledge entails truth.

As for God's actually assigning an obligation that is beyond the ability of the one who is obligated, the Ash'arites invoke their doctrine of acquisition (*kasb*). As explained earlier, this doctrine asserts that God creates the acts of people, but at the time of creating a person's act He also creates in the person a power of which the created act is the object. So although the person does not really create the act, it *appears* to him as if he does; all he actually does is "acquire" the act. According to this doctrine, no one really has the power to fulfill an obligation when the obligation is assigned; a

9. The Māturīdiyya school of Islamic theology was founded by Abū Manṣūr Muḥammad al-Māturīdī (d. AH 333/944 CE). The Māturīdites agree with the Ash'arites on many, but not all, issues. The Ḥanafite jurists tend to be Māturīdite in their theology. Ash'arite theology, however, remains the dominant Islamic theology. (For a brief account, see Amīn, *Ẓuhr al-Islām*, vol. IV, pp. 76–79; and for a complete description of Māturīdite theology, see al-Māturīdī, *Kitāb al-Tawḥīd*, or al-Ghaznawī, *Kitāb Uṣūl al-Dīn*.)

person is given the relevant power only at the moment the obligatory act is performed. Thus obligations are assigned to people who do not have the power to fulfill these obligations until they do so.

Al-Ghazālī gives not only all the standard arguments but other arguments as well (which are, to the best of my knowledge, unique to him) to conclude that God can and does assign obligations that are impossible to fulfill, whether because they are beyond the ability of those who are obligated or because they are impossible by virtue of something extraneous to their essence. However, he does not stop here. He crosses a boundary that almost no one else has crossed. Al-Ghazālī asserts that God may assign an obligation that is impossible by virtue of its own essence. Although the cases of impossible obligations that he discusses all concern divine commands whose fulfillment is impossible by virtue of conditions extraneous to the commands themselves, he says that there might be divine commands that are impossible to fulfill by virtue of their own essence. The two types of commands are analogous in many ways. They both can be spoken by God, they are both requirements, and they both can be deemed good or bad from our point of view. According to al-Ghazālī, an obligation is a type of speech that is a requirement residing in one's mind and is addressed to someone who is lower in rank than the addresser. Whether the obligation cannot be fulfilled by virtue of itself or by virtue of another is irrelevant to this definition. Thus if God can assign an obligation whose fulfillment is impossible by virtue of a condition extraneous to it, He can equally assign an obligation whose fulfillment is impossible by virtue of something intrinsic to it.

Most Muʿtazilites assert that God is obligated to care for the well-being of His creation and to compensate fairly those that are wronged or harmed through no fault of their own. Many Islamic theologians, however, would deny that God is obligated to do so, but would still assert that caring for the well-being of the creation and compensating in the hereafter those that are wronged or harmed unfairly in this worldly life are constraints on the divine will.

These constraints are typically invoked in defending a Muʿtazilite theodicy, embraced by other theologians as well, which affirms the absolute goodness of God. God is not the source of moral evil. The source of moral evil is finite beings who have free will. There is only one infinite being, who is God, and He performs no evil acts. Free finite beings are agents who are imperfect, and hence capable of committing evil acts. God neither wills nor creates any of these evil acts: their agents do. The only "evil" that God can be the source of is "natural evil" or worldly harm. God creates worldly harm for reasons that He in His infinite wisdom understands even if they are difficult for us. Sometimes, as an act of grace, He reveals His reasons to some people.

God's goodness implies (or necessitates or requires, depending on how the constraint is interpreted) that all created beings are treated with fairness and grace. So He does two things: He cares about the well-being of the creation *as much as His wisdom permits*, and those beings that are wronged or harmed unfairly in this worldly life are compensated in the hereafter to the extent needed to render the evil or harm that was inflicted upon them insignificant. In other words, from the viewpoint of the victims, no evil is genuine evil and no harm is genuine harm, because the reward that awaits the victims in the hereafter is so great as to render any harmful worldly experience desirable. Although this "removes" the evil or harm from the viewpoint of the victims, moral evil has not become good. The agents who commit evil are truly evildoers and will be punished in the hereafter, and this is a good thing too. The Muʿtazilites believe that this notion of fair compensation is universally applicable to all created beings that are capable of experiencing harm. As one tradition goes, if a horned goat injures another goat that has no horns, the second goat will be resurrected on the Day of Judgment and compensated fairly and graciously.

The evil that free agents inflict on other created beings is moral evil. A theodicy must deal with the question why God allows moral evil to exist in the world, when He has the ability to prevent it. There is much disagreement among the Islamic theologians who subscribe to the general Muʿtazilite theodicy about this issue. Without wading into their conflicting views, we extract three positions that are directly relevant to this question. All agree that moral evil is an outcome of there being free finite beings. The difference between these positions lies in the way 'outcome' is interpreted.

Some theologians say that it is an *essential quality* of free acts that they can be produced only through the will and power of the agent who performs these acts. According to this position, God *cannot* prevent a free agent from creating his freely willed acts, if he has the power to create these acts. This is so even though God created him and endowed him with free will and the power to create his freely willed acts. In other words, by creating free, powerful agents, God has placed a whole class of acts outside His power. It follows that God cannot prevent moral evil without annihilating all free finite beings. However, He can "correct" its consequences by graciously compensating its victims in the hereafter.

A second group of theologians asserts that creating free agents and holding them responsible for their freely willed acts place an obligation on God to allow for the free exercise of this will. God can prevent moral evil but He is obligated to allow it; and since God does not violate any of His obligations, He does not prevent moral evil. The last group says that although God can prevent moral evil and is under no obligation to allow it, He nevertheless allows it because it is good both to allow free agents to exercise their free will and to hold them responsible for their freely willed acts. As with the first case, the consequences of this moral evil are all good in the long run since the victims of moral evil will be fairly and graciously compensated and the perpetrators of moral evil will be justly punished.

According to all versions of this theodicy, therefore, not only is no innocent creature made to suffer in the hereafter, but also all innocent creatures that are wronged or harmed unfairly in this life will be compensated and rewarded in the hereafter. In this sense God cares about the well-being of all creation; it is only that it sometimes takes a second life for this care to produce its fruit. I will focus my discussion below on the constraint that God wills to care for the well-being of all His creation, assuming that fair and gracious compensation in the hereafter is part of caring for the well-being of the creation.

Al-Ghazālī's arguments against this constraint are of two types. The first type is the familiar one. He invokes his definitions of 'good', 'bad', and 'obligatory' to argue that we cannot say that God is obligated to care for the well-being of the creation, that God's bringing suffering upon the innocent is bad, or that God's compensating those that are wronged or harmed unfairly is good. God's acts cannot be described as obligatory, good, or bad. Furthermore, no one is required to do what is good for another.

The second type of argument is to show that this constraint is *actually* false; God does cause the innocent to suffer and He is not concerned with the well-being of all people. Al-Ghazālī does not offer an example of God's inflicting suffering upon innocent creatures *in the hereafter*; he does not cite a tradition, a *ḥadīth*, or a Qur'ānic verse suggesting that some innocent creatures will be tormented in the hereafter. He only says that bringing suffering upon animals, children, and insane people, who are innocent of any crime, is something we observe and perceive daily. But this is hardly an adequate response to the defenders of the Mu'tazilite theodicy, for the Mu'tazilites do not deny that innocent creatures are actually wronged or harmed unfairly in this worldly life but maintain, as a central component of their theodicy, that God "corrects" these injustices in the hereafter.

I suggest that we interpret al-Ghazālī's argument within the Ash'arite theological tradition. This does not convict the argument of question-begging, because al-Ghazālī is entitled to invoke central Ash'arite doctrines that he defends in the Second Treatise of the *Iqtiṣād*. If one presupposes the Ash'arite doctrine of occasionalism, then every innocent creature that is tormented at the hands of created beings is actually tormented directly by God. So if we set aside worldly harm, which both groups agree is caused by God, and focus only on moral evil, we find, according to the Ashʿarites, that God is the direct source of this evil. The so-called "free agents" do not actually create these evil acts, God does. Since God is the sole originator and creator of all the acts that are attributed to created beings, and since we observe and perceive creatures being subjected to unnecessary suffering, God actually wills to inflict unnecessary suffering on the creation. Whether such suffering is inflicted in this life or in the hereafter makes no difference, since there is no reason that can be given for God's inflicting unnecessary suffering on the creation in this life. Said differently, if God wills to torment innocent creatures in this life for no apparent reason, then no reason can be given why He should not torment innocent creatures in the hereafter.

As for showing that God is not actually concerned with the well-being of all creation, al-Ghazālī employs an example similar to that of the "three brothers," with which, according to the tradition, Abū Ḥasan ʿAlī al-Ashʿarī challenged his Muʿtazilite teacher, Abū ʿAlī Muḥammad al-Jubbāʾī, in AH 300/912 CE. When arguing either that God does not reward and punish on the basis of desert or that He is not concerned with the well-being of all people, almost all Ashʿarites invoke similar examples. Al-Ghazālī is no exception. However, unlike the original example of al-Ashʿarī, which posits the three ranks of the brothers in the hereafter as something a Muʿtazilite would affirm, al-Ghazālī's example presents its three ranks as something that actually happens.

Al-Ghazālī's example runs as follows. Imagine three children. The first died a Muslim in his youth; the second lived to maturity and died a Muslim; and the third lived to maturity and died an infidel. The mature infidel would be condemned to hell forever, and the mature Muslim would have a rank in paradise higher than that of the Muslim youth. Al-Ghazālī first presents these ranks as something required by the Muʿtazilites' conception of divine justice. But later he asserts that these divisions actually exist.

A dialogue ensues between the Muslim youth and God. The youth asks why he was given a rank in paradise lower than that of his Muslim brother. God might answer that the second brother toiled in worshiping and obeying Him during his life, while the youth did not toil because he died young. The youth might object that had God allowed him to reach maturity he, too, would have toiled in worshiping and obeying Him, and hence would have been rewarded a high rank like his second brother; his best interest, therefore, was not served by God's letting him die young. God's only feasible answer, according to al-Ghazālī, is to say that He knew that had He let the youth live to maturity, the youth would have sinned and died a sinner, and thus he would have been subject to God's punishment; so his best interest was, indeed, served by letting him die young. At this point the third, infidel brother might complain that since God knew that he would grow up to become an infidel, his best interest would have been served by God's letting him die in his youth, just like his first brother. If God is committed to serving his servants' best interest, He would not be able to answer the third brother's complaint. Al-Ghazālī concludes: "It is common knowledge that these three divisions exist, and this example shows conclusively that serving the best interest of all God's servants is not obligatory for God, nor does it happen."

Another possible constraint on the divine will is that of just consequences. God, in the end, will pay everyone what he deserves. Those who lived their lives as righteous and good will be rewarded fairly and graciously, and those who spread evil and destruction on earth will be punished accordingly. There are some Qur'ānic verses that suggest that there is an element of grace in rewarding people with eternal bliss—no one actually deserves that kind of reward—but the wicked are given exactly what they deserve. In other words, punishment fits the crime, though reward exceeds desert.

Al-Ghazālī rejects this constraint. He claims instead that God may do as He pleases: He may reward the righteous, punish them, or annihilate them and never resurrect them; He does not care whether He forgives all the infidels and punishes all the believers; and none of these acts contradict any of the divine attributes. Note that al-Ghazālī does not merely claim that it is *possible* for God to punish the believers and forgive the infidels, but rather that He *does not care* whether He punishes the believers and forgives the infidels. It is not only a claim about what is logically possible; it is a claim about God's relation to His creation.

In fact, al-Ghazālī agrees that in a certain sense it is "necessary" (*wājib*) that God reward the righteous and punish the wicked. The necessity follows from His revealed promise. God promised in the revelation that He will reward the righteous and punish the wicked. Thus if He does not do this, His promise would be false; and it is impossible for God's promise to be false. The point, however, is that God was not constrained to make this promise. He could have refrained from making this promise, and in which case punishing the righteous and rewarding the wicked would not be impossible, and, as al-Ghazālī tells us, would not be incompatible with any of His attributes. His choice to reward the righteous is purely an act of grace bestowed on the righteous. Al-Ghazālī would say that God could have decided to bless the infidels and bestow His grace upon them by rewarding them in the hereafter.

Al-Ghazālī's position on this issue conflicts even with the view of some who subscribe to Sunni orthodoxy: the Māturīdites affirm that God would not punish the righteous and reward the wicked because doing so is unbefitting His perfection. They invoke several texts that lend support to this view, for instance, the Qurʾānic verse: *Or do those who commit evil deeds suppose that We will treat them as equal to those who believe and do righteous deeds, equal in their life and death? Bad is their judgment* (45:21). These texts are important not because they promise reward for the righteous and punishment for the wicked—almost all Islamic theologians agree that belief in this promise is fundamental—but rather because they indicate that to assume the opposite is to make a *bad* judgment. So there is something bad about punishing the righteous and rewarding the wicked. Al-Ghazālī 's ethical egoism would have some difficulty accommodating this use of 'bad'.

It is natural to interpret assertions about what is befitting and what is unbefitting God's perfection as constraints on the divine will. A Muʿtazilite relies on the principle that God would not will to do what is not good in order to justify other constraints on the divine will. Similarly, the Māturīdites' reliance on the principle that God would not will to do what is unbefitting His perfection in order to account for God's unwillingness to perform certain types of acts can be seen as placing constraints on the divine will—even if they refuse to use the term 'constraint' (*taqyīd* or *ḥajr*). It is likely that al-Ghazālī has groups like the Māturīdites in mind when he declares that none of these acts contradicts any of the divine attributes.

Al-Ghazālī's first argument is designed to invoke the basic categories of his ethical egoism. We are by now familiar with his denial that anything is obligatory for God and with his affirmation that no act of God can be described as good or bad in a moral sense. He uses the same strategy to deal with the objection that God would not will to punish the righteous because it is bad for one who is able to give rewards to assign obligations to people and then to refrain from rewarding those who fulfill those obligations, or even worse, to punish them. Al-Ghazālī asks about the meaning of 'bad' here. Is it bad for the one who obligates or for the one who is obligated? If it is bad for the one who obligates, then it does not apply to God, for, after all, nothing is bad for God. God has no interests, and hence nothing can be contrary to His interest. On the other hand, if it is bad for the one who is obligated, this may be conceded, but what is good and what is bad for the one who is obligated are equally of no concern to a God who is not concerned with the well-being of the creation.

Moreover, al-Ghazālī questions the justification for saying that punishing the wicked is a constraint on the divine will. According to some Muʿtazilites, this constraint is justified because it is good to punish the wicked—it is a manifestation of justice. This justification presupposes a retributive theory of punishment, which al-Ghazālī thinks "shows ignorance of generosity and magnanimity, and of reason, habit, revelation, and all matters." It shows ignorance of generosity, magnanimity, habit, reason, and revelation, because to overlook and forgive is more generous and noble than to punish and avenge. People habitually praise the forgiver and deem good the act of pardoning. The revelation also enjoins people to forgive and considers an act of forgiveness a demonstration of one's good character and refined soul. Al-Ghazālī asks: "How is it, then, that to pardon and be gracious are deemed bad and a prolonged retribution is deemed good?"

Before discussing al-Ghazālī's deterrence theory of punishment, we should describe his arguments against the claim that there is a retributive justification for punishing the wicked with eternal torment. First, if retribution implies a punishment that fits the crime, then finite evil must be assigned finite punishment. How could it be justified then, even on retributive grounds, for finite evil to receive infinite punishment? Furthermore, if one declares his unbelief in God and His messengers, then according to orthodoxy, whether Sunni or Shīʿī, he will be condemned to eternal torment. Uttering a few words, therefore, can lead to eternal punishment. To say that it is good that such a person is punished eternally, which is what a retributivist would have to say, is highly irrational no matter what the person's conception of the good is. Al-Ghazālī writes sardonically: "A mental asylum is more suitable than gatherings of scholars for one whose intellect leads him to deem good such an extreme response."

Second, one might argue, as some theologians do, that God's eternal punishment is a fitting retribution for people's unbelief and major sins, because these acts are violations of God's rights, which are infinitely great. Al-Ghazālī says that this argument is cogent only if God is harmed and His rank is lowered by people's unbelief and disobedience. But this is impossible. Insofar as His divinity and loftiness are concerned, faith and unbelief, obedience and disobedience are on a par in their effect on God.

Third, one might give a consequentialist justification for retribution. One might argue that the victim of a crime typically feels intense resentment and rage, which are painful emotions. Subjecting the perpetrator of the crime to a punishment that fits the crime usually relieves those painful feelings, and relieving the victim's pain is a good thing. Moreover, fairness requires that the perpetrator of the crime feel pain instead of the victim. Thus retribution serves a good and just cause. Al-Ghazālī is willing to accept this argument as possible grounds for retribution but he thinks that the victim's desire for seeing the one who wronged him punished is "indicative of a deficiency of the victim's intellect and of his being controlled by anger."

At any rate, when the retributivist's argument is applied to the case of God's punishment, it entails that God punish the evildoers in the hereafter on behalf of their victims. The argument does not address two questions. First, why does God torment the perpetrators of crimes for eternity, when presumably finite punishment is adequate for relieving the victims' pain? And second, why does God punish those who did not harm any creature but simply refused to accept His message or committed certain major sins (such as having a consensual premarital affair) in which no one is harmed?

This argument also seems to conflict with the Muʿtazilites' principle of fair compensation, which was discussed previously. If God compensates the victims of crimes with eternal bliss, would this not be more than adequate for relieving the victims' pain? There seems to be no convincing reason for insisting that a victim's pain can only be relieved by punishing the one who wronged him. One might respond to the retributivist's argument by agreeing with al-Ghazālī's statement that the desire to punish is indicative of deficient intellect and untempered passion. God should not act on behalf of such victims. Rewarding the victims with eternal bliss and consigning the villains to, say, a place of neither bliss nor torment are consistent with both fair and gracious compensation for the victims and generosity and forgiveness for the perpetrators of the crimes. After all, the revelation enjoins people to compensate their victims fairly, and although it gives the victims the right to have the perpetrators of the crimes punished, it encourages them to forgive and pardon. The Qur'ān says: *The retribution for an injury is an injury equal thereto; but if a person forgives and makes reconciliation, his reward is due from God; verily He loves not those who are unjust. Indeed, if any avenge themselves after they have been wronged, there is no cause of blame against them. . . . But he who bears with patience and forgives surely complies with divine resolve* (42:40, 41, 43).

Al-Ghazālī defends an alternative to the retributive theory of punishment. He proposes a deterrence theory. This should not be surprising in light of the consequentialist account he gave of the good (egoism is a form of consequentialism, since an act is deemed good for a certain person by virtue of its consequences for that person). Punishing a person for a crime he already committed is deemed good just in case it serves a future interest of deterring further crimes. The punishment here is good (for most people) because it serves the future interest of most people by deterring others from committing similar crimes and by, hopefully, deterring the perpetrator of the crime from repeating the deed. If no such interest is served, then the punishment is bad, because it is harmful to the interest of the perpetrator of the crime and it serves no other person's interest. The victim's *real* interest lies in forgiving the villain and not having him punished (in this case "his reward is due from God"); the villain's interest lies in being forgiven and set free; and on the assumption that this punishment fails to deter, no one's future interest is harmed by forgiving the villain.

Given this theory of punishment, it is clear that God's punishing evildoers in the hereafter serves no one's interest and harms the interest of those who are punished. The crimes have already been committed, and there are no future crimes to be deterred by this punishment. Eternal punishment, therefore, is *not good* for any person. Since it is against the interest of those who are punished, it is *bad* for them. Thus if God's will is, as the Muʿtazilites' say, constrained by doing only what is good, He would not will to punish anyone. The conclusion, therefore, that follows from this theory and the Muʿtazilites' fundamental constraint on the divine will is that God will forgive everyone in the hereafter. This conclusion, however, is contrary to the Muʿtazilites' core belief and it is, of course, contrary to the revelation.

In sum, al-Ghazālī first argues that a retributive justification for God's punishment in the hereafter is without merit. He then defends a deterrence justification for human punishment. If this justification is applied to the acts of God and if the Muʿtazilites' fundamental constraint on the divine will—namely, that God would not will an act that is not good—is true, we have to conclude that God will not punish anyone in the hereafter. This conclusion is contrary not only the fundamental Islamic belief but also to the core Muʿtazilite belief. So if one maintains the Muʿtazilites' fundamental constraint on the divine will, he has no option but to deny that a deterrence justification is applicable to God's punishment. Hence neither a retributive nor a deterrence justification can be applied to God's punishment in the hereafter. Since these are the only possible justifications for punishment in general, someone who maintains the Muʿtazilites' fundamental constraint on the divine will must concede that al-Ghazālī's original declaration that God does not care whether He punishes all the believers and forgives all the infidels in the hereafter is true. Simply put, no reason can be identified for God's reward and punishment, and hence no constraint can be placed on God's will regarding His reward and punishment. The Muʿtazilite, therefore, is in awkward predicament: if he maintains the constraint that God would not will an act that is not good, he must liberate the divine will from any constraints concerning reward and punishment; and if he gives up the constraint that God would not will an act that is not good, he loses the fundamental constraint that he invokes to justify the other constraints.

## IV

The Fourth Treatise, which carries no title, is the least theoretical part of the book. It is divided into four chapters. The First Chapter is aimed at establishing the prophethood of Muḥammad. This must be seen as part of the argument of the *Iqtiṣād*, since some aspects of God's attributes and acts can only be learned from revelation. The demonstration is a standard argument from miracle, in which al-Ghazālī discusses the miracle of the Qur'ān and other miracles attributed to the Prophet Muḥammad.

The Second Chapter enumerates some matters about the afterlife, in which, according to al-Ghazālī, it is obligatory to believe, since they are mentioned in the revelation and deemed possible by reason. The chapter is divided into an introduction and two sections. The introduction describes the classification of necessary truths into three categories: those that are known through reason but not through revelation, those that are known through revelation but not through reason, and those that are known through both. For instance, the existence of the Maker of the world is of the first category, resurrection is of the second, and that God is seeable is of the third. The existence of the Maker of the world cannot be known through revelation, since one needs to believe in the existence of God prior to his acceptance of revelation. Thus that the world has a maker must be established by a demonstrative proof that does not invoke revelation. No demonstrative proof can be given of resurrection other than that it is affirmed in the revelation, and that whatever is affirmed in the revelation must be true. This qualifies as a demonstration if the revelation is accepted on the basis of a demonstrative proof and if there is no reason to offer a metaphorical interpretation of the verses that affirm the occurrence of the resurrection. The seeability of God is known through revelation and reason, since reason establishes that God is seeable (God is an existent, every existent is knowable, whatever is knowable is seeable) and the revelation affirms that the righteous will see God in the hereafter.

Al-Ghazālī offers an epistemic principle regarding how to interpret the scripture. On the one hand, if the scripture affirms something that reason deems possible, then it must be interpreted literally, and the belief in it is obligatory. On the other hand, if the scripture affirms something that reason deems impossible, then it must be interpreted metaphorically, and the belief in the metaphorical interpretation is permissible (since different scholars might offer different metaphorical interpretations). In previous treatises, al-Ghazālī says that if there is only one possible metaphorical interpretation that meets the dictates of reason, then to believe in it is obligatory. As for truths that reason deems necessary and are affirmed in the revelation, every rational person must believe in them regardless of whether he accepts the revelation or not, since a demonstration is sufficient reason for believing in these truths.

The first section of the Second Chapter discusses such affairs of the afterlife as resurrection and congregation and the torment of the grave. In all of them, al-Ghazālī argues that since revelation affirms them and reason deems them possible, it is obligatory to believe in them. Most of his polemics is directed against some Muʿtazilites and others who deny the possibility of these affairs. The second section is an apology for not addressing in this book certain issues that other theology books address. He divides these into intellectual, semantical, and legal issues, and he discusses a representative issue of each type. There is one aspect of this discussion that is of particular interest to al-Ghazālī's defense of occasionalism.

It is a remarkable fact about the *Iqtiṣād* that al-Ghazālī does not waver from his commitment to strict occasionalism: all occurrents, including all humans' and animals' acts, are directly and exclusively created by God. He is very explicit about this in the chapter on the divine attribute of power in the Second Treatise. Furthermore, he consistently employs occasionalist language to describe what is ordinarily considered causal relations: when he speaks about "causal regularities," he uses the expression 'the habitual course of events' (*majrā al-ʿāda*); when he talks about miracles that "violate causal laws," he describes them as acts that transcend what is habitual (*khāriq li-l-ʿāda*); when he talks about acts that "are produced by humans," he says that they proceed from them (*taṣdur ʿan hum*). Al-Ghazālī explicitly reaffirms his commitment to strict occasionalism in his discussion of the intellectual issue of the second section of the Second Chapter of this treatise.

In "An Intellectual Issue," al-Ghazālī considers the question whether one dies at his predestined time if he is killed. The opinion he is arguing against is one that posits a predestined time for each natural object, where the predestined time of an object is the time at which God directly causes the termination of the object's existence, and that allows natural occurrents to terminate the existence of natural objects. For instance, the predestined time for a wall might be ten years, at the end of which God would cause the wall to collapse. But the wall might be demolished by an ax after one year. In this case, it would be said that the wall was destroyed before its predestined time, since the ax, and not God, destroyed that wall. Following the same logic, Zayd's predestined time might be sixty years, at the end of which God would directly cause the death of Zayd. Hence if a sword severed his head at the age of twenty, then we ought to say that Zayd died before his predestined time. Al-Ghazālī, as expected, rejects this reasoning. The way he argues against this reasoning is most interesting because it is in total conformity with strict occasionalism.

Al-Ghazālī says that co-occurrent events are of two types: those that have correlation between them and those that do not. Non-correlated things are such things as the death of Zayd and the occurrence of a lunar eclipse. Either can occur or fail to occur without entailing the occurrence or non-occurrence of the other. Correlated events are further divided into three categories. The first is that of equivalent things, such as left and right. It is inconceivable that one thing be to the left of another without the latter being to the right of the former. Such a correlation is logical, and hence the correlated events occur or fail to occur together. The second category of correlation is also logical, but here the second event is a necessary condition for the first event. So if the second fails to occur, the first also fails to occur. Al-Ghazālī gives the example of life and knowledge. Knowledge is not a necessary condition for life (there are many living beings that have no knowledge), but life is a necessary condition for knowledge: an inanimate object cannot have knowledge. Observe that life is not the cause of knowledge, but it is necessary for it.

The third category of correlation is that of cause-and-effect. If A is the *only* cause of B, then the absence of A entails the absence of B. In other words, the occurrence of B entails the occurrence of A. Al-Ghazālī says that someone who believes in natural causation would infer the death of Zayd from the severing of his head if no other cause of death is known. Hence such a person would say that the severing of the head caused the death, and that had the severing of the head not occurred, the death would not have occurred either, which means that Zayd died before his predestined time, since the sword, and not God, caused his death. Al-Ghazālī says that the followers of the Sunna do not accept the severing of the head as the cause of death: for them, God is, for "God is the exclusive originator . . . , and no created thing is the cause of a created thing." Al-Ghazālī concludes:

> [The answer to this question] must be sought in the canon we mentioned regarding the omnipresence of God's power and the annulment of generation. On the basis of this, it must be said about the one who is killed that he died at his predestined time, for this predestined time is the time at which God (Exalted is He) created his death, whether it was accompanied with the severing of the head, a lunar eclipse, the falling of rain, or not. All of these, for us, are co-occurrents and not causes, but some co-occur repeatedly according to the habitual course of things (*bi-l-ʿāda*) and some do not.

I cite this passage to make it clear that some of the recent interpretations of al-Ghazālī that suggest that he left it open whether he is committed to strict Ashʿarite occasionalism downplay the textual evidence in the *Iqtiṣād*.[10]

10. Griffel (2009, p. 204) is a case in point. Although he acknowledges al-Ghazālī's "openly occasionalist language" in *al-Iqtiṣād fī al-Iʿtiqād* (he translates the title of the book

The Third Chapter is on the imamate. It argues that an appointment of an imam is obligatory; it investigates the requirements of the imamate; and it describes the Sunni orthodoxy regarding the schisms that took place between the Prophet's companions in the early decades after his death. Al-Ghazālī explains that such a discussion does not really belong to a book on theology, but he includes it because it is customary for theological books to conclude with a discussion of the imamate.

The final chapter describes the canon according to which someone might be charged with infidelity. The canon al-Ghazālī specifies is denying the complete truthfulness of the Prophet Muḥammad. To attribute a lie to the Prophet, whether in one's heart or overtly, is to be burdened with unbelief and all its consequences. This is the same canon al-Ghazālī specifies in *Fayṣal al-Tafriqa bayn al-Islām wa-l-Zandaqa* (*The Decisive Differential between Islam and Unbelief*), which is his most elaborate treatise on this subject. In the *Iqtiṣād*, al-Ghazālī is content with a general description of this canon without elaborating the sense in which someone can be said to disbelieve the Prophet. According to this canon, believing that the Prophet uttered a lie is on par with not believing in something whose existence is affirmed by the Prophet.

In the *Iqtiṣād*, al-Ghazālī is concerned with the various levels of unbelief. For example, the atheists are the worst infidels because they believe that almost everything any prophet said is a lie and they deny the existence of the one who sends messengers, while those who deny the possibility of prophecy are second in rank to the atheists since they are willing to believe in God but they attribute lies to the messengers of God. Al-Ghazālī continues his classification of degrees of unbelief until he reaches the Islamic philosophers, whom he also charges with infidelity. The philosophers, he says, believe in God and in his messengers and accept as true a great deal of what the Prophet says. Nevertheless, they are infidels because they believe that the messengers used untrue representations to make the intelligibles accessible to the masses, who are incapable of comprehending the intelligibles. For example, the Prophet used bodily descriptions of the pleasures and pains in the hereafter to entice people to obey the divine law and to frighten them away from disobeying God's commands in order to achieve their happiness in this world and in the hereafter. But the philosophers do not believe in bodily resurrection. So strictly speaking, the philosophers

---

as *The Balanced Book on What-to-Believe*), he nevertheless claims that "al-Ghazālī shows no signs that he committed himself exclusively to an occasionalist cosmology . . . as in most of his works, al-Ghazālī wishes to leave open whether these events are created directly by God or are the results of secondary causes."

believe that these bodily descriptions of pleasures and pains are false, which means that they believe that the Prophet uttered lies.

It is incorrect to say, according to al-Ghazālī, that the philosophers do not consider them false but rather imaginative representations. For him, 'imaginative representations' is an invented term to avoid saying that these bodily descriptions are false. An imaginative representation cannot be equated with metaphor, since there is no similarity at all between the affairs of the soul and the affairs of the body. Precisely speaking, according to al-Ghazālī, the philosophers consider these imaginative representations to be false statements employed by the Prophet to motivate the masses to follow the path of their happiness in this world and in the hereafter. He could have achieved the same goal by telling them the truth, had their intellect been capable of comprehending the intelligibles. But given their limited intellect, he had to rely on falsehood in order to achieve the same goal. In sum, the philosophers attribute lies to the Prophet, and thus they are infidels.

In *Fayṣal al-Tafriqa*, al-Ghazālī elaborates the meaning of saying that the Prophet affirms the existence of something. He first gives five different levels for existence: real (*dhātī*), sensory (*ḥissī*), imaginative (*khayālī*), intelligible (*'aqlī*), and analogous (*shibhī*). A real existence is an existence independent of perception and the mind, such as the existence of the ordinary physical objects. A sensory existence is an existence that is derived from sense experience without necessarily corresponding to external reality, such as the existence of objects in one's dreams. An imaginative existence is a mental existence in one's imagination without necessarily corresponding to sense experience, such as the existence of an imagined winged horse. An intelligible existence is a conceptual existence that is abstracted from a certain type of object, such as the existence of circularity. Analogous existence is an existence that bears some similarity to something else, such as the existence of God's wrath, since this wrath has no real, sensory, imaginative, or conceptual existence, but is only a metaphor for God's punishment, which bears similarity to the usual effect of wrath.

Al-Ghazālī then explains under what conditions something whose existence is affirmed by the Prophet might be understood according to one or more of these levels. Someone might err in attributing a level of existence to something the Prophet affirms, when he should attribute to it a different level. Such an error does not make the person an infidel. Al-Ghazālī says that, in this case, the person made a mistake in independent opinion (*ijtihād*). A person is correctly charged with infidelity if he fails to attribute any level of existence to something whose existence is affirmed by the Prophet. This is the meaning of attributing a lie to the Prophet. Al-Ghazālī concludes the *Iqtiṣād* by explaining that almost all the different Islamic theological schools, such as the Muʿtazilites and the anthropomorphists, have erred in their interpretations of Islamic texts or in their theoretical reflections on the attributes or acts of God. All such errors can be considered an outcome of independent opinion. None of them attributed a lie to the Prophet, and hence none of them should be charged with infidelity.

# Bibliography


'Abd al-Jabbār, al-Qāḍī abū al-Ḥasan ibn Aḥmad. *Al-Mughnī fī Abwāb al-Tawḥīd wa-l-'Adl*, twenty volumes. Edited by Khiḍr Muḥammad Nabhā. Beirut: Dār al-Kutub al-'Ilmiyya, 2012.

Abu Zayd, Abdu-r-Rahman. *Al-Ghazali on Divine Predicates and Other Properties*. New Delhi: Kitab Bhavan, 1994. (First published by Sh. Muhammad Ashraf, Lahore, 1970.)

Al-Āmidī, Abū al-Ḥasan 'Alī (Sayf al-Dīn). *Abkār al-Afkār fī Uṣūl al-Dīn*, three volumes. Edited by Aḥmad Frīd al-Mazyadī. Beirut: Dār al-Kutub al-'Ilmiyya, 2003.

———. *Ghāyat al-Marām fī 'Ilm al-Kalām*. Edited by Aḥmad Frīd al-Mazyadī. Beirut: Dār al-Kutub al-'Ilmiyya, 2004.

Amīn, Aḥmad. *Ḍuḥā al-Islām*, three volumes. Beirut: Dār al-Kutub al-'Ilmiyya, 2004.

———. *Fajr al-Islām*. Beirut: Dār al-Kutub al-'Ilmiyya, 2006.

———. *Ẓuhr al-Islām*, four volumes. Beirut: Dār al-Kutub al-'Ilmiyya, 2004.

Al-Asfarāyīnī, Abū al-Muẓaffar Shāhfūr. *Al-Tabṣīr fī al-Dīn wa-Tamyīz al-Firqa al-Nājiya 'an al-Firaq al-Hālikīn*. Edited by Majīd al-Khalīfa. Beirut: Dār Ibn Ḥazm, 2008.

Al-Ash'arī, Abū al-Ḥasan 'Alī. *Al-Ibāna 'an Uṣūl al-Diyāna*. Edited by 'Abd Allāh Maḥmūd Muḥammad 'Umar. Beirut: Dār al-Kutub al-'Ilmiyya, 2005.

———. *Maqālāt al-Islāmiyyīn wa-Ikhtilāf al-Muṣallīn*, two volumes. Edited by Na'īm Zarzūr. Beirut: al-Maktaba al-'Aṣriyya, 2009.

Austin, J. L. *How to Do Things with Words*. 2nd edition. Edited by J. O. Urmson and M. Sbisá. Cambridge, MA: Harvard University Press. 1962.

———. *Philosophical Papers*. Edited by J. O. Urmson and G. Warnock. Oxford: Oxford University Press, 1970.

Badawī, 'Abd al-Raḥmān. *Madhāhib al-Islāmiyyīn*. Beirut: Dār al-'Ilm li-l-Malāyīn, 1996.

———. *Mu'allafāt al-Ghazālī*. Kuwait: Wikālat al-Maṭbū'āt, 1977.

Al-Baghdādī, 'Abd al-Qāhir. *Al-Farq bayn al-Firaq*. Edited by Muḥammad Muḥyī al-Dīn 'Abd al-Ḥamīd. Beirut: al-Maktaba al-'Aṣriyya, 2004.

Al-Barnasī, Abū al-'Abbās Aḥmad (Zarrūq al-Fāsī). *Sharḥ 'Aqīdat al-Ghazālī*. Edited by Yūsuf Aḥmad. Beirut: Dār al-Kutub al-'Ilmiyya, 2006.

Black, Deborah L. "Al-Fārābī." In *History of Islamic Philosophy*, two parts. Edited by Seyyed Hossein Nasr and Oliver Leman. London: Routledge, 1996, part I, pp. 178–197.

Cottingham, John, Robert Stoothoff, Dugald Murdoch, and Anthony Kenny. *The Philosophical Writings of Descartes*, three volumes. Cambridge: Cambridge University Press, 1984, 1985, 1991.

Davis, Dennis Morgan, Jr. "Al-Ghazālī on Divine Essence." Ph.D. dissertation, University of Utah, 2005.

Al-Fārābī, Abū Naṣr Muḥammad. *Kitāb Arā' Ahl al-Madīna al-Fāḍila*, 8th edition. Edited by Albert Naṣrī Nādir. Beirut: Dār al-Mashriq, 2002.

———. *Kitāb al-Ḥurūf*. Edited by Muḥsin Mahdī. Beirut: Dār al-Mashriq, 2004.

Al-Ghazālī, Abū Ḥāmid Muḥammad. *Bidāyat al-Hidāya*. Edited by 'Abd al-Ḥamīd Muḥammad al-Darwīsh. Beirut: Dār Ṣādir, 1998.

———. *Faḍā'iḥ al-Bāṭiniyya*. Edited by 'Abd al-Raḥmān Badawī. Cairo: Al-Dār al-Qawmiyya, 1964.

———. *Fayṣal al-Tafriqa bayn al-Islām wa-l-Zandaqa*. Edited by Sulaymān Dunyā. Cairo: Dār Iḥyā' al-Kutub al-'Arabiyya, 1961.

———. *Iḥyā' 'Ulūm al-Dīn*, five volumes. Edited by Muḥammad Wahbī Sulaymān and Usāma 'Ammūra. Damascus: Dār al-Fikr, 2006.

———. *Iljām al-'Awām 'an 'Ilm al-Kalām*. Edited by Muḥammad al-Mu'taṣim bi-Allāh al-Baghdādī. Beirut: Dār al-Kitāb al-'Arabī, 1985.

———. *Al-Iqtiṣād fī al-I'tiqād*. Edited by Anas Muḥammad 'Adnān al-Sharafāwī. Jeddah: Dār al-Minhāj, 2008.

———. *Al-Iqtiṣād fī al-I'tiqād*. Edited by Ibrahim Agâh Çubukçu and Hüseyin Atay. Ankara: Nur Matbaasi, 1962.

———. *Al-Iqtiṣād fī al-I'tiqād*. Cairo: Maktabat Muṣṭafā al-Bābī al-Ḥalabī, 1966. (First edition published in 1891.)

———. *Kitāb al-Arba'īn fī Uṣūl al-Dīn*. Beirut: Dār al-Kutub al-'Ilmiyya, 1988.

———. *Majmū'at Rasā'il al-Ghazālī* (a collection of 24 epistles by al-Ghazālī), seven volumes, 5th edition. Beirut: Dār al-Kutub al-'Ilmiyya, 2011.

———. *Maqāṣid al-Falāsifa*, 2nd edition. Edited by Sulaymān Dunyā. Cairo: Dār al-Ma'ārif, 1960.

———. *Al-Maqṣad al-Asnā fī Sharḥ Asmā' Allāh al-Ḥusnā*. Edited by Aḥmad Qabbānī. Beirut: Dār al-Kutub al-'Ilmiyya, 2010.

———. *Minhāj al-'Ābidīn ilā Jannat Rabb al-'Ālamīn*. Edited by Muḥmūd Muṣṭafā Ḥalāwī. Beirut: Dār al-Bashā'ir al-Islāmiyya, 2006.

———. *Mishkāt al-Anwār* (*The Niche of Lights*). A parallel English-Arabic text translated, introduced, and annotated by David Buchman. Provo: Brigham Young University Press, 1998.

———. *Mi'yār al-'Ilm*. Edited by 'Alī Bū Malḥam. Beirut: Dār al-Hilāl, 1993.

———. *Mīzān al-'Amal*. Edited by 'Alī Bū Malḥam. Beirut: Dār al-Hilāl, 1995.

———. *Al-Munqidh min al-Ḍalāl*. Edited by Jamīl Ṣalībā and Kāmil ʿAyyād. Beirut: Dār al-Andulus, 1956.

———. *Al-Murshid al-Amīn ilā Mawʿiẓat al-Muʾminīn min Iḥyāʾ ʿUlūm al-Dīn*. Cairo: Maktabat Muṣṭafā al-Bābī al-Ḥalabī, 1969.

———. *Al-Qisṭās al-Mustaqīm*, 3rd edition. Edited by Victor Shalḥat. Beirut: Dār al-Mashriq, 1991.

———. *Tahāfut al-Falāsifa*, 7th edition. Edited by Sulaymān Dunyā. Cairo: Dār al-Maʿārif, 1987. (First edition published in 1947.)

Al-Ghaznawī, Aḥmad ibn Muḥammad. *Kitāb Uṣūl al-Dīn*. Edited by ʿUmar Wafīq al-Dāʿūq. Beirut: Dār al-Bashāʾir al-Islāmiyya, 1998.

Genequand, Charles. "Metaphysics." In *History of Islamic Philosophy*, two parts. Edited by Seyyed Hossein Nasr and Oliver Leman. London: Routledge, 1996, part II, pp. 783–801.

Griffel, Frank. *Al-Ghazālī's Philosophical Theology*. Oxford: Oxford University Press, 2009.

Hourani, George F. "A Revised Chronology of Ghazālī's Writings." *Journal of the American Oriental Society* 104 (1984): 289–302.

Hume, David. *An Enquiry Concerning Human Understanding*. Edited by Eric Steinberg. Indianapolis: Hackett Publishing Company, 1993.

———. *A Treatise of Human Nature*. Edited by P. H. Nidditch. Oxford: Oxford University Press, 1978.

Ibn Ḥazm, Abū Muḥammad ʿAlī. *Al-Fiṣal fī al-Milal wa-l-Ahwāʾ wa-l-Niḥal*, three volumes, 3rd edition. Edited by Aḥmad Shams al-Dīn. Beirut: Dār al-Kutub al-ʿIlmiyya, 2007.

———. *Al-Uṣūl wa-l-Furūʿ*. Edited by ʿAbd al-Ḥaqq al-Turkumānī. Beirut: Dār Ibn Ḥazm, 2011.

Ibn Khaldūn, ʿAbd al-Raḥmān ibn Muḥammad. *Lubāb al-Muḥaṣṣal fī Uṣūl al-Dīn*. Edited by Rafīq al-ʿAjam. Beirut: Dār al-Mashriq, 1995.

Ibn Rushd, Abū al-Walīd Muḥammad (Averroës). *Kitāb Faṣl al-Maqāl wa-Taqrīr mā bayn al-Sharīʿa wa-l-Ḥikma min al-Ittiṣāl* (*The Book of the Decisive Treatise Determining the Connection between the Law and Wisdom*). A parallel English-Arabic text translated with introduction and notes by Charles E. Butterworth. Provo: Brigham Young University Press, 2001.

———. *Tahāfut al-Tahāfut*. Edited by Maurice Bouyges. Beirut: Dār al-Mashriq, 2003.

Ibn Sīnā, Abū ʿAlī al-Ḥusayn (Avicenna). *Al-Ishārāt wa-l-Tanbīhāt*. Edited by Mujtabā al-Zāriʿī. Qum: Bustān Kitāb, 2002.

———. *Al-Najāt*, two volumes. Edited by ʿAbd al-RaḥmānʿUmayara. Beirut: Dār al-Jīl, 1992.

———. *Al-Shifāʾ: al-Ilāhiyyāt*, two volumes. Edited by Father Georges C. Anawati, Saʿīd Zāyid, Muḥammad Yūsuf Mūsā, and Sulaymān Dunyā, introduction by Ibrāhīm B. Madkūr. Cairo: Public Committee for the Affairs of al-Amīriyyah Press, 1960.

Ibn Taymiyya, Aḥmad ibn ʿAbd al-Ḥalīm. *Kitāb al-Asmāʾ wa-l-Ṣifāt*, two volumes, 2nd edition. Edited by Muṣṭafā ʿAbd al-Qādir ʿAṭā. Beirut: Dār al-Kutub al-ʿIlmiyya, 2007.

———. *Al-Risāla al-Ṣafadiyya*. Edited by Abū ʿAbd Allāh Sayyid ibn ʿAbbās al-Julaymī and Abū Maʿādh ibn Ghārif al-Dimashqī. Riyadh: Maktabat Aḍwāʾ al-Salaf, 2002.

Al-Jurr, Khalīl. *Lārūs*: *al-Muʿjam al-ʿArabī al-Ḥadīth*. Paris: Librairie Larousse, 1973.

Al-Juwaynī, Abū al-Maʿālī ʿAbd al-Malik. *Al-ʿAqīda al-Niẓāmiyya*. Edited by Muḥammad Zāhid al-Kawtharī. Cairo: Maṭbaʿat al-Anwār, 1948.

———. *Kitāb al-Irshād*. Edited by Muḥammad Yūsuf Mūsā and ʿAlī ʿAbd al-Munʿim ʿAbd al-Ḥamīd. Cairo: Maktabat al-Khānjī, 1950.

Kant, Immanuel. *Critique of Pure Reason*. Translated and edited by Paul Guyer and Allen W. Wood. Cambridge: Cambridge University Press, 1998.

Khalidi, Muhammad Ali, ed. *Medieval Islamic Philosophical Writings*. Cambridge: Cambridge University Press, 2005.

Khalīl, Aḥmad Khalīl. *Mawsūʿat Lalande al-Falsafiyya*: *Muʿjam Muṣṭalaḥāt al-Falsafa al-Naqdiyya wa-l-Taqaniyya*. Beirut: Dār ʿUwaydāt, 2008.

Locke, John. *An Essay Concerning Human Understanding*. Edited with an introduction by Peter H. Nidditch. Oxford: Oxford University Press, 1975.

Al-Makkī, Abū Ṭālib Muḥammad. *Qūt al-Qulūb*, two volumes. Beirut: Dār al-Kutub al-ʿIlmiyya, 1997.

Al-Maqdisī, Aḥmad ibn Muḥammad. *Mukhtaṣar Minhāj al-Qāṣidīn*. Edited by Muḥammad Wahbī Sulaymān. Beirut: al-Maktaba al-ʿAṣriyya, 2002.

Marmura, Michael E. "Ghazālī's Chapter on Divine Power in the *Iqtiṣād*." *Arabic Sciences and Philosophy* 4 (1994): 279–315.

Al-Māturīdī, Abū Manṣūr Muḥammad. *Kitāb al-Tawḥīd*. Edited by Bekir Topaloğlu and Muhammed Aruçı. Beirut: Dār Ṣādir, 2007.

McCarthy, R. J. *Deliverance from Error*. Louisville: Fons Vita, 1980. (Translation of al-Ghazālī, *al-Munqidh min al-Ḍalāl*.)

*Al-Munjid fī al-Lugha*, 39th edition. Beirut: Dār al-Mashriq, 2002.

Muṣṭafā, Ibrāhīm, Aḥmad Ḥasan al-Zayyāt, Ḥāmid ʿAbd al-Qādir, and Muḥammad ʿAlī al-Najjār. *Al-Muʿjam al-Wasīṭ*, 2nd edition. Istanbul: al-Maktaba al-Islāmiyya, 1972. (First edition published in 1960.)

Nadler, Steven. *Occasionalism*: *Causation Among the Cartesians*. Oxford: Oxford University Press, 2011.

Nasr, Seyyed Hossein, and Oliver Leaman, eds. *History of Islamic Philosophy*, two parts. London: Routledge, 1996.

Ormsby, Eric L. *Theodicy in the Islamic Thought: The Dispute over al-Ghazālī's "Best of All Possible Worlds."* Princeton: Princeton University Press, 1984.

Al-Qāsimī, Muḥammad Jamāl al-Dīn. *Maw'iẓat al-Mu'minīn min Iḥyā' 'Ulūm al-Dīn,* two volumes. Edited by Na'īm Zarzūr. Beirut: al-Maktaba al-'Aṣriyya, 2005.

Al-Rāzī, Fakhr al-Dīn. *Kitāb al-Arba'īn fī Uṣūl al-Dīn.* Edited by Aḥmad Ḥijāzī al-Saqqā. Beirut: Dār al-Jīl, 2004.

Ṣalībā, Jamīl. *Al-Mu'jam al-Falsafī,* two volumes. Qum: Dhawī al-Qurbā, 1965.

Searle, John. *Speech Acts: An Essay in the Philosophy of Language.* Cambridge: Cambridge University Press, 1969.

Al-Shahrastānī, Abū al-Fatḥ Muḥammad. *Al-Milal wa-l-Niḥal,* two volumes. Edited by Amīr 'Alī Mahnā and 'Alī Ḥasan Fā'ūr. Beirut: Dar al-Ma'rifa, 1995.

———. *Nihāyat al-Iqdām fī 'Ilm al-Kalām.* Edited by Aḥmad Farīd al-Mazyadī. Beirut: Dār al-Kutub al-'Ilmiyya, 2004.

Spinoza, Benedict. *The Ethics.* Translated by R. H. M. Elwes. New York: Dover Publications, 1955. (Originally published by George Bell and Sons in 1883.)

Strawson, P. F. "Intention and Convention in Speech Acts." *Philosophical Review* 73 (1964): 439–460.

Al-'Uthmān, 'Abd al-Karīm. *Sirat al-Ghazālī wa-Aqwāl al-Mutaqaddimīn fīh.* Damascus: Dār al-Fikr, 1960.

Al-Zabīdī, Muḥammad al-Ḥusaynī (Murtaḍā). *Itḥāf al-Sāda al-Muttaqīn bi-Sharḥ Iḥyā' 'Ulūm al-Dīn,* fourteen volumes. Beirut: Dār al-Kutub al-'Ilmiyya, 2009.

Al-Zuḥaylī, Wahba. *Al-Tafsīr al-Munīr: Fī al-'Aqīda wa-l-Sharī'a wa-l-Manhaj,* seventeen volumes. Damascus: Dār al-Fikr, 2003.

# Index of Qur'ānic Verses

# Index of *Ḥadīths*

# Subject Index